**DO NOT REMOVE
CARDS FROM POCKET**

ALLEN COUNTY PUBLIC LIBRARY

FORT WAYNE, INDIANA 46802

You may return this book to any agency, branch,
or bookmobile of the Allen County Public Library.

DEMCO

The Casuistical Tradition

*in Shakespeare, Donne,
Herbert, and Milton*

CAMILLE WELLS SLIGHTS

*Princeton University Press
Princeton, New Jersey*

To William and Jessica

What man knoweth the things of a man, but the Spirit of man which is in him. That is his own Conscience.

—Robert Sanderson,
Several Cases of Conscience

 We are pilgrims in this world, our life is our journey: God also hath appointed our conscience to be our companion and guide, to shewe us what course we may take and what we may not.

—William Perkins,
A Discourse of Conscience

Contents

The contrast between the high regard in which Renaissance Englishmen held casuistry and the contempt with which the modern mind regards it is a measure of the distance between us. While today theologians and laymen alike tend to think of casuistry as rigid and sophistical, men as different as William Ames and John Donne, Archbishop Laud and Francis Bacon, James I and John Milton, all thought of casuistry as a necessary part of moral theology and moral life. The distance can be exaggerated, of course. Donne was aware of dangers and limitations inherent in casuistry, and the emergence of situational ethics in recent years indicates a renewed interest in a casuistical approach to moral problems. But the gap is there, and this study is an attempt to bridge it.

In the following chapters, I have tried to show that English casuistry was a distinctive religious and literary phenomenon of the Renaissance. To the medieval mind, all human actions were reenactments either of Adam falling or Christ redeeming. Poets related particular human actions to these great dramas of the soul through conventional schemes and symbols. The Renaissance inherited the habit of seeing the world *sub specie aeternitatis,* but it also exhibited a notably increased interest in the temporary and mutable in human experience. In England, the poets of the sixteenth and seventeenth centuries portrayed human action in relation to transcendent realities, but they attributed real significance to the uniqueness of individual experience. Although the imaginative creations of the major poets are the most brilliant expressions of this focus on the particularity of human life, casuists too were concerned with the uniqueness as well as the typicality of a given act. Casuistry is case divinity—the application of moral law to particular cases. While casuists agreed that moral law was universal and immutable, they also acknowledged that the uniqueness of actual human situations often complicated or obscured the moral quality of particular actions. Casuists were exceptional among moralists in their constant attention to the problems of actual experience among infinitely varying circumstances. Their cautious adjustment of traditional moral law to the needs of individual predicaments is an impressive expression of the characteristic Renaissance ability "to separate the eternal and absolute from the contingent and changing, to distinguish those things that constitute the unalterable, 'natural' circumstances of human life from those that are subject to adjustment by human effort." [1]

Like the great preachers, English casuists tried to correct manners and morals and lead men to God, but their primary concern was not to elucidate the great moral truths or to soften stony hearts but rather to disentangle the mingled good and evil in particular and actual situations. Because they were trying to solve difficult moral problems, the casuists addressed themselves to men's intellects rather than to their emotions. Sir Philip Sidney had maintained that "our erected wit maketh us know what perfection is, and yet our infected will keepeth us from reaching unto it." The casuists were less certain that men knew what perfection was in every particular case. Because they defined the conscience as a faculty of the enlightened understanding and because they understood that the web of good and evil in a fallen world is tangled and the circumstances complex, their casuistry proceeded with caution. Although it is not without passages of charming personal reminiscence and reflection, impassioned eloquence, and wit, for the most part it consists of painstaking considerations of various convolutions of circumstances and minute distinctions of moral responsibility.

The casuists' vision of the complexity of actual moral decisions, together with their insistence on a rational approach to all areas of experience, has often proved offensive to modern readers. While hair-splitting discussions about such topics as the necessity of kneeling or of not kneeling at prayers and the extent of a father's authority over his children's marriages may have been meaningful examinations of urgent problems to pious Englishmen in the seventeenth century, today they appear as so much quibbling over inessentials. The laborious specificity of the casuist becomes tedious, and, to the suspicious, his involved reasoning

[1] Arthur B. Ferguson, *The Articulate Citizen and the English Renaissance* (Durham, N.C.: Duke University Press, 1965), p. xvi.

about the precise extent of a moral obligation can seem cold-hearted at best and an attempt to rationalize selfish motives at worst. Since, in the area of forgotten or unfashionable modes of thought, familiarity more often defeats than breeds contempt, knowledge of the intentions and accomplishments of the casuists should make accessible to us this neglected part of the past. Their rigorous analysis may degenerate into the ostentatious display of logical facility and learning, but the complexities in the practical divinity of such casuists as William Perkins, William Ames, Robert Sanderson, Jeremy Taylor, and Richard Baxter are not, in Taylor's phrase, "tricks and devices to dance upon the ropes" but rather reflections of careful attempts to see life whole. The usefulness of the casuist depended upon his accuracy in approximating the specific situations that men actually encountered, and the best casuists felt their responsibility too keenly to allow oversimplification.

Since casuistry proceeds by examining particular cases, it is intimately linked to contemporary conditions and topical problems and so is a valuable source of information about how men saw what was happening in their world during this crucial period in English social, political, and literary history. More important, the leading casuists' discussions of such key terms as "conscience" and "doubt" and their analyses of particular doubtful actions or cases of conscience provide valuable insight into the habit of mind with which men approached the process of making moral decisions. Renaissance casuists are interesting today not so much for their answers to specific questions as for the method and form they developed to clarify the experiential chaos of moral dilemmas. Although the concepts central to casuistry—divine law, the inviolable conscience, reason as a problem-solving faculty, the significance of particular circumstances—are not peculiar to English Protestant casuistry, the casuists' emphasis on this combination in the context of doubtful moral action and their dual stress on intellectual clarity and practical action define a distinctive approach to a particular kind of experience.

Designed to give specific moral guidance while developing independence in the individual conscience, cases of conscience employed certain structural and stylistic strategies to express a carefully articulated vision of human experience. The form, however, was never a pure one. Cases were resolved orally, and they were imbedded in sermons, essays, and personal letters.

There were no rules for writing cases of conscience and no conventions to be transformed by individual casuists. Whether the case of conscience, then, is a literary genre in the sense that epic and tragedy are, or in the sense that the sermon and Theophrastan character are, depends on a more precisely developed theory of genre than we have. I have found that a more accurate and useful concept than genre is "literary paradigm," the term Isabel MacCaffrey proposes for a structural and thematic principle that can inform generically diverse works. "What we are dealing with," she suggests, in discussing Louis Martz's *The Paradise Within,*

> is actually a nameless principle neither generic, stylistic, nor rhetorical, but structural and thematic simultaneously: a literary paradigm, convention, or fiction in which a particular kind of thematic concern expresses itself habitually in— implies or demands—particular structural characteristics. . . . As the pastoral paradigm can enter into and affect the structure of *Arcadia, The Faerie Queene VI,* and Frost's *Directive,* so the meditative paradigm can enter into such generically diverse works as those treated in Mr. Martz's book.[2]

So too the formal and conceptual characteristics of casuistry constitute a distinctive way of understanding experience that can enter into generically diverse works. The casuistical paradigm, in which the self-conscious turning back of the mind on itself is united with a focus on specific, practical action, can be expressed in many genres, including lyric poetry, verse satire, and drama, as well as theological treatises and prose cases of conscience. The following pages survey the casuistical tradition in English and trace its influence in the imaginative literature of the period.

Renaissance casuistry is part of a larger tradition. It developed out of the casuistry of the medieval Church, and it continued to exert influence throughout the eighteenth century. Even today we read a debased form of case divinity in the advice columns of modern newspapers. But the casuistry of the medieval Church and of the Renaissance Roman Church, designed for the priest, not the layman, differed from Protestant casuistry in intention and form. Later versions of the tradition have largely dispensed

[2] Isabel G. MacCaffrey, "The Meditative Paradigm," *ELH* 32 (1965): 390.

with the carefully enunciated theological substructure and the tortuous reasoning process characteristic of Renaissance casuistry and have approached moral dilemmas in a pragmatic, common-sensical fashion. In England, casuistry as a self-conscious theological discipline was peculiar to the sixteenth and seventeenth centuries. Thus I have limited this study to the period spanned by William Perkins's lectures on the conscience delivered at Cambridge during the 1590s and Richard Baxter's publication of *A Christian Directory* in 1673, when major English theologians turned their attention to providing a method for dealing with difficult moral problems. Events during these turbulent years continually produced new problems and changed perspectives for moral theology. The casuists were Puritans and Anglicans, conservatives and radicals. Although they were not great original theoreticians, they were often heterodox in doctrine and independent in judgment. But in spite of their many differences, they developed a remarkably homogeneous body of principles and procedures for resolving cases of conscience. In Chapter I, therefore, I have largely ignored the biographical, doctrinal, and chronological differences and instead tried to clarify the fundamental conceptual framework common to the major casuists.

In Chapter II, where I survey the structural and stylistic characteristics of the casuistical paradigm, I have tried to do more justice to the differences among casuists by suggesting something of the variety in subject, organization, and quality possible within the basic form. Although this variety means that there is no completely representative case of conscience, the casuists' emphasis on the importance of unique combinations of circumstances means that a detailed examination of a case is necessary to understand the casuistical habit of mind. Since there are cases of conscience on everything from usury to witchcraft, no single case can be representative in terms of subject matter. I have, therefore, discussed at some length one of Robert Sanderson's cases not as a typical case of conscience but as an especially interesting one to illustrate the conceptual and structural characteristics of the casuistical paradigm. "The Case of the Engagement" concerns an issue that received considerable contemporary attention, and so it is possible to look at the case in the context of its intellectual and political circumstances. Because this information is available and because Sanderson is a skillful casuist, the case demonstrates clearly the strengths and weaknesses of the form at its best.

Since so much of English casuistry was originally oral, it is impossible to establish precise lines of influence in pre-Caroline literature, but it is clear that casuistical ideas were germinating in England during the reigns of Elizabeth and James I and that the casuistical form of moral reasoning had its effect on the imaginations of poets even before William Perkins's pioneer works of casuistry were published. My intention is not to prove specific casuistical sources for the imaginative literature I discuss but to show how the processes of thought and language the casuists developed to deal with problems of doubtful action inform the English literature of the late sixteenth and early seventeenth centuries. Awareness of this habit of mind and familiarity with the literary form embodying it sheds light, I think, upon a rich area of English literary history and on many poems still inadequately understood. If I am right that casuistry explains how men characteristically approached moral doubt, then anywhere that moral choice is an issue the tradition of casuistry provides a relevant historical context. The writers I discuss illustrate the broad spectrum of thought and the generic diversity showing the imprint of casuistry. Although their approaches to theological, political, and aesthetic questions differ widely, Shakespeare, Donne, Herbert, and Milton all demonstrate interest in casuistical procedures and give imaginative form to the problems of conscience that are the province of casuistry.

Shakespeare is less directly involved in theological questions than Donne, Herbert, and Milton, but since his plays give "speaking pictures" of men choosing to act in specific circumstances, they have obvious similarities to the case of conscience as an individual model of a universal process. In Chapter III, I hope to show that the casuists' analysis of conscience and their method of resolving moral problems illuminate the portrayal of the decision-making process and its consequences in *Richard III, Julius Caesar, Hamlet,* and *Macbeth.* Chapter IV examines John Donne's adaptations of the casuistical paradigm. *Biathanatos* and *Pseudo-Martyr* draw directly on the casuistical tradition in method of argument and presentation. In the *Satyres,* Donne fuses the casuistical paradigm with the form of the classical verse satire to dramatize and evaluate the casuistical approach to moral doubt. Chapter V analyzes the casuistical paradigm in George Herbert's poetry. Here I argue that casuistry supplies a helpful context for poems where Herbert tries to understand the implications of Christian doctrine, for poems where he struggles with doubt, and, more generally for his problem-solving, self-analytic style. The final chapter examines the pervasive casuistical habit of mind in Milton's works. The treatment of actual problems of conscience in *Areopagitica* and the divorce pamphlets shows the impact of casuistry, and *Paradise Lost* and *Paradise Regained* present the mythic source of the casuists' assumptions about moral choice. But it is *Samson Agonistes* that is most profoundly casuistical in its drama of the doubt, struggle, and triumph of the individual conscience.

These four writers, then, illustrate the casuistical paradigm in a variety of prose and poetic genres ranging chronologically from Donne's *Satyres* in the 1590s, when cases of conscience were just beginning to appear in print, to *Samson Agonistes,* written late in the development of English casuistry. My discussions are not intended as a comprehensive or exhaustive treatment of the influence of casuistry on Renaissance literature but as a demonstration of the variety of shapes the casuistical paradigm takes and the possibilities this approach offers. Throughout, I have tried not to reduce the fictional works I discuss to theology, even to the practical theology of case divinity, but to use English casuistry as a tool that helps us to understand them.

Although casuistry has not gained widespread currency among students of the English Renaissance, it has received some scholarly attention to which I am greatly indebted. There are useful general discussions of casuistry by R.M. Wenley in the *Encyclopedia of Religion and Ethics* and by Benjamin K. Nelson in the *Encyclopedia Britannica.* George L. Mosse's provocative study emphasizes Puritan casuistry.[3] William Ames's casuistry has been treated by Keith L. Sprunger and William Perkins's by Louis B. Wright, Ian Breward, and Thomas F. Merrill.[4] Anglican casuistry is discussed by H. H. Henson and in indispensable studies by

---

[3] George L. Mosse, *The Holy Pretence: A Study in Christianity and Reason of State from William Perkins to John Winthrop* (Oxford: B. Blackwell, 1957).

[4] Keith L. Sprunger, *The Learned Doctor William Ames: Dutch Backgrounds of English and American Puritanism* (Urbana: University of Illinois Press, 1972); Louis B. Wright, "William Perkins: Elizabethan Apostle of 'Practical Divinity'," *Huntington Library Quarterly* 3 (1940): 171-196; Ian Breward, ed,. *The Works of William Perkins,* The Courtenay Library of Reformation Classics (Appleford, Eng.: The Sutton Courtenay Press, 1970); Thomas F. Merrill, ed., *William Perkins 1558-1602: English Puritanist* (Nieuwkoop: B. DeGraaf, 1966).

H. R. McAdoo and Thomas Wood.[5] Until recently, students of literature have ignored the tradition of casuistry. They enjoy the religious musings of Thomas Browne, but few read Robert Sanderson. They have rediscovered Donne's sermons and devotions, but have failed to explore the casuistical tradition of *Biathanatos*. William Ames is known for his influence on New England Puritans, not for his casuistry. Jeremy Taylor's sermons and devotional works are read, but his casuistical *magnum opus* is little known. In analyzing the influence of casuistry on Thomas Fuller, Walter E. Houghton, Jr., comments perceptively on the subject matter and form of casuistry,[6] but other early treatments by literary scholars focus rather narrowly on particular casuistical elements: Lily B. Campbell brings the casuistry on despair to bear on *Doctor Faustus,* and Wylie Sypher, interpreting casuistry as cynical playing with moral cruxes, reads *Measure for Measure* from that point of view.[7] Recently, such scholars as A. E. Malloch, Sheridan D. Blau, George Starr, and Dwight Cathcart have begun to explore in more depth the influence of casuistry on individual authors.[8]

Although I have tried to record in notes my indebtedness to these and other scholars, I know that many of those I have learned most from are acknowledged inadequately or not at all because they have shaped my way of thinking about literature so fundamentally that I can no longer point to specific debts. I owe much to Ralph Wardle and Robert Harper, who introduced me to literary study, and to Ross Garner, who taught me to read Donne and Milton. I am grateful to David Novarr for directing my first

[5] H. H. Henson, *Studies in English Religion in the Seventeenth Century* (London: John Murray, 1903); H. R. McAdoo, *The Structure of Caroline Moral Theology* (London: Longmans, Green and Co., 1949); Thomas Wood, *English Casuistical Divinity During the Seventeenth Century: With Special Reference to Jeremy Taylor* (London: S.P.C.K., 1952).

[6] Walter E. Houghton, Jr., *The Formation of Thomas Fuller's 'Holy and Profane States'* (Cambridge, Mass.: Harvard University Press, 1938).

[7] Lily B. Campbell, "*Doctor Faustus*: A Case of Conscience," *PMLA* 67 (1952): 219–239; Wylie Sypher, "Shakespeare as Casuist: *Measure for Measure*," *Sewanee Review* 58 (1950): 262-280.

[8] A. E. Malloch, "John Donne and the Casuists," *Studies in English Literature* 2 (1962): 57-76; Sheridan D. Blau, "The Poet as Casuist: Herbert's 'Church-Porch'," *Genre* 4 (1971): 142-152; George Starr, *Defoe and Casuistry* (Princeton: Princeton University Press, 1971); Dwight Cathcart, *Doubting Conscience: Donne and the Poetry of Moral Argument* (Ann Arbor: University of Michigan Press, 1975).

study of casuistry and for continuing to give me valuable advice and kind encouragement, to Ephim Fogel for generously sharing with me his imaginative grasp of the implications of casuistry for the study of Renaissance poetry, and to Arthur E. Barker for his provocative suggestion about Samson's case of conscience. Ann and David Hiatt, Robert Ian Scott, John Shawcross, Raymond Waddington, John Wallace, and Joseph Wittreich read parts of the manuscript at various stages of its development, and their generous and learned criticisms have been invaluable to me.

My debts to institutions are also large. The libraries of Cornell University, the University of Illinois, the Union Theological Seminary, the Henry E. Huntington Library, and the Bodleian Library supplied the books I needed. I received financial assistance from the Henry E. Huntington Library and from the National Endowment for the Humanities. Chapters I and II contain ideas and paragraphs that appeared in my essay, "Ingenious Piety: Anglican Casuistry of the Seventeenth Century," *Harvard Theological Review* 63 (1970). Chapter III incorporates material from my essay, "Murder, Suicide, and Conscience: The Cases of Brutus and Hamlet," in *Familiar Colloquy: Essays Presented to Arthur Edward Barker,* ed. Patricia Brückmann (Ottawa: Oberon Press, 1978). Part of Chapter IV appeared in " 'To Stand Inquiring Right': The Casuistry of Donne's 'Satyre III'," *Studies in English Literature* 12 (1972). Some of the material in Chapter VI is reprinted by permission of the Modern Language Association of America from "A Hero of Conscience: *Samson Agonistes* and Casuistry," *PMLA* 90 (1975).

My daughter Jessica's generosity has given me the time to devote to this book, and her love and gaiety have given me the heart for it. My largest debt is to my husband William, who listens to my cases of conscience, scholarly and otherwise, and resolves them with wit and wisdom.

The Casuistical Tradition

Chapter I

THE TRADITION

In *A Priest to the Temple, or, The Country Parson,* George Herbert portrays his ideal parish priest as a man who "greatly esteemes also of cases of conscience, wherein he is much versed," because "herein is the greatest ability of a Parson to lead his people exactly in the wayes of Truth." [1] The case of conscience that the pastor of Bemerton praised so highly was, in the seventeenth century, the characteristic form of casuistry or case divinity, the branch of theology that attempts to provide the perplexed human conscience with a means of reconciling the obligations of religious faith with the demands of particular human situations. In the case of conscience, the casuist poses, or is posed with, a difficult moral problem and then solves it, often with a startling display of erudition and logical ingenuity. The problems considered in Renaissance casuistry include virtually every kind of human activity: whether or not a Protestant may marry a Roman Catholic, whether a man must point out the defects of the goods he is trying to sell, whether a man condemned to prison can in good conscience try to escape, whether a promise made under the threat of force is valid. Casuists—Roman Catholic, Anglican, and Puritan alike—assumed that Christian ethics should regulate all human activity and offered solutions to myriad problems arising in men's domestic, professional, political, and financial lives.

In a broad sense, casuistry is the process of applying fundamental moral principles to the activities of daily living. Thomas DeQuincey points out:

After morality has done its very utmost in clearing up the

[1] George Herbert, *A Priest to the Temple, or, The Country Parson,* in *The Works of George Herbert,* ed. F. E. Hutchinson (Oxford: Clarendon Press, 1941), p. 230.

grounds upon which it rests its decisions—after it has multiplied its rules to any possible point of circumstantiality—
there will always continue to arise cases without end, in the
shifting combinations of human action, about which a question will remain whether they do or do not fall under any
of these rules. . . . The name, the word, Casuistry, may be
evaded, but the thing cannot; nor *is* it evaded in our daily
conversations.[2]

Casuistry in this sense is, of course, never absent whenever men
try to live by their principles. In the narrower sense of a distinctive literary form requiring training and skill and commanding
the attention of leading theologians, casuistry in England was a
phenomenon of the late sixteenth and the seventeenth centuries,
a response to the crisis of conscience and authority that was fundamental to the religious and political experience of the period.

When Henry VIII discovered that he had doubts about the
lawfulness of his marriage to Katherine of Aragon, he was posing
a case of conscience,[3] but the political and ecclesiastical crisis that
it provoked did not immediately give rise to a significant body
of English casuistry. The literature justifying Henry's divorce
took polemical rather than casuistical form, and the casuistry of
the Roman Church was written in Latin and intended primarily
to guide the priest in the confessional. The upheaval of the
Reformation destroyed the traditional system of moral and ecclesiastical discipline: the reformers rejected the sacrament of
penance, the confessional fell into disuse, and the Roman body
of casuistry became suspect. Because the Roman Catholic system
was rejected and the Genevan system of discipline was not
adopted, the English Church was left without a well-articulated
program for guiding men's consciences. It was slow, moreover,
to develop a casuistry of its own to fill the vacuum: England produced no major casuists until the end of the sixteenth century.
In fact, in 1589, Francis Bacon, who finally stumbled in the tan-

---

[2] Thomas DeQuincey, "Casuistry," in *The Collected Writings of Thomas
DeQuincey,* ed. David Masson, 14 vols. (Edinburgh: A. and C. Black, 1889-
1890), VIII, 313, 315.

[3] For the view that conscience rather than sex or statecraft motivated Henry
VIII's divorce, see Lacey Baldwin Smith, "A Matter of Conscience," in *Action
and Conviction in Early Modern Europe: Essays in Memory of E. H. Harbison,*
ed. Theodore K. Rabb and Jerrold E. Seigel (Princeton: Princeton University
Press, 1969), pp. 32-51.

gles of seventeenth-century ethics, criticized English theologians for failing to provide adequate moral direction:

> The word (the *bread of life*) they toss up and down, they break it not. They draw not their directions down *ad casus conscientiae;* that a man may be warranted in his particular actions whether they be lawful or not.[4]

The English casuists agreed with Bacon's complaint. William Ames's address to the reader observes that in Protestant churches both in England and on the continent, "this Practicall teaching was much wanting, and that this want was one of the chiefe causes of the great neglect, or carelessenesse in some duties which neerely concerne Godlinesse, and a Christian life." [5] Regretting that Englishmen were forced to rely on Roman Catholic casuistry, he calls for the development of a specifically Protestant case divinity:

> If such things were handled in the meetings of Preachers, according to the variety of Cases that fall out; and the more remarkeable decisions set downe in writing; the children of Israel should not neede to goe downe to the Philistims (that is, our Sutdents [*sic*] to Popish Authors) to sharpen every man his Share, his Mattocke, or his Axe, or his weeding Hooke, as it fell out in the extreame necessity of Gods people.[6]

According to Jeremy Taylor, the "scarcity of books of conscience" was primarily due to the tenuous position of the Church in the early years of the English Reformation.[7] Routine parish duties prevented the conscientious among the overworked and ill-paid clergy from the task of building an English casuistry, even if they had the requisite training and ability. More impor-

---

[4] Francis Bacon, "An Advertisement Touching the Controversies of the Church of England," in *The Letters and the Life of Francis Bacon,* ed. James Spedding, 7 vols. (London: Longmans, 1861-1872), I, 92.

[5] William Ames, *Conscience with the Power and Cases Thereof* (1639), sig. A3r-v.

[6] Ames, *Conscience,* sig. A4. The analogy that the English are driven to use Roman Catholic casuistry as the Israelites were to use Philistine forges is used again by Thomas Fuller in *The Holy State* (Cambridge, 1642), p. 90, and by Jeremy Taylor in the preface to *Ductor Dubitantium: or the Rule of Conscience,* in *The Whole Works of the Right Rev. Jeremy Taylor,* ed. Reginald Heber, 15 vols. (London, 1828), XI, 346.

[7] Taylor, *Ductor Dubitantium,* XI, 345.

tant, the great theologians of the sixteenth century were busy defending the Church against her enemies. Since the first task facing the apologists of the Church during Elizabeth's reign was the opposition of Roman Catholicism, Bishop Jewel's work was directed against Rome. By the time Richard Hooker entered the field in its behalf, the established Church was most dangerously threatened by Puritan critics, and his *Of the Laws of Ecclesiastical Polity* grew out of the conflict between Canterbury and Geneva.

A deep-rooted suspicion of casuistry within the Church itself, however, is more basic to the problem than the need to counter the fire of rival theologies. The great Roman casuists of the Renaissance were the Jesuits, who continued to be feared in England as actively subversive national enemies. When English theologians turn to casuistry, such Jesuitical terms as "equivocation," "mental reservation," and "probabilism" are used consistently in a derogatory sense, and English casuists are at pains to dissociate their work from the Jesuit variety. They charge the Roman casuists with excessive subtlety and complexity:

> What God had made plain, men have intricated; and the easy commandment is wrapped up in uneasy learning; and by the new methods, a simple and uncrafty man cannot be 'wise unto salvation.'

They also charge them with laxity:

> They have made their cases of conscience and the actions of their lives unstable as the face of the waters, and immeasurable as the dimensions of the moon; by which means their confessors shall be enabled to answer according to every man's humour, and no man shall depart sad from their penitential chairs.[8]

The allegation that Catholic casuistry in fact amounted to a complicated system of ratiocination designed to show men how to avoid their clear moral duties was not merely an expression of patriotic feeling against a national enemy. Rather, the attitude grows out of the Protestant fear of placing barriers between man and God. Human intervention, men feared, could only make obscure and difficult what God had made plain and easy. George Herbert recommends cases of conscience for leading people

---

[8] Ibid., pp. 353-354, 352.

"exactly in the wayes of Truth"; but to many Englishmen the "wayes of Truth" were clearly set forth. They saw no need for perfecting the intricate methods of casuistical divinity when the plain truth could be found in scripture. A man confronted with a problem was advised to consult his Bible in order to find a parallel case and to act only with scriptural warrant. Before the English Church produced a casuistry of its own, then, it had to become interested theoretically in the problem of moral authority, and it needed to move away from biblical literalism.

By the end of the sixteenth century, moral norms and the methods for discovering them had become subjects of violent debate. Significantly, the pioneers in English casuistry were the Puritans William Perkins and William Ames, who were in conflict with the established ecclesiastical authority over questions of biblical interpretation and the nature of authority and man's moral duty. Perkins lectured on casuistry at Cambridge at the end of the sixteenth century, and his *A Discourse of Conscience* (1596) and *The Whole Treatise of the Cases of Conscience* (1606) are the first systematic treatments of the subject in English. His student, William Ames, continued Perkins's work in *De Conscientia, eius Jure et Casibus* (1630). Richard Baxter wrote his *A Christian Directory: or a Summ of Practical Theology and Cases of Conscience* after the Restoration when he was forbidden to preach. Meanwhile, a reaction against rigid scripturalism was growing stronger within the Church. The so-called "Arminian" or High Church party surrounding Archbishop Laud stressed the importance of the tradition of human wisdom and viewed with skepticism the extension of scriptural authority into all practical religious matters. This reexamination of the nature of religious authority from a variety of perspectives fostered the development of casuistry in England.

Throughout the seventeenth century, the hundreds of published cases sufficiently attest to the popularity of casuistry. Walter Houghton illustrates the shift of interest from doctrinal controversies to practical morality by noting that "while King James dabbled in theology, his son cultivated and encouraged the study of Casuistry." [9] The flourishing of English casuistry, moreover, was part of a European movement toward concentra-

---

[9] Walter E. Houghton, Jr., *The Formation of Thomas Fuller's 'Holy and Profane States'* (Cambridge, Mass.: Harvard University Press, 1938), p. 71.

7

tion on practical divinity during this period. Henry Hallam observed that at about the end of the sixteenth century on the continent, "casuistical literature burst out, so to speak, with a profusion of fruit," and that throughout the seventeenth century the Roman Catholic Church produced a casuistry of unprecedented richness.[10] A. E. Malloch reports that more than six hundred collections of cases of conscience appeared between 1564 and 1660.[11]

Political history concurred with ecclesiastical and doctrinal developments to foster English casuistry when the struggle between king and parliament erupted into civil war. Between 1640 and 1660, first the Anglican and then the Puritan establishment was destroyed, and Englishmen were forced to confront serious moral questions at the same time that familiar political and religious institutions were being uprooted and basic assumptions about the nature of man's moral existence were being debated ruthlessly. The debate between the claims of the crown and those of parliament was carried on largely in terms of conscience. In the early years of the war, men like Henry Parker and John Goodwin appealed to conscience to justify resistance to tyranny, while royalists like Henry Ferne and Sir Dudley Digges based their support of the monarchy on the obedience demanded by the Christian conscience. The experience of the Commonwealth, the responsibility of leadership, and the failure of the godly to agree upon the form of the new Jerusalem they would build in England diminished Puritan confidence in the ease with which scriptural models could be transferred to contemporary situations. The civil war also underminded the old hierarchy of authority, and those actively loyal to the Church of Charles I were pushed into a stance of civil disobedience. A new relationship between Church and State had to be dealt with in practice even if it were not acknowledged in theory, and inevitably problems of conscience resulted. Nor were these problems the monopoly of ardent partisans. Many who in normal times would have lived without

---

[10] Henry Hallam, *Introduction to the Literature of Europe in the Fifteenth, Sixteenth, and Seventeenth Centuries,* 7th ed., 4 vols. (London: John Murray, 1864), III, 132. Cited by Houghton, *The Formation,* p. 71.

[11] A. E. Malloch, "John Donne and the Casuists," *Studies in English Literature* 2 (1962): 58. Malloch's source is Hugo von Hurter's *Nomenclator literarius recentioris theologiae catholicae* as cited in Edouard Hamel, "Valeur et limites de la casuistique," *Sciences ecclésiastiques* 11 (1959): 165.

undue soul searching as law-abiding citizens and churchmen were forced by the dramatic shape of events to examine their basic allegiances. No tidy Elizabethan world picture and no personal apathy can secure a man sucked involuntarily into the vortex of civil war. There were, of course, people who lived out their lives relatively untouched by the affairs of the great world, but for many Englishmen, internecine war meant agonizing choices concerning their king, their Church, their family and friends, and their most deeply held and cherished beliefs. Cases of conscience were at the height of their popularity during this period.

The pressing need for systematic and learned theological treatment of the complications produced by the friction of man's worldly life against his spiritual life seems to have disappeared in England with the seventeenth century. Several of the major works of English casuistry did not appear in print until after 1650, and even then men complained of their scarcity.[12] The demand for casuistry remained strong immediately following the Restoration, but cases of conscience were becoming rather old-fashioned by the nineties. Only some fifty years after the major works of the English casuists, Alexander Pope, banishing Belinda's lock to a celestial haven for trivialities, furnished this lunar sphere with such meaningless inconsequentials as

> Cages of gnats, and chains to yoke a flea,
> Dried butterflies, and tomes of casuistry.

The eighteenth century solved its moral dilemmas in other terms, and succeeding generations have followed suit. The judgment of history has often, in fact, been harsher than mere disregard. In *Lettres Provinciales*, Pascal condemned Jesuit casuists for using the confessional to teach men what they might do with legal impunity rather than to guide them in a true search for a peaceful conscience through virtuous action. Casuistry has never recovered from his scathing attack. In the twentieth century, casuistry retains the connotations of tedious and futile quibbling

---

[12] Robert Sanderson's 1647 Oxford lectures on the conscience, *De Obligatione Conscientiae,* and an English translation by Robert Codrington, *Several Cases of Conscience Discussed in Ten Lectures,* were both published in 1660. Also in 1660, Jeremy Taylor published *Ductor Dubitantium: or the Rule of Conscience.* Richard Baxter's *A Christian Directory: or a Summ of Practical Theology and Cases of Conscience,* written largely in 1664 and 1665, was published in 1673.

that it held for Pope as well as the association with hypocritical legalism that it had for Pascal. While to a Renaissance man of affairs like Bacon it was the most practical kind of theology, to the twentieth-century mind, casuistical divinity seems fruitless and rather sinister. While casuistry is not wholly innocent of the charges against it, the kind of experience it is concerned with continues to be of real importance, and the casuist's method of resolving moral dilemmas and imposing form on the chaos of experience can add significantly to our understanding of how men during the sixteenth and seventeenth centuries approached the moral complexities of their lives and used language in trying to deal with them.

THE THEORY OF CASUISTRY

The supremacy of the individual conscience is the key idea in casuistry.[13] For the casuist, the conscience is the mind of man operating morally. It prods the reluctant, accuses and torments the guilty, and comforts the innocent. According to Jeremy Taylor, a good conscience produces the "most certain, clearest, and undisturbed felicity," but a bad conscience may reduce man to abject terror: "Then every bush is a wild beast, and every shadow is a ghost, and every glow-worm is a dead man's candle, every lantern is a spirit." An evil conscience is a "secret tormentor [that] shakes the mind, and dissolves it into indiscrimination and confusion"; it "gnaws perpetually, and consumes not, being like the fire of hell, it does never devour, but torments for ever" (XI, 404, 393, 395, 398). Its activities are varied, and its effects sometimes extreme; nevertheless, to the Renaissance mind the con-

---

[13] Throughout this chapter, wherever practical I will cite parenthically in the text the following editions of the major expositions of the principles of English casuistry: William Perkins, *A Discourse of Conscience* and *The Whole Treatise of the Cases of Conscience*, in *The Workes of That Famous and Worthy Minister of Christ . . . Mr. William Perkins*, 3 vols. (London, 1612-1613); William Ames, *Conscience with the Power and Cases Thereof* (1639); Robert Sanderson, *Several Cases of Conscience Discussed in Ten Lectures* (London, 1660); Jeremy Taylor, *Ductor Dubitantium: or the Rule of Conscience*, in *The Whole Works of the Right Rev. Jeremy Taylor*, ed. Reginald Heber, 15 vols. (London, 1828), vols. XI-XIV; Richard Baxter, *A Christian Directory: or a Summ of Practical Theology and Cases of Conscience* (London, 1673). In quoting seventeenth-century texts, I have changed u to v, i to j, and ō to on to accord with modern usage.

science was less the still, small voice that disturbs the sleep of the sinful than the intellectual and practical activity of judging past actions and legislating future ones. Robert Sanderson, for example, defines the conscience traditionally, as *"a faculty, or a habit of the practical understanding, by which, the mind of Man doth by the discourse of reason apply that light with which he is indued to his particular moral Actions (Lectures,* p. 3).[14] Emphasizing its intellectual and practical nature, he insists that it is a function not of the speculative intellect nor of the will but of the practical intellect that "doth agree with the *Speculative* in this, that it doth look on *Truth,* and with the *Will* in this, that it inclineth to operation" (*Lectures,* p. 25). William Perkins distinguishes the conscience from other parts of the mind by the comprehensiveness of its function:

> The proper end of conscience is, to determine of things done. And by this conscience is distinguished from all other gifts of the mind, as *intelligence, opinion, science, faith, prudence. Intelligence,* simply conceives a thing to be or not to be: *opinion,* judgeth a thing to be probable or contingent: *science,* judgeth to be certen and sure: *faith,* is a perswasion, whereby we beleeve things that are not: *prudence,* discerneth what is meete to be done, what to be left undone; but *conscience* goes further yet then all these: for it determines or gives sentence of things done, by saying unto us this was done, this was not done, this may be done, this may not be done; this was well done, this was ill done. . . . Conscience . . . deales in particular actions, and that not in some few, but in all. (I, 517)

Conscience, then, is the rational means by which man relates moral law to his own actions.

The conscience is composed of two parts: the *synteresis,* the storehouse of truth or moral law, and the *conscientia* or *syneidesis,* the judge that applies this law to particular actions, either excusing and absolving or accusing and condemning. Thus con-

---

[14] The casuists' definition of the conscience as primarily a rational faculty derived from St. Thomas Aquinas. See Thomas Wood, *English Casuistical Divinity During the Seventeenth Century: With Special Reference to Jeremy Taylor* (London: S.P.C.K., 1952), pp. 67-70, and H. R. McAdoo, *The Structure of Caroline Moral Theology* (London: Longmans, Green and Co., 1949), pp. 66-69.

science is both a repository of truth and an instrument for implementing it. It has a dual obligation: to conform passively to God's will and to direct actively all actions. The moral truth with authority over every act is one's understanding of God's will. "Conscience is of a divine nature," Perkins says, "a thing placed of God in the middest betweene him and man, as an arbitratour to give sentence. . . . It is (as it were) a little God sitting in the middle of mens hearts" (I, 517, 519). Since the conscience is the image of God in man, to ignore its dictates is to sin against God. Casuists admit that conscience, operating through fallible human reason, may lead man to sin, but they postulate that a man who acts against his conscience, even to commit an intrinsically innocent act, inevitably sins. The conscience, in short, supersedes all human authorities: it "is immediatly subject to God, and his will, and therefore it cannot submit it selfe unto any creature without Idolatry" (Ames, Bk. I, p. 6).

In casuistical theory, the conscience could be classified as right or wrong according to its relationship to divine law and as sure or unsure according to its function in practical application. The conscience, therefore, could be right and sure, sure but wrong, right but unsure, or simply unsure. A conscience both sure and right was called a "right" conscience, while one that was sure but wrong was called an "erring" conscience. A right but unsure conscience was labeled "scrupulous," and a conscience that was unable to decide whether a proposed action was lawful was known as a "doubtful" or "doubting" conscience.[15]

A right conscience is the basis for all virtuous action:

For *this is the beginning of a good worke, that the con-*
science first of all gives her judgement truly, that the thing
may be done, & is acceptable to God. Rom. 14.23. *Whatsoever*
is not of faith, that is, whatsoever is not done of a setled
perswasion in judgement and conscience out of Gods word,
howsoever men judge of it, *is sinne.*   (Perkins, I, 537)

Since the conscience is a faculty of the intellect, the right conscience judges a past or proposed action lawful on the basis of

15 Taylor lists five kinds of conscience by distinguishing between the doubtful conscience and the probable or thinking conscience. The main difference between the two is that, while neither can assent fully to either side of a question, the probable conscience can choose, while the doubtful cannot. *Ductor Dubitantium* (XII, 31-172).

reason. According to Jeremy Taylor, men who think that "our reason is blind in things divine, and therefore . . . of little or no use in religion" err; a right conscience is "right reason reduced to practice" (XI, 434, 428).

The erring conscience presents a theoretical dilemma for casuists. They agree that man must always follow his conscience, even if it judges falsely. "He that does a good thing while he believes it to be evil, does choose the evil, and refuse the good" (Taylor, XII, 5). But the man who follows his erring conscience into evil is also guilty. Conscience may make an innocent action evil, but it cannot make an evil action good. The erring conscience must be reformed, usually through rational persuasion.

Man should also use reason to overcome the hesitations of the "scrupulous conscience," which is convinced of the right course to follow but continues to worry and fret irrationally. Whereas a scrupulous conscience is rationally persuaded by one side of a question in spite of fears pulling it to the other side, a doubting conscience assents to neither side: it "stickes and staggers betweene assent and dissent, not knowing which to doe" (Ames, Bk. I, p. 17). Although casuists engage in theoretical discussion of the relative sinfulness of erring consciences and offer advice on how to correct an erring or scrupulous conscience, they are sought by men who are torn between conflicting loyalties, not by men who are confidently deceived. Most casuistry, then, is devoted to the doubting conscience. The case of conscience arises when a man is doubtful about what he ought, or ought not, to do, and the casuist's goal is to turn a doubting into a right conscience.

Thus, the second fundamental assumption of the casuist is that he is dealing with problematical material. Unless there is some doubt, some question about the right thing to do, there is no case of conscience. The casuist's treatment of doubtful action derives from his conception of the conscience, just as does his concern with the harmony between action and divine law and between action and individual conscience.

Casuists are usually classified according to their position on the process of accumulating and assessing evidence in cases of doubt. The most rigorous position was tutiorism, which demanded that the doubting conscience choose the alternative with the least possibility of sin, without regard to the degree of sin, the extent of personal suffering, or the evidence that the action in question was really innocent. The piety of this course was admired, but to demand that man always assume himself bound to obey when there is any possibility that a law might apply was clearly impractical. And so tutiorism was rejected by most Renaissance casuists. The alternatives to tutiorism were probabiliorism and probabilism. While probabiliorism demanded that one follow the strongest probability in doubtful cases, probabilism maintained that *any* probability is sufficient ground for action. That is, probabilists held that in a doubtful case, one may act without regard for a moral law when he can discover any real probability that it does not apply in his case, even when its applicability is more probable.

Although probabilism was clearly open to abuses, it is an intelligible concept when examined from the proper perspective.[16] If one assumes that, while truth is absolute, human understanding is fallible, and that doubts about lawful action must be seen in the context of the whole body of opinion about the subject, then probabilism can be seen as a necessary safeguard for individual freedom of action. In this view, the opinion of the majority of respected theologians has the highest probability of being correct in a difficult situation, but it remains possible that a less popular point of view is actually correct. Probabilism, therefore, allows man to act on the less probable opinion; it has the advantage of freeing him to act in especially difficult cases, even against usual theological opinion. The doctrine rests, nevertheless, on the assumption that a moral judgment can be made with reference to an external body of rules and need not issue from personal conviction. The result of this formulation of moral choice is to separate law from truth, the practical from the speculative intellect, the moral agent from himself. Probabilism was associated with, though not confined to, the Jesuits, and English casuists usually condemned it as an excrescence of Jesuitical laxity and cynicism.

Probabiliorism, the position held by most Protestant casuists, allowed the individual to act only when the strongest probability favored liberty. While the probabilists did not demand that moral action issue from perfect personal assent, the probabiliorists assumed that certainty could be reached in doubtful cases by the exercise of reason. Jeremy Taylor defines this position:

[16] In this discussion I am indebted to A. E. Malloch's helpful analysis of probabilism in "John Donne and the Casuists," pp. 57-76. See also McAdoo, *Structure of Caroline Moral Theology*, pp. 88-97, and Wood, *English Casuistical Divinity*, pp. 74-78.

In probabilities, I prefer that which is the more reasonable, never allowing to any one a leave of choosing that, which is confessedly the less reasonable in the whole conjunction of circumstances and relative considerations.　　　(XI, 359)

An accumulation of probable arguments, probabiliorists maintained, could change a doubtful into a right conscience.

Probable arguments are like little stars, every one of which will be useless as to our conduct and enlightening; but when they are tied together by order and vicinity, by the finger of God and the hand of an angel, they make a constellation, and are not only powerful in their influence, but like a bright angel to guide and to enlighten our way. And although the light is not great as the light of the sun or moon, yet mariners sail by their conduct: and though with trepidation and some danger, yet very regularly they enter into the haven. This heap of probable inducements is not of power as a mathematical and physical demonstration, which is in discourse as the sun is in heaven, but it makes a milky and a white path, visible enough to walk securely.　　　(Taylor, XII, 36-37)

The third fundamental assumption of the Renaissance English casuist is that the circumstances of human affairs are so varied that no action can be defined categorically as sinful or virtuous. The infinite variety of cases is due to differences in circumstances and not to moral relativity. What is just for one man would be just for all men in like circumstances. "But," Taylor points out,

men are infinitely differenced by their own acts and relations, by their understandings and proper economy, by their superinduced differences and orders, by interest and mistake, by ignorance and malice, by sects and deceptions. And this makes that two men may be damned for doing two contradictions: as a Jew may perish for not keeping of his sabbath, and a Christian for keeping it; an Iconoclast for breaking images, and another for worshipping them.　　　(XI, 419)

Circumstances may charge an otherwise neutral action with moral significance. While moral law requires certain actions and prohibits others, many actions are morally neutral or indifferent. Indifferent actions "in themselves beeing neither good nor evill, may be done or not done without sinne; In themselves I say, for in their circumstances they are, & may be made either evill or good" (Perkins, II, 3). In addition, there are degrees of sin, and "the circumstances of time, place, person, and manner of doing, doe serve to enlarge or extenuate the sinne committed" (Perkins, II, 10). Sometimes circumstances exempt men from a general rule. For example, Taylor argues that men are morally obligated to obey human laws but that when circumstances change so that a law intended for the public good becomes instead an oppressive burden, the obligation of the law ceases (XIV, 251). Circumstances may also create moral obligation:

> . . . others [moral duties] are not commanded to all, but to some only, and that is not expresly and immediatly, but consequently, and upon the supposition of certaine circumstances, by which it comes to passe that (*hic* & *nunc*) in some particular case, they partake of the nature of precepts.
>
> (Ames, Bk. III, p. 83)

Thus the conscience cannot automatically apply general rules to particular instances but must take into account all the variety of circumstances encountered in the real world. In extremely difficult cases, when the doubting conscience confronts alternatives that seem equally pious and equally probable, consideration of circumstances should determine choice. Taylor argues that, although some men say that in such cases understanding must remain suspended between two equally probable opinions, to suspend judgment is in fact to choose one opinion. Instead, one should weigh "accidents, circumstances, and collateral inducements" and then act (XII, 80).

The casuists' insistence on the inviolability of the individual conscience, the relevance of particular circumstances to moral absolutes, and the role of reason in resolving problems of moral doubt led them to a shared conception of casuistical method. They saw the operation of the conscience as essentially the process of discovering proper relationships among various kinds of knowledge. Perkins suggests that the etymology of "conscience" describes its function of joining introspection with knowledge of universal truths. Conscience "signifieth a knowledge, joyned with a knowledge. . . . First, because when a man knowes or thinkes any thing, by meanes of Conscience, hee knowes what he knowes and thinkes. Secondly, because by it, man knowes that thing of himselfe, which God also knows of him" (II, 11). Robert Sanderson echoes Perkins and suggests a further significance in the word. Conscience is well-named, he says, because "science" plus "con" suggests the idea of man knowing many things. The conscience "addeth *Science* unto *Science,* that is, the universal knowledge, or the knowledge of Law, and Right, to the particular knowledge, or the knowledge of the fact by applying one unto the other" (*Lectures,* p. 7).

Thomas Barlow reports that, when asked to specify the training necessary for a casuist, Sanderson recommended not only a thorough grounding in Greek, Hebrew, and Latin and a "sufficient knowledge of the arts and sciences" but an additional two fields of study. According to Barlow's report, Sanderson believed that the first essential is an understanding of the nature of human action:

> Every Case of Conscience being only this—"Is this action good or bad? May I do it, or may I not?"—he who *in thesi* knows not how and whence human actions become morally good and evil, never can *in hypothesi* rationally and certainly determine, whether this or that particular action be so.

The second requisite for a casuist is a

> convenient knowledge of the nature and obligation of Laws in general. . . . For every Case of Conscience being only this—"Is this lawful for me, or is it not?" . . . he who *in thesi* knows not the nature and obligations of Laws, never can be a good Casuist, or rationally assure himself or others of the lawfulness or unlawfulness of actions in particular.[17]

According to the casuists, the foundation of moral action is the will. Echoing St. Augustine, they insist that no human action can be either good or evil unless it is voluntary. Man must submit his will, which is directed by the conscience, to God's will. Fear, threats, or physical force set no limits to man's responsibility, for *"the will cannot be constrained"* (Perkins, II, 5). Because man is responsible for choosing good, knowledge has great moral significance. Since man lives in a world where "there is good and evil in confusion of imperfect mixture," reason and knowledge must be the basis of choice. If this were not so, Taylor adds, it would be to "no purpose to write cases of conscience" (XIV, 280).

17 William Jacobson, ed., *The Works of Robert Sanderson,* 6 vols. (Oxford: Oxford University Press, 1854), VI, 358-359.

Since only willed action has moral significance, ignorance may limit moral responsibility: "Ignorance . . . if it be unvoluntary both in it selfe and in its cause . . . doth make the action meerly casuall and unvoluntary and so excuseth from sin" (Ames, Bk. III, p. 92). More often, however, ignorance is an additional sin rather than an extenuation of it. The law of God is sufficiently revealed that man cannot plead ignorance of his essential duty. In particular cases, a man may not know enough, but he is required to use "moral diligence" in trying to discover his duty.

There are three aspects of any action that one must consider in the process of making a moral decision: the intrinsic nature of the action, the intention of the agent, and the circumstances surrounding the act. An action may violate the law of God in any of three ways. No action can be justly said to be morally good, unless "the *matter* [is] lawfull, the *intention* right, and the *circumstances* due" (Sanderson, *Lectures,* p. 48).[18] Thus man is responsible not only for knowing God's law but for carefully searching his own motives:

> A good intention by it selfe cannot make a good action, because goodnesse is a perfection, and doth arise from the perfection and integrity of all the causes. . . . Yet an evill intention doth make an action evill.
>
> (Ames, Bk. III, pp. 83-84).

One must also carefully examine the possible implications and consequences of his actions in his particular circumstances. Giving scandal, for example, is a sin because man does not work out his salvation in a vacuum. Man is not guilty of scandal merely because someone is scandalized in the modern sense of being shocked or morally outraged. Scandal is behavior that brings discredit on religion or presents a stumbling block to the faith of others, causing them to sin. Actions that a man performs only indirectly constitute another area requiring careful scrutiny of such surrounding circumstances as political structures and particular responsibilities and expectations. There are, for example, social crimes in which "a man's will is deeper than his hand," and man is morally responsible for the sins that others commit in his name with his approval (Taylor, XIV, 305).

---

[18] Sanderson cites Aquinas when he uses the axiom *Bonum ex causa integra, Malum ex partiali* in his sermons (see *Works,* II, 58, 107).

Although casuistry's emphasis on the individual conscience and on flexibility in applying moral law to individual cases makes it susceptible to the abuse implied in the pejorative connotations that the word "casuistry" has today, casuistical analysis of human action is designed to prevent such laxity and hypocrisy. Richard Baxter warns that there are two kinds of hypocrites: "gross hypocrites," who consciously deceive others, and "close hypocrites," who are self-deceived (Bk. I, p. 210). A major part of the casuist's job is to show men how to avoid deceiving their consciences in matter, intention, or circumstance. Baxter warns against the dangers of oversimplification:

> He that will walk uprightly, must have both a *solid* and a *large understanding,* to know things *truly* as they are, and to *see all particulars* which must be taken notice of, in all the cases which he must determine, and all the actions which his integrity is concerned in. (1) There is no walking uprightly in the dark. Zeal will cause you to go apace; but not at all to go Right, if Judgement guide it not. . . . (2) And the understanding must be *large,* or it cannot be *solid:* When many particulars are concerned in an action, the over-looking of some one may spoil the work. Narrow minded men are turned as the weather-cock, with the wind of the times, or of every temptation; and they seldome avoid one sin, but by falling into another. (Bk. IV, p. 3)

Jeremy Taylor offers rules to help guard against this disaster. First, one should suspect his conscience if he is unwilling to inquire into the case. "He that searches, desires to find, and so far takes the right course; for truth can never hurt a man, though it may prejudice his vice, and his affected folly." Second, inquiring into particulars only after one has firmly resolved upon a conclusion probably indicates that he is not really searching for truth but trying to confirm his own opinion. Third, one should ask advice of wise men instead of following the crowd. And fourth, one should examine his decisions when they apparently serve selfish ends (XI, 411).

The individualism inherent in the concept of the conscience is controlled by the concept of the law. All the English casuists could have endorsed Sanderson's description of the power of the individual conscience:

God hath given to every particular man a proper Conscience
to be as a God unto him, which in Gods steed, as the Preacher
of his eternal Law, should dictate to him what he ought to do.

(*Lectures,* p. 36)

They also supported Baxter's caution:

> *Make not your own judgements or Consciences your Law
> or the maker of your duty; which is but the Discerner of the
> Law of God, and of the duty which he maketh you, and of
> your own obedience or disobedience to him.* (Bk. I, p. 134)

The conscience acts as legislator, witness, and judge: the *synteresis*
discerns the moral norms by which each action is judged; the
syneidesis or *conscientia* examines all facets of a particular action
and passes judgment, directing the will toward virtue. Since sin
is "a want of conformitie to the Law of God," man needs to
understand which laws have valid claims on him and how they
operate (Perkins, II, 3). Thus, the second area of knowledge
necessary for solving cases of conscience is the nature of law.

Although they disagree about the precise significance of various
kinds of law, casuists agree that God is the only power over the
conscience and that the divine will is the basis for all morality.
According to Sanderson, who gives the clearest and most systematic exposition of the obligation of the conscience to law, God has
revealed His will to man in three ways: "the *light innate,* the
light inferred, and the *light acquired;* or the *light of nature,* the
light of Scripture, and the *light of Doctrine*" (*Lectures,* p. 131).[19]

The light innate or light of nature is the knowledge of divine
will that man is born with, a concept assuming the traditional
theory of a hierarchy of laws as expounded by Thomas Aquinas
and Richard Hooker. This knowledge of eternal law is natural
law, "a transcript of the wisdom and will of God written in the
tables of our minds" and given to man "for the conservation of
his nature, and the promotion of his perfective end" (Taylor, XII,
212, 213). The light from natural law has been obscured in man

[19] Sanderson's three "lights" provide a useful terminology for talking about
concepts essential to all English Protestant casuists, but admittedly his formulation would not have been acceptable to Puritan casuists, who regarded
scripture as the only source of law binding the conscience and treated reason
and tradition as useful but unreliable tools for interpretation. See pp.
29-31.

since "that grievous ruine which folowed the fall of *Adam*, . . . [but] in the common wrack it hath come off more unhurt than many other of the Faculties." It consists of many "divers *practical principles* which not withstanding are reduced to one first and universal Law . . . *viz. Good is to be done, Evil is to be avoyded*" (Sanderson, *Lectures*, pp. 131, 132, 133). This universal law and other subordinate laws are conserved in the *synteresis*. As the subordinate laws become more particular and circumstantial, they also become less clear and sure.

The light inferred comes from the revelation of God's will in scripture. More perfect than the inward light, God's written word instructs men in the fundamentals of faith. The Old and New Testaments clarify and supplement the law of nature and are the chief rule of all human actions. The Old Testament contains ceremonial, judicial, and moral laws. The law of the New Testament is more perfect, interpreting the moral law of the Old Testament and adding the two great duties of *"loving our enemies,* and *taking up the cross"* (Sanderson, *Lectures*, p. 143).

Since applying biblical texts to actual moral dilemmas is difficult and potentially dangerous, casuists give directions for interpreting scripture. Jeremy Taylor, for example, explains in detail twenty rules for interpreting scriptural commandments, such as "1. *In negative Precepts the Affirmatives are commanded; and in the affirmative Commandments, the Negatives are included*"; and "7. *When any Thing is forbidden by the Laws of Christ, all those Things also, by which we come to that Sin, are understood to be forbidden*" (XII, 465; XIII, 6). Casuists warn particularly against the uncritical use of biblical examples as precedents for right conduct because the actions even of good men are not always imitable and because biblical examples often demonstrate special divine commandments to particular people in particular situations, as in the story of Abraham and Isaac. They also make distinctions among the obligatory powers of scriptural commandments. Richard Baxter advises:

Observe well in Scripture the difference between Christs Universal Laws, (which bind all his Subjects in all times and places) *and those that are but local, personal or alterable Laws.* . . . The *particular local* or *temporary* Laws are those, which either resulted from a *particular* or *alterable nature* of

21

> *persons* and *things* as *mutually related* . . . or those which
> God *supernaturally* enacted only for some *particular people*
> or *person,* or *for a time*.   (Bk. III, p. 685)

Cases also occur where two divine laws are contradictory. In
such cases "the lesser commaundement gives place to the greater"
(Perkins, I, 520). If, for example, a city should catch fire on a
Sunday, the commandment to rest on the Sabbath gives way to
the commandment to help our neighbors. Indeed, sometimes
man can lawfully violate the letter of God's law:

> For if we shall omit the doing of any law, I. without hin-
> drance of the end & particular considerations, for which the
> law was made: II. without offence giving, as much as in us
> lieth: III. without contempt of him that made the law, we
> are not to bee accused of sinne. . . . God made a law, that
> the Priests onley should eat of the Shew-bread: now David
> beeing no priest, did upon urgent occasion eate of it without
> sin. . . . For as there is a keeping of a law, & a breaking of
> the same; so there is a middle or meane action betweene
> them both, which is, to do a thing (a) *beside the law,* and
> that without sinne.   (Perkins, I, 531)

Thus, while scripture is the most perfect expression of divine
will, it is not a complete guide for "what is lawfull for a pious
and prudent man to do lawfully, or to leave undone, at *such a
time,* or in *such a place*" (Sanderson, *Lectures,* p. 125, incorrectly
numbered as p. 124). It contains fundamental principles of
virtuous conduct rather than detailed legislation. In Sanderson's
formulation, the light innate and the light inferred are supple-
mented by the light acquired, "the *Discourse of Reason* and
Authority; the last of which is the Judgement, and the Practice
of the Church" (*Lectures,* pp. 143-144).

Although there are differences in their accounts of how to
discover the law of God, casuists are at one in insisting that only
God has the power to put the conscience under direct obligation.
They also agree that there are other authorities with claims for
men's obedience: the law of nature leads men to join together
in societies, and scripture teaches that a visible Church is necessary for the preservation of Christian faith. But neither natural
law nor scripture prescribes in detail the government of human
societies. Men choose their forms of government, make laws, and

impose obligations on themselves through vows and promises, according to general axioms of scripture and reason. Man-made laws create problems that are especially perplexing for the moralist, and this was particularly so during the radical transformations of English law in the seventeenth century.

The "greatest case of conscience in this whole matter," Taylor declares, is "whether it be a matter of·conscience as well as of prudence and security, to obey the laws of man" (XIII, 231). On the one hand, only God has authority over the conscience: *"You are bought with a price, be you not made the servants of men* [1 Cor. 7: 23]; that is, do not submit your Consciences to be governed by the Authority of any man" (Sanderson, *Lectures,* p. 102). On the other hand, man is also told, "you must be subject, not because of anger only, but for conscience sake" [Rom. 13:5]. The casuists resolve this paradox by concluding that human law binds the conscience indirectly through the scriptural commandments to obey one's superiors. Obedience to human authority is commanded by divine law, and obeying the laws made by that authority is the form that obedience takes.[20] Thus violations of human laws are indirectly violations of God's law.

While this formulation makes a moral matter of the individual's relation to human authority, it does not really resolve the tension between lawful authority and individual conscience. While providing the rationale for the obedience children owe to fathers, servants to masters, and subjects to princes, it also lays the foundation for civil disobedience, conscientious objection, and revolution. Divine law is always obligatory; human laws may cease to bind the conscience in particular circumstances.

> For the laws of God are wiser and plainer, few and lasting, general and natural, perceived by necessity, and understood by the easiest notices of things; and therefore men have more need to be called upon to obey, than taught how; and there-

[20] This distinction is the usual Protestant position: "For if we must obey rulers not only because of punishment but for conscience's sake [Rom. 13:5], it seems to follow from this that the rulers' laws also have dominion over the conscience. . . . I reply: we must first distinguish here between genus and species. For even though individual laws may not apply to the conscience, we are still held by God's general command, which commends us to the authority of magistrates." John Calvin, *Institutes of the Christian Religion,* ed. John T. McNeill, trans. Ford Lewis Battles, The Library of Christian Classics, 2 vols. (Philadelphia: The Westminster Press, 1960), II, 1183-1184.

fore here the preacher's office is most necessary and most required. But human laws are sometimes intricate by weakness, sometimes by design, sometimes by an unavoidable necessity: they are contingent, and removed far from the experiences of most men; they are many and particular, difficult and transient, various in their provisions, and alterable by many parts and many ways: and yet because the conscience is all the way obliged, she hath greater need of being conducted than in the other, where every wise man can better be a guide in the little intrigues, and every child can walk in the plain way. (Taylor, XIII, 231)

Casuists, then, are most needed in problems relating to human laws, where the relations between authority and personal conscience are especially complex. Conscience, the voice of God in man, is again the key to the casuistical approach. Since the moral force of human authority derives from divine law, the individual's understanding of God's will supersedes all human commands. Human law has no moral force if it contradicts the law of God. The power of kings is "a power of doing right, but not of doing wrong" (Taylor, XIII, 427). The principle that unjust laws are not morally binding, however, receives considerable qualification. *"Think not,"* Baxter warns, *"that it is unlawful to obey in every thing which is unlawfully commanded"* (Bk. IV, p. 25). In order to discriminate among the circumstances that make unjust laws binding or not, casuists must define the nature of an unjust law. A law may be unjust, they explain, because it was not made by lawful authority, because it does not contribute to the public good, or because it is contrary to divine law.

Since no one can obey a law he never heard of, adequate promulgation is necessary if a law is to create any obligation. The law binds according to the will and intention of the lawmaker, and he is responsible for making his intention widely and easily known. Ignorance of the law or its meaning, however, does not always excuse disobedience. The subject is responsible for seeking without negligence or laziness to know his superior's intention. Innumerable problems arise involving this shared responsibility, but casuists maintain that honest goodwill and careful, logical attention to details can resolve them.

A mathematical certitude, which is manifest by Demonstration, and impossible to be false, is in vain to be expected *in morals,* by reason of the infinite variety of Circumstances, and uncertainty of Humane affairs, nevertheless a certain *logical* certitude may oftentimes be had of the Intention of the Law-maker, which is to be collected from the words of the Law it self, from which, his Intention may so perspicuously appear, that there needeth not any further Evidence.

(Sanderson, Lectures, pp. 293-294)

Since the moral sanction of human law depends on the god-given authority of the lawmaker, no law made by an individual or institution without lawful authority can impose moral duty. Although there is no casuistical position on what constitutes lawful authority, the major casuists approach problems in this sensitive area with more caution and conservatism than logical rigor. They deny that the power of the sword alone legitimizes authority, but they acknowledge too that history offers few cases of political rulers with clear and unquestioned rights to power. Generally they recommend that subjects may, and sometimes must, obey the de facto power.

A law may also be considered unjust when it is detrimental to the public good. William Ames explains: "Legall Justice taken strictly, considereth the words just as they are written, but Equity considereth the End, scope and intent of the Law, and so hath more Law in it, then Legall Justice, when taken strictly" (Bk. V, p. 111). The ultimate intention of any just human law is *"the good of the Commonalty,* or the publick peace and tranquillity" (Sanderson, *Lectures,* p. 310). Ordinarily responsibility for determining what is necessary for the safety and welfare of the country rests on the ruler, that is, the established authority whatever the form of government. Generally speaking, the individual citizen is in no position to judge the common good and should comply with a law even though it seems unwise. In certain extreme circumstances, however, a man may dispense with his obedience to a particular law in the interests of the common good. In such a case, the ultimate intention of the lawmaker is assumed to supersede the immediate intention of the words of the law. Ames provides a standard example:

So the Law of not opening some City gates in time of Warre, doth immediatly consider the not letting in of the Enemies, which is the immediate End: but it hath another remote End, to wit, the safegaurd [sic] and preservation of the Citie. . . .

25

For if it be certaine that upon admission of some part of the hostile Forces into the Citie, the safeguard of the Citie, and Victory would follow, it is more just to open the Gates so farre, then to keepe them still shut." (Bk. V, p. 111)

A law demanding the impossible is tyrannical and void. In addition, the concept of equity relaxes the law's rigor by releasing the subject from the unduly severe letter of the law. Except in cases of great public need, a man is not obligated to obey the letter of a law that is "so extremely burthensome as to bring with it the certain ruine of his whole Estate, or the imminent danger of his life" (Sanderson, *Lectures,* p. 205). In these circumstances, the mind and intention, rather than the words, of the lawmaker are to be followed, and the ultimate intention of the lawful ruler is assumed to be the preservation of his people. Finally, a law that commands an action contrary to the law of God does not bind the conscience to obedience. Immoral laws cannot be justified in terms of the public good because the purpose of government is not power but "the preservation of the people in Tranquillity, and peace, with all Godlinesse and Honesty" (Sanderson, *Lectures,* pp. 208-209). Any time one is ordered to violate divine law, his duty is clear: he must disobey human authority.

> *No humane Power is at all to be obeyed against God: For they have no power but what they receive from God: And all that is from Him, is for Him.* . . . No man must commit the least sin against God, to please the greatest Prince on earth, or to avoid the greatest corporal suffering.
>
> (Baxter, Bk. IV, p. 24)

Other branches of law raise particular difficulties and involve differences and exceptions, but generally the casuistical treatment of oaths, vows, and promises and of the rules governing economic, ecclesiastical, and family structures is analogous to its treatment of political law. Casuists place human law in the context of a hierarchy of laws in which human authority is subordinate to divine law. The judgment of the individual conscience is inviolable, but it is by no means autonomous. Renaissance casuistry does not provide a blueprint for rebellion. Equity and Christian liberty allow scope in the interpretation of law, but they do not justify defiance of lawful authority. Some circumstances dissolve the moral obligation to cooperate with a harsh and destructive law, but man is morally bound to prefer the common good to his own profit and advantage. Normally a man must suffer an injustice rather than commit a sin of disobedience. If, for example, a tyrannical king unjustly demands inordinately high taxes, the king is unjust and the law is unfair, but the subject must obey. Only when obedience entails sin is disobedience required, and even then, man is not free from his obligation to his lawful superiors. He must submit to the power of his superior without resistance and patiently endure whatever punishment is inflicted: "For though in some cases it is lawful not to obey, yet in all cases it is necessary not to resist" (Taylor, XIII, 454).

In extreme cases an individual may assume the responsibility to violate a particular law in the interests of the welfare of the country, but only when he can obtain or rationally assume the permission of the lawmaker. Pernicious laws should be changed, but only with great discretion. Casuists are characteristically not millenarians; they have little use for dreams of a "*Platonick* or an *Eutopian* Commonwealth; we are to think we have done well enough, if we stick not too deep in the mire" (Sanderson, *Lectures,* p. 320). Each man's responsibility is to live virtuously and to love God in an imperfect world, not to create a new Jerusalem in England. The major theoreticians of English casuistry, Perkins, Ames, Sanderson, Taylor, and Baxter, place more emphasis on the duty of compliance with the law than on its dangers, but they never close the door to the prerogatives of individual moral judgment. Paul's admonition with respect to teachers, Sanderson suggests, may as aptly be applied to the commands of superiors: "*Try all things, and keep that which is good*" (*Lectures,* p. 211).

This summary of the theoretical basis of English Protestant casuistry is far from exhaustive. By describing the conception of law and conscience outlined by the leading Renaissance casuists I have hoped to illuminate the habit of mind with which they approached the process of making moral decisions. I have neglected such important areas as their treatment of economics and family problems and their theories of repentance. I have not tried to survey the particular problems they discuss or to define the variations found within this conceptual framework.

An aspect of this topic that needs detailed study is the question of individual variation among the casuists. For example, the

major casuists all insist that the end never justifies the means and
that when they condone latitude of conduct in particular situations they do so on the basis of avoiding sin by obeying a higher
law. Nevertheless, George Mosse argues that the tradition of
casuistry that began with Perkins and culminated with Taylor
absorbed the Machiavellian concept of "policy"—the acceptance
of "an expedient but wicked action for reason of state." [21] Only
Robert Sanderson rigorously rejects policy and "insists that good
intention does not provide a sufficient foundation for peace of
conscience." [22] The integrity, clarity, and rationality of Sanderson's casuistry are impressive, and for that reason I have frequently drawn on his exposition of the operation of the conscience in this chapter. None of the major casuists, however,
accepts the principle that a good intention alone constitutes a
good action. Sanderson, moreover, shares the emphases on practical action, circumstances, the hierarchy of laws, and the concept
of intention that, according to Mosse's analysis, "made possible
the assimilation of 'policy' and reason of state into the framework
of Christianity." [23] A careful study of the relation between individual casuists' theory and practice and comparisons of their
treatments of similar problems is needed to discover what differences exist and whether they are due to theoretical distinctions,
to laxity in the application of principles, or simply to personal
temperaments.

Another question that needs fuller investigation is the relation
between Puritan and Anglican casuistry. Robert Sanderson, who
lost his professorship at Oxford because of his refusal to sign the
Solemn League and Covenant, and William Ames, who fled to the
Netherlands as a Puritan exile, obviously disagreed on important
doctrinal and ecclesiastical matters. Casuistry, however, shows no
clear Puritan/Anglican split. For example, Puritans and High
Church Anglicans reach different conclusions in cases of conscience involving such ceremonial matters as kneeling for prayer,
but their casuistical methods are remarkably similar. Whereas
Ames holds that external worship must be based on "the infallible
word of God," and believes it unlawful to require kneeling with-

---

[21] George L. Mosse, *The Holy Pretence: A Study in Christianity and Reason
of State from William Perkins to John Winthrop* (Oxford: B. Blackwell, 1957),
p. 14.

[22] Ibid., p. 141.

[23] Ibid., p. 135.

out scriptural warrant for such compulsion, Taylor argues that because scripture does not prescribe the forms of worship, ecclesiastical authority may lawfully impose decent and orderly forms. Thus they differ on whether kneeling is properly classified as an indifferent action or one prohibited by scripture, but they agree that God's word takes precedence over ecclesiastical law and that laws about genuinely indifferent things bind the conscience.

Puritans tend to ascribe more authority to Old Testament law than do Anglicans, but among the casuists this difference seems more rhetorical than substantial. The Anglican Robert Sanderson, for example, holds that the Old Law—moral, ceremonial, and judicial—was given to the Jews in their particular circumstances and therefore is not binding on the Christian conscience (*Lectures,* p. 138). William Perkins, in contrast, says that Mosaic judicial law is binding in some circumstances, that ceremonial law is positively prohibited for Christians, and that moral law "bindes the consciences of all men at all times" (I, 520). Sanderson's position on the abrogation of the Old Law, however, is qualified by the assertion that parts of it continue to bind men's consciences "not because *Moses* so commanded, but because that which hath been commanded by him is either agreeable to the Law of Nature, or confirmed in the new Law by Christ" (*Lectures,* p. 138). Thus the moral law contained in the Ten Commandments binds the Christian conscience "by *reason of the matter,* as it is the *Declarative* of the *Law of Nature*" (*Lectures,* p. 142). Similarly, Perkins says that the moral law is "the very law of nature written in all mens hearts . . . and therefore it bindes." Some judicial laws continue to bind Christians because "so farre foorth as they have in them the generall or common equitie of the law of nature [they] are morall; and therefore binding in conscience, as the morall law" (I, 520).

Puritan casuists also differ from Anglicans in their scripturalism. Robert Sanderson describes the conscience as being guided by the "light of the mind," which is called "right, or rectified Reason," and analyzes that light according to its sources in nature, scripture, and human tradition. He scoffs at the idea that scripture alone could be a sufficient authority to guide the conscience "insomuch that it is not lawful to take up a straw, unless it be by the prescribed word of God" (*Lectures,* p. 229), while Perkins insists that the authority of the written word does extend to the most minute details of daily life:

> Gods word ministers sufficient direction for all actions what-
> soever: so as if a man bee but to receive a morsell of bread
> into his mouth, it can so farre forth direct him that in doing
> of it, he shall be able to please God.   (I, 537)

He peremptorily rejects any authority over the conscience but
scripture:

> That which is done without good direction of Gods word,
> is a flat sinne. . . . And here by the Word, I meane no thing
> but the Scriptures of the olde and new Testament, which
> containe in themselves sufficient direction for all actions. As
> for the law of nature though it affoarde indeede some direc-
> tion; yet it is corrupt, imperfect, uncerten: and whatsoever is
> right and good therein, is contained in the written word of
> God. And as for the best unwritten traditions, let all the
> Papists in the world answere if they can, how I may in con-
> science be perswaded that they are the word of God. (I, 537)

In spite of the scripturalism that these passages suggest, however, Perkins's discussions of a hierarchy of laws, of a distinction
between the letter and the intention of the law, and of natural
law as the basis for distinguishing general from particular commandments in scripture show that he includes reason and natural
law within his concept of scripture as the only law having supremacy over the conscience. Throughout his works Perkins draws on
Church tradition, quoting freely from patristic and scholastic
writers. In fact, his position has been cited as the universal
English Protestant viewpoint on the issue:

> There be two kindes of writings in which the doctrine of the
> Church is handled, and they are either *Divine* or *Ecclesi-
> asticall*. Divine, are the bookes of the olde and new Testa-
> ment. . . . And the authority of these bookes is *divine,* that
> is, absolute and soveraigne . . . and beeing the onely foun-
> dation of faith, and the rule and canon of truth.
>
> *Ecclesiasticall* writings are all other ordinarie writings of
> the Church consenting with Scriptures. These may be called
> the *word* or *truth of God,* so farre forth as their . . . sub-
> stance is consenting with the written word of God. (I, 122) [24]

[24] Cited by Charles H. and Katherine George, *The Protestant Mind of the
English Reformation: 1570-1640* (Princeton: Princeton University Press, 1961),
pp. 347-348.

The differences that exist in the casuits' treatments of reason, tradition, natural law, and scripture seem to be matters of emphasis rather than contradiction, and they do not correspond exactly with labels of Anglican or Puritan.

Although in general, Anglican faith in natural reason contrasts with Puritan insistence on the total corruption of natural man, Jeremy Taylor, in most ways associated with Laudian or High Church Anglicans, is akin to Perkins and Ames in stressing revelation rather than reason.[25] Reason, he says, "is such a box of quicksilver that it abides no where; . . . it is like a dove's neck, or a changeable taffata; it looks to me otherwise than to you, who do not stand in the same light that I do" (XII, 209). He describes the law of nature as the wisdom inscribed in men's minds to conserve and help to perfect his nature, but he argues that natural law binds man to obedience only through the express commandments of God in scripture (XII, 211-227). It becomes clear that, whatever their particular doctrinal and ecclesiastical bent, the casuists all finally approached moral problems without a single authority to follow unquestioningly and that their casuistry required skillful balancing of the claims of reason, scripture, and tradition in the context of particular circumstances.

The selection of cases in volumes of casuistry is another point at which the casuist's emphasis seems to correlate roughly with his ecclesiastical position. The Anglicans, Sanderson, Joseph Hall, and Thomas Barlow, consider as questions of conscience political, economic, matrimonial, and religous problems that imply some form of external action. They resolve such problems as whether a man is obligated by a rash vow to disinherit his disobedient daughter, whether it is lawful to change interest on a loan, and whether Christians may lawfully seize the lands of pagans by force. In addition to cases of this sort, the Puritan casuists include cases that solely concern the spiritual life of the individual. They treat such questions as how a man may be assured of his salvation and how a man may attain true faith in Christ.

To this slight extent, the Anglicans separate ascetic from moral theology. Sanderson states the principle behind the practice. Human actions, he says, can be considered in two ways, "as they

[25] On the contrasting views of human nature, see J.F.H. New, *Anglican and Puritan: The Basis of Their Opposition, 1558-1640* (Stanford, Calif.: Stanford University Press, 1964); and on Taylor's distrust of reason, see McAdoo, *Structure of Caroline Moral Theology*, pp. 37-38.

are spiritual, that is to say, whether they are done out of *Charity,* and directed to a *supernatural* end" and "as they are *moral,* that is, whether they be *good* or *evil, lawfull* or *unlawful, free* or *necessary*" (*Lectures,* p. 121, incorrectly numbered as p. 221). The distinction provides a way of acknowledging the efficacy of divine grace, the transcendence of faith over reason, and the complete authority of scripture in matters of faith, while focusing on the significance of human will and intellect in questions of morality.

Puritan casuists make this distinction less clearly. The conscience judges human actions on the basis of the law and gospel. Moral law, Perkins says, consists of "duties of love, partly to God and partly towards our neighbour" (I, 519). The gospel promises righteousness and eternal life to all believers and imposes the duties of faith. Ames divides theology into spiritual and moral parts, but he too sees them as equally within the scope of casuistry:

> Now every question, or case of Conscience . . . is either about the state of man before God, or about those actions which in that state he doth put forth, and exercise.
>
> The state of man belongs to the first part of Divinity, which is about *Faith,* and the actions to the second part which is about *obedience.*   (Bk. II, p. 2)

The danger inherent in divorcing moral from spiritual matters is that morality may become sterile and legalistic, an effort to avoid punishment by satisfying the minimum requirement of the law. This is the accusation frequently directed against post-Tridentine Roman Catholic theology in which moral and ascetic theology are rigidly separated.[26] The opposite danger is that intellectual subtleties and moral responsibilities may be submerged in the doctrine of faith, resulting in a casuistry that transforms self-righteousness into a moral principle capable of justifying any expediency. Although Perkins has been accused of this, English casuists on the whole avoid both extremes. Puritan casuists are aware of the intellectual rigor and diligence demanded by many of the moral complexities men face, and they are exacting in their definitions of men's obligations to God and their neighbors; Anglican casuists explicitly deny that casuistry can be separated from spiritual growth:

26 McAdoo, *Structure of Caroline Moral Theology,* p. 10; Wood, *English Casuistical Divinity,* p. 64.

In men as they are Christians, the *object* of the *Conscience* is . . . not only [to] oblige them to the performance of their duties, as they are men, but to believe the mysteries of Faith revealed in the Word of God, as they are Christians.

(Sanderson, *Lectures,* p. 28)

Careful study of the cases of conscience published during the Renaissance should yield significant information about the scope of casuistry and about how political and ecclesiastical allegiances influenced the approach to moral questions. It would not, I believe, prove the existence of separate Puritan and Anglican casuistries.[27]

Puritan and Anglican casuists alike based their work on the conceptual foundation summarized in the preceding pages. They recognized that their emphasis on reason and on the force of circumstances to alter cases could lead to a sterile intellectualism that obscured more than it clarified. Thus Jeremy Taylor reminded his readers:

Truth is easy, error is intricate and hard. If none but witty men could understand their duty, the ignorant and idiot could not be saved; but in the event of things it will be found that this man's conscience was better guided while simplicity held the taper, than by all the false fires of art, and witty distinctions. "Qui ambulat simpliciter, ambulat confidenter," saith Solomon. It is safer to walk on plain ground, than with tricks and devices to dance upon the ropes.   (XI, 422)

But although casuists warned against making unnecessary complications, they believed that oversimplification was an even greater danger to moral clarity. Thus Richard Baxter answered

[27] English casuists wrote with the intention not of correcting the work of their predecessors but of amplifying it. Perkins was echoed by Sanderson and Taylor as well as by his expressed disciple Ames. See Gilbert Walker, *Bishop Sanderson and His Writing on Conscience* (London: S.P.C.K., 1911), p. 20. Sanderson was admired not only by Bishops Barlow, Hall, and Taylor but by Baxter, who expresses the common attitude: "Long have our Divines been wishing for some fuller Casuistical Tractate: *Perkins* began well. Bishop *Sanderson* hath done excellently . . . *Amesius* hath exceeded all, though briefly . . . Bishop *Jer. Tailor* hath . . . but *begun* the copious performance of the work. And still men are calling for more, which I have attempted" (*A Christian Directory,* sig. A3).

objections to the complexity of case divinity by observing that it is

> *ambiguity* and *confusion* that *breedeth* and feedeth almost all our pernitious Controversies: And even those that bring in error by vain distinction, must be confuted by better distinguishers, and not by ignorant Confounders. . . . *Discerning* both good and evil, is the work of long and well exercised senses. (sig. Aa)

Because men must use their wits to discover the path of virtue among the tangled affairs of the world, the casuist used his to blaze a trail.

Despite the abuses to which casuistry was susceptible, then, eminent theologians valued it as a worthwhile discipline. Most of their contemporaries agreed with Robert Sanderson on the paramount importance of practical divinity:

> When all is done, positive and practique Divinity is it must bring us to Heaven: that is it must poise our judgments, settle our consciences, direct our lives, mortify our corruptions, increase our graces, strengthen our comforts, save our souls.[28]

And they looked to casuists to play two important roles in this process: to act as physicians giving comfort and healing aid to troubled consciences and to act as guides leading men to moral action. Although sixteenth- and seventeenth-century Englishmen held themselves responsible for their own decisions, they sometimes needed help in understanding how to deal with difficult moral problems. Ames, Perkins, Sanderson, Taylor, and Baxter published their casuistical works to fill that need.

[28] Sanderson, *Works,* II, 105.

Chapter II

METHOD AS FORM

CASES OF CONSCIENCE

While the moral theology I have described as the basis for Renaissance Protestant casuistry derives from medieval moral theology, English casuistry differs markedly from continental Roman Catholic casuistry. The heart of casuistry is not theoretical theology but the resolution of practical problems. Roman Catholic casuistry was designed to guide the clergy in the confessional. Usually written in Latin, it consisted of surveys of authoritative opinions on hundreds of moral problems or cases of conscience. In contrast, Protestantism assumes that ultimately everyone is his own casuist and must think through every moral doubt for himself. English casuists were probabiliorists, believing that full intellectual assent was a necessary prerequisite for virtuous action. Their task, then, was not to arrange collections of cases for quick reference by confessors but to teach laymen as well as clergy a sound method for resolving moral conflicts. Thus they needed to develop their own form of case divinity.

English casuists agreed that they needed to clarify the principles on which a Protestant casuistry could proceed. Both Jeremy Taylor in his preface to *Ductor Dubitantium* (1660) and Richard Baxter in his preface to *A Christian Directory* (1673) lamented the failure of the English church to provide guidelines for solving cases of conscience. In spite of the beginnings made by Perkins, Ames, and Sanderson, Protestants still had to rely on Roman Catholic casuistry, which they found a confusing maze of rules and exceptions based on an unacceptable concept of authority.

So that there is a wood before your doors, and a labyrinth within the wood, and locks and bars to every door within that labyrinth; and after all we are like to meet with unskil-

ful guides; and yet of all things in the world, in these things
an error is the most intolerable.   (Taylor, XI, 354-355) [1]

But they concluded that rewriting the handbooks of cases from
a Protestant perspective would be futile. Taylor warned his
readers not to expect "a collective body of particular cases of
conscience":

> For I find that they are infinite, and my life is not so; and I
> shall never live to write them all, or to understand them all:
> and if I should write some and not all, I should profit I know
> not whom, and do good but to a very few, and that by chance
> too; and, it may be, that their cases, being changed by cir-
> cumstances, would not be fitted by my indefinite answers.
> (XI, 363)

They wanted to clarify the theoretical basis for moral action
and to avoid endless catalogues of particular cases, but they also
knew that the strength of casuistry is its fidelity to the concrete
particularity of actual experience. As a result of this view of their
responsibility, English casuists usually wrote in English rather
than Latin and, instead of citing authoritative opinions, they
combined exposition of the principles of casuistry with models
of procedure.

In *The Whole Treatise of the Cases of Conscience,* William
Perkins outlines the theoretical foundations of casuistry in an
introductory section and then illustrates general discussions of
moral virtue with particular cases. He divides questions of conscience into three groups: cases about (1) "man as he is considered
apart by himself," (2) man in relation to God, and (3) man in
relation to other men. The third group includes "all those
Questions of Conscience . . . which doe belong unto man, as he
is a member of some societie, whether it bee the Familie, the

[1] Throughout this chapter, wherever practical I will cite parenthetically in
the text the following editions of the major expositions of the principles of
English casuistry: William Perkins, *A Discourse of Conscience* and *The Whole
Treatise of the Cases of Conscience,* in *The Workes of That Famous and
Worthy Minister of Christ . . . Mr. William Perkins,* 3 vols. (London, 1612-
1613); William Ames, *Conscience with the Power and Cases Thereof* (1639);
Robert Sanderson, *Several Cases of Conscience Discussed in Ten Lectures* (London, 1660); Jeremy Taylor, *Ductor Dubitantium: or the Rule of Conscience,*
in *The Whole Works of the Right Rev. Jeremy Taylor,* ed. Reginald Heber,
15 vols. (London, 1828), vols. XI-XIV; Richard Baxter, *A Christian Directory:
or a Summ of Practical Theology and Cases of Conscience* (London, 1673).

Church, or the Commonwealth" (II, 112). Ames follows Perkins's lead, combining theory with illustrative cases grouped under the headings "the state of man," "man's duty in general," "man's duty to God," and "man's duty to his neighbor."

After these beginnings, English casuistry was for a time devoted to urgent practical problems. In 1647, Robert Sanderson lectured at Oxford on the obligations of the conscience, but he modified his original plan for these theoretical lectures in order to respond to the current debate on the political implications of the *salus populi suprema lex doctrine*. His cases of conscience were resolutions of actual problems. Written over a period of many years, they were prepared for circulation in manuscript form and were collected and published posthumously.[2] Thomas Barlow also was a highly esteemed casuist whose resolutions of actual cases of conscience were circulated in manuscript and published posthumously.[3] The one full-scale volume of casuistry published in the middle of the century was Joseph Hall's *Decisions of Divers Practical Cases of Conscience* (1650), which includes no extended discussion of conscience and law but continues the practice of classifying cases by subject matter. It contains forty-three cases divided into four groups: (1) cases of profit and traffic, (2) cases of life and liberty, (3) cases of piety and religion, (4) cases pertaining to matrimony.

Jeremy Taylor and Richard Baxter combined systematic exposition of the principles and methods of Protestant casuistry with illustrative cases of conscience. Taylor organized *Ductor Dubitantium* into four books that analyze the moral nature of human action. Book I explains the conscience, the formal cause of sin and virtue. Books II and III discuss the material cause, the laws

---

[2] Sanderson's cases, written between 1634 and 1660, are printed in William Jacobson, ed., *The Works of Robert Sanderson*, 6 vols. (Oxford: Oxford University Press, 1854), V. One case was published anonymously in 1636, a collection of five cases was published anonymously in 1666, two more were printed in 1668 with the author's name, and editions in 1673 and 1678 each added one case. Jacobson adds two more cases that he obtained from manuscripts, affirming that "many other Cases were known to be in existence fifteen years after our Author's death" (*Works*, I, xv).

[3] Barlow's cases were published in 1692 with the title *Several Miscellaneous and Weighty Cases of Conscience*. . . . According to the bookseller's preface, *"the Bishop gave these Cases to his Friends, when first writ, with his leave to print them; yet they, fearing some of them might prejudice his further Promotions in the Church in those Days, forbore Publication of them."*

of God and man. Book IV outlines the rules relating to the concepts of "will" and "motive," the efficient and final causes of human action. In *A Christian Directory*, Baxter used the traditional method of organizing by subject matter. Book I explains private duties, Book II family duties, Book III church duties, and Book IV duties to rulers and neighbors. Taylor's "general instrument of moral theology" and Baxter's "sum of practical theology" order moral theology into general "rules" or "directions" designed to provide directors of conscience and individual Christians with the means to resolve particular cases of conscience for themselves.

While the format of their cases of conscience varied considerably, English casuists would have all agreed with Baxter that the purpose of casuistry is

> the resolving of *practical Cases of Conscience,* and the reducing of Theoretical knowledge into *serious Christian Practice* and promoting a *skilful facility* in the faithful exercise of universal obedience, and Holiness of heart and life.
>
> (sig. A2ᵛ) [4]

Their answers to a question of conscience might range from a brief "yes" or "no" to a discursive essay,[5] and the "case of con-

---

[4] Most cases of conscience were discussed orally and never published. George Herbert's opinion that every clergyman should be well versed in casuistry in order to discharge his pastoral duties was echoed by Bishop Sprat, Bishop Gardiner, and Bishop Stillingfleet (see Thomas Wood, *English Casuistical Divinity During the Seventeenth Century: With Special Reference to Jeremy Taylor* [London: S.P.C.K., 1952], pp. 31-33). At least some clergy followed their advice. Because of "his known abilities in resolving cases of conscience," Mr. March, Vicar of Newcastle, "drew after him a great many good people, not only of his own flock, but from remoter distances who resorted to him as to a common oracle, and commonly went away from him entirely satisfied in his wise and judicious resolutions" (see Overton, *Life in the English Church,* p. 333, as cited by Wood, *English Casuistical Divinity,* pp. 33-34). Richard Baxter reports that at Kidderminister every Thursday evening neighbors gathered in his home to propose their cases of conscience and hear him resolve their doubts (see Matthew Sylvester, ed., *Reliquiae Baxterianae, Mr. Richard Baxter's Narrative of the Most Memorable Passages of his Life and Times* [London, 1696], p. 83).

[5] For example, the following question and brief answer signed by several churchmen including Henry Hammond, Gilbert Sheldon, Sanderson, and Taylor was widely circulated in 1647.

> *Qu* Whither upon any necessity or exigence
> of state it bee lawfull for a Christian
> Prince, beside the Religion established, so

science" label might be applied to everything from theoretical treatises to political polemics. But, for all the variety of the casuists' activities and the looseness with which the term "case of conscience" was used, the casuists' conception of moral experience was reflected in a distinctive use of language, and their cases share certain defining characteristics.

The purpose of the case of conscience—the application of moral law to an individual action in a unique and bewildering set of circumstances—created a special relationship between the casuist and his audience. While the preacher or the orator may assume an audience hardened in sin or complacent in its prejudices and in need of being jolted out of moral apathy, the casuist addresses a distressed and confused individual in need of moral guidance. He characteristically assumes that his audience is well-intentioned, receptive of advice, but perplexed and fearful. The casuist is at once a comforter, healer, and guide. His goals are to bring rest to the weary, health to the sick, and to resolve difficulties by untangling knotty problems. Thus, in the dedicatory letter to *The Whole Treatise of the Cases of Conscience,* Thomas Pickering praises Perkins's casuistry because "first, it serveth to discover the cure of the dangerousest sore that can be, the *wound*

---

to tolerate the exercise of other religions
in his Kingdome, as to oblige himself not
to punish any subject for the exercise of
any of them?
Answe That
Although every Christian Prince bee obliged
by all just and Christian wayes to maintein
and promote to his power the Christian
religion in the truth and purity of it,
yet in case of such exigence and concernment
of Church and state as they cannot in humane
reason probably be preserv'd otherwise, We
cannot say that in conscience it is unlawfull,
but that a Christian Prince hath in such
exigents a latitude alowed him, the bounding
whereof is by God left to him. (Sanderson,
Works, VI, 459-460)

At the other extreme is a letter from Taylor to Mrs. Katherine Phillips, "the matchless Orinda," who wrote inquiring about the lawfulness of friendship for a Christian. Taylor's reply was not the usual intricately constructed analysis but a graceful and courtly essay on friendship (see "A Discourse of the Nature, Offices, and Measures, of Friendship," XI, 299-335).

of the Spirit. . . . Secondly, it giveth for all particular Cases, speciall and sound direction." Similarly, Ames honors his mentor for teaching "how with the tongue of the Learned one might speake a word in due season to him that is weary . . . by untying and explaining diligently, CASES OF CONSCIENCE" (sig. A3).

This relationship between speaker and audience determines the rhetoric of the case of conscience. The tone is occasionally sharp when reprimanding sin, but normally it is calm and re-assuring. Since the goal is to make clear what is obscure and perplexing, the language is relatively plain and unadorned. Taylor says that his style "is according as it happens; sometimes plain, sometimes closer" and explains, "I was here to speak to the understanding, not to win the affections; to convince, not to exhort" (XI, 360). The material is by definition difficult, and the argument is often a tortuously intricate analysis developed through fine distinctions and logical deductions.

Since the conscience is a rational faculty, it relates universal laws to particular actions by means of logic. In fact, the operation of the conscience can be reduced to two interlocking syllogisms: the law is the first premise; the particular facts or actions con-stitute the minor premise; and a statement of the relation between them is the conclusion, which then serves as the first premise of the second syllogism. Sanderson gives the following illustration:

> *Every thing that is unjust is to be eschewed.*
> *Every Theft is unjust,* therefore
> *Every Theft is to be eschewed.*

Let this be the first Syllogism, the first proposition whereof is known of it self by the light of Nature: *Reason* doth prove the *Minor,* and the Conscience doth bring in the conclusion; which conclusion it presently takes up to be the beginning of the following Syllogism, and applying it to some particular Fact, according as the Will shall propound unto it, it argues in this manner.

> *All Theft is to be eschewed.*
> *This which is now propounded to me to be*
> *done is a Theft,* therefore, *it is to be*
> *eschewed.*

And the Name of the Vice being changed, it proceedeth in this manner.[6]

---

[6] Sanderson, *Lectures,* p. 14. Compare Ames, Bk. I, p. 3; Perkins, I, 535-556; Taylor, XI, 383. Sanderson was Reader in Logic at Oxford before the civil war.

The operation of the conscience, of course, is not as simple as the syllogistic paradigm suggests. The relation between act and law is not self-evident, as Ames suggests when he defines a case of conscience as "a practicall question, concerning which, the Conscience may make a doubt" (Bk. II, p. 1). The difficulty arises in the formulation of the minor premises. In order to set up the first syllogism, the casuist must select the appropriate moral law. In practice this involves analyzing various moral principles and discriminating among the conflicting claims of the relevant ones. In order to draw a conclusion from the second syllogism, he must decide whether or not the proposed action violates that law. Given the casuist's assumptions about the double intention of the law and the relevance of the motive, circumstances, and anticipated consequences of the action, this procedure typically involves him in intricate psychological and social analysis as well as legal and logical complexities. Perhaps it is significant that leading casuists such as Ames and Perkins were also associated with Ramistic logic. The Ramistic emphasis on dialectical demonstration, disjunctive arguments, and on the use of "specials" or individual cases seems especially suited to the casuists' efforts to demonstrate universal truth in particular cases by making fine distinctions.[7] Certainly the practice of casuistry demanded skill as a logician in addition to moral sensitivity, theological erudition, psychological acuity, and social and political awareness.

A simple example of the form is provided by Perkins's treatment of the question, "Whether a man may with good conscience and a meeke Spirit, defend himselfe by law, for wrongs that are done unto him?" (II, 118). He answers the question affirmatively: "A man may, with good conscience, defend himselfe against great injuries, by the benefit of law." He bases this conclusion on two general principles drawn from scripture.

Magistracy is Gods ordinance, for the good of men, Rom.

His lectures, published as *Logicae Artis Compendium*, went through eleven editions and were the standard work on logic at Oxford for many years. See George Lewis, *Robert Sanderson* (London: S.P.C.K., 1924), p. 7.

[7] On Ramism see Rosemond Tuve, *Elizabethan and Metaphysical Imagery: Renaissance Poetic and Twentieth-Century Critics* (Chicago: The University of Chicago Press, 1947); Walter J. Ong, *Ramus: Method and the Decay of Dialogue* (Cambridge, Mass.: Harvard University Press, 1958); Wilbur S. Howell, *Logic and Rhetoric in England, 1500-1700* (Princeton: Princeton University Press, 1956); Perry Miller, *The New England Mind: The Seventeenth Century* (Cambridge, Mass.: Harvard University Press, 1939).

13.4. and therefore men may use the benefit of authority, judgement, and jurisdiction of Magistrates, without breach of conscience. Againe, it is the expresse law of God, that when a false witnes riseth up against a man, to accuse him of a trespasse; that both the accuser and the accused, should stand before Gods, that is, before his Priests & Judges for the time beeing, and have remedy at their hands. An example of which judiciall defence, we have in Paul, who in case of wrong, makes his appeale to the judgement seate of Rome, Act, 25.10. (II, 118)

Perkins uses the rest of the case to defend his judgment against anticipated objections. For example, to the objections raised by Luke 6:29, "*To him that smiteth thee on the one cheeke, offer also the other,*" and Math. 5:40, "*If any man will sue thee at the law, and take away thy coate, let him carrie thy cloake also,*" he answers that these passages concern "private persons," who without the help of the public magistrate must suffer rather than take private revenge. In answer to the argument that Paul condemned recourse to law—"*There is utterly a fault among you, because ye goe to law one with another*" (1 Cor. 6:7)—Perkins again distinguishes between cases on the basis of circumstances: "We must distinguish betweene things themselves, and the manner of doing them" (II, 118). Paul, he argues, condemned the Corinthian manner of going to law as a fault because they did so upon slight causes, because they acted out of passionate rage and envy, and because they caused scandal by suing each other before heathen judges. He counters more general arguments for Christian meekness by insisting on a less simple conception of Christian duty: "So Christ commaundeth that we should be *simple as doves,* Math. 10.16. and yet withall, he commaundeth us *to be wise as Serpents,* to defend our owne heads, and to save our selves" (II, 119). In a sense, this case is continued in the next question, "How is a man to defend himselfe by law?" Perkins answers with numbered rules instructing the reader to go to law only as the last resort and then only to seek peace and justice, without envy, malice, or impatience.

In this typical case, Perkins has constructed a form to serve the needs of Protestant casuistry. Protestant casuists accused Roman Catholic casuists of being, in Taylor's phrase, "hard in the case, but easy in the action" (XI, 349): too hard, because they legalistically applied a confusing mass of rules and precedents to unique moral problems; too lax, because they released the individual conscience from the responsibility for its own moral judgments and conceived of the priest as a judge with power to absolve or condemn. Perkins acts not as judge or magistrate but as guide.[8] By stating clearly the general principles that his resolution of the case rests on and by following this implicit deductive argument with a series of objections and answers, he tries both to provide specific guidance and to remove the lingering reservations or doubts that his reader might have. He constructs a case that is general and typical enough to be of use to the general public and simultaneously acknowledges that circumstances make each individual case different. His case is designed not merely to answer a question about moral law but to provide a model of his reasoning process.

"THE CASE OF THE ENGAGEMENT"

Perkins's case on legal defense concerns a particular problem in the sense that it appears as part of a discussion of clemency or meekness, the virtue that "serves to moderate wrath and revenge," and in the sense that it stands as a qualification of the general duty to forgive one's enemies. It formulates the general rule that a Christian may in good conscience go to court to defend his rights, but it stipulates enough limiting circumstances in terms of the situation and manner of acting that it leaves any individual case open to discussion. In order to understand the casuistical habit of mind, however, we need to examine in detail a case written about an actual historical problem. Robert Sanderson's "The Case of the Engagement" is one of the most interesting and historically important cases of conscience and illustrates nicely a case applying orthodox Christian doctrine to an unprecedented situation.

[8] Thomas Wood and H.R. McAdoo offer sympathetic discussions of this emphasis on method rather than conclusion, but Elliot Rose argues that the failure to tell people exactly what they ought to do is the weakness of Protestant casuistry. See Wood, *English Casuistical Divinity;* McAdoo, *The Structure of Caroline Moral Theology* (London: Longmans, Green, and Co., 1949); and Elliot Rose, *Cases of Conscience: Alternatives Open to Recusants and Puritans Under Elizabeth I and James I* (Cambridge, Eng.: Cambridge University Press, 1975), pp. 186-200.

This case raises the fundamental casuistical problem of the tension between individual conscience and external authority. The particular moral dilemma that Sanderson tries to untangle involves the chronic problem of the loyalty oath. After the execution of the King, Parliament, frightened by Charles II's negotiations with the Scots and by the growing royalism of the Presbyterians, imposed a new oath of allegiance:

> I Do declare and promise, That I will be true and faithful to the Commonwealth of England, as it is now Established, without a King or House of Lords.[9]

The imposition of this so-called "Engagement Oath" intensified the controversy precipitated by the King's execution and forced all male citizens to come to terms in one way or another with the question of obedience to the revolutionary government. Historians disagree on the import of the oath. One calls it "the slightest test of allegiance that any government could require," while to another it was "as foolish as it was tyrannical." [10] The government had considered and rejected the more severe wording: "to maintain the same as it is now established against King and Lords." [11] Still, even in its final moderate form, the oath could hardly have been welcomed by Englishmen horrified by the death of the King. Staunch Anglicans like Henry Hammond and Gilbert Sheldon, who were attempting to present solid and unyielding resistance to the new order, opposed subscription to the oath. The strongest resistance came from the Presbyterians who had been instrumental in curtailing the power of the King but were opposed to his execution and against legitimizing the existing regime. In spite of the vocal opposition, however, many who

[9] C. H. Firth and R. S. Rait, eds., *Acts and Ordinances of the Interregnum, 1642-1660,* 3 vols. (London: H. M. Stationery, 1911), II, 325. In February 1649, the Engagement Oath was required of the Council of State. In October, a similar oath was extended to include such groups as soldiers, ministers, and schoolmasters, and in January 1650, another was extended to all men over the age of eighteen.

[10] Henry Hallam, *The Constitutional History of England,* 7th ed., 3 vols. (London: J. Murray, 1854), II, 234; Samuel Rawson Gardiner, *History of the Commonwealth and Protectorate 1649-1660,* 3 vols. (London: Longmans, Green and Co., 1894), I, 216.

[11] See Robert S. Bosher, *The Making of the Restoration Settlement: The Influence of the Laudians 1649-1662* (Westminster, Eng.: Dacre Press, 1951), p. 14.

did not accept the legitimacy of the Cromwellian government took the oath.[12]

Among those puzzled about how to react to the new oath was Thomas Washbourne, the son-in-law of Dr. John Fell and a rector in Gloucestershire, who wrote to Robert Sanderson to ask his advice. Explaining with pathos but with puzzling imprecision that refusing to take the oath might endanger his church living and his ability to support his wife and "five or six small children," he poses his dilemma: "I would not be flattered into a conceit that I may safely, without making shipwreck of a good Conscience, take the Engagement . . . so would I not precipitately ruin myself in my temporal estate by an over-preciseness in refusing what is not repugnant to the Rule of Faith." [13] He asks Sanderson's opinion of a list of the "most common Arguments" used to justify compliance.

Washbourne's summaries do not develop a consistent argument, but they indicate the context of ideas in which contemporaries saw the question. He begins and ends with the kind of technical, legalistic quibbling that was attributed to Jesuit casuistry by English casuists and that is today associated with casuistry in general.

> That it is only a Promise, not an Oath, and consequently not so obliging the Conscience, but only *pro tempore.* . . . Whether, upon supposition that the words of the Engagement may bear a double construction, I may take it in my own sense or in the Imposer's? and whether I ought to ask his interpretation before I subscribe?

Another argument essentially justifies the means by the end, suggesting William Prynne's charge that Royalists took the oath on the basis of "a most wicked and base Maxime" that *"He is a fool that will not take it, and he is a knave that will not break it."* [14] Washbourne's version is:

> That by not subscribing I become a prey to them, and

[12] On the controversy surrounding the oath, see Bosher, *The Making of the Restoration Settlement;* Gardiner, *History of the Commonwealth;* and John Wallace, *Destiny His Choice: The Loyalism of Andrew Marvell* (Cambridge, Eng.: Cambridge University Press, 1968), pp. 43-68.

[13] Washbourne's letter and Sanderson's case are printed in Sanderson, *Works,* V, 17-36.

[14] Quoted by Wallace, in *Destiny His Choice,* p. 50.

thereby am made utterly unable, in a civil capacity, to serve the rightful Prince, if he should come in place to demand my assistance.

While these arguments attempt to minimize the obligations created by the new oath, others suggest that even a Royalist was no longer required to act on his conviction that the Stuarts were the lawful rulers of England. These include the rumor that the King had given his subjects permission to take the oath and the argument that since oaths "bind not to impossibilities" and since changed circumstances make defence of the lawful ruler impossible, previous oaths of allegiance to the King no longer bind. Most of the arguments Washbourne proposes for consideration advocate the moral lawfulness of obedience to any existing power, regardless of how that power was acquired.

That it is but just to promise fidelity, though to an unjust Power, under whom I live and from whom I have protection. . . . That the present Power, though usurped, is the only Power exstant; and we must be subject to that or none. And how can it be sin to promise what I cannot choose but perform?

These questions make clear that people in 1650 were as eager as anyone to eat their cake and have it too, but they also indicate that they saw political action more as a matter of conscience and less as the effective manipulation of power for the achievement of a desired goal. This summary of the prevalent arguments in the Engagement controversy also indicates the extent to which the context of ideas had changed during the years of civil war and the inadequacy of traditional concepts of order for solving moral dilemmas.

In compiling his list, Thomas Washbourne drew on a new political theory that based lawful authority on possession of power rather than on hereditary right or popular consent. This theory, developed primarily by Anthony Ascham, Francis Rous, and John Dury to justify the status quo and prevent further civil turmoil, gradually replaced those based on precedent and popular sovereignty in the debate over the Engagement Oath.[15]

15 On this line of argument, see Wallace, *Destiny His Choice* and "The Engagement Controversy 1649-1652: An Annotated List of Pamphlets," *Bulletin of the New York Public Library* 68 (1964): 384-405; Perez Zagorin, *A*

Its proponents advised subscription to the oath not by claiming the government's right to power but by arguing that since it had power, subjects had the duty to obey. According to Ascham, people must obey whatever government has power to perform its essential functions: "We of the People must be contented with those governours, into whose full possessions it is our destiny to fall." Allegiance to a ruler ends when he loses plenary power, ceases, in fact, to rule. Changes in government are not the capricious deeds of blind fortune but acts of God. "We are bound," says Ascham, "to owne Princes so long as it pleases God to give them the power to command us, and when we see others possest of their powers, we may then say, that the King of Kings hath chang'd our Vice-Roys." [16] In essence, all earlier loyalties dissolved in the overwhelming flood of present reality. Because God had awarded victory to Cromwell's army, the English people owed obedience to the Commonwealth as the plenary power of England by act of providence.

Thomas Washbourne obviously drew heavily on these ideas in compiling his list, and Sanderson's response to them illuminates his own moral position as well as his casuistical procedure.[17] He touches on most of the points Washbourne raised, but he does so within his own frame of reference. Sanderson consistently condemned the policies of equivocation and mental reservation as destructive of the very purposes of speech and oaths among men. He scorned men who "play fast and loose with Oaths" and can swear to one thing on Monday and its opposite on Tuesday. To

---

History of Political Thought in the English Revolution (London: Routledge and Kegan Paul, 1954), pp. 63-77; and Quentin Skinner, "History of Ideology in the English Revolution," *The Historical Journal* 8 (1965): 151-178, and "Conquest and Consent: Thomas Hobbes and the Engagement Controversy," in *The Interregnum: The Quest for Settlement 1646-1660*, ed. G. E. Aylmer (Hamden, Conn.: Archon, 1972), pp. 79-98.

[16] Anthony Ascham, *Of the Confusions and Revolutions of Government* (London, 1649), pp. 115, 99.

[17] Sanderson was a natural choice for a case on oaths. *De Juramenti Promissorii Obligatione*, his lectures on oaths and vows delivered at Oxford in 1646, was frequently reprinted between 1647 and 1719 and reputedly translated by Charles I. In 1647, he played a large part in supplying the rationale for Oxford's resistance to the Solemn League and Convenant (see his *Reasons of the Present Judgment of the University of Oxford* [*Works*, IV]). See also Jacobson's preface to *Works*, I, ix-xi, xvii, and Lewis, *Robert Sanderson*, pp. 100-101. In addition, Sanderson's refutation of Ascham's *Of the Confusions and Revolutions of Government* was published in 1650 (*Works*, VI, 372-374).

take an oath with such general reservation as "So far as lawfully
I may" or "So far as it is agreeable to the Word of God" does not
eliminate guilt; rather it creates "a new guilt of most vile and
abominable Hypocrisy" (IV, 422). In "The Case of the Engagement," he indignantly condemns such subterfuges and denies a distinction between promises and oaths. All promises are acts done
in the sight of God whether or not they expressly call Him in as
witness. Sanderson also subordinates considerations of the consequences of engaging, since they become relevant only if the
action can be shown to be innocent. He denies that a change in
circumstances can change the moral force of an oath and rejects
the argument that previous oaths to the King are dissolved
because he no longer exercises power. Sanderson admits of no
relevant exceptions to the duty of obedience to the lawful sovereign. For the Royalist, taking an oath of loyalty to the Commonwealth is lawful only if it is compatible with full allegiance to
the King. Clearly Sanderson does not believe that Puritan military
success has indicated God's endorsement of their authority, and
he does not even consider the possibility that men could be
morally bound to subscribe to the Engagement because it was
commanded by the de facto power. He rejects the arguments
based on the concept of necessity. When everyone else was talking
about "the present power," Sanderson submitted a piece of
English prose to rigorous textual analysis.

Sanderson, then, wrote as a Royalist and Anglican, explicitly
dissociating himself from the Jesuit casuistry on the subject of
oaths and from Ascham's and Dury's support of the Commonwealth. But casuistry is broader than party allegiance, and Sanderson's casuistical approach allies him with his contemporaries.
There were cases of conscience that opposed the Engagement
Oath entirely and cases that defended it in terms of Ascham's
theories. As John Wallace demonstrates, Ascham's approach was
casuistical, not a simple-mined assertion that might makes right.
Ascham, Rous, and Dury were attempting to find a peaceful and
sane solution to a difficult problem in a nation exhausted by war.
They tried to remove men's doubts about the lawfulness of
obedience to an unlawful power, not in order to foster cynicism
but in order to avoid further bloodshed.

Casuistry was not a particular doctrinal or political position
but a particular way of looking at human experience, a way
involving both the recognition of the problematical nature of

human action and the attempt to discover rational solutions to moral problems. In Sanderson's hands the casuistical method was a remarkably subtle tool. He condemns intentional deception, but, like all casuists, he recognizes that to tell all the truth at all times is impossible and that to say nothing is sometimes dangerous or even sinful. His position lies between recommending deception and naively admonishing his readers to tell the truth. Like Ascham, he gives considerable weight to the circumstances of living in the midst of revolution and tries to show men how to live with peaceful consciences in the confusion of contemporary politics. He rejects Ascham's argument based on necessity and his treatment of oaths, while at the same time assuming the central thesis that one may obey the lawful command of an unlawful power.[18]

When placed in the context of the Engagement controversy, Sanderson's case is notable more for its subtlety in applying traditional moral principles to experience than for the originality of its political philosophy. Like Perkins's case on lawsuits, "The Case of the Engagement" gives literary form to the decision-making process. Since it was written as part of a political debate, approaching the form through the categories of rhetoric would seem natural, but traditional rhetoric fails to explain its structure. Sanderson's introduction is not the elaborate classical exordium or the briefer survey of the context of the subject recommended by some Renaissance handbooks. There is no proposition and no division, and his solution to the problem, the proposition that the case attempts to prove, is not even given until the end. Although the body of the case offers proof for Sanderson's conclusions and refutes their contraries, there is no separate confutation or confirmation. The case reaches a kind of

---

[18] In his lectures on the conscience, Sanderson gives three reasons justifying obedience to an unlawful power. First, prudence, a man's duty to protect his life, liberty, and property, may necessitate accommodation with an illegitimate government as long as it entails nothing sinful. Second, the citizen has some obligation to any government under whose protection he lives. Third, since the purpose of civil government is the tranquillity and security of human society, the behavior of every citizen must be conducive to that end and should not interfere with even an unlawful power's attempt to defend the country against foreign enemies, to administer justice, and to secure the economic life of the country. See *Lectures*, pp. 168-173.

emotional peak in the last section, yet it does not end with a stirring peroration.

The structure of the case is not that of a call to action or that of a defense of a particular view of government. Rather, Sanderson's focus is on the conscience, and his goal is to reconcile human action with divine law, to discover the lawfulness of acting or not acting in stipulated circumstances. This approach required considerable modification of traditional forms, and the process of moral discovery offered a shaping principle.

A list of various incompatible arguments such as Washbourne's could not offer a satisfactory principle of organization because acting for the wrong reason was sinful and the conscience could be satisfied only by a clear line of reasoning from first principles. So Sanderson begins by warning readers not to separate his conclusion from his complete analysis of the problem:

> If I should allow it in any case lawful, what ill use would certainly be made thereof by multitudes of people, apt to be so far scandalized thereby, as . . . to swallow it whole without chewing, (that is, resting themselves upon the general determination of the lawfulness to take it hand over head, without due consideration either of the true meaning of it or of other requisite cautions and circumstances).   (V, 20)

After thus cautioning that the case must be understood as a whole, his first step in the process of discovery is to formulate the problem accurately. While an introductory note stresses the dangers of opposing "those that have all power," the first section of the case proper makes explicit the other horn of the dilemma: man sins against his conscience, the voice of God in him, by taking an oath contrary to full allegiance to his lawful sovereign. In Part I, Sanderson clarifies the moral absolutes and spiritual dangers involved in the political action by briefly summarizing the nature of political allegiance. He assumes that the law of nature has implanted in all men the knowledge that they owe allegiance to their country and to its sovereign power and that any act contrary to that allegiance is sinful. Thus any man who believes that the King and his heirs constitute the sovereign power of England and who believes that the Engagement Oath is a repudiation of allegiance to the King may not subscribe without sinning against his conscience. The problem exists, of course, because this danger is only doubtfully present. In Part II, therefore, Sanderson shows that legitimate doubt exists because the ambiguity of language and the compliance of some men close to the King indicate the possibility that the Engagement Oath may be interpreted as compatible with allegiance to the King.

Having shown Washbourne how to set up the question, Sanderson devotes the rest of the case to showing him how to answer it. The process of resolution moves unfalteringly from the universal to the particular. Part III is a short lecture on the obligations of oaths. Sanderson postulates that all vows, oaths, and promises must be taken with an honest intention of compliance, that they must be interpreted according to the ordinary use of language, and that only this normal use of language binds the swearer, even when external knowledge indicates an ulterior intention on the part of the framers of the oath. In Part IV, Sanderson raises the particular question of ambiguity in the Engagement Oath, and, in Part V, he attempts to decide on the proper interpretation of the oath. His argument that the most reasonable interpretation is compatible with allegiance to the King necessitates recourse from theological principles to the world of experience and a careful weighing of conflicting evidence.

In the last section, the particularizing process continues. Sanderson moves from universal principles, to the particular act proposed, and then to the individual agent. Since the act itself, the circumstances, and the intention of the agent must each be considered, in Part VI Sanderson concentrates on the mind of man in action. He organizes his conclusion around the possible states of conscience—the erring, the doubting, and the right conscience. He gives in turn his opinion on the act of subscribing by a man who believes he may take an unlawful oath, a man who is doubtful of the oath's legality, and a man who is sure that it is lawful.

This final section serves simultaneously as the last step in the decision-making process and as a summarizing conclusion. In order to review the principles and method by which man must judge his action in this case, Sanderson divides his condemnation of acting against one's own judgment of the oath's unlawfulness into three parts. First, taking the Engagement while intending to break it is unlawful. Second, taking the Engagement while understanding it to require a promise of unlawful action is sinful. Third, the Engagement Oath does require a promise of unlawful action if it is understood as contrary to one's true allegiance.

These three conclusions review the principles of the sanctity of oaths, the inviolability of natural allegiance, and the necessity of following one's own conscience.

Sanderson's next conclusion is condemnation of any man with a doubting conscience who subscribes for prudential reasons. Here he reviews the criterion for resolving a doubting conscience, "some probable ground of reason" that the proposed action is lawful. Finally, he concludes that a man who is firmly convinced that the words of the Engagement intend nothing contrary to his allegiance and do not prohibit him from exercising his loyalty to the King should the opportunity arise may take the Engagement rather than incur physical or economic hardship. This last recommendation serves as both a prototype of the mature, enlightened conscience and an indirect plea for individual freedom of action in this particular case.

"The Case of the Engagement" is a didactic work exhorting men to virtue, a description of various kinds of human evil and good, and a detailed argument justifying compliance with an act of Parliament. It is structured differently from most works with these ends, however, in that it is not primarily descriptive or persuasive. The process of discovering a solution to a problem gives the case its shape. Sanderson starts by setting up an unanswered question and by indicating the moral laws that may or may not prevent the proposed act. He then indicates the theological principles governing cases of this particular kind and demonstrates the deductive process by which man should relate his actions to general rules and the inductive process by which questions of fact can be decided. Finally, he tries to lead men to explore their own consciences. The most distinctive feature of the case is its attempt to imitate the process by which man can reach right decisions, that is, to embody the mode of thinking it recommends.

The casuist's conception of the decision-making process determines his presentation of his subject matter. Sanderson's belief in the supremacy of the individual conscience permeates his treatment of the Engagement Oath controversy. He does not discuss the oath on its intrinsic merits as a piece of governmental policy. Because the essential problem for him is the relationship between the oath and divine law, he devotes most of the case to demonstrating that the act of subscribing to the Engagement may be in harmony with the will of God. More significantly, he assumes that subscription can be judged morally only by knowing the conscience of the man who subscribes. Even if the act is essentially lawful, it becomes evil for anyone not fully convinced of its innocence. Thus, in the last section, Sanderson actually gives no absolute answer to the question but concludes instead with five particular and more limited opinions. Thus the decision of whether subscribing is lawful or unlawful remains perforce with Mr. Washbourne, but the casuist can show him how to proceed.

This focus on the individual decision produces one of the most obvious stylistic features of the case of conscience—a personal quality often reflected in the use of the epistolary form. Thomas Washbourne appeals to Sanderson, whom he did not know personally: "I desire you would supply the place of a father in your counsel" (V, 17). Sanderson replies appropriately with a letter that begins with informal remarks on the weather, sometimes refers directly to Washbourne in the course of the analysis of the problem, and ends gracefully with messages of friendship to his family. More important, Sanderson works with the political and religious assumptions of his audience. He makes no effort to prove that Charles is the lawful King of England or to refute current arguments that taking the oath is morally obligatory. He tailors his analysis to the conflict of conscience proposed by Washbourne, a Royalist trying to decide whether cooperation with the new establishment will involve repudiating deeply held beliefs.

Yet this personal quality should not be exaggerated. Casuistry is not simply fatherly advice of the "if I were you" sort. Sanderson clearly thought that his analysis applied to more people than Thomas Washbourne and gave explicit permission for his letter to be used by others with similar doubts. Since the conscience is a faculty of the conscious intellect, not a religious emotion, he takes pains to present his decision as the product of an incontrovertible logical process. He relies most heavily on the enthymeme, which Aristotle calls the most effective of the modes of persuasion and recommends as particularly useful for the forensic orator who is concerned with the justice or injustice of actions. The logical structure of Sanderson's argument is readily apparent: if the Engagement is a repudiation of the subject's allegiance to his sovereign, taking it is unjust; if the declared intention of the oath is compatible with true allegiance, taking it is lawful;

if the declared intention of the oath is the more liberal of the possible interpretations, it is compatible with allegiance to the King. The more liberal interpretation is the most probable, and, therefore, anyone so understanding it may lawfully engage.

Sanderson stresses the continuity of his line of thought and maintains a semblance of dialogue with his questioner by anticipating new steps in his analysis with rhetorical questions. He emphasizes his logical structure with such logical connectives as "First, then," "For if," and "Wherefore," and calls attention to the inevitability of the dialectical machinery he has set in motion with such phrases as "the next Inquiry must be," and "there are two things more to be done." Similarly, he often labels his unproved premises: "I take that for a clear truth," "the reason whereof is manifest." All this produces a dense prose style that carries forward a closely reasoned argument. Numbered sections and subdivisions outline the argument and create the sense of a systematic and exhaustive treatment.

This clarity and rationality do not mean that Sanderson disdained artfulness. He is writing for Anglicans and therefore directs his appeals to their prejudices. His conclusion was open to the criticism of encouraging compliance with regicides and of using Jesuitical sophistries, so he carefully dissociates himself from both enemy camps with emotionally charged passages prior to commiting himself to controversial opinions. In Part I, he roundly condemns those who took the Solemn League and Covenant; and in Part II, where he first admits of ambiguity in the oath and charitably judges men who have taken it, he indulges in a largely irrelevant jibe at the Presbyterians. Before concluding in Part III that one may interpret an ambiguous oath to his own advantage, he castigates "the impudence of the Jesuits" (V, 24) for justifying equivocations. Thus Sanderson uses traditional rhetorical techniques, but his polemical skill is effective more because of its infrequency than because of its originality. On the whole, his is the calm, unruffled voice of the academician even when taking a controversial stand on a bitterly debated contemporary problem. Frequently reminding his reader of the possibility of doubt and disagreement, he keeps the focus as much on his method of disentangling complexities as on his solution to the problem.

Sanderson's discussion of verbal ambiguity illustrates his ingenious problem-solving approach to moral choice. Having established in Part II that the Engagement Oath has been interpreted in different ways, he proposes in Part III to answer a series of questions:

> Whether, upon supposition that the words of the Engagement will bear more constructions than one, the Subscriber may take it in his own sense? Or is bound to take it in the Imposer's sense? Or whether it be necessary, or expedient, before he subscribe, to ask those that require his subscription, in what sense they require him to subscribe it? (V, 24)

First, Sanderson categorically denies that anyone can in good conscience make a promise if his own interpretation of the promise differs significantly from the meaning expressed and understood by its proposer. The concept of equivocation, he says, undermines the purpose of such promises, "the preservation of faith among mankind." All oaths "ought to be understood *ad mentem Imponentis,* according to the mind and meaning of him to whom the faith is to be given . . . as according to the ordinary use of speech amongst men" (V, 25).

On the other hand, he argues, sometimes words express intention so imprecisely that an oath may be understood in more than one sense without forcing language beyond ordinary usage. In that case it is usually imprudent and unnecessary to ask for clarification. Since a man imposes an oath for his own benefit, the responsibility for making his intention intelligible is also his. Sanderson recognizes still another possibility. A cunning man may purposely word an oath ambiguously because he has "some more remote and secret intention than he is willing to discover." The casuist advises using this duplicity to one's own advantage by disregarding any ulterior meaning, since the prescriber of the oath is free to word it as he wishes and can be assumed to intend no more than the oath states.

Part IV applies these rules for dealing with ambiguity to the oath itself. According to Sanderson, the very leniency of the Engagement Oath introduced "sundry ambiguities." Most basically, "Commonwealth" may mean either "those persons who are the prevalent party . . . and now are possessed of and do exercise the Supreme Power" (V, 28), or simply the whole English nation as distinguished from foreign states. Thus the promise of fidelity may be to the present governors and imply acknowledgment of their right to power, or it may simply pertain to the safety of the nation and imply no more than willingness to live peaceably under the de facto rulers.

The second ambiguity is closely related to this. The final clause, "as it is now established without King and Lords," may signify approval of this form of government, or it may be a mere recital of facts describing the present government. The last ambiguity is the phrase "true and faithful." Here there are three alternative readings. The faith promised may be understood to be that owed to the King; it may be simply that fidelity every man owes his country; or it may be such faith as prisoners of war give to their captors "to remain true prisoners of War, and, so long as they are under their power, not to attempt any thing to their destruction." Finally, on the basis of these ambiguous phrases, Sanderson proposed three readings of the oath ranging from a promise of undying allegiance to the present government to a promise merely "to do what every good member of a Commonwealth ought to do for the safety of my Country, and preservation of Civil Society" (V, 30-31).

In this fashion, Sanderson continues to weave his way through the intricacies of logic, semantics, moral philosophy, psychology, and political theory that are presented by the problem he confronts. For the reader, the result of this procedure is that the interest in reading the case derives as much from the puzzle-solving process as from the applicability of its solution to his life. The focus on the use of reason to resolve doubt distinguishes the case of conscience from related genres. Casuistry often appears within sermons and devotional works that also treat human experience in moral terms and are designed to influence the conscience. Unlike cases of conscience, however, these forms usually attempt to overcome the natural man's resistance to known truths rather than to resolve moral dilemmas. The meditation, for example, moves from a sense perception of the physical universe, through the play of the mind on some tenet of faith, to the directing of the will to action. Sermons, too, are directed at the apostate will rather than the analytic intellect. Neither Donne's funeral sermons nor Browne's *Hydriotaphia* is designed to prove that man must die in order that he may live. Rather they attempt to convince men of the imminence of death, the transience of the mundane, and the reality of the world of the spirit. Sermons often dealt with practical problems, of course, and were used for controversial purposes, but they characteristically focused on an accepted principle of virtuous action rather than on a difficult application of a principle.

Casuistry's concern with practical morality allies it with such genres as the essay, the courtesy book, the book of estates, and the Theophrastan character, but casuistry is distinctive in its detailed attention to the circumstances of particular moral problems.[19] Conduct books teach men that they should be obedient and honest, but they rarely deal with specific issues. The books of estates give general directions for virtuous behavior but are organized around particular callings and do not give detailed instructions for dealing with specific cases. Whether organized in terms of occupation, social position, or basic character traits, the Theophrastan character portrays types of human nature rather than analyzing moral problems. Even such characters as "a hypocritical convert of the times" or "a turn-coat," concentrate on the moral quality of the man rather than of the action.[20] In contrast, the casuist's moral judgment is inseparable from his analysis of a particular action. Thus, in Sanderson's "The Case of the Engagement," swearing to an oath proposed by an unlawful government does not necessarily make a man "a turn-coat" or "a hypocritical convert." Instead, Sanderson demonstrates that understanding the moral nature of an act of accommodation requires detailed investigation of the nature of oaths, the wording of the oath in question, and the surrounding political and ecclesiastical situation. Such particular circumstances determine which of the three possible readings can most reasonably be regarded as the government's "declared intention" in the Engagement Oath.

In Part V, Sanderson acknowledges that a reasonable argument can be presented in support of the strongest interpretation. Assuming that any political power desires to secure and perpetuate itself and that this end can best be achieved by obtaining the widest possible acknowledgment of its right to power, one could argue that the Engagement was designed to achieve this

[19] See Walter E. Houghton, Jr.'s analysis of the interrelations of these traditions in *The Formation of Thomas Fuller's 'Holy and Profane States'* (Cambridge, Mass.: Harvard University Press, 1938).

[20] According to Benjamin Boyce, this type, the polemic character, flourished between 1640 and 1660, a period contemporary with the popularity of cases of conscience. *The Polemic Character 1640-1661* (Lincoln, Neb.: University of Nebraska Press, 1955).

end and must, therefore, be interpreted in the most obligatory sense. But, Sanderson argues, although the strongest interpretation is undoubtedly closer to the present rulers' secret and ultimate intention, it is strongly probable that their declared intention is less binding. He lists six arguments in favor of a more lenient interpretation. First, many conscientious Royalists have taken it, and, second, some of the men imposing the oath are reported to have said that the less rigorous interpretation is correct. Third, the imposers of the oath could have worded it more strongly if they had wanted to. Fourth, they seem to have purposely rejected the stronger phrase "against King and Lords." Fifth, since they are consciously forcing the oath on men who think them to be usurpers, they must in reason be requiring only a promise to live quietly. Sixth, it is a "received Maxim of Political Prudence" for disputed governments to attempt to conciliate their disaffected subjects rather than to increase their hostility. Such governments usually are well satisfied with the assurance that men will live quietly under their rule. Thus, Sanderson argues, the men imposing the Engagement, who have shown themselves to be very effective politicians, probably would not "be so impolitic as not to proceed by the same rules, that all wise and successful persons have ever practised in the managing and for the establishing of an Acquired Power" (V, 34).[21]

My analysis of "The Case of the Engagement" has attempted to demonstrate that the habits of mind evident in casuistical theory produce a distinctive formulation of human moral experi-

---

[21] Evidence about the intention of Parliament is contradictory. Earlier in the year, John Lilburne subscribed to the Engagement when he was elected to the London Common Council with a declaration that by "Commonwealth" he understood "all the good and legal people of England to be meant," not "the present Parliament, Council of State, or Council of the Army" (*The Engagement Vindicated and Explained*). Parliament rejected Lilburne's declaration and invalidated his election (Gardiner, *History of the Commonwealth*, I, 198). On the other hand, John Dury interpreted the Engagement as an oath "to be true and faithfull to the Nation, notwithstanding the absence of the King and House of Lords from the government" (*Declaration of John Durie*). His written interpretation submitted to the government was found satisfactory (see J. Minton Batten, *John Dury: Advocate of Christian Reunion* [Chicago: The University of Chicago Press, 1944], pp. 122-123). At any rate, the question of whether Parliament wanted to purge dissenters or to reassure themselves of a peaceful citizenry is largely irrelevant here since Sanderson's position is that a lawful decision must consider the available information but not secret intentions.

ence when they are applied in particular cases of conscience. The end of Part VI of the case demonstrates the distinctive quality of this kind of prose:

> That if any man, after a serious desire and moral endeavour of informing himself as rightly and impartially as he can, what are the duties and obligations of his Allegiance on the one side, and what is most probably the meaning intended by the words of the Engagement on the other side, shall find himself well satisfied in this persuasion, that the performance in the mean time of what is required by the Engagement, so understood as he apprehendeth it ought to be, is no way contrary (for any thing he can discern for the present) to his bounden Allegiance, so long as he is under such a force, as that he cannot exercise it; and likewise, that whensoever that force is so removed from him, or he from under it, as that he hath power to act according to his Allegiance, the Obligation of the Engagement of itself determineth and expireth; and out of these considerations, rather than suffer extreme prejudice in his Person, Estate, or necessary Relations, shall subscribe the Engagement; since his own heart condemneth him not, neither will I. (V, 34-35)

Although Sanderson is not eloquent, he has created a fitting conclusion for his case by pulling together a bewildering array of considerations. This painstaking prose is less the product of a legalistic mind or of an externally imposed logical framework than of a conceptual system in which thought and act are inseparable. The motives from which a man acts, the information available to him about the circumstances of a proposed action and its consequences, and a standard of moral value are inextricably bound together. Sanderson delicately traces their relations to each other in a particular case and dexterously suspends his final resolution of the case from an intricate network of qualifications and reservations.

CASUISTRY AND ITS PROBLEMS

The case of conscience was not a rigid prose form and was never entirely satisfactory, but it constitutes an interesting and significant, if minor, Renaissance prose form. The characteristics that distinguish "The Case of the Engagement" appear in the writings of other casuists and in Sanderson's other cases. In "The Case of the Use of the Liturgy," for example, Sanderson again demonstrates the proper operation of the conscience by combining an exposition of relevant theological assumptions with a model of the ratiocinative process by which one can relate them to a specific problem. But instead of moving from the problem through the basic principles to the particular action and then to the conscience of the individual agent, Sanderson structures this case on the fundamental tenet that virtuous action must be consistent with the dictates of conscience. He begins by summarizing the question and then describes his own practice in three different situations, thus providing models of the logical process of discovery of a right conscience in three possible sets of circumstances.

Sanderson has been useful in this chapter as a model of the casuist at work because he so admirably combines respect for the freedom of the individual conscience with veneration for moral law, attitudes essential to the casuist's habit of mind. The painstaking precision and ingenuity with which he solves riddles of moral life relate action to thought and thought to the varying and transient conditions of the world as well as to eternal truths. Focusing on one case has been necessary to show how the casuist applies his theory of conscience and law to a particular problem, but it inevitably distorts the view of casuistry as a whole. While Sanderson's case treats the dilemma of an individual within a framework of external authority, many cases adapt the casuistical approach to problems concerning the morally right conduct of authority itself.

Case divinity always concentrates on moral decisions, but problems of personal and of public morality imperceptibly merge. The question of whether I may lawfully sign a loyalty oath is very close to the question of whether the state may lawfully test the loyalty of its citizens in this way. If the breakdown of traditional channels of moral guidance created the need for casuists to treat issues of the first kind, the experience of civil war and the virtual disintegration of established institutions increased the need for answers to issues of the second kind. For example, when Cromwell referred to the Council of State the question of readmitting Jews into England, they called a conference to consider "whether it be lawful to receive the Jews. If it be lawful, then upon what terms is it meet to receive them?"[22] Both Thomas Barlow and John Dury wrote cases of conscience presenting this issue as a problem of moral doubt for the decision makers who risked sin either through refusal to act or through precipitous action.[23] These casuists resolved the dilemma by discussing such general moral principles as the duty of charity and the nature of scandal and then applying them to particular circumstances to prove the lawfulness of allowing nonbelievers to live within a Christian commonwealth.

Although they approached the issue from a distinctively casuistical perspective, the casuists had to modify the form of their approach because they were dealing with government policy rather than with individual action. Their cases include brief discussions of "lawfulness" in a constitutional as well as a moral sense. Once they have established that toleration in general is not prohibited by either human or scriptural law and that the question is one of the lawfulness of tolerating Jews in England in 1655, then their focus shifts almost entirely to the anticipated consequences of the action. They refute prevalent opposition arguments that the presence of Jews will endanger the Church and the economic vitality of England, and they discuss such diverse arguments for readmission as expiation of guilt for past cruelty, probable economic benefits, and the hope that the world-wide dispersal of the Jews and their subsequent conversion will usher in the millennium. All these arguments about the con-

---

[22] Albert M. Hyamson, *A History of the Jews in England*, 2d ed. (London: Methuen, 1928), p. 159; Cecil Roth, *A History of the Jews in England* (Oxford: Clarendon Press, 1941). A valuable contemporary account of the conference is "A Narrative of the Late Proceedings at Whitehall, concerning the Jews" (London, 1656), in *The Harleian Miscellany*, ed. J. Malham, 12 vols. (London, 1808-1811), VI, 445-454.

[23] Barlow's "The Case of the Jews" was, according to the preface to the 1692 edition, "writ at the Request of a Person of Quality, in the late troublesome Times; when the *Jews* made Application to *Cromwel*, for their Re-admission into *England*." The "Person of Quality" has been variously identified as Robert Owen, Robert Boyle, or Thomas Goodwin. See Rev. S. Levy, "Bishop Barlow on the 'Case of the Jews'," *Transactions of the Jewish Historical Society of England: 1896-1898* 3 (1899): 151-156, and Roth, *A History of the Jews in England*, pp. 162-164. John Dury's "A Case of Conscience, whether it be lawful to admit Jews into a christian commonwealth?" was written for Samuel Hartlib and is dated 8 January 1650 (see *The Harleian Miscellany*, VI, 438-444).

sequences of toleration, however, are subordinated to the design that tries to establish its moral innocence.[24]

Cases such as these, obviously intended to influence the course of public events as well as to bring peace to a troubled conscience, became more frequent as democratic ideas developed through the century. In the 1590s, Perkins dealt with the moral duties of the individual as a member of society but did not presume to give moral advice to Elizabeth. But Baxter, writing after the Restoration, says that he omitted "Directions to Princes, Nobles, Parliament-men, and other Magistrates" only because they would not accept his advice (Bk. IV, Preface). And Taylor, an ardent Royalist, advises Charles II in 1660, "you will best govern by the arguments and compulsory of conscience," and includes questions on the proper use of civil and ecclesiastical power (XI, cccxlii).

My analysis of the method and form of the case of conscience has also largely ignored the obvious fact that casuistry could easily be used not to discover truth but to justify what one had already decided to do. All casuists agreed that circumstances alter cases and that prudence is a virtue and overscrupulousness a vice. The godly discretion of casuistry was imperative for salvation as well as worldly survival, but it could also be a way of finding moral loopholes. For all their skill in meeting evil with shrewdness, Ames, Sanderson, Taylor, and Baxter personally confronted situations where conscience prohibited compromise; and they suffered for their principles in the political turbulence of their world. In contrast, Thomas Barlow, who also enjoyed the reputation of skillful casuist,[25] was a master of the art of self-preservation. Not only did he survive the purge of Oxford, which reduced Sanderson to penury, but he furthered his career under the Protectorate. Meanwhile, he maintained his connections with episcopal leaders and adapted as easily to the Restoration as he had to the Commonwealth, becoming Bishop of Lincoln in 1675. Subsequently, his violent anti-Catholicism after the Titus Oates

---

[24] More precisely, Barlow concludes that toleration in this case is permissible, and Dury concludes that it is obligatory.

[25] Thomas Birch writes of Barlow, "The doctor was a man of prodigious reading, and a proportionable memory; he knew what the fathers, schoolmen, or canonists had said upon any question in divinity, or case of conscience; and being with all these accomplishments very communicative of his knowledge, he gained the highest degree of Mr. *Boyle's* esteem and friendship, who used, as long as he lived, to consult him upon cases of conscience." Thomas Birch. *The Life of the Honorable Robert Boyle* (London, 1744), pp. 113-114.

scandal, his compliance with a severe policy toward nonconform-
ists, his effusive endorsement of James II, and his immediate and
willing transfer of allegiance to William and Mary illustrate
Barlow's skill in trimming his sails as the political and ecclesiastical winds shifted.[26]

Although Barlow professed admiration for Sanderson's casuistry, his own cases of conscience manipulate the principles and
procedures of casuistry as a strategy of persuasion rather than as
a model of the decision-making process. He follows Sanderson
in emphasizing the responsibility of the Christian conscience and
in portraying moral absolutes as functions of appropriate thought
and action in particular circumstances. He adopts the epistolary
framework, the controlled rational tone, and the division of his
prose into numbered subdivisions. He usually organizes his cases
by first clarifying the implications of the problem, then proposing
the general principles or laws by which moral doubt can be
resolved and systematically applying these principles to the problem, and finally suggesting specific directions for acting without
sin. His analysis, however, is often logically inconsistent, and the
actual progression of thought does not embody the ostensible
application of general moral principles to a unique human
predicament. He imposes the external characteristics of the case
of conscience on his discussion without actually demonstrating the
process of discovering moral certainty.

Barlow's casuistry, then, marks the limitations of the form. The
reader is annoyed by his parade of erudition and his display of
misleading schematizations. And even in such cases as Sanderson's,
where logic is used rigorously, the cautious and deliberate examination of detail becomes tedious. More serious than the danger
of pedantry, though, is the tension in the case of conscience
between the universal and the particular. While professing the
uniqueness of each case, the casuist must also try to create a model
resolution that will apply to the problems of many men. This
attempt to universalize while preaching particularity leads to a
proliferation of exceptions and qualifications that can try the
patience of even the most sympathetic reader.

Most Renaissance casuists recognized these problems. They
were aware that case divinity, properly the study of how to act

[26] Leslie Stephen and Sidney Lee, eds., *Dictionary of National Biography*,
22 vols. (London, 1885), II, 224-229.

obediently and lovingly in difficult circumstances, could degenerate into quibbles over exceptions to external laws. Thus Taylor
warns that "when men have no love to God, and desire but just
to save their souls, and weigh grains and scruples, and give to
God no more than they must needs, they shall multiply cases of
consciences to a number which no books will contain, and to a
difficulty that no learning can answer" (XI, 366). But the answer
to human weakness and perversity was to provide the proper sort
of case divinity, not to scrap it entirely. "The good man," Taylor
argues, "understands the things of God; not only because God's
Spirit, by secret emissions of light, does properly instruct him;
but because he hath a way of determining his cases of conscience
which will never fail him" (XI, 366).

Casuists also struggled with the tension between their assumptions that individual cases are unique and that model cases may
be generally helpful. Sanderson's lectures and cases are notable
for the subtlety and integrity of their exploration of man's
attempt to live according to divine law in a human world, but
they do not comprise a comprehensive body of casuistry. Taylor's
and Baxter's treatises are the most systematic and comprehensive
expositions of English casuistry. They clarify the relationship
between the individual and moral authority by explaining precisely the hierarchy of moral laws that govern human conduct, the
circumstances that qualify these duties, and the relationship
between these standards of good and evil and man as a free moral
agent defined by his thought as well as his actions, his intentions
as well as the consequences of his deeds. They demonstrate all
this vividly and often persuasively in concrete examples. But
neither Taylor nor Baxter was entirely successful in reconciling
the individualizing and the generalizing impulses in casuistry.
Edmund Gosse sees no merit in the theological structure of
Ductor and praises the illustrative cases as "an entertaining miscellany of stories," while H. R. McAdoo complains that Taylor's
sound exposition of principles is obscured by his "positively
feminine garrulity" in recounting thousands of intricate hypothetical cases.[27] Both the theoretical discussions and the sample
cases are necessary expressions of the view that a holy life results
from the discovery of viable norms by the enlightened reason

---

[27] Edmund Gosse, *Jeremy Taylor* (London: Macmillan and Co., 1904), pp.
165-166; McAdoo, *Structure of Caroline Moral Theology*, p. 67.

and exists in the realization of these values in experience. Nevertheless, the two parts seem mechanically combined rather than unified, and the combination is a huge work that I doubt anyone has read straight through with complete enjoyment.

Closely related to the contradiction involved in supplying a general model for a process that was theoretically unique and personal is the problem of the basis of authority. Casuists applied generally accepted norms to particular problems with varying degrees of success and intellectual integrity. On the whole, they maintained a delicate balance between individual freedom and moral order, but they were never able to resolve the problem of a direct conflict between the individual conscience and lawful authority. Protestant casuists insisted that the individual conscience is supreme, but they also held that authority is divinely sanctioned and that just law is morally obligatory. They taught that laws are intended for the public good and in some circumstances may be disregarded. Thus they allowed considerable scope for individual action with regard to particular laws, but they also denied that the individual could defy the lawful authority of church or state. A man who in conscience could not accept that authority thus had no alternative but to sin. The major English casuists agreed that the conscience is bound only by the word of God, that individual interpretations of God's word differ, and that failing to follow the dictates of one's conscience is sinful. They also warned that men err in interpreting God's word and sin by following an erroneous conscience. Baxter's position is typical:

> If you *follow it* [an erroneous conscience] you break the Law
> of God in doing that which he forbids you: If you *forsake*
> it and *go against* it, you reject the *authority* of God, in doing
> that which you *think* he forbids you. (Bk. I, p. 135)

For this quandary they offered only the futile advice that anyone in error should stop being wrong: "Shall he *follow* his judgement, or *go against it? Neither*, but *change it, and then follow it*" (Baxter, Bk. I, p. 135).

The casuists' occasional failures should not blind us to their more frequent successes. The attempt to construct in prose an example of a difficult moral decision involves the casuist at once in intrinsically interesting and important material. His subject matter includes the human mind, the actual world of particular things, people, and events, and man's conception of truths transcending his own time and place. Like a philosopher, the casuist schematizes the truths of human existence. Like a journalist, he reports the minutiae of public life, and like a psychologist, he studies the way men know and think and feel. Like a poet, he presents the universal through the particular. He is distinctive in his constant acknowledgment of the distance between generalized rules of conduct and the actuality of a single mind operating morally in a particular situation and in his form that embodies the decision-making process. The casuist's preoccupation with generally established moral law and his conception of the conscience as a function of the practical intellect do not lead him to rise to the heights of bold and original thought or to plumb the depths of human passion, but they do allow him to organize in coherent fashion a significant kind of human experience. Coleridge's evaluation of Jeremy Taylor accurately defines the powers and the limitations of the best English casuists. According to Coleridge, Taylor possessed broad and deep erudition, acute and subtle logic, fine yet secure psychological insight, public prudence and practical sagacity; he lacked only the creative faith and imagination that would have made him a great creative genius.[28] In the following chapters I shall examine the works of men who successfully combined the casuistical habit of mind with creative imagination.

[28] E. L. Griggs, ed., *Collected Letters of Samuel Taylor Coleridge,* 6 vols. (Oxford: Clarendon Press, 1956-1971), III, 954-955.

Chapter III

CASES OF CONSCIENCE IN SHAKESPEARE'S TRAGEDIES

Renaissance drama is certainly far removed in mode and style from laborious casuistical prose with its fine distinctions and numbered directions. Indeed, the casuists' tortuous reasoning and emphasis on exceptions to moral law provided a ready target for dramatic satire. In *Epicoene,* Ben Jonson mocked the casuistry of divorce, and Molière, like Pascal, parodied Jesuitical casuistry as *"une science / D'étendre les liens de notre conscience."* [1] But casuistry provided dramatists with more than a butt of satire: the casuists' categories and procedures are often revealingly pertinent to the playwrights' explorations of moral choice. In Webster's *The Duchess of Malfi,* for example, the Bosola plot is a study of a man sinning against his conscience, and the disintegration of Duke Ferdinand's mind and the cold despair of the Cardinal are dramatic investigations of states of mind that the casuists discussed in terms of evil conscience. Beatrice Joanna in *The Changeling* is a fascinating study of the way in which lack of intellectual clarity and responsibility leads to immoral action and the way action produces character. In *Measure for Measure* and *All's Well that Ends Well,* Shakespeare's treatment of unconventional and morally problematic action in complex circumstances suggests casuistry's focus on moral dilemmas. [2] Less obviously, casuistical ways of thinking inform Shakespeare's tragedies. Recent scholar-

---

[1] *Tartuffe,* 4.5.

[2] Although I disagree with Wylie Sypher's interpretation of casuistry and of *Measure for Measure* as "adjusting immediate legalism to ultimate indeterminations," he is surely right to suggest a connection with casuistry. Wylie Sypher, "Shakespeare as Casuist: *Measure for Measure,*" *Sewanee Review* 58 (1950): 262-280; reprinted in *Essays in Shakespearean Criticism,* ed. James L. Calderwood and Harold E. Toliver (Englewood Cliffs, N.J.: Prentice-Hall, 1970), pp. 323-336.

ship has done much to deepen our understanding of the crucial moral choices in the tragedies by freeing us from short-sighted absorption in our own values and in the issues of our time and place, but it has sometimes subordinated the artist's particular moral vision to the intellectual tradition invoked to illuminate it. In order to respond fully to Shakespeare's dramatizations of the act of choice, we need to understand not just Renaissance values but also Renaissance ideas about how values apply to particular circumstances. Recognizing the casuistical habit of mind can help to rescue us from the Scylla of reducing the plays to thesis-ridden expositions of conventional Tudor pieties and the Charybdis of distorting them into anachronistic forerunners of existential nihilism.

SINNING AGAINST CONSCIENCE IN *Richard III*

As early as *Richard III,* Shakespeare constructed a play reflecting the contemporary interest in the problems of conscience that also engaged the first English casuists.[3] For example, Buckingham's speech persuading the Cardinal to seize the young Prince of York exemplifies the sophistical type of casuistry that argues that sin is not sin. Although his mother has taken the young prince into sanctuary and Cardinal Bourchier has said that he will not "be guilty of so deep a sin" as to "infringe the holy privilege/Of blessed sanctuary," Buckingham convinces the Cardinal that in this case sanctuary is not sanctuary:

> You break not sanctuary in seizing him.
> The benefit thereof is always granted
> To those whose dealings have deserv'd the place
> And those who have the wit to claim the place.
> This prince hath neither claim'd it nor deserv'd it,

---

[3] Several studies have focused on the theme of conscience in *Richard III.* See especially Robert Heilman, "Satiety and Conscience: Aspects of *Richard III,*" *Antioch Review* 24 (1964): 57-73, reprinted in *Essays in Shakespearean Criticism,* ed. Calderwood and Toliver, pp. 137-151; Nicholas Brooke, "Reflecting Gems and Dead Bones: Tragedy vs. History in *Richard III,*" *Critical Quarterly* 7 (1965): 123-134, revised and expanded in Brooke, *Shakespeare's Early Tragedies* (London: Methuen and Co., 1968), pp. 48-79; Richard P. Wheeler, "History, Character and Conscience in *Richard III,*" *Comparative Drama* 5 (1971-1972): 301-321; William B. Toole, "The Motif of Psychic Division in *Richard III,*" *Shakespeare Survey* 27 (1974): 21-32.

And therefore, in mine opinion, cannot have it.
Then taking him from thence that is not there,
You break no privilege nor charter there.

(3.1.47-54) [4]

When Richard feigns reluctance to ascend the throne, Bucking-ham plays a similar role, urging that in the circumstances Rich-ard's hesitation is overscrupulous:

My lord, this argues conscience in your Grace,
But the respects thereof are nice and trivial,
All circumstances well considered.

(3.7.174-176)

Richard III exposes the way in which men use the casuistical principle that circumstances alter cases to rationalize the most reprehensible actions, but more centrally it dramatizes the dy-namics of the evil conscience. The casuistical concepts of con-science and moral law constitute the thematic heart of the play. Indeed, William Perkins's dedicatory letter to *A Discourse of Conscience* could serve as a gloss on the central action. Perkins introduces his treatise on conscience by refuting the popular error that "Conscience was hanged long agoe." Although people blithely sin without hesitation or remorse, he says, they can ig-nore their consciences only for a time. Finally, everyone has a conscience he cannot escape.

Indeede Satan for his part goes about by all meanes he can, to benumme the conscience: but all is nothing. For as the sicke man, when he seemes to sleepe and take his rest, is in-wardly full of troubles: so the benummed and drousie con-science wants not his secret pangs and terrours, and when it shall bee roused by the judgement of God, it waxeth cruell and fierce like a wilde beast. Againe, when a man sinnes against his conscience, as much as in him lieth, he plungeth himselfe into the gulfe of desperation: for every wound of the conscience, though the smart of it be little felt, is a deadly wound. . . . Thirdly, he that lieth in sinnes against his

---

[4] Shakespeare quotations are from *The Riverside Shakespeare*, ed. G. Blake-more Evans et al. (Boston: Houghton Mifflin Co., 1974). I have dropped the square brackets used by Evans to indicate his departures from copy-text. References are to act, scene, and line and will be cited parenthetically in the text.

conscience, cannot call upon the name of God: for a guiltie
conscience makes a man flie from God.[5]

The painful waking of the numbed conscience is first worked
out through Clarence. He appears in scene one as "Simple plain
Clarence," the victim of Richard's duplicity, bewildered by the
injustices he suffers. But in scene 3, we are soon reminded of
Clarence's past of bloodshed and perjury. Unlike the troubled
man who consulted Robert Sanderson about the Engagement
Oath in fear he would shipwreck his conscience by searching for
security in politically tumultuous times, Clarence has switched
allegiances and broken oaths without compunction. In defeat, he
experiences "the force and nature of Conscience" that William
Ames reduces to the syllogism:

He that lives in sinne, shall dye:
    I live in sinne;
Therefore, I shall dye.[6]

Clarence dreams of the wreck men make of their lives by pursuing worldly instead of spiritual treasure:

> Methoughts I saw a thousand fearful wracks;
> A thousand men that fishes gnaw'd upon;
> Wedges of gold, great anchors, heaps of pearl,
> Inestimable stones, unvalued jewels,
> All scatt'red in the bottom of the sea:
> Some lay in dead men's skulls, and in the holes
> Where eyes did once inhabit, there were crept
> (As 'twere in scorn of eyes) reflecting gems,
> That woo'd the slimy bottom of the deep,
> And mock'd the dead bones that lay scatt'red by.
>   (1.4.24-33)

This macabre vision of the vanity of earthly riches is only the
prologue to the tempest in Clarence's soul, where his conscience
acts as witness and judge. Memories of his past actions testify
against him:

[5] William Perkins, *A Discourse of Conscience,* in *The Workes of that
Famous and Worthy Minister of Christ . . . Mr. William Perkins,* 3 vols.
(London, 1612-1613), I, 516.
[6] William Ames, *Conscience with the Power and Cases Thereof* (1639),
Bk. I, p. 3.

70

> The first that there did greet my stranger soul
> Was my great father-in-law, renowned Warwick,
> Who spake aloud, "What scourge for perjury
> Can this dark monarchy afford false Clarence?"
> And so he vanish'd. Then came wand'ring by
> A shadow like an angel, with bright hair
> Dabbled in blood, and he shriek'd out aloud,
> "Clarence is come—false, fleeting, perjur'd Clarence,
> That stabb'd me in the field by Tewksbury:
> Seize on him, Furies, take him unto torment!"
>
> (1.4.48-57)

Clarence, who protests the injustice of his condemnation by men, cannot deny the evidence of his conscience:

> Ah, Keeper, Keeper, I have done these things
> (That now give evidence against my soul).
>
> (1.4.66-67)

While Clarence returns to the terrors of sleep troubled by his own judgment of his guilty past, his murderers enter and discuss the other function of conscience: to legislate or guide future action. One of the murderers, restrained by some "dregs of conscience," balks at the last moment, but he remembers the promised reward and decides never again to listen to his conscience:

> I'll not meddle with it, it makes a man a coward. A man cannot steal, but it accuseth him; a man cannot swear, but it checks him; a man cannot lie with his neighbor's wife, but it detects him. 'Tis a blushing shame-fac'd spirit that mutinies in a man's bosom. (1.4.134-139)

Clarence's account of his dream and the murderers' decision to kill dramatize how conscience applies knowledge of good and evil to particular actions, past and future, and how acting against one's conscience is a universal failing among men. When Clarence awakes, the confrontation between killers and victim clarifies the relation of conscience to the laws of man and of God. In spite of the second murderer's recognition that killing Clarence, even with the king's warrant, means "to be damn'd for killing him, from the which no warrant can defend me" (1.4.111-112), they justify themselves to Clarence on the basis of human authority:

> *1 Mur.*   What we will do, we do upon command.
> *2 Mur.*   And he that hath commanded is our King.
>
> (1.4.193-194)

Clarence's reply demonstrates that the individual conscience's warning against murder is an internalization of divine law that supersedes all human authority:

> Erroneous vassals, the great King of kings
> Hath in the table of his law commanded
> That thou shalt do no murther. Will you then
> Spurn at his edict, and fulfill a man's?
> Take heed: for he holds vengeance in his hand,
> To hurl upon their heads that break his law.
>
> (1.4.195-200)

The murderers respond to the threat of divine judgment with the curious inconsistency characteristic of men who choose to act against their own moral judgment. Arguing that Clarence is suffering divine retribution for his sins, they act on the assumption that they are exempt from that reality. The scene ends, as it began, with the pain of self-knowledge. Clarence is killed, and the first murderer, his conscience still numbed by Richard's power, exits to collect his reward. But the second murderer discovers that his conscience will not stay quietly "in the Duke of Gloucester's purse" (1.4.127) and suffers immediately from his guilt:

> A bloody deed, and desperately dispatch'd!
> How fain, like Pilate, would I wash my hands
> Of this most grievous murther!
>
> (1.4.271-273)

The theme of the nature and force of the evil conscience concentrated in the scene of Clarence's murder informs the rest of the dramatic action. The world that Richard of Gloucester bustles in is as the murderer describes it. Conscience "is turn'd out of towns and cities for a dangerous thing, and every man that means to live well endeavors to trust to himself and live without it" (1.4.141-144). Shakespeare has peopled the English court with men who consciously break divine law, oblivious to the moral dangers to themselves but highly articulate in their prophecies of divine retribution for other people's sins. They all refuse to follow their consciences, choosing worldly power instead of obe-

72

dience to the King of kings. Having sinned against their consciences, they live to suffer inwardly, illustrating the moral that Brakenbury draws from Clarence's fate:

> Princes have but their titles for their glories,
> An outward honor for an inward toil.
>
> (1.4.78-79)

Richard rises to power by shrewdly exploiting the greed and ambition of others. As the wheel of fortune turns, his pawns reach the height of their worldly fortunes and fall. One by one, as they begin the descent, they experience a painful moment of self-knowledge when their consciences judge them responsible for their own ruin.

These attacks of conscience run the social scale from Edward IV down to Richard's hired henchmen. When King Edward learns that his precipitous order for Clarence's death has been executed, he charges himself and his courtiers with the guilt:

> O God! I fear thy justice will take hold
> On me and you, and mine and yours, for this.
>
> (2.1.132-133)

The susceptibility of even paid murderers to the ravages of conscience, first seen in one of Clarence's murderers, is echoed in the account of the murder of the princes in the tower. Tyrrel, who undertook the assignment with cool efficiency, concludes that it is the "most arch deed of piteous massacre / That ever yet this land was guilty of" and reports that the actual murderers have fled "with conscience and remorse / They could not speak" (4.3.2-3, 20-21).

Although King Edward never learns that he was a pawn in Richard's plot against Clarence, Hastings and Buckingham know that they betray their consciences in following Richard, and they come to regret their choice. They swear friendship and loyalty to the Queen and her family, reminded by Edward not to dissemble "Lest He that is the supreme King of kings / Confound your hidden falsehood" (2.1.13-14), but on Edward's death, they break their oaths and plot with Richard against the Queen and her allies. Both then lose Richard's favor, are condemned to death, and just before death suffer the accusations of conscience. Hastings regrets his overconfidence and repents of his pride and vindictiveness:

73

> O now I need the priest that spake to me!
> I now repent I told the pursuivant,
> As too triumphing, how mine enemies
> To-day at Pomfret bloodily were butcher'd,
> And I myself secure, in grace and favor.
>   (3.4.87-91)

While Edward's "inward toil" was primarily horror at having killed the brother who loyally served him; Hastings' more generalized insight into the futility of preferring man's will to God's recalls Clarence's emblematic vision of the vanity of earthly power:

> O momentary grace of mortal men,
> Which we more hunt for than the grace of God!
> Who builds his hope in air of your good looks
> Lives like a drunken sailor on a mast,
> Ready with every nod to tumble down
> Into the fatal bowels of the deep.
>   (3.4.96-101)

Buckingham's self-judgment is yet more bitter. He understands that his betrayal by Richard fulfills the curses he hypocritically called upon himself should he break his oath to Edward's queen:

> That high All-Seer, which I dallied with,
> Hath turn'd my feigned prayer on my head,
> And given in earnest what I begg'd in jest.
> Thus doth he force the swords of wicked men
> To turn their own points in their masters' bosoms.
>   (5.1.20-24)

He accepts his death as just punishment for his sins.

> Come lead me, officers, to the block of shame;
> Wrong hath but wrong, and blame the due of blame.
>   (5.1.28-29)

Lady Anne provides the most interesting instance of this pattern of sinning against the conscience followed by internal anguish. Comment on the wooing of Anne usually focuses on Richard's tactics rather than on Anne's moral choice, but Richard's boast of winning her in spite of "Having God, her conscience, and these bars against me" (1.2.234) and Anne's later remorse both show that it is a variation on the basic pattern. Critics tend to write about Anne's capitulation as though she were hypnotized by Richard's verbal brilliance and intellectual agility, captivated by the same qualities that fascinate audiences. But Anne succumbs, of course, not to admiration for Richard's skill in playing whatever role the situation demands but rather to one of the roles itself. And that role is not one of amused, ironic detachment but of passionate involvement. She scorns his denial of guilt; she spits at him when he claims that he will make a better husband for her than the one he killed. Neither his lectures on charity nor his sophistical wit confuse her. His simple flattery and pose as doting lover do not move her. Only when Richard exults in his cold ruthlessness in conjunction with his total submission to her does Anne weaken. Richard insists that he shed no tears at the piteous spectacle of Rutland's death. At the story of his own father's death, his "manly eyes did scorn an humble tear" (1.2.164). But the hard, powerful man who weeps for nothing else has wept for her, kneels before her, gives her his sword, and offers to die at her will. The temptation Richard presents is power over an otherwise invulnerable man. Anne, a woman without husband or father to protect her and hence powerless in a power-mad world, surrenders to the appeal of power in the form of the chance to reform a strong man.[7] She does not seek political power for its own sake as the others do and does not consciously sin against her conscience, but she allows this subtle temptation to confuse her application of moral law to particular cases, to drown the voice of conscience. And as a result, she, like the others, achieves only the glory of a temporary title and much inward toil, condemning herself for grossly surrendering to Richard's honeyed words.

Richard, of course, is the supreme example of the evil conscience. Other characters either deceive themselves that the evil they do is good or reach a point where their consciences revolt. Clarence's perfidy is motivated in part, at least, by loyalty to his brother. Anne accepts Richard only under the illusion that she

[7] The vulnerability of women in this society is reinforced in the next scene by Queen Elizabeth's fears concerning King Edward's death:

> Q. Eliz. If he were dead, what would betide on me?
> Grey No other harm but loss of such a lord.
> Q. Eliz. The loss of such a lord includes all harms.
> (1.3. 6-8)

can direct him toward good. Hastings will not condone usurpation nor does Buckingham cooperate in the murder of the princes. Only Richard sets no limits. He pursues his selfish goals with total determination and without self-deception. And, as many critics attest, this terrible consistency in evil compels from us admiration as well as loathing. He is free from the moralistic cant with which people disguise from themselves undesired directions of conscience. When he mouths pieties, he knows he is playing a role and plays it more skillfully for that awareness.

Although Richard never tries to persuade himself that evil is good, he seems without the basic knowledge that "good is to be chosen, evil avoided" that casuists claimed to be recorded in every person's conscience. Through most of the play he forces other characters to confront their consciences while seeming conscience-less himself. But the design of the play is complete only when Richard too feels the pain of his wounded conscience and fulfills Queen Margaret's most bitter curse:

> The worm of conscience still begnaw thy soul!
> Thy friends suspect for traitors while thou liv'st,
> And take deep traitors for thy dearest friends!
> No sleep close up that deadly eye of thine,
> Unless it be while some tormenting dream
> Affrights thee with a hell of ugly devils!
>
> (1.3.221-226)

When Richard agrees to accept the crown, he protests that he does so "against my conscience and my soul" (3.7.226). His conscientious reluctance is feigned, but, like Buckingham who suffers in earnest what he said in jest, Richard discovers that his hypocritical invocation of conscience was more accurate than his self-image of monstrous amorality. His loss of gaiety and self-confidence after becoming king, his suspicions of Buckingham, and his uneasiness over prophecies concerning Richmond are the first indications that the worm of conscience is disturbing his peace. When Lady Anne complains that Richard's "timorous dreams" have kept her from the solace of sleep (4.1.82-84), we know that he suffers the "secret pangs and terrours" that Perkins attributes to those apparently oblivious to conscience. This secret torment becomes most cruel and fierce at Bosworth field, where Richard is terrorized in his sleep by the ghosts of his victims. Each in turn bears witness to Richard's guilt and calls on him to "Despair and die." When he awakes, Richard accepts this nightmare as the self-judgment of his conscience:

> My conscience hath a thousand several tongues,
> And every tongue brings in a several tale,
> And every tale condemns me for a villain.
> Perjury, perjury, in the highest degree;
> Murther, stern murther, in the direst degree;
> All several sins, all us'd in each degree,
> Throng to the bar, crying all, "Guilty! guilty!"
> I shall despair; there is no creature loves me,
> And if I die no soul will pity me.
> And wherefore should they, since that I myself
> Find in myself no pity to myself?
> Methought the souls of all that I had murther'd
> Came to my tent, and every one did threat
> Tomorrow's vengeance on the head of Richard.
>   (5.3.193-206)

The worst horror of such desperate guilt is the moral paralysis it creates. Clarence could accept his guilt and then display genuine unselfishness:

> O God! if my deep pray'rs cannot appease thee,
> But thou wilt be aveng'd on my misdeeds,
> Yet execute thy wrath in me alone!
> O, spare my guiltless wife and my poor children!
>   (1.4.69-72)

But Richard cannot pray. As Perkins warned, "a guiltie conscience makes a man flie from God." So Richard tries to shake off the frightful memories of guilt and to dismiss conscience as "but a word that cowards use, / Devis'd at first to keep the strong in awe" (5.3.309-310). Although his clear-sighted recognition of the human drive for power has enabled him to manage the external world so expertly, Richard does not know himself. He cannot avoid the voice of God in his own mind, and the worst horror of his mutilated conscience is that he can neither repent nor escape knowledge of guilt.[8]

[8] Robert Heilman, a most acute commentator on conscience in *Richard III,* attributes the shallowness of Richard's self-knowledge and the rigid separation between the characters' ordinary lives and their attacks of conscience to Shakespeare's inexperience in creating drama out of the conflict within human

The concluding movement of the play actualizes Richard's self-judgment to "Despair and die." He leads his troops into battle with desperate pride, "Our strong arms be our conscience, swords our law!" (5.3.311). He is defeated by an army inspired by the thought that "Every man's conscience is a thousand men" (5.2.17), an army led by Richmond who fights for God and justice. Richard's death is divine retribution for human sin, but at the same time it is the human victory of the boldness and confidence of Richmond's good conscience over the fear and frenzy of Richard's evil one.

Thus, in *Richard III* Shakespeare uses the traditional tragic pattern of the rise and fall of a powerful man to dramatize the futility of people's attempts to live as though "conscience [were] hanged long agoe." The thematic conflict is not a contest between abstract forces of good and evil but a struggle between the attempts of men to avoid self-judgment and the facts of their own nature. From this perspective, we can see that Queen Margaret's function is not, as it is often taken to be, to provide an antagonist for Richard but to symbolize in her bitter, unrepentant suffering Richard's unacknowledged destiny, the mental anguish of guilt. Richard's crisis of conscience is short-lived. He dies, presumably to face God's judgment. Margaret embodies the fate he escapes, the lingering perdition that is the only alternative to repentance for those who sin against their consciences.

In the relatively early *Richard III*, Shakespeare explores the guilty conscience, a topic in the casuists' theoretical discussions of the nature and function of conscience. Later he draws on the kinds of experience that elicited the casuists' cases of conscience. The mature tragedies share both the casuists' interest in the

---

consciousness (see his "Satiety and Conscience"). Without denying his point about the greater psychological and moral depth of the mature tragedies, I am suggesting that the design of *Richard III* is neatly symmetrical because Shakespeare is not portraying psychological processes realistically but dramatizing in a formal pattern of action a concept—the futility of the common attempt to pretend that conscience does not exist. Men sin against their consciences easily and often, but the judgment of conscience is inescapable. Richard's incapacity for remorse is both sin and consequence of sin. Compare William Ames: "A *Desperate Conscience* (fully representing all sinnes, together with their exceeding great and unpardonable guilt, and Gods fearful wrath abiding upon Sinners, with the endlesse misery that followes thereon) is Gods most powerfull means to torment the Reprobate; like unto a worme, that most sharply biteth and gnaweth their hearts for ever" (Bk. I, p. 46).

difficulties of moral choice and their focus on the decision-making process. The heroes of the tragedies face problems with fundamentally Christian assumptions, but they live in worlds where complicating circumstances obscure moral duties. They attempt to relate relevant moral laws to their own particular cases, a casuistical procedure that each hero approaches differently.

Evasions of Doubt in *Julius Caesar*

In *Julius Caesar,* the first of the distinctively Shakespearean tragedies of moral choice, right action is usually expressed as the classical conception of integrity and honor, but the opening scene provides a Christian view of the decision-making process.[9] A group of commoners celebrating Caesar's triumph is interrupted by the tribunes Flavius and Murellus, who are loyal to the defeated Pompey and who reprimand the tradesmen for appearing in the streets without the signs of their trade. When asked his trade, the cobbler answers:

A trade, sir, that I hope I may use with a safe conscience,
which is indeed, sir, a mender of bad soles.   (1.1.13-14)

The expression "safe conscience" with the pun on sole/soul wittily suggests the view of human action taken by casuists: "The Conscience of man . . . is a mans judgement of himselfe, according to the judgement of God of him" (Ames, Bk. I, p. 1). Before immersing his audience in the politics of pre-Christian Rome, Shakespeare reminds us in funny but familiar terms that salvation depends upon divine judgment and that man has a conscience that enables him to judge his own actions.[10]

The first scene not only sketches the conditions of moral choice as described by moral theology; it also presents a situation that calls for casuistry, one where conflicting principles and the obscurity and ambiguity of available evidence mean that it is difficult to make decisions that can assure a safe conscience. By accusing

[9] Virgil Whitaker comments on the significant place of *Julius Caesar* in the development of Shakespeare's treatment of moral choice. See his *Shakespeare's Use of Learning* (San Marino: The Huntington Library, 1953), p. 248, and *The Mirror up to Nature* (San Marino: The Huntington Library, 1965), p. 132.

[10] Paul J. Aldus, "Analogical Probability in Shakespeare's Plays," *Shakespeare Quarterly* 6 (1955): 397-414, discusses this scene as an analogue to the entire dramatic action but does not comment on the cobbler's speech.

the tradesmen of a minor infraction of civil law and then deciding to take the law into their own hands by destroying the public displays honoring Caesar, Flavius and Murellus raise questions about obedience to civil authority. By condemning the citizens for gross ingratitude to Pompey in their easy transfer of loyalty to Caesar, the tribunes make clear that political actions are also moral actions. But, although the confrontation between the grim officials and the impudent merrymakers establishes the moral and political ambiguity of the situation, no one expresses doubt or uncertainty about where he stands or what he ought to do. Admittedly, both Murellus's fierce denunciation of their hard hearts and his threat of divine vengeance seem to effect a change of heart in the revellers, but whether they withdraw in remorse, as Flavius assumes ("They vanish tongue-tied in their guiltiness"), or whether they retreat abashed by the display of civil authority and wrath is not obvious from the text. Certainly there is no evidence that they search their minds or reexamine the political situation. It is all thoughtless holiday spirits on one side and unquestioning dedication on the other.

Only once in this first scene does anyone raise a question about the right thing to do. When Flavius suggests stripping the ornaments honoring Caesar from the public statuary, Murellus questions the legality of the plan:

> May we do so?
> You know it is the feast of Lupercal.

But Flavius immediately dismisses the objection:

> It is no matter, let no images
> Be hung with Caesar's trophies. I'll about,
> And drive away the vulgar from the streets;
> So do you too, where you perceive them thick.
>
> (1.1.66-71)

This sequence of action, in which a question is raised and immediately dismissed in order to proceed to action, is a dominant pattern in the design of the play.

After the dramatic prologue, the central action gets under way in act 1, scene 2, where the action consists almost entirely of this kind of confident interpretation of ambiguous evidence. First, Caesar is confronted with the soothsayer's enigmatic warning to beware the ides of March, which he dismisses contemptuously.

Next, Cassius questions Brutus's apparent coolness toward him, readily admits he has misinterpreted his friend's behavior, and immediately proceeds to analyze Brutus's character for his friend's benefit:

> And since you know you cannot see yourself
> So well as by reflection, I, your glass,
> Will modestly discover to yourself
> That of yourself which you yet know not of.
>
> (1.2.67-70)

As the scene develops, the opposition between the two groups of characters intensifies, but without direct conflict. Instead, they are all engaged in interpreting the significance of each other's actions from a distance.

In the longest section of the scene, where Brutus and Cassius are on stage alone, Cassius catalogues Caesar's weaknesses while Brutus worries that the offstage shouts indicate increased power for Caesar. When Caesar and his train return, the two groups cross paths and purposes, each trying to read the external signs of the other. Caesar confides to Antony his distrust of the lean-faced Cassius, while Brutus tries to grasp the significance of the color in Caesar's face and the lack of color in Calphurnia's. Casca answers Brutus's questions, reporting both what happened and his version of what it meant. For example:

> I saw Mark Antony offer him a crown . . . he put it by once;
> but for all that, to my thinking, he would fain have had it.
>
> (1.2.236-240)

Just as Casca remains behind to interpret Caesar's behavior, when Casca exists, Brutus and Cassius remain to interpret his, and when Brutus leaves, Cassius analyzes Brutus.

My point is that throughout the scene, the major characters are aware that they live in a world that requires interpretation. They know that men disagree widely about the significance and value of events and people, that external behavior need not reflect the reality of men's minds, that apparent strengths mask hidden weaknesses and obvious weaknesses belie inner strengths. But whereas the ambiguous evidence and contradictory interpretations prevent the audience from reaching firm conclusions about the relative merits of the versions of truth offered by Caesar and his opponents,[11] the awareness of complexity causes remarkably little doubt among the characters in the play. Caesar's unquestioning belief in his own greatness and his confidence that he has nothing to fear are matched by the conspirators' belief in the rightness of their cause and their confidence of success.

The storm that dominates the next several scenes provides a symbolic center for this pattern of action. The tempest dropping fire and blood during the night before the assassination is fraught with ominous and mysterious significance. Casca is initially sure only that the strange phenomena signify danger, but Cassius soon convinces him that they are signs of the monstrous shape of Rome under Julius Caesar and by means of this interpretation lures Casca into the conspiracy. Calphurnia interprets the tempest and her troubled dream just as the priests interpret the sacrificial animal lacking a heart, as warnings of danger to Caesar. Although Caesar sees these omens as warnings against cowardice, he temporarily agrees to humor Calphurnia's fears, until Decius convinces him that the bleeding statue is an auspicious sign of his greatness, which is to be confirmed that day by the senate's offer of a crown. On each side, then, the extraordinary disturbances of nature are interpreted to support a course of action leading to a predetermined goal. When disagreements over interpretation occur, they produce no real debate or discussion. There is no developing dialectic, no argument that refutes objections through logic or additional evidence, no synthesis that subsumes other points of view. The pattern is one of confident assertion, flat contradiction, and one more step toward catastrophe. Only Cicero warns:

> But men may construe things after their fashion,
> Clean from the purpose of the things themselves.
>
> (1.3.34-35)

And his voice is never heard again.

Julius Caesar, then, presents the kind of world that the casuists write about where human actions have serious practical and moral consequences but where the ambiguity of moral abstractions and the complexity of circumstances make the right course

---

[11] This point is demonstrated by Ernest Schanzer in "The Problem of *Julius Caesar*," *Shakespeare Quarterly* 6 (1955): 297-308, and in *The Problem Plays of Shakespeare* (London: Routledge and Kegan Paul, 1963), pp. 10-70; and by Mildred E. Hartsock, "The Complexity of *Julius Caesar*," *PMLA* 81 (1966): 56-62.

of action problematic. The doubt and perplexity that the casuist tries to resolve, however, is significantly absent from Shakespeare's Rome. His Romans experience no difficulty in applying their principles of virtue and justice to particular actions. Although Caesar's refusal of the crown offered by Mark Antony obscures his intentions, his immediate swallowing of Decius's bait indicates that the hesitation is merely tactical. There is no indication that he reflects upon the moral implications of accepting the crown. His decision to go to the Capitol on the ides of March is only slightly more difficult than his decisions to ignore the soothsayer's warning and Artemidorus's petition. Because, throughout the play, ambiguous evidence is interpreted so readily and genuine questions are raised about means but not ends, we see men acting in confident and thoughtless ignorance with a horrifying clarity of outline.

At first glance, Brutus seems to be a major exception to this generalization. The contrast between Brutus and the other conspirators is a fundamental structural principle in the play. Although Cassius believes that he manipulates his noble friend ("I see / Thy honorable mettle may be wrought / From that it is dispos'd," 1.2.308-310), Brutus is less naive than he supposes. Brutus knows what Cassius is doing and implies that such ideas are not new to him. He responds cautiously to Cassius's attempts to stir him to action.

> What you would work me to, I have some aim.
> How I have thought of this, and of these times,
> I shall recount hereafter. For this present,
> I would not (so with love I might entreat you)
> Be any further mov'd. What you have said
> I will consider; what you have to say
> I will with patience hear, and find a time
> Both meet to hear and answer such high things.
>   (1.2.163-170)

The following scene, in which Cassius easily recruits Casca into the conspiracy, contrasts Casca's emotional and immediate commitment with Brutus's rational hesitation. The contrast is heightened at the end of the next scene when Brutus brings Ligarius into the ranks of the conspirators simply through the force of his own personality. Ligarius commits himself without hearing the plan or its rationale:

> Set on your foot,
> And with a heart new-fir'd I follow you,
> To do I know not what; but it sufficeth
> That Brutus leads me on.
>
> (2.1.331-334)

Between these two episodes we see Brutus in soliloquy defending the decision to kill Caesar not out of unreasoning personal loyalty or bitter enmity but out of thoughtful consideration of the general good:

> It must be by his death; and for my part,
> I know no personal cause to spurn at him,
> But for the general.
>
> (2.1.10-12)

We hear him speak too of the agony that decision costs him:

> Since Cassius first did whet me against Caesar,
> I have not slept.
> Between the acting of a dreadful thing
> And the first motion, all the interim is
> Like a phantasma or a hideous dream.
>
> (2.1.61-65)

This series of scenes pointing up the contrasts among the conspirators presents a dramatically convincing interpretation of the complex of ideas, temperaments, and circumstances that form the fabric of history. It is also a concrete dramatization of casuistical concepts. The differences of motive and decision making among men participating in the same action give living form to the tenet that intention and attendant circumstances as well as the intrinsic nature of an action determine its moral character. The same act, for example, could be good in one set of circumstances and evil in another. An intrinsically good action, the casuists argued, becomes evil when it is performed with an evil intention. Thus the conscience, the part of the practical understanding that judges what one ought to do, cannot judge the lawfulness of a proposed action without considering the nature of the particular action in relation to universal moral law, the individual motives leading to the action, and the specific circumstances of time and place and the probable consequences of the action. In any complicated situation, then, the good conscience proceeds cautiously. When a man reviews his actions honestly, the casuist William Ames warns, "a bare and naked *knowledge* is not sufficient for this act of Conscience, but things must bee weighed over and over" (Bk. I, p. 25).

The audience accepts Antony's judgment that Brutus was "the noblest Roman of them all" (5.5.68) because Brutus acts conscientiously. He applies to a particular political situation the general principle that the public good should take precedence over personal desires. He acts on his own rational judgment, not out of passion or reliance on someone else's authority. While Cassius and Casca are prompted by envy to destroy Caesar, Brutus acts out of concern for the welfare of Rome, without personal enmity toward his victim. He tries to control the surrounding circumstances in order to make the act of killing a sacrifice to justice rather than an act of savage butchery. In deciding to spare Antony and to permit him to address the populace, he shows his awareness that the desired consequences of Caesar's death require that the public understand and accept the conspirators' view of their action. Brutus is not rash and impetuous but calm and deliberate. He resorts to the deception and hypocrisy that his purpose and circumstances require, but he does so with self-awareness and loathing. The conspirators' hands are all equally bloody, but because Brutus acts on principle and with careful thought, he is actually performing a morally different action.

Shakespeare does not, however, present Brutus as a model of a safe conscience. Despite his ostentatious rationalism, Brutus reaches his judgment too easily. He makes what Robert Sanderson is later to condemn as the common mistake of thinking that "*sin* may drive out *sin,* as one nayl doth drive out another, as for example, . . . *Tyranny* by *Sedition*." [12] His descriptions of the decision-making process as "a hideous dream" and "an insurrection" suggest that he has made the arduous intellectual effort to deal with a difficult moral problem but not that he has moved through doubt to clarity and resolution. He decides deliberately, but he decides on the basis that there is some probability that his decision may be just, without full conviction that his facts

[12] Robert Sanderson, *Several Cases of Conscience Discussed in Ten Lectures* (London, 1660), p. 65.

are accurate or his conclusion valid. Caesar, he admits, has not abused his power, but there is strong evidence that success will change his nature.

> Th' abuse of greatness is when it disjoins
> Remorse from power; and to speak truth of Caesar,
> I have not known when his affections sway'd
> More than his reason. But 'tis a common proof
> That lowliness is young ambition's ladder,
> Whereto the climber-upward turns his face;
> But when he once attains the upmost round,
> He then unto the ladder turns his back,
> Looks in the clouds, scorning the base degrees
> By which he did ascend. So Caesar may;
> Then lest he may, prevent.
>
> (2.1.18-28)

Although critics have accused Brutus of illogicality and intellectual dishonesty, his procedure here is essentially what casuists called probabilism, the doctrine that in cases of moral doubt one has the freedom to act when there is some real probability that the action is lawful, even when its unlawfulness is more probable. Recognizing the difficulty of reaching certainty and unanimity in moral judgments and the necessity of acting on some human opinion concerning complex moral situations, probabilists argued that, since even the opinions of the most respected theologians may be false, men may act on a less probable opinion. In a confusing world, probabilism provided certainty.[13]

Probabilism dominated the casuistry of the Church of the Counter-Reformation, but English casuists rejected it in favor of probabiliorism, the doctrine that moral doubts can be resolved only when it is most probable that the proposed action is lawful. They condemned probabilism for allowing cynical evasions of moral duty. More penetratingly, they saw that the combination of speculative doubt and practical certainty relieved even the most sincere and morally sensitive men of the responsibility to search for truth and encouraged them to rely on legalistic codifications of moral duty. By separating intellectual from moral judgment, probabil-

---

[13] A. E. Malloch observes that probabilism not only makes real assent of the self unnecessary, "it also inhibits that condition which is the reverse of real assent—doubt." See "John Donne and the Casuists," *Studies in English Literature* 2 (1962): 74 n.

ism divides a man's thoughts from his actions, encouraging authoritative complacency as well as moral compromise.[14]

Brutus is a subtle portrait of these twin dangers of laxity and rigidity. He passes judgment without full intellectual assent; once decided, he assumes a posture of unquestionable moral authority. In spite of his nobility of spirit, Brutus is finally like his compatriots in his confident ignorance. As a probabilist, Brutus does not require evidence proving that Caesar's future tyranny is most probable. He need only establish that "'tis a common proof / That lowliness is young ambition's ladder" and apply that authority to the present case: "So Caesar may." His crucial decision is tragically wrong not because he chooses public duty over private affection or because he opts for republicanism in a world providentially destined for monarchy but because he decides to act on insufficient evidence and then banishes doubt.

If the first half of the play demonstrates Brutus's moral superiority to his fellows, the second half demonstrates the evil consequences of his action. While Caesar's death divides Rome politically, Brutus's moral assurance without full intellectual conviction creates division within his mind. The separation between intellectual and moral judgment becomes immediately evident in his funeral oration. His speech fails where Antony's succeeds not simply because it lacks Antony's impassioned eloquence but because it presents no evidence for its conclusions. Brutus argues logically from general principle (tyranny must be destroyed) to particular action (because Caesar was a tyrant, his killing is justified). He invites his audience to judge him critically, but first, with fine circularity, he asks them to accept his argument on personal faith: [15]

Believe me for mine honor, and have respect to mine honor,
that you may believe.   (3.2.14-16)

---

[14] For the attitude toward probabilism characteristic of English casuists, see Jeremy Taylor, *Ductor Dubitantium: or the Rule of Conscience,* in *The Whole Works of the Right Rev. Jeremy Taylor,* ed. Reginald Heber, 15 vols. (London, 1828), X, 213-218; XI, 349-350.

[15] Maynard Mack points out that Brutus's argument rests entirely on his own moral authority but concludes that Brutus appeals to reason and Antony to passion. See "Teaching Drama: *Julius Caesar,*" in *Essays on the Teaching of English,* ed. Edward J. Gordon and Edward S. Noyes (New York: Appleton-Century-Crofts, 1960), pp. 320-336, reprinted in *Modern Shakespearean Criticism,* ed. Alvin B. Kernan (New York: Harcourt, Brace and World, 1970), pp. 290-301.

Brutus, then, presents the probabilistic argument that a respected moral authority—himself—finds Caesar's death justifiable. His sincerity is convincing. His argument reassures the citizens bewildered by Caesar's death, but it cannot withstand scrutiny. When Antony gets his audience to test Brutus's key propositions about Caesar's tyranny against their own experience, their faith in Brutus collapses, and they become readily susceptible to Antony's manipulations.

Brutus's simultaneous laxity and rigidity become even more obvious as the division in his mind widens from a separation of intellectual from moral judgment to a separation of thought from action. In his quarrel with Cassius in act 4, his condemnation of tainted money is admirable, even though unattractively self-righteous, but his indignation that Cassius has not shared the ill-gotten gains betrays the extent of his self-deception. Perhaps his irritability and peremptoriness are symptoms of an uneasy conscience, a repressed awareness that he has participated in a treacherous murder instead of a ritual sacrifice, but the mental process that allowed him to decide to kill Caesar without conclusive evidence of guilt also prevents him from facing self-doubt.[16] Like Richard III, Brutus sees his victim's ghost the evening before the decisive battle, but while Richard recognizes the night's horror as the voice of conscience, Brutus, with unquestioning self-assurance, apparently interprets it as a challenge to his courage and as an external source of information about his fate, rather than as moral judgment. When the "monstrous apparition" warns that Brutus will see him at Philippi, Brutus replies with unruffled dignity: "Why, I will see thee at Philippi then" (4.3.286). Defeated at Philippi, he tries to enlist help in his suicide by citing the ghost as evidence that "I know my hour is come" (5.5.20), but he never consciously associates it with guilt for killing Caesar.

The clearest, and of course final, example of Brutus's ability to separate moral certainty from careful thought is his suicide. Shakespeare makes a point of Brutus's principled opposition to suicide. In both North and Amyot, Brutus recalls his past disapproval of Cato's suicide but then rejects his earlier opinion. In

16 On this point, see Elias Schwartz, "On the Quarrel Scene in *Julius Caesar*," *College English* 19 (1958): 168-170.

Shakespeare's play, Brutus is consistent in his condemnation of suicide: [17]

> Even by the rule of that philosophy
> By which I did blame Cato for the death
> Which he did give himself—I know not how,
> But I do find it cowardly and vile,
> For fear of what might fall, so to prevent
> The time of life—arming myself with patience
> To stay the providence of some high powers
> That govern us below.
>
> (5.1.100-107)

But when Cassius draws the obvious conclusion from this statement, Brutus immediately cautions:

> Think not, thou noble Roman,
> That ever Brutus will go bound to Rome;
> He bears too great a mind.
>
> (5.1.110-112)

When he faces defeat and capture, Brutus finds suicide "more worthy" (5.5.24) than dishonor and kills himself without agonizing doubts.

Most commentators interpret Brutus's suicide as noble and courageous, arguing that in the Roman plays Shakespeare always presents suicide as a virtuous act.[18] But a distinction must be made between *Antony and Cleopatra,* where no one condemns suicide, and *Julius Caesar,* where Brutus himself condemns it. Since, in casuistical terms, acting against the conscience, even to commit an otherwise innocent action, is sinful, it is even more important to note the difference between the suicides of Cassius, who consistently maintains that suicide is honorable, and Brutus, who thinks that suicide is the "cowardly and vile" alternative to patience. The noblest of Romans is sometimes defended against

---

[17] Mark Sacharoff demonstrates that Shakespeare altered his source to emphasize Brutus's disapproval of suicide on principle. In North's Plutarch, Brutus describes doubts about Cato's suicide that he felt in the past but that he firmly rejects in the present. See "Suicide and Brutus' Philosophy in *Julius Caesar,*" *Journal of the History of Ideas* 33 (1972): 115-122.

[18] For example, see Maurice Charney, *Shakespeare's Roman Plays* (Cambridge, Mass.: Harvard University Press, 1961), pp. 209-210.

the charge of inconsistency on the grounds that he is against
suicide in general but that he is not opposed to it in certain
instances.[19] Casuistry, which derived its name from its study of
particular cases, certainly recognized that general principles do
not apply in every set of circumstances. But Brutus offers no
explanation of why his case is an exception to "the rule of that
philosophy." One wonders where the general principle against
suicide "For fear of what might fall" would apply, if not to the
dreaded consequences of military defeat. Brutus is consistent only
in his conviction that "He bears too great a mind" to suffer
public humiliation. He applies his principled condemnation of
tyranny to Caesar without establishing its appropriateness in the
particular circumstances, and he commits suicide despite his
principles. Whether deciding to kill himself or a friend, Brutus
chooses the course of action that dramatizes his sense of his own
greatness and obliterates the necessity for inquiry and doubt. He
is not without moral courage, but he has his limits, and the limits
are drawn when he moves from general principle to particular
case. Like his compatriots, Brutus faces the ambiguities of his
life as challenges to his courage and honor rather than as problems to be solved with intelligence and humility.

Julius Caesar does not propose unambiguous answers to the
moral cruxes that it poses. It presents assassination and suicide
not as clear-cut examples of treachery or heroism but as perplexing moral problems, and it finds tragedy not in the hidden corruption of men's motives but in the mistaken application of
general principles to particular situations. Titinius's lament for
Cassius, "Alas, thou hast misconstrued every thing" (5.3.84), is an
apt commentary on the entire dramatic action. *Julius Caesar* is
a play about the gap between intention and consequence: a play
where Caesar goes to the Capitol to show his strength and to
receive adulation, only to be killed without protest as a tyrant; a
play where Brutus kills in order to restore republican justice to
Rome, only to deliver Rome to civil war and the tyranny of the
triumvirate. Shakespeare's Romans exhibit courage and selfless
devotion to the common good, but they repeatedly act in error
and ignorance. Their noble intentions miscarry in action not
simply because of the unavoidable inadequacy of human knowledge but because their heroic self-sufficiency and unquestioning

---

[19] Sacharoff, "Suicide and Brutus' Philosophy," p. 115.

commitment to purpose prevent them from tolerating uncertainty and from struggling with doubt.

STRUGGLES WITH DOUBT IN *Hamlet*

That assassins and victim alike misconstrue everything links *Julius Caesar* with another tragedy of error and ensuing destruction written soon afterward. *Hamlet* too develops a story "Of accidental judgments" and "purposes mistook/Fall'n on th' inventors' heads" (5.2.382-385). In Hamlet's Denmark, as in Brutus's Rome, appearances deceive, and moral issues are bewilderingly complex. Again, the memory of a fallen leader and the questionable authority of a present ruler intensify the common human predicament of having to choose among conflicting values and to act in ignorance of the full chain of consequences. In both tragedies men define their moral being in relation to a moral ideal, but, while the Romans' standards of honor are essentially self-generated, the Danes are acutely conscious of being held accountable to divine law. The chilling account of his doom by the mysterious apparition on the battlements, Hamlet's bowing to the will of the Everlasting and his fear of something after death, Claudius's anguished attempt to pray, and even Laertes' outburst at the priest over Ophelia's funeral—all reflect a view of life as a struggle in which souls are lost and saved. No one forgets the stakes of moral choice, and no one overcomes the ignorance that subverts judgment.

In *Richard III,* moral issues are relatively clear-cut, and no sense of mystery or obscurity complicates the decision-making act. Richard's victims remain unaware of his duplicity until too late, and Richard himself is confident that he knows exactly what he is doing. In *Julius Caesar,* although conflicting values and interpretations of evidence convince the audience of the ambiguity of complex situations and the difficulty of choice, the characters themselves experience little doubt about the significance of events or about what they should do. But Hamlet's world is notoriously one of perplexity and doubt.[20] The play opens in an atmosphere of fear and mystery in which men try to distinguish between

[20] Many critics have built on the discussions of doubt and questioning in Maynard Mack, "The World of Hamlet," *Yale Review* 41 (1952): 502-523, and Harry Levin, *The Question of Hamlet* (New York: Oxford University Press, 1959).

friend and foe, the benign and the hostile. In the first scene, Marcellus, Barnardo, and Horatio all question the nature of the strange apparition and the state of Denmark's health, but they offer explanations only as rumors and tentatively held hypotheses. The common-sensical soldiers and the skeptical Horatio question each other and the ghost itself about the significance of what they see. They recognize the parallel between this portentous figure and the fiery tempest that was harbinger to the fall of "mightiest Julius," but they arrive at no interpretation. They do not conclude, as do the conspirators in the early scenes of *Julius Caesar,* with a plan for violent action and a prediction of success; instead they agree that because of love and duty they are obligated to communicate what they have seen to Hamlet so that he may inquire further.

Although few in Denmark share this uncompromised loyalty or commitment to truth, the bewilderment and recognition of the effort and skill necessary to discover hidden truth are universal. Gertrude, Claudius, Laertes, Ophelia, Polonius, Rosencrantz, and Guildenstern, alone and in combination, try to interpret Hamlet's behavior, while Hamlet tries to penetrate their pretenses and hypocrisy, to solve the mystery of the ghost and the riddle of his own nature.

Through the first half of the play, contradictions and ambiguities increase: the ghost appears as a beloved father and noble king and also as a "guilty thing"; Claudius acts as prudent and judicious king, while other evidence indicates that he is a smiling villain; Hamlet appears as the rose of the fair state and as a madman. People cope with the world of shifting appearances each in his own style, but essentially all resort to secrecy and pretense: Polonius in a fatuous posture of shrewdness, Claudius with more sinister cunning, and Ophelia, Rosencrantz, and Guildenstern in their subservience to authority. All hide their own motives and intentions while trying to discover the reality beneath the disguises that others wear. Ophelia's pathetic bewilderment, Claudius's self-protective suspicion, Gertrude's imperceptive solicitude, and Hamlet's agonized questioning testify to the perplexity they all experience.

This endemic awareness of ignorance and the simultaneous attempts to increase confusion and deception make choice difficult, but the necessity of deciding what to do remains. In *Hamlet,* as in casuistry, people reveal their moral nature by how they act in response to doubt. The characters engage the sympathy or provoke the censure of the audience not simply by what they do but by how they decide to do it. In the first scene, Marcellus and Horatio reach a decision easily. Their awareness of the doubtful nature of the ghost, their respect for authority, and their affection for young Hamlet all lead them to decide to report what they have seen to him. Doubt, duty, and love no longer coalesce so conveniently in their next encounter with the ghost. This time, frightened by Hamlet's apparently reckless determination to follow the ambiguous figure wherever it leads him, they agree that they can no longer defer to his authority.

> *Horatio* He waxes desperate with imagination.
> *Marcellus* Let's follow. 'Tis not fit thus to obey him.
> *Horatio* Have after. To what issue will this come?
> *Marcellus* Something is rotten in the state of Denmark.
> *Horatio* Heaven will direct it.
> *Marcellus* Nay, let's follow him.   (1.4.87-91)

Marcellus's observation that to obey is "not fit" is an ironic echo of the last line of the preceding scene: Ophelia's "I shall obey, my lord" (1.3.136). The contrast is not between obedience and rebelliousness but rather between thoughtful analysis of a particular situation and timid surrender of personal judgment to authority. Marcellus and Horatio obey Hamlet except in this instance where they believe he is better served by defiance. Although Marcellus urges immediate action and Horatio advises trust in God, they both show that they are thinking through an unprecedented and dangerous situation where conventional social and political roles have broken down. They admit ignorance of the cause and consequences of the rottenness afflicting Denmark, but they are certain that they must and can discover the fittest way to act. In contrast, when asked whether she believes Hamlet's expressions of affection, Ophelia confesses, "I do not know, my lord, what I should think" (1.3.104). Against Polonius's cynical warnings, she protests that Hamlet has courted her in honorable fashion, but she never risks interpreting Hamlet's behavior herself. She sets aside doubt and confusion rather than resolving them.

In spite of Ophelia's appealingly youthful timidity, her unthinking acceptance of her father's judgment links her intellectually and morally with Gertrude's unquestioning reliance on custom and habit and with Polonius's automatic platitudinizing. While Ophelia is painfully confused by the bewildering change in Hamlet, Polonius delights in it as an opportunity for demonstrating his shrewdness in detection. But he understands Hamlet's situation no better than Ophelia does and applies generalizations about hot-blooded youth and unrequited love without sufficient evidence and without hesitation. The substitution of traditional authority for personal judgment is made even more explicit by Rosencrantz and Guildenstern. The play directs us to condemn them not because they fail to discern Claudius's villainy or because they revere the majesty of his office but because, having failed to understand Hamlet, they accept without question Claudius's claim that he is dangerously mad and show their willingness to do anything the king asks.

In their various ways, these characters all demonstrate the casuistical premise that moral choice is grounded in knowledge. "Ignorance," Perkins observes,

> is a great and usuall impediment of good conscience. For when the mind erreth or misconceiveth, it doth mislead the conscience, & deceive the whole man.[21]

In *Hamlet,* the men and women that Claudius manipulates err because they do not carefully examine the moral principles by which they judge individual cases and because they do not know enough about the particular circumstances impinging on their decisions. Their ignorance results in self-deception and destructive action. Although the audience should understand the characters' moral failures, the play demands a much greater range of response than casuistry ordinarily permits. While Polonius's self-deception is largely comic, Ophelia's pathetic bewilderment elicits more pity than condemnation. When Polonius, Ophelia, Rosencrantz, and Guildenstern demonstrate by their deaths the danger inherent in abdicating personal responsibility, the audience's awareness of the poetic justice by which mistaken purposes fall on the inventors' heads is balanced with fear and pity at the inadequacy of good intentions.

In Act 5, the substitution of external authority for individual thought and judgment takes more grotesque form in the priests's response to Ophelia's death:

[21] Perkins, I, 516.

> Her death was doubtful,
> And but that great command o'ersways the order,
> She should in ground unsanctified been lodg'd
> Till the last trumpet; for charitable prayers,
> Shards, flints, and pebbles should be thrown on her.
> Yet here she is allow'd her virgin crants,
> Her maiden strewments, and the bringing home
> Of bell and burial.
>
> (5.1.227-234)

Here a doubtful case is settled by a smug judgment in which religious authority is tempered by political power but not by human sympathy. Even more absurd and sinister is Laertes' reception of Hamlet's apology:

> I am satisfied in nature,
> Whose motive in this case should stir me most
> To my revenge, but in my terms of honor
> I stand aloof, and will no reconcilement
> Till by some elder masters of known honor
> I have a voice and president of peace
> To keep my name ungor'd.
>
> (5.2.244-250)

In this case the divorce between personal judgment and external authority is explicit and total. That Laertes does not know whether he forgives Hamlet without asking someone else would be comic were it not for his secret, murderous intention.

Thus the largest group of characters in *Hamlet,* like those in *Julius Caesar,* contribute to the world's havoc and destroy themselves through error that is moral as well as factual. In *Julius Caesar,* they make decisions on the basis of flattering self-images of nobility, while in *Hamlet* they transfer moral responsibility to some external authority. Hamlet's most dangerous adversaries, however, do not confuse conscience with authority but consciously decide to act against the direction of their consciences. In the passage just quoted, Laertes' claim that he makes decisions according to a punctilious code of honor is, of course, spurious. When he dedicates himself to revenge, he repudiates conscience:

> To hell, allegiance! vows, to the blackest devil!
> Conscience and grace, to the profoundest pit!
>
> (4.5.132-133)

Claudius tries to give a veneer of morality to their plotting—"Now must your conscience my acquittance seal" (4.7.1); "No place indeed should murther sanctuarize" (4.7.127)—but Laertes knows that he wants to cut Hamlet's throat in church and kill him with a poisoned foil in order to satisfy his desire for revenge, not honor or justice. In renouncing conscience, he has renounced rational moral judgment altogether.

Laertes decides to kill in disregard of his conscience, and in the course of the play his conscience judges him guilty. Claudius sinned against his conscience in the past by murdering his brother, and our first glimpse of his present inner life reveals the torment he suffers for that sin:

> How smart a lash that speech doth give my conscience!
> The harlot's cheek, beautied with plast'ring art,
> Is not more ugly to the thing that helps it
> Than is my deed to my most painted word.
> O heavy burthen!
>
> (3.1.49-53)

He knows that his deed is detestable and that he cannot escape divine judgment:

> In the corrupted currents of this world
> Offense's gilded hand may shove by justice,
> And oft 'tis seen the wicked prize itself
> Buys out the law, but 'tis not so above:
> There is no shuffling, there the action lies
> In his true nature, and we ourselves compell'd,
> Even to the teeth and forehead of our faults,
> To give in evidence.
>
> (3.3.57-64)

Ironically Claudius gives the play's clearest analysis of the inadequacy of human authority as a moral standard. He understands that political power does not alter the true nature of action and that his own conscience testifies in moral judgment against him. Although repentance is his only hope, he cannot repent. His worst torture is not fear of future punishment but his present incapacity to realize his intention in action:

> My stronger guilt defeats my strong intent,
> And, like a man to double business bound,

I stand in pause where I shall first begin,
And both neglect.

(3.3.40-43)

   Claudius's description of his dilemma fits the situations of most of the dramatis personae. Just as Ophelia's bewildered admission, "I do not know, my lord, what I should think," epitomizes the atmosphere of confusion and doubt, so Gertrude sums up the main action in her two anguished questions: "What have I done . . . ?"; "What shall I do?" (3.4.39,180). *Hamlet* is a dramatization of how people take responsibility for what they have done and how they decide what to do in a confusing, frightening world. Both dilemmas are most acute for Hamlet. From the beginning, he faces the problem of how to behave in Claudius's hypocritical court, initially suffering most from the constraints that inhibit open, direct action. Although he is critical of the shallowness of traditional, customary forms, he bows to familial and political authority, deciding to obey his mother and to hold his tongue. When he sees the ghost, his overriding concern is to discover its implications for action. Its "questionable shape" provokes him to question it, and his queries about its nature, intention, and significance build up to the crucial question: "What should we do?" (1.4.57). The ghost's answer, burdening him with apparently incompatible duties, intensifies and complicates the problem of what course of action to pursue. The way he approaches the dilemma of doubt and responsibility is the center of the dramatic action and distinguishes Hamlet from the other characters in the play and from Shakespeare's other tragic heroes.
   Charged with establishing justice in Denmark, Hamlet, far from being timid and indecisive, is eager to act. His response to the mysterious figure of his father is immediate and impassioned, and he dedicates himself to duty without hesitation:

Remember thee!
Ay, thou poor ghost, whiles memory holds a seat
In this distracted globe. Remember thee!
Yea, from the table of my memory
I'll wipe away all trivial fond records,
All saws of books, all forms, all pressures past
That youth and observation copied there,
And thy commandement all alone shall live

97

> Within the book and volume of my brain,
> Unmix'd with baser matter.
>
> (1.5.95-104)

He remembers the duty to revenge his father's murder, but he also remembers the injunction, "But howsomever thou pursues this act, / Taint not thy mind" (1.5.84-85). He is aware of a fact that Jeremy Taylor makes explicit: when memory is "instructed with notices in order to judgments practical, so it takes the Christian name of conscience." Conscience, Taylor continues,

> is that book, which at doomsday shall be brought forth and laid open to all the world. The memory, changed into conscience, preserves the notices of some things, and shall be reminded of others. . . . Our conscience will be the great scene or theatre, upon which shall be represented all our actions good and bad.[22]

Some scholars, notably Eleanor Prosser, have argued that the ghost's charge is not a moral duty but a temptation for Hamlet, a diabolical enticement to damn himself by undertaking the vengeance properly left to God.[23] But to schematize Renaissance attitudes as a bloody code of revenge in conflict with a Christian prohibition of revenge is to oversimplify. S. P. Zitner has demonstrated that the code of revenge incorporated moral considerations; conversely, moral theology left room for revenge in certain circumstances.[24] The important point is not to second-guess what a Renaissance audience thought Hamlet ought to do, but to understand that they, like Hamlet and like us, saw such questions as perplexing. Killing another man as punishment for crime could be sinful or virtuous depending upon the circumstances. Hamlet's problem is not resisting the temptation to become a

22 Taylor, XI, 387.

23 Eleanor Prosser, *Hamlet and Revenge* (Stanford, Calif.: Stanford University Press, 1967). See also Harold Skulsky, "Revenge, Honor, and Conscience in *Hamlet*," *PMLA* 85 (1970): 78-87.

24 S. P. Zitner, "Hamlet, Duellist," *University of Toronto Quarterly* 39 (1969): 1-18. See also Paul Gottschalk, "Hamlet and the Scanning of Revenge," *Shakespeare Quarterly* 24 (1973): 155-170. Casuists frequently treated questions about the lawfulness of killing. For example, in *Resolutions and Decisions of Divers Practical Cases of Conscience in Continual Use Amongst Men* (1648), Joseph Hall includes the case, "Whether, and in what cases, it may be lawful for a man to take away the life of another?" *The Works of . . . Joseph Hall*, 10 vols. (1863; reprint ed., New York: AMS Press, 1969), VII, 294-298.

bloody avenger or overcoming a temperamental inability to act decisively but deciding what he ought to do in a particular set of circumstances. He sees the complexities and contradictions involved in dual obligations to obey divine law absolutely and to fight evil vigorously. He is aware of the danger of tainting his own mind through active involvement in the power struggles of the Danish court and of the opposite danger of becoming Claudius's pawn. He does not try to avoid these problems by identifying conscience with external authority or by repudiating conscience. Like Brutus, he is challenged to accept responsibility for destroying a source of evil, but, unlike Brutus, he does not rely on the purity of his intentions to obliterate moral doubt. For Hamlet, doubt must be resolved conclusively, not simply set aside. If Brutus's tragedy is that of the moral probabilist in a world where decisions once acted upon are absolute and irrevocable, Hamlet's is the tragedy of the probabiliorist in a world where nothing is quite what it seems.[25]

Hamlet sees himself not as a private person bent on bloody revenge but as the lawful prince born to the responsibility of establishing just authority in Denmark. Yet he knows too that "the dev'l hath power / T'assume a pleasing shape," that his grief and disgust may cause him to deceive himself about the extent of Claudius's treachery, and that "when the mind erreth or misconceiveth, it doth mislead the conscience, & deceive the whole man." He knows that to kill Claudius without establishing the overwhelming probability of his guilt is to court damnation, and thus he must discover grounds more relative than the mysterious accusations of the ghost. Hamlet will not kill, as Brutus does, on the possibility that his victim may be guilty. He knows too that, in a world of hostility and deception, conventional piety offers no alternative and that to avoid the moral risks of action is to acquiesce to the corruption around him and to be used, like Polonius, Ophelia, and Laertes, as an instrument of evil. Hamlet responds to this dilemma in the manner the casuists endorse:

> If it were propounded to any one to commit *two sins,* and most manifest it is unto his Conscience that both of them are *sins,* I do affirm that he is not to make *any choice* of *either,* but to eschew *both* of them.[26]

[25] Professor Ephim Fogel suggested to me the applicability of the probabilism/probabiliorism distinction to Hamlet and Brutus.

[26] Sanderson, *Lectures,* p. 61.

Hamlet refuses to choose either course of action presented to him by the world of powerful evil and duplicity; instead he uses his own intelligence and imagination to devise such strategies as the "mousetrap" and the "antic disposition" that give him temporary moral and physical safety and effectively provide evidence of Claudius's guilt.

Hamlet's treatment of the question of suicide is another striking example of his approach to moral problems. Brutus condemns suicide on principle but decides to kill himself without moral doubt or struggle. Hamlet's conscience operates both more rigorously and more flexibly, continuing to link the particular circumstances of his situation with the concept of a universal moral order. In the "O that this too too sallied flesh" soliloquy, Hamlet, appalled by the sordid, hypocritical world in which he lives, longs for death, but he is prevented from suicide by moral law. He chafes against but does not question the divine law fixed against self-slaughter. When he returns to the question in the "To be, or not to be" soliloquy, his situation has changed. He has accepted the duty to avenge his father's death; he has questioned the reliability of the ghost; he is yet to witness the performance that catches Claudius's conscience. Frustrated and humiliated by the impossibility of acting with complete moral certainty, he wants even more intensely to die, and suicide becomes not a forbidden action but an open question: to be or not to be? To Hamlet, as to Brutus, suicide appears as an active, heroic alternative to passive suffering. When to live is to be imprisoned, bound physically and morally, while smiling villains grow in power and plausibility, then to die by one's own hand seems the most noble, as well as the most reasonable, course of action.

But while Brutus's decision is unhesitating and inflexible, Hamlet thinks his way through his case of conscience. Although he is less certain at this point that traditional formulations of divine law are adequate guides to action, "something after death" is still a spiritual possibility to him. He has not, in fact, obliterated from his memory all but the commandment of his father's image. As a rational creature, he retains his knowledge of natural law, Taylor's "transcript of the wisdom and will of God written in the tables of our minds," [27] and he considers too the possibility

[27] Taylor, XII, 212.

that God's judgment will lay open the entire volume of his brain and that memory as conscience will judge all his actions good and bad. He does not *know* that killing himself is the right thing to do, and he will not act in a state of doubt. His conscience commits him to the world of the living, where thought must precede action and righteous intentions must await proper circumstances. Chafing under these self-imposed restraints, Hamlet, like Richard III, sardonically links conscience with cowardice, but unlike Richard, he does not determine to be a villain and sin against his conscience. He decides for life, not death, and it is Hamlet, not Brutus, who arms himself with patience.

Although the honesty, subtlety, and intensity with which Hamlet explores his cases of conscience demonstrate his intellectual and moral courage, he fails to set the time right without tainting his own mind. After the success of the mousetrap, he has no wish to die and no doubt about his duty to revenge, so the soliloquies that follow do not debate the right thing to do but how to go about obeying the ghost's command. Even with the question of Claudius's guilt settled, the ghost's charge is ambiguous. The nature and purpose of revenge remain problematic. Because personal fidelity and hatred of evil may motivate brutal vindictiveness as well as heroic pursuit of justice, Hamlet's intention and the circumstances of Claudius's exposure and punishment are as significant morally as the evidence of guilt. When doubt of the ghost's reliability ceases to restrain Hamlet's personal hatred, he acts, for the first time, in passionate fury and ignorance.

In his first moments alone after Claudius has fled the reenactment of his crime, Hamlet relishes the idea of revenge as brutal murder:

> Now could I drink hot blood,
> And do such bitter business as the day
> Would quake to look on.
>
> (3.2.390-392)

But Claudius shares the royal bed of Denmark with Gertrude, whose punishment Hamlet must leave

> to heaven,
> And to those thorns that in her bosom lodge
> To prick and sting her.
>
> (1.5.86-88)

As he prepares to answer his mother's summons, he exhorts himself to waken her numbed conscience without physical violence, and the rhetoric of bloody revenge gives way to rational moral discourse:

> Let me be cruel, not unnatural;
> I will speak daggers to her, but use none.
> My tongue and soul in this be hypocrites—
> How in my words somever she be shent,
> To give them seals never my soul consent!
> (3.2.395-399)

His murderous excitement is quieted by understanding that to harm his mother would be unnatural and by the ghost's admonition to leave her to the punishment of heaven and her own conscience. No such moral barriers protect Claudius. Confusing his purpose of setting the time right with the divine prerogative of eternal judgment, Hamlet passes up the opportunity of killing Claudius for reasons that are, as Dr. Johnson observed, horrible. Because Hamlet has gained our sympathy and admiration, we are relieved that he decides not to stab his praying enemy in the back, but the process by which he reaches his decision is morally repugnant. While Claudius unsuccessfully struggles to obey his conscience, Hamlet successfully abandons his for fantasies of diabolic revenge. In the next scene, he acts blindly, without thought, and kills the wrong man. Ironically, while trying to awaken his mother's conscience, he burdens his own with guilt for Polonius's death.

Hamlet, then, is not immune to the accidental judgments and mistaken purposes that plague human action. But he faces the problem of what he has done, as well as the problem of what to do, with an active conscience. It has often been observed, that with Polonius's death on his conscience, Hamlet shows new awareness of divine control of human actions and of the self-destructiveness of evil. We should also note his renewed emphasis on individual reason and resolve. In explaining to Gertrude what she has done, he does not mention the speed or incestuousness of her remarriage or even dwell on his father's murder. He presents her action as a choice between conflicting values. She was not misled by powerful sensuality or faulty sense perception, he insists, but rather she made a conscious judgment for which she must take responsibility. His advice is orthodox: repentance, confession, and a changed life.

> Confess yourself to heaven,
> Repent what's past, avoid what is to come,
> And do not spread the compost on the weeds
> To make them ranker.
>
> (3.4.149-152)

He acts as he advises. While Claudius is unable to act on his desire to repent and Gertrude dissolves in ineffectual self-loathing on seeing her soul's black and grained spots, Hamlet straightforwardly repents and promises to "answer well" for Polonius's death. Like his mother, he is responsible for the choices he has made and must avoid future misjudgments. From the consequences of his sadistic hatred and murderous fury he has gained a clearer understanding of his purpose. There is no more rant about feeding vultures with a slave's offal or drinking hot blood. But awareness of guilt and of death's horror cannot excuse evasion of duty. Hamlet knows that Fortinbras' cause is not his, but he envies the young prince who is translating his idea of honor into action. Reason as well as blood incite Hamlet to avenge "a father kill'd, a mother stain'd," and he is determined not to let his godlike reason "fust . . . unused" (4.4.38-57).

After his return from the sea voyage, Hamlet has a sharpened sense of providential control, but he does not renounce conscience and conscious choice. Although he knows that divinity shapes our ends and that rashness may save as well as punish, he does not rely on nonrational intuitions, and he is not fatalistic. He has actively outwitted Claudius's agents and is ready to kill Claudius. No longer fretting that conscience makes us cowards, he thinks precisely on each event of moral choice, even more determined to act according to his own conscience and more discriminating in his moral judgments in particular cases. In his disquisition on when drowning oneself is or is not suicide, the first gravedigger parodies the sterile legalism into which casuistry can degenerate:

> If the man go to this water and drown himself, it is, will he nill he, he goes mark you that. But if the water come to him and drown him, he drowns not himself; argal, he that is not guilty of his own death shortens not his own life. (5.1.16-20)

But this ridiculous quibbling also prepares us for Hamlet's serious attempts to define more precisely the extent of moral responsibility in particular actions.[28] The available knowledge, the intention, the probable consequences, the time, place, and person involved—all the circumstances surrounding a particular action contribute to his judgments.

In the fourth soliloquy, Hamlet saw that his case of passively suffering the outrages of fortune was analogous to those of all people bearing "the whips and scorns of time"; after his return to Denmark his understanding of the limits of human power has deepened. No man knows the future, except that death is the common end. But this recognition of human limitations does not imply a vision of life as a grotesque dance of death where godlike reason is useless and moral distinctions absurd. If there is special providence in the fall of a sparrow, surely a man's efforts to distinguish guilt from innocence have significance. Hamlet accepts the responsibility for Polonius's death and for his outburst at Laertes, but not for Ophelia's death and not for treachery against Laertes.[29] Rosencrantz and Guildenstern are morally responsible for their own actions: they willingly allowed themselves to be used as instruments of murder and are not near Hamlet's conscience. He will kill Claudius not because he has received, from an inexplicable apparition, a dread command that confirms his intuitive revulsion, but because he has ample proof that Claudius killed his king and father, corrupted his mother, seized the throne, and tried to kill him, and because allowing this moral poison to continue to spread is damnable.

> He that hath kill'd my king and whor'd my mother,
> Popp'd in between th' election and my hopes,

28 Mark Rose points that the inadequacy of the gravedigger's discussion of suicide emphasizes the problematic nature of Ophelia's death and Hamlet's final act. See *Shakespearean Design* (Cambridge, Mass.: Harvard University Press, 1972), p. 121.

29 Hamlet's analogy of shooting an arrow and inadvertently killing his brother (5.2. 241-244) is typical of the casuists' hypothetical examples. For example, Taylor uses the arrow analogy to explain the effect of ignorance: "He that shoots an arrow at a stag, and hits his enemy whom he resolved to kill when he could well do it, but knew not at all that he was in the bush. . . . To this I answer, that the ignorance excuses that action, but not that man. . . . But if the man have no malice to the unfortunate man that is killed, then he is entirely innocent, if his ignorance be innocent" (XIV, 378).

Thrown out his angle for my proper life,
And with such coz'nage—is't not perfect conscience
To quit him with this arm? And is't not to be damn'd,
To let this canker of our nature come
In further evil?

                                        (5.2.64-70)

Hamlet's conscience directs him not to shed blood, his own or another's, merely out of a sense of his own purity and the corruption around him, but it obliges him to kill in other circumstances when the victim's guilt is proved and his own life and the welfare of his country are directly threatened. After amassing incontrovertible evidence against Claudius, Hamlet kills, turning his own poisoned weapons against Claudius in "perfect conscience."

Obviously, Shakespeare does not present in *Hamlet* a thorough and convincing exposition of why killing is justified in some cases and not in others anymore than in *Julius Caesar* he demonstrates the moral nature of tyrannicide. What he does do is to make dramatically convincing the tragedy of a man of acute moral reason who resolves perplexing moral problems with rigor and discrimination. Hamlet commits errors and suffers from the unintended consequences of his actions, but he does not deceive himself morally. By struggling with doubt and guilt, he loses his life, but not before achieving the peace of mind of a good conscience. As he goes to confront his mighty opposite for the last time, he senses the danger ahead but refuses to act on a vague premonition: "Since no man, of aught he leaves, knows what is't to leave betimes, let be" (5.2.223-224). He can accept not knowing without bitterness because he has gained a quiet assurance that he knows all he needs to in order to act virtuously in whatever circumstances he finds himself—"the readiness is all." The problems the prince of Denmark faces and the solutions he reaches are outside the scope of the prose casuists, but the way he applies values to particular sets of circumstances resembles their discussions of the decision-making process. And they would have understood perfectly his dying concern that Horatio survive to report his cause correctly. Hamlet's story is not simply about the corpses that litter the stage in the final scene but rather about how and why he decided to act as he did, with all the "occurents more and less / Which have solicited—the rest is silence" (5.2.357-358).

EQUIVOCATION AND CONSCIENCE IN *Macbeth*

Since action is the heart of drama and human action entails choice, any play could conceivably be subjected to analysis in casuistical terms. I hope that my readings of *Richard III, Julius Caesar,* and *Hamlet* do not merely substitute these terms for more widely used critical vocabularies, but that, in addition, they show how contemporary ideas about conscience inform and illuminate the central themes and dramatic actions of these plays. Although Richard II experiences guilt more surely and poignantly than does Richard III, conscience is not an explicit issue in the later play. Moral decisions are crucial to all the tragedies, but *Julius Caesar* and *Hamlet* dramatize the conscious struggle to discover morally right action in a way that *Othello* and *Lear,* for example, do not. We see how Othello's perceptions of reality are distorted and his moral judgment consequently corrupted, but the decision-making process itself is not an issue. Othello's doubt is about the facts of the case; he does not pause to debate what he ought to do if Desdemona proves unfaithful. Lear's tragedy is set in motion by a crucial misjudgment of a particular case, but the dramatic focus is not on how he decides but on the terrible knowledge that results. The last play I will try to place in the context of casuistry is *Macbeth,* another tragedy where conscience is a major theme and moral choice a significant part of the dramatic action.

Indeed, the most famous direct references to casuistry in Shakespeare are the drunken porter's remarks on the casuistical concept of equivocation. Although demonstrations of the dramatic effectiveness and thematic relevance of the scene have countered Coleridge's strictures against this intrusion of low comedy, the place of casuistry in the moral vision of the play remains unclear.[30] In Mark Rose's terms, the porter's soliloquy is a speaking picture, a dramatic emblem of the significance of the action.[31] Macbeth has murdered Duncan. Ominous knocking

---

[30] Thomas Middleton Raysor, ed., *Coleridge's Shakespearean Criticism,* 2 vols. (Cambridge, Mass.: Harvard University Press, 1930), I, 75-78. The seminal defense is Thomas DeQuincey, "On the Knocking at the Gate in *Macbeth,*" in *The Collected Writings of Thomas DeQuincey,* ed. David Masson, 14 vols. (London: A. & C. Black, 1897), X, 389-394. Kenneth Muir's introduction to the Arden (10th) edition of *Macbeth* (London: Methuen and Co., 1974) offers a thoughtful discussion of the scene.

[31] Rose, *Shakespearean Design,* p. 40.

offstage has interrupted Lady Macbeth's anxious desire to clear away incriminating evidence and Macbeth's frantic effort to hide from himself what he has done. As the guilty couple exit, a drunken porter stumbles on stage and identifies the moral location of the action: [32]

> Here's a knocking indeed! If a man were porter of Hell Gate, he should have old turning the key. (*Knock.*) Knock, knock, knock! Who's there, i' th' name of Belzebub? Here's a farmer, that hang'd himself on th' expectation of plenty. . . . Faith, here's an equivocator, that could swear in both scales against either scale, who committed treason enough for God's sake, yet could not equivocate to heaven. . . . Faith, here's an English tailor come hither for stealing out of a French hose. . . . But this place is too cold for hell. I'll devil-porter it no further. I had thought to have let in some of all professions that go the primrose way to th' everlasting bonfire. (2.3.1-19)

With the murder of Duncan, Macbeth's castle has become hell, and the porter's farcical perspective both demeans and universalizes Macbeth's crime. When he decided to kill Duncan, Macbeth joined the farmer, the equivocator, and the tailor on "the primrose way to th' everlasting bonfire." He is a thief like the tailor, and clothing imagery recurs throughout to express the self-diminishing consequences of his crime.[33] Like the farmer, he gluts himself on his country's loss and ultimately despairs when prosperity and fertility return with Malcolm. The parallel between Macbeth and the equivocator, however, is more puzzling.

The description of the equivocator who practiced duplicity for God's sake but could not equivocate to heaven alludes to the 1606 trial of Father Henry Garnett, who was condemned and executed for complicity in the Gunpowder Plot.[34] Among the

[32] Glynne Wickham and others have shown that the porter's similarity to the porter of Hell Castle in the mystery cycles identifies Macbeth's castle as hell on the night of Duncan's murder. *Shakespeare's Dramatic Heritage* (London: Routledge and Kegan Paul, 1969), pp. 214-224.

[33] On clothing imagery, see Caroline Spurgeon, *Shakespeare's Imagery* (Cambridge, Eng.: Cambridge University Press, 1935), pp. 324-327, and Cleanth Brooks, *The Well Wrought Urn* (New York: Reynal and Hitchcock, 1947), pp. 30-37.

[34] Most editions explain the allusion to Garnett's trial. The fullest accounts of the role of equivocation in the trial and in *Macbeth* are Henry N. Paul, *The Royal Play of "Macbeth"* (New York: The Macmillan Co., 1950), pp.

most damaging evidence against Father Garnett was his defense of equivocation. The doctrine of equivocation was developed by Jesuit casuists to deal with situations where telling the literal truth did not serve the cause of justice. Equivocation could take the form of amphibology, where ambivalent grammatical structure or double senses of words create ambiguity. Jeremy Taylor gives this example:

> Titius, the father of Caius, hid his father in a tub, and to the cut-throats that inquired for him to bloody purposes, he answered "Patrem in doliolo latere:" now that did not only signify a little tub, but a hill near Rome, where the villains did suspect him to be, and were so diverted.[35]

Equivocation also involved the concept of mental reservation. Drawing on Aristotle's observation that a proposition can be partly stated and partly unstated, some casuists held that in certain situations one could in conscience deceive others by uttering only part of a true statement and completing the sense mentally. For example, to the question, "Do you know Mr. Brown?" one could answer aloud, "No," and add mentally "not to the end of telling you," thus concealing information from men and telling the truth before God, who knows thoughts as well as words. Jesuits like Father Garnett defended the use of equivocation as a means for a persecuted minority to avoid self-incrimination. For example, a treatise used as evidence in Father Garnett's trial carried the following title:

> A treatise of Equivocation, wherein is largely discussed the question whether a Catholic or any other person before a Magistrate being demanded upon his oath whether a Priest were in such a place, may (notwithstanding his perfect knowledge to the contrary) without Perjury and securely in conscience answer, No: with this secret meaning reserved in his mind, That he was not there so that any man is bound to detect it.[36]

According to its proponents, equivocation was justifiable only for a good purpose and in certain extreme circumstances, but,

---

237-247, and especially Frank L. Huntley, "*Macbeth* and the Background of Jesuitical Equivocation," *PMLA* 79 (1964): 390-400.

[35] Taylor, XIII, 379.

[36] Quoted by Paul, *The Royal Play*, p. 238.

since interrogation by an English court and defense of co-religion-
ists were among those justifiable situations, these qualifications
did not lessen English outrage at the casuistical practice of calling
a lie the truth, especially in the atmosphere of horror and fear
following the discovery of the plot to blow up the King in
parliament. Many Roman Catholics as well as Protestants saw
equivocation as the tool of treason and diabolical treachery and
associated it with Jesuitical hypocrisy and cunning. The Roman
Catholic Christopher Bagshawe condemns Jesuits on these
grounds:

> They are so delighted with equivocation, or a subtile dis-
> sembling kind of speech, as that to the scandall of others
> they are not ashamed to defend it in their publick writings.[37]

Although Macbeth certainly commits treason enough to justify
the application of the porter's words, he does not fit the stereotype
of the equivocator. His betrayal of the king he professes to love
and serve involves deceit, but he embraces duplicity for his own
sake, not God's. Lacking Brutus's tortuous reasoning, Macbeth's
commitment to evil is remarkably unequivocal. He knows that
murdering Duncan will earn him condemnation by God and
man. Nor is Macbeth a notably cunning villain. Admittedly, he
must put on a false face to cover his false heart, but he is an
unsuccessful hypocrite. From the beginning, Lady Macbeth fears
his transparency:

> Your face, my thane, is as a book, where men
> May read strange matters.
>
> (1.5.62-63)

In fact, he does not deceive anyone for very long. In contrast to
the praise heaped on "honest Iago," suspicion surrounds Macbeth
from the moment Duncan's body is discovered until he betrays
himself completely in the banquet scene. He has none of Richard
of Gloucester's delight in exploiting the ambiguities of language.
Richard equivocates with his victim, assuring Clarence:

> Well, your imprisonment shall not be long,
> I will deliver you, or else lie for you.
> (*Richard III*, 1.1.114-115)

[37] Quoted by Huntley, "*Macbeth* and the Background of Jesuitical Equivocation," p. 395.

But Macbeth, in his last conversation with Banquo, gathers useful information with scant subtlety and direct lies. The truth mingled with falsehood in Macbeth's speeches is unintended and subsequently reverberates against him, not his victim. His murderous plots rely less and less on deception and more and more on sheer power: from the secret, midnight slaying of Duncan, through the hired assassination of Banquo, to the savage daylight massacre of Macduff's household.

Macbeth, then, is a brutal tyrant, not a subtle dissembler, but if he does not characteristically resort to equivocation to gain his ends, he certainly is a victim of the equivocation of the fiend. The spirits' prophecies that Macbeth cannot be killed by a man born of woman and that he will not be destroyed until Birnam wood comes to Dunsinane equivocate on double senses of "born" and "come." These prophecies can also be analyzed as equivocations where part of the meaning is unstated, as Huntley suggests:

> (1) No man born of woman can harm you, Macbeth [not counting a Caesarian section];
> (2) You will not be vanquished till Birnam woods move to Dunsinane [omitting of course the exigencies of military camouflage].[38]

However the statements are described, they, like all equivocations, present partial truths as though they were whole truths. Macbeth is tempted, deceived, and destroyed when he guides his actions by flattering half-truths instead of grappling with the complexities of himself and the world he lives in.

Thus, Shakespeare exploited the contemporary interest in equivocation aroused by Garnett's trial but did not merely rely on stereotypical associations. Instead of presenting equivocation as an effective technique of traitors imposing on the innocent, he shows its danger as symptomatic of a self-corrupting mode of thought. Equivocation was usually condemned for its external destructiveness, its capacity for subverting language and destroying social cohesion. Jeremy Taylor sums up the typical objections:

> The thinking one thing, and speaking it otherwise, is so far from making it to be true, that therefore it is a lie, because the words are not according to what is in our mind: and it is a perverting the very end and institution of words, and

[38] Ibid., p. 398.

evacuates the purpose of laws, and the end of oaths, making them not to be the end of questions, and the benefit of society.[39]

In contrast, Shakespeare has used the equivocation motif to investigate the growth of evil within the mind. Macbeth equivocates most effectively and dangerously with himself. While diabolical ingenuity and subtlety were the stock qualities associated with equivocation, Shakespeare associates it with the origin of evil in the narrowing of perception and the simplifying of response.

An equivocation reveals only one part of a complex truth, while the rest remains hidden like the submerged and dangerous bulk of an iceberg. The obverse of equivocation is paradox, the apparent contradiction that asserts the complexity of reality.[40] While equivocation oversimplifies, paradox stimulates thought by pointing to the mixed nature of human experience. It has been well established that the world of *Macbeth* is paradoxical, but it is often incorrectly assumed that the endemic paradoxes in the language of the play reflect the evil that Macbeth unleashes on the world. G. I. Duthie, for example, argues that paradox defines the conception of evil in *Macbeth*, a situation where "a given entity is both one thing and the opposite simultaneously," and that Macbeth is largely responsible for this state of affairs. In Lawrence Danson's analysis, paradoxes are examples of unnatural language reflecting Macbeth's unnatural deed, and the weird sisters' paradox "Fair is foul, and foul is fair" focuses the central question of the play: whether Macbeth destroys all rational order so that the referents of "foul" and "fair" lose their identities, or whether he merely confuses the true order of things temporarily, so that those things that are really "fair" are called "foul" until the true order of things is revealed and normal language returns. Margaret Burrell's rhetorical study of the play goes so far as to suggest that good characters such as Duncan speak paradoxically

[39] Taylor, XIII, 375-376.

[40] Rosalie Colie points to the relationship between paradox and equivocation, showing that paradox is necessarily equivocal or ambiguous. *Paradoxia Epidemica: The Renaissance Tradition of Paradox* (Princeton: Princeton University Press, 1966), *passim,* but see especially pp. 6, 483. My point is that equivocation in the casuistical sense of a means of deception can succeed only while unrecognized. As soon as its double senses are recognized, it becomes paradox.

because they breathe the atmosphere contaminated by Macbeth and Lady Macbeth.[41]

These interpretations are incorrect, I think, both because they present paradox as a symptom of unusual moral disorder and because they present evil as an alien force introduced by Macbeth. It is true that Macbeth destroys order and harmony in the individual soul and the state, but neither microcosm nor macrocosm is a Scottish paradise of Edenic innocence. The harmony is a blending of potentially discordant forces, and the order is the just but precarious subordination of passion to reason, of self to the common good. Duplicity and treachery are already active in Scotland before Macbeth commits himself to evil, but when treason and rebellion occur, they are defeated by a wise king and loyal subjects. Macbeth's world, like all Shakespeare's fictional worlds, is a mixture of good and evil where appearances deceive and "There's no art / To find the mind's construction in the face" (1.4.11-12), where a person or an event may be either fair or foul, good or ill, depending on the surrounding circumstances. It is, in short, an ambiguous, confusing place, and paradoxes are an accurate way of describing its complexity. The weird sisters' "Fair is foul, and foul is fair" and "When the battle's lost and won" are immediately translated into concrete human situations, as the wounded soldier reports the fair outcome of the foul rebellion and the winners deal out just and cruel punishment to the losers. The Thane of Cawdor, "that most disloyal traitor," who in defeat "set forth / A deep repentance" (1.2.52; 1.4.6-7) illustrates the mixed good and evil inherent in the individual soul. The rewards and obligations of peaceful human intercourse are no less paradoxical than the fortunes of war. While in war, the source of comfort becomes the source of discomfort, in peace, trouble and sorrow can be joyful forms of love:

> *Duncan* My plenteous joys,
> Wanton in fullness, seek to hide themselves
> In drops of sorrow.
>
> (1.4.33-35)

[41] G. I. Duthie, "Antithesis in *Macbeth*," *Shakespeare Survey* 19 (1966): 25-33; Lawrence Danson, *Tragic Alphabet: Shakespeare's Drama of Language* (New Haven and London: Yale University Press, 1974), pp. 124-131; Margaret Burrell, "*Macbeth*: A Study in Paradox," *Shakespeare Jahrbuch* 90 (1954): 171, 173.

Duncan The love that follows us sometime is our trouble,
Which still we thank as love. Herein I teach you
How you shall bid God 'ield us for your pains,
And thank us for your trouble.

(1.6.11-14)

In the early scenes, then, paradoxes establish the complexity of human experience by calling attention to the varied nature of the physical world, human nature, and human society. Not a monster of perversity like Richard III, Macbeth combines strength and weakness, vice and virtue. Initially he recognizes and struggles with the paradoxes of experience. He knows that the witches' prophecies are both fair and foul. He has murderous thoughts and is horrified by them:

> This supernatural soliciting
> Cannot be ill; cannot be good. If ill,
> Why hath it given me earnest of success,
> Commencing in a truth? I am Thane of Cawdor.
> If good, why do I yield to that suggestion
> Whose horrid image doth unfix my hair
> And make my seated heart knock at my ribs,
> Against the use of nature?

(1.3.130-137)

Yet he begins immediately to equivocate with himself, suppressing part of the paradoxical truth. His letter to Lady Macbeth, reporting the confirmation of the prophecy that he would be Thane of Cawdor and his belief in the prophecy that he will be king, does not mention the paradoxes addressed to Banquo:

> Lesser than Macbeth, and greater.
> Not so happy, yet much happier.
> Thou shalt get kings, though thou be none.

(1.3.65-67)

This tendency in Macbeth to suppress unwelcome paradoxes is a settled habit of mind in Lady Macbeth. She is aware of the mixture of fair and foul in herself and others, but has the kind of mind that wants to see reality as simple and straightforward. To her, Macbeth's fair-foul nature is simply a contradiction to be resolved: he "wouldst not play false / And yet wouldst wrongly win" (1.5.21-22). Her determination to deny human paradoxes

113

controls her conception of sexual identity: a man is strong and fearless, both morally and physically; a woman is compassionate, weak, and timid. To achieve the strength needed for their daring enterprise, she must deny her womanhood and shame Macbeth out of any unmanly hesitation to take what he wants ruthlessly. In her literal-minded, absolutist view of the world, people are either wholly masculine or wholly feminine, either strong or weak, honorable or contemptible, and anything other than concrete, physical reality is unreal, mere fantasy. Demonstrable physical and political power is the only possible goal, and moral considerations are merely excuses for cowardice. She dismisses as "brain-sickly" illusion the voice of conscience crying to Macbeth, "Sleep no more! / Macbeth does murther sleep." For her, only physical reality exists: "A little water clears us of this deed" (2.2.43, 32-33, 64).

At the beginning of the play, Macbeth's view of experience is more complex; it includes his own potential for good and evil in an ambiguous world where choice is difficult. He knows that the same situation, desire, or action may be fair and foul, that being a man involves more than narrowly defined "masculine" qualities, and that "what is not" is just as real a part of his experience as "what is." When, in response to his wife's determination to act quickly and efficiently, he tries to set aside spiritual considerations—to "jump the life to come" (1.7.7)—and to confine his reflections to calculations of worldly success, the knowledge that when murder is done it is not done forces its way into his thoughts. He knows that to murder Duncan would be to violate all human and social order and that moral judgment before and after action is an inescapable part of the human condition: "in these cases / We still have judgment here" (1.7.7-8). He knows that virtue, which seems weak and vulnerable, will become strong and triumphant through natural human pity, and that evil, while apparently strong, is ultimately futile. But these paradoxes disappear under the pressure of Lady Macbeth's determined reduction of complexity to a one-dimensional world of material reality where the voice of conscience is unmanly cowardice. As A. C. Bradley points out, Lady Macbeth offers Macbeth a straightforward plan of action that can replace "the terror and danger of deliberation." [42] So Macbeth chooses the false security

[42] A. C. Bradley, *Shakespearean Tragedy*, 2d ed. (London: Macmillan and Co., 1905), p. 367.

of over-simplification, denying the reality of the doubts and ambiguities of experience. Unwilling to sustain the tension between fair and foul in himself, he chooses to become totally foul, wearing a false face to hide a false heart.

Macbeth's vision of a dagger as he goes to murder Duncan dramatizes his last chance to change his mind.

> Is this a dagger which I see before me,
> The handle toward my hand? Come, let me clutch thee:
> I have thee not, and yet I see thee still.
> Art thou not, fatal vision, sensible
> To feeling as to sight? or art thou but
> A dagger of the mind, a false creation,
> Proceeding from the heat-oppressed brain?
> I see thee yet, in form as palpable
> As this which now I draw.
> Thou marshal'st me the way that I was going,
> And such an instrument I was to use.
> Mine eyes are made the fools o' th' other senses,
> Or else worth all the rest.
>
> (2.1.33-45)

The dagger is paradoxically real and unreal, but to Macbeth it is either the creation of the brain, and hence false, or physically real, in which case sight is his only trustworthy sense. He cannot accept the dagger as an incorporeal but true creation of the moral imagination. So far, Macbeth has kept the act of murder abstract and remote, euphemistically thinking of killing Duncan as "it," "this business," "surcease," or "his taking off." [43] Now the bodiless creation of his mind gives visual form to the actual physical details of murder:

> I see thee still;
> And on thy blade and dudgeon gouts of blood,
> Which was not so before.
>
> (2.1.45-47)

Rejecting this disturbingly real unreality, the image that points the way to murder with repellant vividness, Macbeth substitutes

[43] This point is made by Paul A. Jorgensen, *Our Naked Frailties: Sensational Art and Meaning in "Macbeth"* (Berkeley and Los Angeles: University of California Press, 1971), pp. 47-50, and Ruth Nevo, *Tragic Form in Shakespeare* (Princeton: Princeton University Press, 1972), p. 229.

the unambivalently sinister rhetoric of stage villainy and seeks comfort in a securely physical world and unambiguous commitment to horror:

> There's no such thing:
> It is the bloody business which informs
> Thus to mine eyes. Now o'er the one half world
> Nature seems dead, and wicked dreams abuse
> The curtain'd sleep; witchcraft celebrates
> Pale Hecat's off'rings; and wither'd Murther,
> Alarum'd by his sentinel, the wolf,
> Whose howl's his watch, thus with his stealthy pace,
> With Tarquin's ravishing strides, towards his design
> Moves like a ghost. Thou sure and firm-set earth,
> Hear not my steps, which way they walk, for fear
> The very stones prate of my whereabout,
> And take the present horror from the time,
> Which now suits with it. Whiles I threat, he lives:
> Words to the heat of deeds too cold breath gives.
> (2.1.47-61)

He tries to release himself from torturing internal conflicts by replacing the paradoxical dagger with his physical dagger and physical action. Rejecting any reality other than the material, denying the kindness and gratitude in his nature, defying the judgment of his conscience, Macbeth leaves the stage to kill Duncan: "I go, and it is done" (2.1.62). By repressing his understanding that "done" means "finished" as well as "performed," he equivocates himself to hell. He kills, as he says later, "to gain our peace" (3.2.20), and so loses peace forever.

Macbeth sins against his conscience, murdering Duncan in full knowledge of the moral nature of his action. From this point on, his impossible goal is to escape his conscience. The moral universe he inhabits is described by Perkins: "We must passe thorough three judgements; the judgement of men, the judgement of our conscience, and the last judgement of God." [44] Macbeth may temporarily ignore the judgment of men and of God, but his judgment of himself is immediate and terrible: his "Amen" sticks in his throat, and he hears the cry "Sleep no more! / Macbeth does murther sleep." His terrible self-knowledge stops him from

[44] Perkins, I, 553.

seeking God's blessing and cuts him off from nature's restorative processes. The mental traits evident in Macbeth and his wife before the murder are intensified in their reactions to the voice of Macbeth's conscience. Lady Macbeth busies herself with practical action and counsels against thinking more deeply:

> Consider it not so deeply.
> (2.2.27)

> These deeds must not be thought
> After these ways; so, it will make us mad.
> (2.2.30-31)

Macbeth struggles not to know what he knows:

> I am afraid to think what I have done;
> Look on't again I dare not.
> (2.2.48-49)

> To know my deed, 'twere best not know myself.
> Wake Duncan with thy knocking! I would thou couldst!
> (2.2.70-71)

As several critics have observed, this desperate flight from self-knowledge never takes the form of self-justification. Rather than deny the evil he has done, Macbeth tries to escape awareness of the paradoxical complexities of good and evil in himself and his world. As he kills Duncan to gain peace, so he kills Banquo to gain safety, an end to the doubts and uncertainties that torment him. His fears and doubts come partly from the paradoxical prophecies which promised that Banquo's descendants will reign, but his insecurity and his motive for murder are not primarily political. Although Banquo suspects Macbeth, he gives no evidence of plotting against him. He is content to let fate crown his children if it will have them kings. Although he has ambitions, he will not compromise his conscience to achieve them. And it is this combination that tortures Macbeth. Macbeth defends his murder of Duncan's grooms by denying the possibility of combining wisdom and passion:

> Who can be wise, amaz'd, temp'rate, and furious,
> Loyal, and neutral, in a moment?
> (2.3.108-109)

He is lying, of course, but he is also describing human nature

117

as he wants it to be. Banquo is a living refutation of this simplified psychology:

> 'Tis much he dares,
> And to that dauntless temper of his mind,
> He hath a wisdom that doth guide his valor
> To act in safety. There is none but he
> Whose being I do fear; and under him
> My Genius is rebuk'd, as it is said
> Mark Antony's was by Caesar.
>
> (3.1.50-56)

Macbeth feels rebuked by Banquo not simply as Iago does by the
beauty of Cassio's life but specifically for combining wisdom and
valor. Because Macbeth has chosen to be dauntless and valiant
instead of wise and thoughtful, he is tortured by the living
evidence that the choice was unnecessary.

While Banquo reminds Macbeth and the audience of the fuller
humanity that Macbeth sacrifices, the hired murderers function
like the farmer, equivocator, and tailor in the porter's speech,
embodying the limited understanding underlying the histrionic
trappings of Macbeth's diabolism. The murderers respond with
inexpressive, one-sentence answers both to Macbeth's allusions
to Christian virtue and to his attempt to impart grandeur to
the murder.[45] They reject his offer of privacy to debate and
resolve the question, answering in unison, "We are resolv'd, my
lord" (3.1.138). In contrast to the hired murderers in *Richard
III,* these men do not debate whether to act against their consciences, for they are determined not to think. Weary and bitter,
they are "reckless," resolved to set their lives "on any chance"
(3.1.109-113). Although we sometimes think of evil as an extension of human possibilities beyond normal limits—as a transcendence of barriers—Shakespeare, in both the anonymous
murderers and in Macbeth, shows evil as essentially a diminish-
ment of man's potential. Although Macbeth's choice of evil has
tremendously far-reaching consequences, he does not have a
grandly aspiring mind. He subjects his mind to evil not as a bold
and daring plunge into the unknown and forbidden but as a
willful over-simplification of the demands of an ambiguous and

---

[45] On echoes of Matt. 5, see Muir's introduction to the Arden *Macbeth,*
p. lx, and his note to 3.1. 87-88.

complex world, a deadening of perception to escape from the tensions of a complex human nature.[46]

Banquo's death, of course, does not alter the basic conditions of Macbeth's world. He cannot obliterate the ambiguities of experience by killing Banquo or destroy his conscience by defining himself as totally evil. As Perkins explains, although men may think that "conscience was hanged long agoe . . . *hanged conscience will revive and become both gibbet & hangman to them.*" [47] Macbeth's moral self-knowledge revives in the accusing figure of Banquo's ghost. Although some of the play's best critics have argued that Banquo's ghost is not a manifestation of Macbeth's conscience but a real ghost or an evil spirit in Banquo's form, I am not persuaded that its precise ontological status is a fruitful question to pursue.[48] The ghost is obviously a nonphysical expression of Macbeth's guilt. As Lady Macbeth recognizes, it has the same paradoxically real-unreal status as the bloody dagger. Characteristically, she dismisses it as effeminate, cowardly fantasy:

> This is the very painting of your fear;
> This is the air-drawn dagger which you said
> Led you to Duncan. O, these flaws and starts
> (Impostors to true fear) would well become
> A woman's story at a winter's fire,
> Authoriz'd by her grandam.
>
> (3.4.60-65)

Macbeth's first, frightened reaction—"Thou canst not say I did it; never shake / Thy gory locks at me" (3.4.49-50)—shows that he fears it as a figure of judgment. But again he deflects moral self-analysis with greater horror at this violent assault on his tenuous grasp of a one-dimensional, predictable reality:

> The time has been,
> That when the brains were out, the man would die,
> And there an end; but now they rise again

---

[46] A useful discussion of Macbeth's flight from self-knowledge is in Robert Heilman, " 'Twere Best not Know Myself'," in *Shakespeare 400*, ed. James G. McManaway (New York: Holt, Rinehart and Winston, 1964), pp. 89-98.

[47] Perkins, I, 516.

[48] Willard Farnham argues that it is a "real ghost" as distinct from an internal force. See *Shakespeare's Tragic Frontier: The World of His Final Tragedies* (Berkeley and Los Angeles: University of California Press, 1950), p. 123. Paul Jorgensen believes that it is the devil or a spirit in the form of Banquo. See *Our Naked Frailties*, p. 125.

With twenty mortal murthers on their crowns,
And push us from our stools. This is more strange
Than such a murther is.

(3.4.77-82)

Since the experience is too powerful to dismiss entirely as an "Unreal mock'ry," Macbeth translates it into the physical terms in which he wants to view the world. Refusing to understand Banquo's ghost as an expression of moral reality, a nonmaterial form confronting him with the fact of his guilt, he instead interprets it as another manifestation of a known, if unusual, feature of physical nature:

It will have blood, they say; blood will have blood.
Stones have been known to move and trees to speak;
Augures and understood relations have
By maggot-pies and choughs and rooks brought forth
The secret'st man of blood.

(3.4.121-125)

This second disturbing vision intensifies Macbeth's effort to force the mysterious complexities of experience into a simplified pattern of evil that can be fully known, and hence predicted and controlled. While Hamlet responds to his blood-guilt and to the reappearance of the ghost with increased uncertainty about the extent of human knowledge and with intensified moral reflection and self-scrutiny, Macbeth becomes even more determined to know but not to think. He is "bent to know, / By the worst means, the worst," but rejects the possibility of redeeming the past by looking within: "Returning were as tedious as go o'er" (3.4.133-134; 137). In contrast to Hamlet, who kills Polonius, admits his guilt, repents, and continues to struggle with moral problems in an ambiguous world, Macbeth fails to face his cases of conscience honestly and becomes increasingly corrupt. Because he is unwilling to deal with the moral paradoxes of his nature, he destroys the good in himself and chooses to believe the prophecies conjured by the weird sisters.

Taken as a whole, the apparitions presented by the weird sisters are paradoxical rather than equivocal in the casuistical sense of leaving essential meaning unexpressed. If the second apparition tells Macbeth to "laugh to scorn / The pow'r of man," the first tells him to "beware Macduff." The prophecies that "none of

120

woman born / Shall harm Macbeth" and that "Macbeth shall never vanquish'd be until / Great Birnan wood to high Dunsinane hill / Shall come against him" equivocate by exploiting Macbeth's desire to see nature as simple (4.1.71-94). But the apparitions themselves are evidence of a more complex reality. While the second and third apparitions suggest that Macbeth is invulnerable, the parade of kings followed by Banquo clearly indicates the transience of Macbeth's power. When Macbeth banishes fear on the basis of these visions, he dupes himself. Essentially it is Macbeth who equivocates with Macbeth. Looking for assurance in the unalterable laws of nature, he blocks from consciousness his knowledge of nature's complexity and ferociously repudiates the compassion and sense of justice in his own nature. Finally he deals 1) with the contradictory advice to beware and to be bold, 2) with his contradictory impulses both to trust spirits that vanish in air and to rely on the predictable solidity of physical nature, and 3) with his contradictory decisions to kill Macduff and to let him live, by refusing to think or to exercise moral judgment at all:

> From this moment
> The very firstlings of my heart shall be
> The firstlings of my hand. And even now,
> To crown my thoughts with acts, be it thought and done:
> The castle of Macduff I will surprise,
> Seize upon Fife, give to th' edge o' th' sword
> His wife, his babes, and all unfortunate souls
> That trace him in his line. No boasting like a fool;
> This deed I'll do before this purpose cool.
> But no more sights!
>
> (4.1.146-155)

In flight from the fear and doubt that such paradoxical sights evoke, Macbeth replaces thought with action.[49]

[49] Lawrence Danson also relates Macbeth's tragedy to the doctrine of equivocation, but, while I want to argue that Macbeth equivocates with himself by repressing awareness of ambiguity and substituting action for thought, Danson argoes that Macbeth generates evil by hypostatizing thought: "As to the Jesuitical equivocators a thought could be a speech, so to Macbeth a thought can be a deed." Danson sees Macbeth confusing fantasy with reality until fantasy overwhelms reality, while I see him repudiating the complex vision of reality that fantasy or imagination provides. See Danson, *Tragic Alphabet,* pp. 134-135.

The simplistic certainty demanded by Macbeth contrasts sharply with the doubt and confusion of the other characters. We should notice not only that Banquo remains innocent while Macbeth becomes evil but that he does so in terms which show that he must struggle with the evil in himself—"the cursed thoughts that nature / Gives way to in repose!" (2.1.8-9)—and resists temptation by understanding that fair may be foul (1.3.122-126) and honor may involve dishonor (2.1.26-27). Banquo's understanding of complexity and his willingness to live with doubt and uncertainty are reiterated in Macbeth's next victims, Lady Macduff and her child. In her fear and anger, Lady Macduff tries to interpret experience as either fair or foul: her husband as motivated by either fear or love; actions as either wise or foolish; people as either liars or honest men. But, as her son never doubts, she knows better. She remembers that:

> I am in this earthly world—where to do harm
> Is often laudable, to do good sometime
> Accounted dangerous folly.
>
> (4.2.75-77)

She recognizes not just that appearances deceive but that conventional moral categories may be inadequate to actual human dilemmas. Thus, Macduff's abandonment of his family and disloyalty to his king may be "to do good."

The scene at Macduff's castle, then, contrasts the narrowing and rigidifying of Macbeth's mind with the breadth and flexibility of mind that characterize the good characters in this play. Awareness of the ambiguity of language reflects this comprehension of the ambiguity of experience. In the immediately preceding scene, Macbeth convinces himself that no man can be motherless; in contrast, Lady Macduff summarizes her child's situation with the paradox that Macbeth fails to see: "Father'd he is, and yet he's fatherless" (4.2.26).[50] Throughout the scene, the child himself demonstrates his awareness that words must be interpreted in the light of the circumstances in which they are spoken. When his mother tells him his father is dead, he knows she does not mean what she says literally. She expresses her exasperation, and he teases her in response. When she says his

[50] L. C. Knights suggests comparing this riddle with the equivocation about Macduff's birth. See *Explorations* (New York: Chatto and Windus, 1946), p. 26.

father is a traitor, he jokingly quibbles on the multiple meanings of words. But when a hostile stranger calls his father a traitor, he responds unequivocally, "Thou li'st, thou shag-ear'd villain!" (4.2.83), and is killed.

Macbeth's confidence in deceptive half-truths contrasts most strikingly with Malcolm's shrewdness. Malcolm is identified as an obstacle to Macbeth's ambitions as early as act 1, scene 4. Upon discovering Duncan's murder, Malcolm immediately sees his danger and the need for unconventional measures to protect himself: "There's warrant in that theft / Which steals itself, when there's no mercy left" (2.3.145-146). When we next see Malcolm in act 4, scene 3, evil is triumphant and danger everywhere. Although violence, deception, and disorder did not originate with Macbeth, under his tyranny they have become the norm rather than the exception. In these circumstances, deciding how to act is abnormally difficult, and Malcolm's announcement that he will act only on what he believes and believe only what he knows is admirable. His suspicions of Macduff are reasonable coming from a man who knows that Macbeth's spies have infiltrated every household and that Macbeth and the previous Thane of Cawdor were also once regarded as honest men. Even though Malcolm's doubt of a man who would leave his wife and child unprotected echoes Lady Macduff's charge that flight is unnatural and "against all reason" (4.2.14), we should not conclude that Macduff made the wrong decision. Instead, we should understand that Macduff faced an agonizing case of conscience in deciding what to do.

All the characters are in morally similar, if personally less terrible, predicaments. Banquo, Rosse, and Lennox also have to decide how to act in circumstances where good and evil, falsehood and truth are hard to distinguish and where moral issues cannot be obvious. In the minor characters, the focus is on the difficulty of decision rather than the correctness of choice. As a result, some critics argue that the minor characters are most notable for their total innocence, while others judge them at least partially guilty.[51]

---

[51] A. C. Bradley finds evil in Banquo, while A. P. Rossiter sees him as the symbolic Good Man. D. A. Traversi refers to Macduff's unpardonable carelessness, while G. R. Elliott defends Macduff's decision but criticizes the time-serving of Rosse and Lennox. Rossiter and Roy Walker see the characters in general as innocent antitheses to the evil of Macbeth and Lady Macbeth, but G. Wilson Knight and Robert Ornstein hold that they are all tainted

The critic, of course, is free to make personal moral judgments, but Shakespeare does not guide our judgment in every case. Just as we cannot deduce Shakespeare's opinion of suicide or tyrannicide from *Julius Caesar,* we cannot derive from *Macbeth* his judgment of how one ought to act under the rule of an oppressive usurper. Since the play does not dramatize the decision-making process, we cannot judge Macduff, Rosse, and Lennox as we can Brutus, Hamlet, and Macbeth, on how they arrive at their decisions. But if we cannot judge their decisions, we can appreciate their dilemmas. Rosse describes the situation of all Scotland when he tells Lady Macduff:

> But cruel are the times when we are traitors,
> And do not know ourselves; when we hold rumor
> From what we fear, yet know not what we fear,
> But float upon a wild and violent sea
> Each way, and move.

(4.2.18-22)

The consequences of Macduff's decision to leave his family unprotected in Scotland in order to join Malcolm in England do not prove that his action was morally wrong, but the slaughter of his family puts beyond question the seriousness and difficulty of the decision.

The scene in the English court begins in an atmosphere of horror and confusion, but Malcolm's doubt and fear are balanced by his effectiveness in coping with this dangerous, bewildering world. Macbeth's antithesis, he is willing to grapple with complexities as well as to endorse the kingly graces that Macbeth so conspicuously rejects. He knows that his bleeding country needs the healing care of a virtuous king and that innocence alone will not rescue Scotland. Thus, in order to protect himself and to test Macduff's worth as an ally, he adopts the pious fraud of

---

with the pervasive evil. See Bradley, *Shakespearean Tragedy,* pp. 384-385; A. P. Rossiter, *Angel with Horns,* ed. Graham Storey (London: Longmans, Green and Co., 1961), pp. 231-232; D. A. Traversi, *An Approach to Shakespeare,* 3d ed. rev., 2 vols. (Garden City, N.Y.: Doubleday, 1969), II, 133; G. R. Elliott, *Dramatic Providence in "Macbeth"* (Princeton: Princeton University Press, 1958), pp. 105-106, 161-165; Rossiter, *Angel with Horns,* p. 219; Roy Walker, *The Time is Free* (London: Andrew Dakers Ltd., 1949), p. xv; G. Wilson Knight, *The Wheel of Fire,* 4th ed. rev. (London: Methuen and Co., 1949), pp. 150-152; Robert Ornstein, *The Moral Vision of Jacobean Tragedy* (Madison: The University of Wisconsin Press, 1960), p. 233.

lying, accusing himself of evil that would make him unfit to rule. In adopting this "false speaking" while claiming to "delight / No less in truth than life" (4.3.129-130), Malcolm presents a paradox that becomes common in casuistry. English casuists who contemptuously denounced the equivocator's confounding of truth with falsehood also argued that in some circumstances deception is prudent and right. Jeremy Taylor, for example, endorses traditional praise of truth as the virtue "in which we are to endeavour to be like God" but continues:

> The affairs of men are full of intrigues, and their persons of infirmity, and their understandings of deception; and they have ends to serve which are just, and good, and necessary; and yet they cannot be served by truth, but sometimes by error and deception.[52]

In Taylor's analysis of the problem, "to deceive our neighbour to his hurt" is intrinsically evil, but one may lawfully deceive someone for his own good out of charity, as Malcolm does Macduff, and may use his wit for "simulation and dissimulation" in a just war, as Malcolm does when he directs his soldiers to use the trees of Birnam wood for camouflage.[53]

Although Malcolm's relations with the saintly English king who heals his countrymen's evil through grace associates him with supernatural good just as Macbeth's dealings with the weird sisters connect him with nonhuman evil, both Malcolm and Macbeth are men with limited human knowledge who must act in ambiguous and bewildering circumstances. While Macbeth chooses to blind himself to complexity with a vision of impenetrable evil, Malcolm realizes the power of evil without falling

[52] Taylor, XIII, 350-351.

[53] Quotations are from Taylor, XIII, 351-374. Shakespeare's use of Holinshed supports the conclusion that he deliberately emphasized Malcolm's shrewdness as well as his virtue. Although Shakespeare omitted the episodes where Holinshed portrays Duncan as wily and deceptive, he retained the accounts of Malcolm's deception of Macduff and of his military strategem. In Holinshed, Malcolm accuses himself of lust, avarice, and deceit. Shakespeare uses the pattern of three speeches of almost equal length, each answered by Macduff, but the third, instead of singling out deception as the worst of vices, professes generalized virtuousity in evil: "the division of each several crime." Compare Arden *Macbeth*, ed. Muir, Appendix A, pp. 176-178 with *Macbeth* 4.3. 91-99. For a different account of the change, see Paul, *The Royal Play*, pp. 359-366.

into cynicism. He knows that "Though all things foul would wear the brows of grace, / Yet grace must still look so" (4.3.23-24). We see nothing of Malcolm's inner life, so he does not fascinate or move us as Shakespeare's more fully developed characters do, but he is more engaging than many of the survivors left to restore order after tragic catastrophe. His adherence to principle and his grasp of complexity in particular circumstances promise a workable moral alternative to Macbeth's conduct—an alternative more reassuring than Richmond's unconvincing purity, Fortinbras's single-minded concentration on military honor, or Octavius Caesar's expedient grasp of political power.

A similar multiple awareness characterizes the men who follow Malcolm against Macbeth. When Rosse reassures Macduff that his wife and children are well before revealing the horror of their deaths, his lies serve no obvious purpose, but they suggest a complex, albeit confused, human response that contrasts with Macbeth's simplistic reduction of himself to unconsidered brutality. Macduff meets the paradoxes within and without even more impressively. When his hopes for Scotland are first destroyed and then revived, he feels the difficulty of reconciling such "welcome and unwelcome things at once" (4.3.138). When he learns what he has lost, he is overwhelmed with horror, grief, anger, bitterness, and guilt, but he does not repudiate his humanity to escape this pain and confusion. He reconciles conflicting emotions by understanding that as a man he must both feel and fight against the evil he suffers.

In the last act, Malcolm and Macduff triumph. Their victory is morally and emotionally ambiguous, costing young Siward's life as well as Macbeth's severed head, but by making friends of foes and measuring the value of life by its quality as well as its quantity, Macbeth's opponents seem capable of establishing an ordered and productive human community where violence and egotism will be held in control though not abolished. In this last movement of the action, Macbeth and his wife are destroyed by the paradoxical reality that they have tried to simplify and control. As the porter explains in his speech on drink as an equivocator with lechery, equivocation cancels gain with loss. It

> makes him, and it mars him; it sets him on, and it takes him off; it persuades him, and disheartens him; makes him stand to, and not stand to; in conclusion, equivocates him in a sleep, and giving him the lie, leaves him. (2.3.32-36).

Victims of equivocation, Macbeth and Lady Macbeth gain temporary strength from their concentrated singleness of vision and purpose but eventually must confront the complexities that they tried futilely to evade. Because they cannot will out of existence their own consciences and because they cannot destroy all life's good and grace by brute force, the "judgment here" that Macbeth foresaw and tried to forget inevitably overtakes them.

Lady Macbeth, the first to deny her own nature by acting against her conscience, is also the first to feel the full horror of her accusing conscience. She is no more morally blind than Macbeth. The extreme violence of language with which she commits herself to her goal implies that she understands how radically she is proposing to alter her nature. Indeed, the fact that she associates with her very womanhood the pity and remorse that she wishes to extirpate indicates how natural these feelings are to her. But she dismisses these "compunctious visitings of nature" as weaknesses more easily than Macbeth does. After committing herself to evil, she consistently voices the most simple-minded kind of common sense, advising Macbeth to fight the scorpions of the mind by avoiding solitary thought, keeping a firm grasp on material reality, and getting a good night's sleep. She knows that what she has done is repugnant to her physical, emotional, and moral nature, but she never fully understands that what is done is not done—that she cannot escape the consequences of this self-violation. As Coleridge saw, her attempt to *"bully* [her] conscience" into silence fails.[54] In her last scene, the paradoxes of her nature assert themselves horribly in a sleep that is not sleep, in eyes that look but do not see. She knows that she is in a hell of her own making but is still pathetically trying to remove moral guilt by physical means.

The tragic irony of Macbeth's end is that his suffering is a measure of his success in diminishing his own nature. After his last visit to the witches, he perceives only a one-dimensional material world without resonance or ambiguity. He conquers doubts and fears with courage derived from his conviction of invulnerability in a world where trees cannot move and all men

[54] Raysor, ed., *Coleridge's Shakespearean Criticism,* II, 270-271. Coleridge's insistence that Lady Macbeth is a woman with a conscience seems to me entirely accurate and a salutary corrective to the still-frequent conception of the character as a sexless monster. I do not agree with his further remark that she has a "visionary and day-dreaming turn of mind."

are born of women. Relying on the spirits' equivocal pronouncements about the future, Macbeth no longer struggles to interpret ambiguous experience, to reconcile conflicting values, or to make difficult decisions. When Malcolm's stratagem and the circumstances of Macduff's birth demonstrate that trees move and men are born in more ways than one, Macbeth is forced to realize that the unnatural may be natural and that "th' equivocation of the fiend" (5.5.42) is a partial truth that constitutes a lie. Directly confronted with paradoxical complexity, he begins to doubt and fear again, but even then he perceives little freedom of choice:

> There is nor flying hence, nor tarrying here.
> (5.5.47)

> They have tied me to a stake; I cannot fly,
> But bear-like I must fight the course.
>
> (5.7.1-2)

His final decisions not to "play the Roman fool" and not to yield are less the deliberate choices of whether to seek life or death than they are unreasoning, automatic responses to seek oblivion in action.

The horror of Macbeth's suffering is that although he succeeds in reducing life to bare physical existence and himself to animal ferocity, he cannot quite escape his conscience. He knows what he has done; even worse, he knows what he has become, and in Menteth's words, "all that is within him does condemn / Itself for being there" (5.2.24-25). By act 5, Macbeth has become so hardened to sin that he almost seems free from the anguish of conscience, but Menteth's analysis of Macbeth's state of mind, just before he reappears on stage after an absence of several scenes, alerts us to his repressed self-condemnation.[55]

---

[55] Critics have disagreed about whether "conscience" is an appropriate word to describe the functioning of Macbeth's mind in act 5. William Rosen and Ruth Nevo, for example, argue that Macbeth deliberately destroys his conscience and is then unaffected by it, while Willard Farnham believes that Macbeth is tortured by conscience throughout the play. Paul identifies the stages of Macbeth's deterioration with the three kinds of conscience described in *Basilicon Doron*: the sound, the superstitious, and the "leaprose" or seared conscience. Paul Jorgensen acknowledges that Macbeth has many symptoms of a guilty conscience and may have a seared conscience but argues that he does not have an active conscience. A. L. and M. K. Kistner examine Macbeth's state of mind in the light of Alexander Hume's *Ane Treatise of Conscience* (1594). They find close parallels between Macbeth's conscience and Hume's

Consciousness of guilt does not always produce remorse. As we saw in *Richard III*, it may cause a guilty man to flee desperately into further evil. According to Perkins, a "stirring conscience" may lead to repentance, but a "seared conscience" has "no feeling or remorse" and leads to "an *exceeding greedines to* all manner of sin." [56] Even closer to Macbeth's condition is the guilty conscience described by William Fenner. According to Fenner, if they do not kill themselves, men "swallowed up in despair" either

> runne desperately into all abominable courses: Their consciences telling them there is nothing to be expected but damnation, they give themselves desperately to commit sinne with greedinesse . . . or else they grow senseless of it. They see they are wrong, but they are not sensible of it. . . . A kind of sorrow they have, but they cannot mourn; a kind of sad dolour, but they cannot weep.[57]

In acts 3 and 4, Macbeth, expecting damnation, sins greedily. By act 5, he exemplifies Fenner's category of men who know they are wrong but cannot feel their guilt or respond emotionally to the sorrow of their lives.[58] In putting himself beyond doubt and fear, Macbeth also puts himself beyond hope. He bitterly asks the physician to "minister to a mind diseas'd" (5.3.40), but he knows there is no physical cure for the sickness of his wife, his country, or his own heart. He knows he has cut himself off from the "honor, love, obedience, troops of friends" (5.3.25) that might have been the harvest of time. He has "supp'd full with horrors" (5.5.13) and can no longer react. Having refused to struggle with the bewildering mixture of fair and foul in himself and his world, he comes to see his life as simply foul—"full of sound and fury, / Signifying nothing" (5.5.27-28).

---

description of the wounded conscience and suggest similarity between Macbeth in act 5 and the seared or cauterized conscience. William Rosen, *Shakespeare and the Craft of Tragedy* (Cambridge, Mass.: Harvard University Press, 1960), pp. 87-88; Nevo, *Tragic Form in Shakespeare,* p. 246; Farnham, *Shakespeare's Tragic Frontier,* pp. 107-127; Paul, *The Royal Play,* pp. 134-135; Jorgensen, *Our Naked Frailties,* pp. 181-184; Kistner, "*Macbeth*: A Treatise of Conscience," *Thoth* 13 (1973): 27-43.

[56] Perkins, I, 550.

[57] William Fenner, *The Soules Looking-glasse . . . with a Treatise of Conscience* (1640), p. 182.

[58] Compare Rosalie Colie's description of Macbeth's guilt "which he knows he has, but also knows he cannot feel." See Colie, *Paradoxia Epidemica,* p. 234.

In concluding his book on *Macbeth*, Paul Jorgensen warns:

> Anyone who today, in the middle of warring armies of critics, ventures upon a theological approach to Shakespeare must say of his venture, "I am afraid to think what I have done;/ Look on't again I dare not." [59]

If any theological approach is cause for fear, my admittedly moral concerns undoubtedly invite alarming attacks from warring critics on many sides. My defense must be that I have found the casuists helpful in clarifying Shakespeare's portrayal of tragic choice and hope that others will too. In using the casuistical paradigm to discuss *Richard III, Julius Caesar, Hamlet,* and *Macbeth,* I do not mean to suggest that moral approval or disapproval of the characters is an adequate response. None of the heroes is merely despicable and none is entirely innocent. But they all suffer and die as a result of their own choices of action, and focusing on their moral reasoning illuminates the causes and implications of those choices. Approaching the plays with knowledge of the casuistical discussions of conscience reveals with new fullness and precision not only the pervasiveness of Shakespeare's interest in conscience but also the range and subtle variety of his presentation of the problems of conscience.

A much more comprehensive study than this would be necessary for any generalizations about Shakespeare's moral vision, but in these four plays at least, Shakespeare dramatizes moral decision-making as the action of conscience or moral understanding and emphasizes the difficulty of applying moral absolutes to the complex circumstances of actual human predicaments. The particular moral cases of his fiction are not, of course, reproduced in prose casuistry, but the understanding of moral judgment implicit in the plays is strikingly similar to that of the casuists. The assumptions shared with the casuists do not limit the plays to a bland orthodoxy or a naive piety. Instead, the emphasis on the supremacy of the individual conscience, the uniqueness of particular circumstances, and the need for reason in resolving moral doubt provides a basis for searching portrayals of how men confront tragic dilemmas. The conception of conscience does not vary significantly in these four plays, but the chronological sequence from *Richard III,* through *Julius Caesar* and *Hamlet,* to *Macbeth*

[59] Jorgensen, *Our Naked Frailties,* p. 218.

shows increasing emphasis on the ambiguity of circumstances, the difficulty of choice, and the inadequacy of simple good intentions. This growing attention to doubt and confusion correlates with a movement of dramatic focus into the minds of the characters. In *Richard III*, we observe the play of external events around the pivot of human conscience; in *Julius Caesar* and *Hamlet*, we watch men consciously struggling to make decisions; in *Macbeth*, we see people thinking and choosing to act and we also observe how they choose to think.

The plays are informed by, but not confined within, the casuistical paradigm, so that the same assumptions about the moral decision-making process yield strikingly different dramatic forms. While *Richard III* demonstrates the existence of moral judgment in even the most selfishly amoral society, *Julius Caesar* and *Hamlet* dramatize the difficulty of moral choice for even the most noble people. Hamlet and Brutus try to act virtuously but fail not only to achieve the results they intend but also to live up to their own moral standards. Both risk becoming like the men they seek to destroy: after Caesar's death, Brutus is unwilling to tolerate dissent and insists on an almost superhuman image of his virtue; like Claudius, Hamlet disguises murderous thoughts under a deceptive appearance, and, like Claudius, he kills. Yet the differences are crucial. While Brutus becomes increasingly self-righteous and rigid, Hamlet grows in humility and flexibility. Brutus chooses his role as noble patriot in the drama of Roman history, and, like an actor who always plays an idealized image of himself, never consciously deviates from his interpretation. The discovery that other people do not accept the form he has tried to impose on life and that they interpret the "lofty scene" differently brings him disillusionment and confusion. Where Brutus sees certainty, Hamlet sees perplexing moral problems that he examines from several perspectives. He plays such varied roles as rejected lover, madman, mourner, penitent, and revenger, and he produces a scene that is not intended to impose his interpretation of experience on others but to discover truth. The discovery that he shares the ignorance and guilt of the human lot frees him to resolve his doubts—and so to act and to die in "perfect conscience."

Richard III and *Macbeth* both deal with guilty consciences, but, while *Richard III* shows how commonplace it is—how easy to ignore the judgment of conscience—*Macbeth* makes us understand the excruciating pain of such denial of one's own judgment. The essentially optimistic effect of *Richard III* in large measure results from the repeated pattern of willful self-deception and subsequent moral recognition: despite the universal denial of conscience, no one can avoid knowledge of good and evil. By looking at similar moral and psychological material from another perspective, *Macbeth* creates a much more disturbing impact: despite our capacity for understanding moral complexity, people destroy themselves by seeking a simpler commitment to power.

Shakespeare's tragedies afford no pat solutions for the moral questions they raise. They suggest no guarantee of success or promise of heavenly reward for those who struggle diligently to join knowledge of fact with knowledge of value and to act in accordance with their own judgment. But the enactments of tragic self-discovery do suggest that any attempt to evade or simplify the operation of conscience is a violation of the self and that heroic virtue is the manifestation of complex knowledge in action.

Chapter IV

JOHN DONNE AS CASUIST

John Donne's interest in casuistry is well documented. His prose is sprinkled with references to such contemporary casuists as Juan Azor, Ludovico Carbo, and Robert Sayr, and, according to Izaak Walton, he answered Thomas Morton's urging that he take holy orders with an appeal to the judgment of "the best of *Casuists*":

> . . . that *Gods Glory should be the first end, and a maintenance the second motive to embrace that calling;* and though each man may propose to himself both together; yet the first may not be put last without a violation of Conscience, which he that searches the heart will judge. And truly my present condition is such, that if I ask my own Conscience, whether it be reconcileable to that rule, it is at this time so perplexed about it, that I can neither give my self nor you an answer. You know, Sir, who sayes, *Happy is that man whose Conscience doth not accuse him for that thing which he does.*[1]

In addition to studying the body of Roman Catholic casuistry and meeting personal crisis with casuistry, Donne wrote a collection of cases. Walton testifies that Donne was in the habit of keeping his own solutions "of divers Letters and cases of Conscience that had concerned his friends," and Donne twice refers to a book of cases of conscience.[2] Although this putative volume of cases has been lost, two surviving works, *Biathanatos* and

[1] Izaak Walton, "The Life of Dr. John Donne," in *Lives*, The World's Classics (London: Oxford University Press, 1927), pp. 34-35.

[2] Walton, *Lives*, p. 68; Edmund Gosse, *The Life and Letters of John Donne*, 2 vols. (London: William Heinemann, 1899), II, 151-152. Subsequent references to this work will be cited parenthetically in the text.

Pseudo-Martyr, are in the casuistical tradition. Moreover, since the habit of mind with which Donne devoured contemporary theology and resolved cases of conscience also finds expression in his poems, his relation to the casuistical tradition provides an illuminating context for his poetry.

Besides maintaining the casuists' assumption that the individual conscience is the center of man's moral life, Donne also shared their absorption in the doubts and problems resulting from the conjunction of moral absolutes with the immediate circumstances of personal experience. In terms resembling Sanderson's warning that *"a mathematical certitude,* which is manifest by Demonstration, and impossible to be false, is in vain to be expected in *morals,"* [3] Donne records his understanding of the problematical nature of experience: "Except demonstrations (and perchance there are very few of them) I find nothing without perplexities" (Gosse, II, 16). This vision of complexity, moreover, leads to positive emphasis on rigorous intellectual effort:

> To come to a doubt, and to a debatement in any religious duty, is the voyce of God in our conscience: Would you know the truth? Doubt, and then you will inquire: And *facile solutionem accipit anima, quae prius dubitavit,* sayes S. Chrysostome.[4]

The attraction of intellectual inquiry, with its emphases on logical procedures, fine distinctions, and abstruse knowledge, does not absorb Donne either in the intricacies of doctrinal disputes or in incommunicable mystical experience. Rather, as poet and preacher, he insists on applying the truths the mind perceives to the practical difficulties of daily life. His exhortation to express knowledge of God in holy living could serve well as a motto for casuistry: "let us make *Ex scientia conscientiam,* Enlarge science into conscience: for, *Conscientia est Syllogismus practicus,* Conscience is a Syllogisme that comes to a conclusion" (*Sermons,* IX, 248).

Throughout his life, Donne was intrigued with casuists' attempts to untangle knotty problems of conscience. He refers to

[3] Robert Sanderson, *Several Cases of Conscience Discussed in Ten Lectures* (London, 1660), p. 293.

[4] George R. Potter and Evelyn M. Simpson, eds. *The Sermons of John Donne,* 10 vols. Berkeley and Los Angeles: University of California Press, 1953-1962), V, 38. Subsequent quotations of the sermons are from this edition.

their classification of kinds of conscience in an early letter (Gosse, I, 170), and later, in one of his sermons, he explains the kinds of conscience and advises consulting a casuist in doubtful cases (*Sermons*, IV, 223). In his sermons, he generally avoids detailed discussion of controversial religious and political cases, but he acknowledges their existence and attempts to teach his parishioners the general principles by which they can be solved. For example, this advice:

> Howsoever the affections of men, or the vicissitudes and changes of affairs may vary, or apply those two great axiomes, and aphorisms of ancient Rome, *Salus populi suprema lex esto,* The good of the people is above all Law, and then, *Quod Principi placet, lex esto,* The Pleasure of the Prince is above all Law, howsoever I say, various occasions may vary their Laws, adhere we to that Rule of the Law, which the Apostle prescribes, that we always make *Finem praecepti charitatem, The end of the Commandement charity.*
>
> (*Sermons,* III, 185)

Donne devoted one sermon at least to a detailed discussion of what Geoffrey Bullough calls "one of those cases of conscience dear to Donne's heart." [5] In a sermon on Esther 4:16, Donne uses the procedures of English case divinity to analyze what Esther did "in a perplexed and scrupulous case" (*Sermons*, V, 217). He carefully sets up the problem, explaining the ethical questions that create doubt. When Esther learned that Haman had the king's permission to destroy the Jews, she went to the king, her husband, to plead that he save her people, in spite of the king's edict that no one enter his presence unsummoned on penalty of death. Donne emphasizes the difficulties that the decision to disobey the king presents:

> There is in every Humane Law, part of the Law of God, which is obedience to the Superior. That Man cannot binde the conscience, because he cannot judge the conscience, nor he cannot absolve the conscience, may be a good argument; but in Laws made by that power which is ordained by God,

[5] Geoffrey Bullough, "Donne the Man of Law," in *Just So Much Honor: Essays Commemorating the Four-Hundredeth Anniversary of the Birth of John Donne,* ed. Peter Amadeus Fiore (University Park: The Pennsylvania State University Press, 1972), p. 86.

man bindes not, but God himself: And then you must be subject, not because of wrath, but because of conscience. . . . In all true Laws God hath his interest; and the observing of them in that respect, as made by his authority, is an act of worship and obedience to him; and the transgressing of them, with that relation, that is, a resisting or undervaluing of that authority, is certainly sinne. How then was *Esthers* act exempt from this? for she went directly against a direct Law, *That none should come to the King uncalled.*

(*Sermons,* V, 225)

In addition, by willingly risking death, Esther neglected the natural law of self-preservation.

Donne resolves these doubts and defends the rightness of Esther's decision on the basis of the casuistical concepts of the hierarchical nature of law, the intention of the law, and the significance of particular circumstances. "Whensoever divers Laws concur and meet together," he explains,

that Law which comes from the superior Magistrate, and is in the nature of the thing commanded, highest too, that Law must prevail. If two Laws lie upon me, and it be impossible to obey both, I must obey that which comes immediately from the greatest power, and imposes the greatest duty.   (*Sermons,* V, 225-226)

Esther was bound by the king's law and also by "the fix'd and permanent Law, of promoting Gods glory." She would not have been justified in breaking a positive law on pretense of fulfilling her duty to God, Donne cautions, unless her conscience was completely satisfied that she was not violating the intention of the law. She considered carefully the purpose of the law, the exceptions mentioned in the body of the law, the imminence of the danger, and her relationship to the king. On the basis of these circumstances, she concluded that the law "intended onely for the Kings ease, or his state, reached not to her person, who was his wife, nor to her case, which was the destruction of all that professed her Religion" (*Sermons,* V, 227). Only then did she

come to that, which onely can excuse and justifie the breaking of any Law, that is, a probable, if not a certain assurance, contracted *Bona fide,* in rectified conscience, That if this present case, which makes us break this Law, had been known and considered when the Law was made, he that made the Law would have made provision for this case.

(Sermons, V, 226)

Similarly, Donne justifies Esther's exposing herself to danger on the grounds of a higher duty and of attendant circumstances. She "was under two Laws, of which it was necessary to obey that which concerned the glory of God" (*Sermons*, V, 227). She did not risk her life in a spirit of pride and reckless abandon but with humility and hope, prepared with prayer and fasting.

Donne's sermon on Esther 4:16, then, uses the tools of casuistry to provide a model of "what every Christian Soul ought to do, when it is surprised and overtaken with any such scruples or difficulties to the Conscience" (*Sermons*, V, 217). This casuistical purpose and method, however, is unique among Donne's sermons. Although one could gather enough relevant passages from the sermons to construct a fairly comprehensive description of his theory of casuistry, the sermons, for all their learning and wit, are primarily directed to move the apostate will, not to enlighten the conscience. Donne's interest in the problems and methods of casuistry is more central to *Biathanatos* and *Pseudo-Martyr*, which are both extended discussions of traditional cases of conscience.

DONNE'S PROSE CASUISTRY: *Biathanatos* AND *Pseudo-Martyr*

Biathanatos, Donne's demonstration that "Self-homicide is not so naturally Sin, that it may never be otherwise," clearly belongs to the body of casuistical literature, but just how it fits into that tradition is puzzling. Scholars have treated it variously as a bold challenge to traditional Christian thought, as a conventional case of conscience, and as a parody of casuistical reasoning and cases of conscience.[6]

---

[6] George Williamson interpreted *Biathanatos* as an intermediate step in Donne's scepticism of human reason "between his earlier scepticism and naturalism and his later scepticism and mysticism" ("The Libertine Donne," *Philological Quarterly* 13 [1934]: 276-291). But Charles Coffin found *Biathanatos* animated by a modern spirit in its argument for the reinterpretation of traditional ideas by individual reason (*John Donne and the New Philosophy* [New York: The Humanities Press, 1958], pp. 253-259). Like Coffin, Robert Ornstein sees it as a defense of human reason, but he traces Donne's ideas to "traditional and quite respectable ethical theories" ("Donne, Montaigne, and

The question of whether causing one's own death is justified in any circumstances is a standard problem in casuistry, and Donne handles the problem with traditional casuistical methods, examining the doubtful action in relation to natural law, positive law, and divine law. He grants that natural law, man's knowledge as a rational being that he should avoid evil and seek good, ordinarily forbids suicide. But, he argues, since any law binds according to its intention, the "reason upon which it was founded," and binds only "so long as the reason lives," the natural law of self-preservation ceases to bind when man intends a greater good through his death.[7]

His demonstration that human law does not make self-homicide wrong in all circumstances is similar. Acknowledging that civil legislation prohibits suicide, he argues that any human law may be broken when it conflicts with a higher law. Thus, although a man cannot lawfully kill himself to secure any physical or spiritual good for himself (for example, release from suffering or avoidance of temptation), he may take his own life when he intends "only or primarily the glory of God" (p. 99).

The strongest prohibition against self-homicide is divine law as set forth in scripture: Thou shalt not kill. Again, Donne argues that the general law does not apply in all circumstances and that the higher must take precedence over the lesser good. For example,

> If perchance a publique exemplary person, which had a just assurance that his example would governe the people, should be forced by a Tyrant, to doe an act of Idolatry, (although by circumstances he might satisfie his owne conscience, that he sinned not in doing it,) and so scandalize and endanger

---

Natural Law," *Journal of English and Germanic Philology* 55 [1956]: 213-229). Joan Webber describes it as "a somewhat half-hearted, somewhat unsuccessful satire on scholastic and casuistical reasoning," while Helen Gardner and Timothy Healy call it "a long and careful piece of casuistry" (Webber, *Contrary Music* [Madison: University of Wisconsin Press, 1963], p. 5; Gardner and Healy, *John Donne: Selected Prose* [Oxford: Clarendon Press, 1967], p. 25). The most adequate description is Rosalie Colie's: "*Biathanatos* is a book of casuistry in both neutral and pejorative senses" (*Paradoxia Epidemica: The Renaissance Tradition of Paradox* [Princeton: Princeton University Press, 1966], p. 499).

[7] *Biathanatos* (New York: The Facsimile Text Society, 1930), pp. 47, 49. Subsequent quotations are from this edition and will be cited by page number in the text.

them, if the matter were so carried and disguised, that by no
way he could let them know, that he did it by constraint,
but [not?] voluntarily, I say, perchance he were better kill
himselfe.   (P. 166)

While this brief summary indicates Donne's debt to traditional
casuistry, it overstates the argument for *Biathanatos* as an orthodox case of conscience. Donne explicitly criticizes the casuistical
approach. He condemns the tortuous legalism of casuists "applying rules of Divinitie to particular cases: by which they have
made all our actions perplex'd and litigious" (p. 33). In the
Preface, he acknowledges that he has encumbered his prose with
lengthy discussions of others' opinions and defends this "multiplicity of not necessary citations" as standard practice: "I did it
the rather because scholastique and artificiall men use this way
of instructing; and I made account that I was to deale with such"
(p. 23). Indeed, Donne adopts the external characteristics of these
"scholastique and artificiall men" with such zeal and with so
little apparent connection with his actual reasoning process that
he seems to be mocking the intricate legalism of the casuists.[8]
His prose is divided into numbered sections, his sentences are
often compressed syllogisms, and logical connectives such as
"therefore," "so," "for," and "since" are frequent. But the divisions and subdivisions in the text do not always correlate with
the development of the argument, the logical steps do not appear
in orderly sequence, and the argument itself seems in danger of
collapsing under the weight of the lengthy citations of authorities
and of the numerous and frequently bizarre examples. For example, since Donne argues that self-preservation, "the foundation
of generall naturall Law" (p. 49), is simply man's innate preference for good and may admit of desiring death in certain circumstances, his long proof that suicide is common and therefore
natural seems irrelevant, and such examples as *"Hippionas* the
Poet rimed *Bubalus* the Painter to death with his Iambiques"
(p. 53) appear as tongue-in-cheek spoofs of the legalistic marshal-
ing of evidence.

  The simultaneous use and mockery of the tools of casuistry
reflect Donne's ambivalence toward contemporary Roman Catholic casuistry. Although he frequently cites casuists approvingly,

[8] Webber, *Contrary Music*, pp. 5-12.

Donne explicitly condemns the casuistical doctrine of probabilism as encouraging intellectual apathy and hypocrisy:

> . . . so many doctrines have grown to be the ordinary diet
> and food of our spirits, and have place in the pap of cate-
> chisms, which were admitted but as physic in that present
> distemper, or accepted in a lazy weariness, when men so they
> might have something to rely upon, and to excuse themselves
> from more painful inquisition, never examined what that
> was. To which indisposition of ours the casuists are so indul-
> gent, as that they allow a conscience to adhere to any prob-
> able opinion against a more probable, and do never bind
> him to seek out which is more probable, but give him leave
> to dissemble it and to depart from it, if by mischance he
> come to know it.   (Gosse, I, 174)

A. E. Malloch has shown that Donne's fundamental objection
was to the probabilists' externalization of moral choice.[9] While
Donne believed that right action is necessarily based on personal
assent, probabilism rests on the assumption that moral judgment
can be made with reference to an external body of opinion and
need not issue from personal conviction. Counter-Reformation
casuistry, which separated lawful action from individual judgment, was quantitative and external, as Malloch explains:

> It claims in its treaties to be comprehensive, but it seeks
> comprehensiveness through a multiplying of the individual
> cases of conscience discussed. It copes with the variety and
> complexity of human existence not by speaking to the indi-
> vidual person and directing him how to proceed to moral
> judgment in whatever situation engages him, but by attempt-
> ing to register and analyze as many "cases" (i.e., combination
> of circumstances) as possible. In this tendency we can again
> see moral action drawn out from the world of the self and
> reconstituted in a non-personal world where cases and their
> attendant probable opinions are multiplied almost indefi-
> nitely.[10]

Donne, Malloch concludes, "insists that moral action must pro-

[9] Malloch's important article, "John Donne and the Casuists," *Studies in English Literature* 2 (1962): 57-76, first called general attention to the relevance of casuistry to Donne studies.
[10] Ibid., p. 70.

ceed from an assent of the self and yet he toys constantly with a literature of casuistry which sets moral action within a legal arena and allows little room for the self." [11]

In *Biathanatos,* Donne's distrust of the externality of Roman Catholic casuistry takes two forms. He warns his readers directly against relying on authorities: "trust neither me, nor the adverse part, but the Reasons" (p. 19). He argues that one discovers what he should do in any particular situation through reason, not through the mechanical application of rules, and he insists on the inviolability of the individual conscience. Indirectly, he satirizes the legalism of the casuists by parodying their elaborate schemes for categorizing particular actions and their multiple citations of authorities and precedents. This combination of serious moral analysis with satire of an inadequate casuistical method is not wholly successful, in spite of Donne's acute grasp of casuistical procedures and his considerable satiric skill, because his central argument relies too heavily on the methods he condemns.

In *Biathanatos,* Donne's failure to distinguish his own casuistical method from the object of his satire is not the inevitable result of his ambivalence toward Roman Catholic casuistry. As Barbara Lewalski has demonstrated, the traditions of English Protestantism are generally more helpful in elucidating Donne than continental Roman Catholic thought,[12] and English Protestant casuistry departs from that of the Counter-Reformation along lines remarkably similar to those that Donne suggests. As we have seen, Jeremy Taylor also condemns Roman Catholic casuistry for its hair-splitting intellectuality and for its too accommodating morality. Like Donne, Taylor traces these weaknesses to probabilism, "the foundation on which their doctors of conscience rely," [13] and insists that one must accept and act on the most probable conclusion.

Although the published casuistry that Donne knew was Roman Catholic, Malloch is wrong, I believe, in suggesting that Protestant casuistry cannot illuminate Donne's casuistry because it "avoided the legal complexity and the precision which seem for

[11] Ibid., p. 75.

[12] Barbara Kiefer Lewalski, *Protestant Poetics and the Seventeenth-Century Religious Lyric* (Princeton: Princeton University Press, 1979), Chapter 8.

[13] Jeremy Taylor, *Ductor Dubitantium: or the Rule of Conscience,* in *The Whole Works of the Right Rev. Jeremy Taylor,* ed. Reginald Heber, 15 vols. (London, 1828), X, 213-214.

Donne to have been the fascinations of casuistry." [14] Legal complexity and precision are essential to any casuistry, as Sanderson's cases and Taylor's *Ductor Dubitantium,* as well as Juan Azor's *Institutiones morales* will attest. Protestant casuists, who rejected probabilism for probabiliorism and insisted on the full assent of the self in right action, tried to show men how to proceed in their own moral dilemmas by stressing their reasoning process instead of by citing authorities. They presented individual cases not in an attempt to be comprehensive but in order to provide models of the process by which moral law can be applied to individual cases rooted in the unique circumstances of one particular moment in history. This emphasis does not relieve men of the intellectual effort to make fine distinctions among varying combinations of circumstances and to understand the complexities of moral law.

Donne's sermon on Esther's decision enunciates casuistical principles and resolves a case of conscience with logical clarity in a way similar to other Protestant casuists. But in *Biathanatos,* Donne does not construct a model case, nor does he systematically clarify the principles by which such a case can be solved. He relies instead on the methods of the despised probabilists, building his argument in terms of the body of opinion on the subject. The satiric impulse is inadequately integrated with the central intention of the work not because of Donne's ambivalence about the casuistical use of right reason in resolving moral dilemmas but because he was unable to resolve his ambivalence about the lawfulness of suicide.

What he really demonstrates with logical consistency is the orthodox casuistical judgment that, in certain circumstances—those of Christian martyrs, for example—causing one's own death is lawful and virtuous. Joseph Hall mentions such cases of legitimate self-homicide as dying to protect the sovereign's life, relinquishing the only plank to another survivor of a shipwreck, and those "infinite examples of deadly sufferings for good causes, willingly embraced for conscience' sake." [15] The concrete cases Donne fully approves are similar. He cites the death of Samson:

[14] Malloch, "John Donne and the Casuists," p. 59, n. 4.

[15] Joseph Hall, *Resolutions and Decisions of Divers Practical Cases of Conscience in Continual Use Amongst Men* (1648), in *The Works of . . . Joseph Hall,* 10 vols. (1863; reprint ed., New York: AMS Press, 1969), VII, 323. Unlike Donne, however, Hall condones only "indirect," not "direct," suicide.

A man so exemplar, that not onely the times before him had him in Prophecy, (for of him it is said,) [*Dan shall judge his people,*] and the times after him more consummately in Christ, of whom he was a Figure, but even in his own time, other nations may seeme to have had some Type, or Copy of him, in *Hercules*.

And he adds,

That hee intended not his owne death principally, but accidentally . . . can remove no man from our side; for wee say the same, that this may be done onely, when the honour of God may bee promoved [sic] by that way, and no other.

(Pp. 199-200)

But throughout *Biathanatos* there is the constant implication that Donne is justifying other kinds of suicide as well, proving that there is nothing sinful in escaping the evils of this world by fleeing to God with dispatch. The autobiographical remarks in the Preface suggest that his original interest in the problem of self-homicide was of this sort: "whensoever any affliction assailes me, mee thinks I have the keyes of my prison in mine owne hand, and no remedy presents it selfe so soone to my heart, as mine own sword" (p. 18). By calling *Biathanatos* a paradox, Donne suggests that it challenges conventional opinion, and modern readers usually interpret it as a defense against the orthodox con-demnation of suicide.[16]

The overall impression is that while Donne is strongly com-pelled by the idea that man has within his power the means to escape the pain of mortal existence and to find eternal life he is simultaneously committed to the orthodox position that killing oneself to escape the burdens of life is to despair of God and therefore is sinful. Because this contradiction remains unresolved, Donne avoids treating the personal problem directly, but it is always there as a disrupting pressure on the logical consistency of the argument. Thus, *Biathanatos* lacks the detailed attention to particular circumstances and rigorous distinctions evident in Donne's treatment of Esther's case of conscience. In the latter,

16 Rosalie Colie argues that although Donne protects himself by relying on the conventional view that paradoxes are intended to provoke refutation, *Biathanatos* paradoxically denies this convention of paradox by undercutting instead of inviting refutation. Colie, *Paradoxia Epidemica*, pp. 500-501.

he carefully explains that the principle by which honor to God
takes precedence over human law does not justify Puritan defiance of laws governing religious observances in England because
the circumstances differ. In *Biathanatos,* he declines to specify
the kinds of circumstances and conditions that make self-homicide
lawful:

> I abstained purposely from extending this discourse to par-
> ticular rules, or instances, both because I dare not professe
> my self a Maister in so curious a science, and because the
> limits are obscure, and steepy, and slippery, and narrow,
> and every errour deadly, except where a competent dilligence
> being fore-used, a mistaking in our conscience may provide
> an excuse. (P. 216)

For all its intricacy, *Biathanatos* proceeds not by making, but
by blurring, distinctions. Donne, for example, offers elaborate
proof that we cannot judge whether suicide is sinful because we
cannot know other men's motives or whether or not they are
penitent. He argues for the ultimate identity of natural, positive,
and divine law. Most important, he obliterates the differences between wishes, passive deeds, and direct action, so that the com-
monness of the desire for death becomes proof of the compati-
bility of suicide with natural law and so that the willingness to
risk death becomes equivalent to driving a knife through one's
heart. Donne concludes that we should be willing to think about
so complex a topic with open minds and that we should be char-
itable to both the suicide and to those who write books defending
the suicidal act. But the constant blurring of distinctions and the
repeated attacks on the certainty of judgment have the further
effect of suggesting the impossibility of clear perception or sure
judgment by the individual conscience. Donne seems to be trying
to establish some degree of probability for the lawfulness of suicide within the body of theological opinion rather than striving
to provide the means for full assent by the individual conscience.
In this context, his attack on the externality of probabilistic casuistry weakens his argument; satire becomes self-parody, and the
case of conscience becomes paradox.[17]

Pseudo-Martyr, probably written a year or so after *Biathanatos,*
also deals with a recurrent casuistical problem. Like Sanderson's

[17] Compare Colie, *Paradoxia Epidemica,* pp. 497-507, where she argues that
the self-contradictions are intentional and successfully controlled.

"Case of the Engagement," it attempts to resolve the problems of conscience created by a loyalty oath. After the discovery of the Gunpowder Plot, James I imposed an Oath of Allegiance on all English Catholics in order to make "a trew distinction betweene Papists of quiet disposition, and in all other things good subjects, and such other Papists as in their heartes maintained the like violent bloody *Maximes,* that the Powder-Traitours did." [18] Initially many Catholics, including the archpriest George Blackwell, complied, but the Pope subsequently issued two breves condemning the oath. The Pope's prohibition not only intensified the controversy between his Jesuit supporters and several Catholic writers opposed to Papal claims of temporal jurisdiction but it also created a moral dilemma for many English Catholics.[19] In *Pseudo-Martyr,* Donne argues that English Catholics should take the Oath of Allegiance to James I in spite of the Pope's prohibition and that those who refuse the oath suffer not as Christian martyrs but as disloyal subjects.

Pseudo-Martyr, then, is a political discussion carried on, like most seventeenth-century political controversy, in terms of conscience. Essentially Donne defends James's position that it is improper for the Pope "to meddle betweene me and my Subjects, especially in matters that meerely and onely concerne civill obedience," [20] but Donne's casuistical habit of mind shapes his defense of the King's rights in terms of the conscience of his Catholic subjects. He violently attacks the leaders of the opposition to the oath, the Jesuits, as:

> nourishing jelowsies in Princes, and contempt in Subjects, dissention in families, wrangling in Schooles, and mutinies in Armies; ruines of Noble houses, corruption of blood, confiscation of States, torturing of bodies, and anxious entangling and perplexing of consciences.[21]

But he stresses his respect for the Roman Church, acknowledging it as for long "the head, that is, the *Principall* and *most eminent,*

---

[18] Charles H. McIlwain, ed., *The Political Works of James I* (Cambridge, Mass.: Harvard University Press, 1918), p. 113.

[19] On this controversy, see R. C. Bald, *John Donne: A Life* (New York: Clarendon Press, 1970), pp. 212-227.

[20] McIlwain, *Political Works,* p. 72.

[21] *Pseudo-Martyr* (London, 1610), pp. 127-128. Subsequent quotations are from this edition and will be cited by page number in the text.

examplar member" (p. 135) of the universal Christian Church. He bases his argument against the temporal jurisdiction of the Pope, not on English law, but on a detailed analysis of canon law and of the authority of Papal breves, and he analyzes the wording of the oath to show that it in no way *"violates the Popes spirituall Jurisdiction"* (p. 347).

Donne's attitude toward casuistry is more straightforward in *Pseudo-Martyr* than it is in *Biathanatos*. Again, he both attacks and employs the methods of casuistry, but here he carefully distinguishes his own conception of the conscience from that of his adversaries. According to Donne, Jesuit casuistry incites men to suffer and die in a false martyrdom, but the roots of casuistry go deeper into Christian tradition than Jesuit sedition:

> For, their *Casuists,* which handle *Morall Divinitie,* and waigh and measure sinne (which for all that perplexitie and entangling, we may not condemne too hastily, since in purest Antiquitie there are lively impressions of such a custome in the Church, to examine with some curiositie the circumstances, by which sinnes were aggravated or diminished) . . . have filled their bookes with such questions as these, *How Princes have their jurisdiction, How they may become Tyrants, What is lawfull to a private man in such a case,* and of like seditious nature. (P. 144)

These casuists, he charges, instead of guiding and forming independent consciences, make endless rules that allow them to decide particular cases however they want. Thus they so obscure issues that in a particular case it is impossible to

> unentangle our consciences by any of those Rules, which their *Casuists* use to give, who to st[r]engthen the possession of the *Romane* Church, have bestowed more paines, to teach how strongly a conscience is bound to doe according to a *Scruple,* or a *Doubt,* or an *Opinion,* or an *Errour,* which it hath conceived, then how it might depose that *Scruple,* or cleare that *Doubt,* or better that *Opinion,* or rectifie that *Errour.* (Pp. 226-227)

He then sets out to show that, even according to their own rules of casuistry, taking the oath is lawful. The doctrine of probabilism, he argues, justifies taking the oath in spite of doubts or scruples:

For when it comes to that, we shall finde it to be the *common* opinion of *Casuists,* which the same *Summist* [Ludovico Carbo] delivers, *That there is no matter so waighty, wherein it is not lawfull for me, to follow an opinion that is probable, though I leave the opinion which is more probable; yea though it concerne the right of another person:* as in our case of obedience to the *King* or the *Pope.* And then, wheresoever I may lawfully follow an opinion to mine advantage, if I will leave that opinion with danger of my life or notorious losse, I am guilty of all the damage I suffer. For these circumstances make that Necessary to me then, which was *indifferent* before: the reasons upon which *Carbo* builds this Doctrine of following a *probable* opinion, and leaving a more *probable,* which are, *That no man is bound, Ad melius & perfectius, by necessity, but as by Counsell:* And that this Doctrine hath this commoditie, *that it delivers godly men, from the care and solicitude, of searching out, which is the more probable opinion,* shew evidently, that these Rules give no infallible direction to the conscience, and yet in this matter of Obedience, considering the first native certaintie of subjection to the King, and then the damages by the refusall to sweare it, they encline much more to strengthen that civill obedience, then that other obedience which is plainly enough claimed, by this forbidding of the Oath. (Pp. 230-231)

While he is willing to construct this argument in the probabilists' terms, he is eager to distance himself from this kind of reasoning, and continues:

So that in these perplexities, the *Casuists* are indeede, *Nubes Testium:* but not in that sense as the holy Ghost used the Metaphore. For they are such *clouds* of witnesses, as their testimonie obscures the whole matter. And they use to deliver no more, then may beget farther doubts, that so every man may from the *Oracle* of his *Confessors* resolution, receive such direction, as shall be fit at that time, when hee gives the aunswere.   (P. 231)

In opposition to the intricate legalism that relieves man of the responsibility of searching out the truth and reduces him to dependence on his confessor's instructions, Donne's definition of conscience stresses the inseparability of knowledge and conscience, personal judgment and lawful action.

> Since the *conscience* is by *Aquinas* his definition, *Ordo scientiae ad aliquid,* and *an Act by which wee apply our knowledge to some particular thing,* the *Conscience* ever presumes *Knowledge*: and we may not, (especially in so great dangers as these) doe any thing upon *Conscience,* if we doe it not upon *Knowledge.* For *it is not the Conscience itselfe that bindes us, but that law which the Conscience takes knowledge of, and presents to our understanding.* (P. 237)

His central argument is that men know on the basis of scripture and natural law that they owe obedience to their king, that searching examination of the oath and its political and religious context reveals nothing evil in the intention, matter, or consequences of the oath, and that therefore refusal to take the oath is sinful. Although Donne's demonstration that Roman Catholics might lawfully take the oath to a Protestant king is too complicated to treat adequately here, his primary strategy is to contrast the certain duty of civil obedience with the doubtful and debatable authority of Paul V's breves and of the Jesuit casuists' opinions. He consistently assumes that the *"Conscience,* which we must defend with our lives, must be grounded upon such things, as wee may, and doe not onely know, but know *how* we know them" and on this basis argues "That it is the *safest,* in both acceptations, both of *spirituall safety,* and *Temporall,* and in both *Tribunals,* as well of conscience, as of civill Justice, to take the Oath" (p. 246).

Pseudo-Martyr gives Donne's fullest exposition of his conception of casuistry and the most detailed application of these principles to a particular case. However, in spite of Donne's impressive analysis of the relevant ecclesiastical, political, and religious issues and of his sensitive understanding of the recusant conscience, *Pseudo-Martyr* is less engaging today than the casuistry of lesser writers. As a casuist, Donne is handicapped by his political position: he is not a priest advising his flock but rather an aspiring courtier supporting his king. He makes effective rhetorical use of the fact that he himself has gone through the process he advocates, surveying *"the whole body of Divinity, controverted betweene ours and the Romane Church"* (sig. B3) before accepting the established Church of England. Still, this dual Roman Catholic and Anglican perspective prevents *Pseudo-Martyr* from having the economy and force that Sanderson's case achieves through the unrelenting drive of a single, logical progression. Donne's own position is that taking the Oath of Allegiance is a moral duty, but he spends much of *Pseudo-Martyr* merely trying to convince Catholic readers that taking the oath is not sinful. Because he concentrates on the legal complexities of one particular issue, his casuistry lacks the scope and general applicability of comprehensive discussions of principles like Taylor's and Baxter's. At the same time, by addressing himself variously to a heterogeneous audience whose assumptions differ from his own, he loses the implicit dramatic tension of cases of conscience addressing an individual problem and presenting a model of the decision-making process.

The Satirist's Cases of Conscience

Donne, then, drew freely on the ideas and techniques of casuistry in his prose, but ironically his casuistry lacks the concrete economy and dramatic immediacy achieved by casuists who were not also poets. More intriguing, though less easily definable, is the connection between casuistry and Donne's poetry. In his poetry, Donne was more successful at combining his interest in the laws governing human action with the particular circumstances of individual cases. We can see the casuist transformed into the poet with special clarity in his verse satires. In a valuable article exploring "Donne's conviction that the energies of the mind precede and largely determine the good man's virtuous choices," Sister M. Geraldine perceptively suggests that Donne's lost cases of conscience would have provided us with a commentary on the satires.[22] As she suggests, the satires are explicitly concerned with the moral value of reason, and their approach to sin and folly grows out of the traditions of case divinity as well as those of verse satire.

The relation between the satiric point of view and its objects is a key question about any literary satire, and the speaking voice has been the focal point of much of the relatively little critical attention Donne's satires have received. Although his critics have

[22] Sister M. Geraldine, "John Donne and the Mindes Indeavours," *Studies in English Literature* 5 (1965): 115, 116. See also her "Donne's *Notitia*: The Evidence of the Satires," *University of Toronto Quarterly* 36 (1966): 24-36, which traces Donne's characteristic focus on the activity of the mind in the satires and in *Ignatius His Conclave*.

by no means agreed in their descriptions of Donne's satiric persona, their responses indicate that Donne's classical models do not provide a sufficient guide for the critic attempting to account for the complexity of tones and attitudes the poems present. Donne's is not wholly the urbane, ironically detached, witty Horatian voice nor the direct, outraged, savage Juvenalian voice characteristic of most formal verse satire in English. N.J.C. Andreasen sees the speaker of the satires as an idealist defending spiritual values against the creeping materialism of the sixteenth century, and to Wesley Milgate, he is "Moral Man who can rise at times to the heroic and dare greatly," escaping the "rather repellent superciliousness" implicit in this "necessary pose of moral supeɩiority" only by his humor. To others he is less completely detached from the vice and folly he attacks. According to Earl Miner, he joins the bitterness, indignation, and detachment of the classical satirists with a distinctively private voice, angry with tne establishment and "angry with himself for his partial involvement with it." John Shawcross reads "Satyre I" as a dialogue of body and soul in which the speaker struggles with his own gross impulses, and Wilbur Sanders finds the strength of the satires in the speaker's participation in the preposterous world he observes and in Donne's ability to direct his attack at the satirist as well as at the obvious satiric butts. Other critics are struck by the speaker's capacity for self-judgment. A. F. Bellette argues that the originality of the satires lies in the satirist's abandonment of the traditional pose of moral superiority and his awareness of his own involvement in the corrupt and corrupting world. While Bellette finds this self-awareness confined to satires one, three, and four, other recent studies focus on the speaker's developing awareness through the five poems. John Lauritsen argues that the satires are unified by the speaker's progression from a stance of moral superiority to the discovery of his own involvement in the fallen world. Richard Newton, Emory Elliot, and M. Thomas Hester trace his struggle to understand the moral implications of his role as Christian satirist, but while Newton and Hester see him finally achieving a balanced satiric vision, Elliot argues that in the fifth satire he abandons the role of satirist.[23]

[23] N.J.C. Andreasen, "Theme and Structure in Donne's *Satyres*," *Studies in English Literature* 3 (1963): 60; W. Milgate, ed., *John Donne: The Satires, Epigrams and Verse Letters* (Oxford: Clarendon Press, 1967), pp. xxi-xxii; Earl Miner, *The Metaphysical Mode from Donne to Cowley* (Princeton:

The differences in these descriptions are partly due to the wit and verve of Donne's agile shifts in tone and technique, but they also demonstrate our need for a fuller understanding of the speaker's relation to the sin and folly he sees and to the moral and intellectual standards by which he judges human conduct. If we see Donne's speaker in the context of the ideas and concerns of casuistry, we recognize that he is at once a man struggling with doubts about how he ought to live and a satirist trying to solve the problem of how best to use language to lead others to right action. This double concern with the satirist's own case of conscience and with the question of how to direct the consciences of others accounts for the voice of the satires and for their sometimes bewildering structure. It also helps to distinguish Donne's satires from other Elizabethan satires where the focus is more wholly on the objects of the satirist's scorn.

"Satyre I" presents the satirist's problem in its broadest terms: Should he become responsibly involved in human society, or should he detach himself from the corruptions of worldly affairs? [24] Since Donne is writing poetry rather than prose casuistry, he does not pose a formal case of conscience but creates a dramatic situation from which the moral problem gradually emerges. The speaker, who identifies himself as a student and poet, is interrupted by an invitation from a frivolous acquaintance. This intrusion by a "fondling motley humorist" (l. 1) distracts him from his volumes of theology, philosophy, statecraft, and poetry, and he must decide:

Princeton University Press, 1969), pp. 10-11; John Shawcross, "All Attest His Writs Canonical: The Texts, Meaning and Evaluation of Donne's Satires," in *Just So Much Honor*, ed. Fiore, pp. 253-254; Wilbur Sanders, *John Donne's Poetry* (Cambridge, Eng.: Cambridge University Press, 1971), pp. 33-36; A.F. Bellette, "The Originality of Donne's *Satires*," *University of Toronto Quarterly* 44 (1975): 130-140; John R. Lauritsen, "Donne's *Satyres*: The Drama of Self-Discovery," *Studies in English Literature* 16 (1976): 117-130; Richard C. Newton, "Donne the Satirist," *Texas Studies in Literature and Language* 16 (1974): 427-445; Emory Elliot, "The Narrative and Allusive Unity of Donne's *Satyres*," *Journal of English and Germanic Philology* 75 (1976): 105-116; M. Thomas Hester, " 'Zeal' as Satire: The Decorum of Donne's *Satyres*," *Genre* 10 (1977): 173-194.

[24] My discussion assumes the traditional ordering of the satires. For discussion of the evidence for this numbering of the satires, see Milgate's "Textual Introduction" in *The Satires, Epigrams and Verse Letters*, and Shawcross, "All Attest His Writs Canonical," pp. 245-247. Quotations from the satires are from Milgate's edition and will be given by line number in the text.

> Shall I leave all this constant company,
> And follow headlong, wild uncertaine thee?
> (Ll.11-12)

His irritable response is an indication of the significance he
sees in this apparently trivial decision. By remaining with his
books, he can pursue his vocation: "With God, and with the
Muses I conferre" (l. 48). By running headlong after his fickle,
unpredictable friend, who may well disappear at the first distraction, he abandons worthwhile activity, possibly for nothing. His
vocation demands and his temperament welcomes the contemplative life. The fashionable world has a kind of spurious glamour,
but the "course attire" (l. 47) of the scholar is closer to a life of
simple virtue. Nevertheless, the satirist cannot simply dismiss his
friend with a curt "Away" or "Leave mee" (ll. 1-2). He has responsibilities to the busy world of men outside the solitude of the
study.

Although he is less explicit about this horn of his dilemma, it
is implicit in everything he says. His wish to live and die in
studious isolation is ironically hyperbolic:

> let me lye
> In prison, and here be coffin'd, when I dye.
> (Ll. 3-4)

The images of confinement and death express his awareness of
how self-destructive total withdrawal from the human community
would be.[25] His brief characterizations of the authors he reads—
"grave Divines," "jolly [arrogant] Statesmen," "Giddie fantastique
Poëts" (ll. 5-10)—are not entirely admiring, for authors have
value through their relationship with reality outside their own
minds as "Gods conduits" or "Natures Secretary" (ll. 5-6), as
chroniclers of other men's deeds or teachers of the body politic.
When the satirist, then, decides to accompany his friend, despite

---

[25] In a sermon, Donne condemns withdrawal from social responsibility as
a kind of suicide: "Every man hath a *Politick life*, as well as a *natural life*;
and he may no more take himself away from the world, then he may make
himself away out of the world. For he that dies so, by withdrawing himself
from his calling, from the labours of mutual society in his life, that man *kills
himself*, and God calls him not" (*Sermons*, I, 209-210). Milgate quotes this
passage in connection with Donne's stress on active virtue in the verse letters
(*The Satires, Epigrams and Verse Letters*, p. xxxvii).

his announced preference for dedicated learning over ephemeral pleasure, he acts on his commitment to a life of active virtue.

He also shows his eagerness to guide others to virtue when he subordinates the question of what he himself should do to the opportunity to instruct and reform his companion. As he warns his friend against folly and demands a promise of reformation, he gives a dramatic version of the casuistical principles that apparently trivial actions are morally significant and that intellectual effort must precede moral action. For example, in discussing the question "are not some actions not only in their whole kind, but in their circumstances and limitations also, merely indifferent?" [26] Jeremy Taylor insists that most actions, even those indifferent in themselves, become either good or evil when chosen by the will.

> Whatsoever we do, we do it for a good end or an evil; for if we do it for no end, we do not work like men. . . . And this doctrine is to great and severe purposes taught by our blessed Saviour; "Of every idle word that a man shall speak, he shall give account in that day." . . . The effect of this question is very great: for it engages us upon a strict watchfulness over all our words and actions. . . . Every thing we do must twice pass through the conscience; once, when it is to be done,—and again, when it is done. And not only whatsoever is not of faith, is sin, so that we sin if we are not persuaded it is lawful;—but it becomes a sin, when we are careless and consider not at all . . .[27]

Similarly, Donne's speaker advises that taking a stroll with a friend—"indifferent" in itself—becomes in practice a moral action requiring commitment and sound judgment. His vivid caricatures of "a briske perfum'd piert Courtier" and "a velvet Justice with a long / Great traine of blew coats" (ll. 19, 21-22) illustrate the need to discriminate between superficial and substantial worth. His farfetched analogies between his giddy friend and an adulterer, a "superstitious puritan," and a "needy broker" (ll. 26-30) point to genuinely similar failures of loyalty and value. The witty malice with which he compares his friend's calculation

26 Taylor, XIV, 287.
27 Ibid., pp. 292, 294, 296, 297.

of social worth with the practised appraisal of a seedy pawnbroker hits off precisely the confusion of value with cost in both:

> when thou meet'st one, with enquiring eyes
> Dost search, and like a needy broker prize
> The silke, and gold he weares, and to that rate
> So high or low, dost raise thy formall hat.
>
> (Ll. 29-32)

While these displays of wit save the speaker from pomposity, they should not blind us to his serious moral purpose.

After explaining the personal and moral implications of frivolous inconstancy and exacting from the "motley humorist" a promise to mend his ways, the satirist decides to act:

> But since thou like a contrite penitent,
> Charitably warn'd of thy sinnes, does repent
> These vanities, and giddinesses, loe
> I shut my chamber doore, and 'Come, lets goe.'
>
> (Ll. 49-52)

Although he decides to accompany his friend, he still has doubts about the promised reformation:

> But sooner may a cheape whore, that hath beene
> Worne by as many severall men in sinne,
> As are black feathers, or musk-colour hose,
> Name her childs right true father, 'mongst all those:
> . . . .
> Then thou, when thou depart'st from mee, canst show
> Whither, why, when, or with whom thou wouldst go.
>
> (Ll. 53-56, 63-64)

His friend cannot be trusted because he is nonrational. He does not think about or understand the motives, consequences, or moral nature of his actions. The word of a man who does not think is worthless, regardless of how sincerely the promise is given. In addition, acknowledging his friend's untrustworthiness leads to a serious self-accusation.

> But how shall I be pardon'd my offence
> That thus have sinn'd against my conscience?
>
> (Ll. 65-66)

Since he knows the futility of trying to teach virtue to someone unwilling to think, his decision to go is contrary to his own best judgment. He is guilty of inconsistent, nonrational behavior—ironically the very things he condemns so scathingly. In Taylor's terms, the friend sins because he is "careless and consider[s] not at all"; the speaker sins because he is "not persuaded it [his action] is lawful."

Thus, the first section of "Satyre I" (ll. 1-48) presents an unresolved dilemma. The speaker feels responsible to act as his companion's moral guide, but he also believes that involvement in such frivolous company is irresponsible abandonment of the life of simple virtue. His ambivalence marks the pivotal second section (ll. 49-66), where he decides to act. He speaks of penitence and sin in an exasperated but amused voice, for he knows that his lecture is falling on deaf ears and that, while he should not go, neither should he stay.

The third section (ll. 67-108) is not directly concerned with analysis of the satirist's dilemma but narrates the consequences of his decision. The giddy young man fulfills his predictions. Images of motion chart his unstable progress. Although he chooses to be "imprison'd, and hem'd in" close to the wall for dignity's sake and is immobile when meeting a "grave man," he grins, smacks, shrugs" at "Every fine silken painted foole" (ll. 69-74). Moving through the world of tawdry pretension, he stoops and leaps, dances and droops, ogles and chatters, wanders away and returns, until:

> At last his Love he in a windowe spies,
> And like light dew exhal'd, he flings from mee
> Violently ravish'd to his lechery.
>
> (Ll. 106-108) [28]

The satirist describes this cavorting in language that fixes its value precisely, but in action, he restricts himself to witty but largely unregarded jokes at his companion's ignorance and excesses. His images express feelings both of responsibility and of

---

[28] Cf. Perkins: "If we must give an account of every idle word, then also of every idle gesture and pace: and what account can be given of these paces back-ward and forward, of caprings, jumps, gambolds, turnings, with many other friskes of lightnes & vanitie, more beseeming goates and apes, of whom they are commonly used, then men." See William Perkins, *A Discourse of Conscience,* in *The Workes of That Famous and Worthy Minister of Christ . . . Mr. William Perkins,* 3 vols. (London, 1612-1613), I, 539.

futility. This "fondling motley humorist" is as thoughtless and directionless as "light dew," but he is also a "lost sheep" (l. 93).

The first satire shows the influence of the casuistical tradition in its analysis of the moral and intellectual dimensions of men's actions and in its stress on the difficulty of making moral decisions in particular circumstances. Its structure, however, is not that of a case of conscience. Instead of exemplifying the movement from doubt to certainty, the speaker raises a moral question, decides to act without resolving his doubts, and thus raises more questions about the relation of thought to action and the efficacy of moral instruction. The last four lines of the satire provide an epilogue to his dilemma. The results of his decision to leave his books are frustration for the would-be guide and pain and humiliation for his friend:

> Many were there, he could command no more;
> He quarrell'd, fought, bled; and turn'd out of dore
>   Directly came to mee hanging the head,
>   And constantly a while must keepe his bed.
>
> (Ll. 109-112)

The consequences of his action are as inconclusive as his analysis of the problem. The young man is constant only in having to keep to his bed "a while." The description of his return, bloody and bowed, concludes the poem with the speaker's ironic detachment and continued involvement.

The second satire builds directly on the unresolved doubts of the first, debating in moral terms the alternatives of detachment and direct involvement in worldly affairs. Again, Donne begins in casuistical fashion with a specific question about what to do and secures formal unity and dramatic force by linking satire of a variety of sins and follies with the immediate problem. The specific question, however, is new. The young man has presumably just said something roughly equivalent to, "I'm not getting anywhere with that poetry rot; I think I'll take up law. There's more money in it anyway." While in the first satire the speaker addressed a "fondling motley humorist" in a derisive but affectionate tone, he now replies sternly to a "bold soule," acknowledging that his friend's posture as poet has been ridiculous but warning that taking up the law for selfish motives is even more despicable:

When sicke with Poëtrie, 'and possest with muse
Thou wast, and mad, I hop'd; but men which chuse
Law practise for meere gaine, bold soule, repute
Worse then imbrothel'd strumpets prostitute.

(Ll. 61-64)

In "Satyre I," the speaker first raised a question of where his responsibility lay and then shifted his attention to the behavior of his fictional audience. In "Satyre II," he considers directly only what his audience ought to do, but as he analyzes the question of occupational choice, he indirectly struggles with personal doubts about his responsibility as a poet.

He begins his response to the proposed transition from poet to lawyer by examining the poet's role. While in the first satire he assumed the innocence of poetry, here he ironically endorses charges against it. The sin of poetry, he concedes, brings famine and danger from Spain, presumably by being so addictive that hordes of men drop their ploughshares and swords to take up the pen. Like the plague and like Petrarchan love, poetry mysteriously overwhelms its victims until it is starved out of their systems. Yet these poor wretches are harmless: "their state / Is poore, disarm'd, like Papists, not worth hate" (ll. 9-10).

Donne's satire is thus double-edged. His tongue-in-cheek exaggerations effectively mock Puritan charges that poetry is socially harmful, but his contempt is for poets, not their attackers. Far from being a threat to the well-being of the commonwealth, the poet is totally ineffectual. Even the poet of the commercial theaters who provides a livelihood for actors cannot support himself. Hoping to win love by writing verses is as misguided as hoping to get rich, and those who turn poet for the sake of political preferment or the sake of fashion are obviously pathetic. In each case, the butt of the satirist's ridicule is not a type of poetry so much as a type of poet: those who "would move Love by rimes," "they who write . . . rewards to get," and "they who write, because all write" (ll. 17, 21, 23). His disdain is not for the sin of failure but for the self-serving motives of contemporary poets. Still, those who write poetry for worldly ends are not really worthy objects of moral outrage because they harm only themselves: "these do mee no harme" (l. 31); "these punish themselves" (l. 39). Even the plagiarist, "who (beggarly) doth chaw / Others

157

wits fruits" (ll. 25-26), is not worth getting excited about because talent cannot be counterfeited; plagiarism is its own reward:

> For if one eate my meate, though it be knowne
> The meate was mine, th'excrement is his owne.
> (Ll. 29-30)

Next, the satirist turns his attention from the vocation his friend would abandon to the profession he would adopt. Having dismissed those who write poetry for the wrong reasons as too pitiful to hate, he vents his anger on Coscus, a poet turned lawyer. He reverses the strategy of "Satyre I," where he insisted on the moral significance of the cut of men's clothes and the depth of their bows. In "Satyre II," he makes distinctions among degrees of evil:

> there's one state
> In all ill things so excellently best,
> That hate, towards them, breeds pitty towards the rest.
> (Ll. 2-4)

> the insolence
> Of Coscus onely breeds my just offence.
> (Ll. 39-40)

Coscus represents an evil worse than the irrationality of flatterers and plagiarists because he is far more harmful to others. Consequences, as well as intentions, contribute to the moral quality of our actions. Both poetasters and corrupt lawyers pervert language from its proper end of truth, but bad poets, however greedy, harm only themselves. As a poet writing love poetry in legal jargon, Coscus is merely absurd; as a lawyer, he is all too effective in twisting language to serve his purpose. He lies to clients and to judges. He ruins improvident heirs ("Satan will not joy at their sinnes, as hee," l. 80) by securing title to their lands in long, detailed contracts. In other transactions, his legal chicanery takes the form of significant verbal omissions. When selling land, he leaves out the clause assuring legal title to the buyer's heirs so that the land reverts to him. Exploiting other men's sins and their naiveté, Coscus is always on the make, and he is thriving.

His destructiveness is not confined to individuals or even to families. The greed he embodies threatens the whole country:

> Shortly ('as the sea) hee'will compasse all our land;
> From Scots, to Wight; from Mount, to Dover strand.
>
> (Ll. 77-78)

Since Coscus does not live in these ill-gotten estates, he does not fulfill the landlord's traditional responsibilities of economic and moral protection and support. The woods disappear from the countryside without returning in the form of new construction or hospitable fires in the manor house.

Obviously Coscus is not an attack on a particular individual but a portrait of all who live for success rather than service. Donne acknowledges that Coscus's motives and methods are not confined to the legal profession through a series of similes linking his sins with similar actions at every social level. His hypocritical representation of innocence is like that of prisoners who "whole months will sweare / That onely suretiship hath brought them there" (ll. 67-68). He lies "Like a Kings favorite, yea like a King" (l. 71); he is "more shamelesse farre / Then carted whores" (ll. 72-73). And his sophisticated legal maneuvering resembles the intellectual dishonesty of commentators who skip over difficult passages and of theologians who ignore the evidence against their arguments. Coscus is merely *primus inter pares*. Greed, calculated mendacity, and the shameless degradation of human talents for base ends permeate society. The satirist would substitute for parasitic greed and fashionable ostentation an ideal of moderation and social responsibility:

> meanes blesse; in rich mens homes
> I bid kill some beasts, but no Hecatombs,
> None starve, none surfet so . . .
>
> (Ll. 107-109)

But the whole town is corrupt, and good works are "out of fashion now" (l. 110).

In the second satire, as in the first, Donne's speaker is more concerned with showing the moral dangers inherent in practical decisions than with resolving doubts or discovering an innocent course of action. Again he tries to guide his audience toward virtue, but he makes no effort to bind his friend with a promise of amendment and no longer tries to educate his charge by accompanying him through the streets. Although he stresses the lawyer's culpability, he does not actually advise the young man what he ought to do. Instead, he demonstrates how to analyze the moral quality of what men do by specifying the motives and possible consequences should this "bold soule" act as poet or lawyer.

This analysis also bears on the satirist's case of conscience, clarifying without resolving the problem. Although he refers directly to his own doubts only in the last two lines, throughout the poem the satirist is concerned with the appropriateness of his response to the evils he observes, distinguishing carefully between his contempt for the dishonest poet and his hatred for the more destructive lawyer. He attacks poets who write for the wrong reasons but himself takes on the role of the satiric poet, castigating sin and folly and proposing an ideal of sanity and virtue. Thus, in a sense, he again contrasts the poet's innocence with the corruption of worldly men, although now he sees the poet's separation from other men as a problem as well as a protection. The days of faith in the efficacy of poetry to destroy evil are over,[29] and good works of more than one kind are "out of fashion now." His argument that Coscus is less harmful as a poet than as a lawyer indirectly disparages the effectiveness of all poets, while his descriptions of increasingly sinister perversions of language—from the idle chatter of "Satyre I," through the silly effusions of poetasters and the stolen words of plagiarists, to the lies and legal traps of the lawyer—show the need for someone to tell the truth. He fears his efforts are futile but concludes asserting the poet's innocence: "my words none drawes/ Within the vast reach of th'huge statute lawes" (ll. 111-112).

"Satyre III" has received more helpful and more favorable critical attention than the rest of Donne's satires. While most critics complain that the first two are structurally loose and only mechanically unified, they have praised the thematic coherence and structural clarity of the third. But the general neglect of the relation of "Satyre III" to the rest of the sequence and the failure to understand what I believe to be its dramatic context has obscured its imaginative vitality. The poem is central to the sequence thematically as well as numerically. Once again, the general themes of detachment and involvement and sin and virtue are particularized in a specific problem of doubt. This

[29] See Robert C. Elliott, *The Power of Satire: Magic, Ritual, Art* (Princeton: Princeton University Press, 1960), p. 36.

time the satirist achieves a satisfactory mode of discourse to fulfill his responsibilities to the young worldling he addresses, and in doing so he clarifies his own case of conscience about his vocation.

In "Satyre III," the poet addresses himself to the young man's religious doubts. The complexities and contradictions of institutionalized religion are apparently leading him to cynicism, accompanied, perhaps, by a swaggering bravura. The satirist's personal response is more complex than in the first two satires. The scorn of "Satyre I" and the pity and anger of "Satyre II" merge in his reaction to this thoughtless, self-defeating, yet willful cynicism. But he knows the futility of scornful laughter and tearful chastisement, and he doubts the effectiveness of the satirist's bitter railing:

> Kinde pitty chokes my spleene; brave scorn forbids
> Those teares to issue which swell my eye-lids;
> I must not laugh, nor weepe sinnes, and be wise,
> Can railing then cure these worne maladies?
>
> (Ll. 1-4)

Since the shallow cynicism of his fictional audience involves a question of belief and intellectual doubt, it raises the genuinely difficult question of the authority for moral judgments. To deal with the particular confusion honestly and helpfully, the poet must confront directly the theoretical relations among individual conscience, human institutions, and ultimate truth. To do this, he rejects the traditional satiric stances and assumes the voice and method of a casuist. Ironic wit is subordinated to rational discourse, and logical analysis replaces dramatic contrast as a structural principle.

He begins by explaining both the basic terms of the problem and the stakes for its solution, skillfully adapting his language to the character of his audience.

> Is not our Mistresse faire Religion,
> As worthy'of all our Soules devotion,
> As vertue was to the first blinded age?
>
> (Ll. 5-7)

What horrible irony, he laments, if pagan philosophers should be saved on the basis of a good life directed by reason unaided by revelation, while you throw away the chance of salvation. "O if thou dar'st," he taunts the young man, "feare this" (l. 15), implying that the battle to save one's soul from the world, the flesh, and the devil requires far greater courage than all of a young gallant's vain struggles against illusory enemies. Having clarified the nature of the problem and selected reason as the method for solving it, he draws the inevitable conclusion that one's duty is to "Seeke true religion."

The general conclusion raises another, more particularized problem: Where in the actual world is true religion to be found? The casuist's approach is to concentrate, not on solutions to the problem, but on methods of resolving it. First, he offers examples of inadequate methods, continuing to choose his metaphors from the "lecherous humors" (l. 53) of the fashionable world. Mirreus and Crants attempt to identify the bride of Christ by the style of her clothes. Acting as probabilists, they decide the form of their religion on the basis of inadequate external authority. Graius, like the docile boy who accepts whatever woman his legal guardian chooses for him, simply thinks whatever the established authorities "bid him thinke" (l. 57). Like the shallow young cynics of Jacobean comedy who believe that all females are cuckolders and hence cannot recognize an honest woman, Phrygius foolishly cuts himself off from the possibility of discovering the true Church because some Christian sects must be in error. With similar lack of discrimination and intellectual rigor, Graccus arrives at the opposite conclusion that all are equally right. Applying the "they're all the same in the dark" approach to religion, he decides that because the Church of England, the Church of Rome, and the Church of Geneva are all churches, it is futile to choose among them.

The casuist thus has shown that all conclusions are ridiculous if they are based on external authority, on unthinking indifference, or on fashionable cynicism instead of on the most reasonable analysis of available evidence. After he has demonstrated the folly of choosing any, none, or all of the major existing churches on the basis of inadequate authority, Donne discusses how the dilemma can be resolved. He does not propose a solution but suggests a method for discovering one. Like Jeremy Taylor, who insisted that "God had made the way to heaven plain and simple"[30] before the Jesuit casuists obscured it, Donne as casuist claims that "easie wayes and neare/To follow" (ll. 14-15) have been revealed to the Christian. Still, he acknowledges that the

---

[30] Taylor, IX, 353. .

necessity of discovering the one true Church is perplexing in the face of the conflicting claims of the churches of the world. He does not pretend to know an infallible arbiter of truth, but advises an honest, strenuous, personal search for it:

> Be busie to seeke her, beleeve mee this,
> Hee's not of none, nor worst, that seekes the best.
>
> (Ll. 74-75)

In an important sense, the true path consists in the process of the search.

> doubt wisely; in strange way
> To stand inquiring right, is not to stray;
> To sleepe, or runne wrong, is . . .
>
> (Ll. 77-79)

He urges his listener to grapple with the problem as a probabilior-ist by attempting to discover truth through reason, weighing all available knowledge. Truth is attainable, but there are no short cuts to it.

> On a huge hill,
> Cragged, and steep, Truth stands, and hee that will
> Reach her, about must, and about must goe;
> And what th'hills suddennes resists, winne so.
>
> (Ll. 79-82)

Like Dante, who in the first canto of the *Inferno* describes being frustrated in his direct assault on heaven and forced to take a less direct route guided by human reason, Donne describes truth standing on a steep, cragged hill that resists the zealous truth-seeker's "suddennes." The way of limited human reason is difficult and circuitous but finally successful. Instead of separating thought from action, the speculative from the practical understanding, Donne conceives of the operation of the conscience or moral reason as action. The verbs he uses to describe the search for truth—"strive," "worke," and "doe"—suggest vigorous activity, and he urges that just as the body can endure difficult physical action, "hard knowledge too / The mindes indeavours reach" (ll. 83-87).

Donne resembles Anglican casuists like Taylor and Sanderson in his approach to the problem of the moral force of human authority as well as in his conception of the individual conscience as the rational faculty that applies universal truth to a personal moral decision. The representatives of the predominant contemporary churches in the third satire epitomize their churches' views of ecclesiastical authority. Mirreus, the Roman Catholic, indulges his taste for external religious trappings and bases his ecclesiastical allegiance solely on tradition. He seeks true religion at Rome simply "because hee doth know / That shee was there a thousand yeares agoe" (ll. 45-46). The Calvinist Crants scorns tradition and chooses his church for the absence of any ceremony or ritual without scriptural sanction. Thus Donne mocks the Roman Catholic and Puritan treatment of indifferent actions. Although he does not actually endorse the Anglican position that the Church could legitimately regulate indifferent actions as long as it did not impose them on men's consciences as doctrine, he does suggest that "To' adore, or scorne an image, or protest, / May all be bad" (ll. 76-77). More directly, he recommends the position that the best authority in religious questions is right reason aided by tradition:

> aske thy father which is shee,
> Let him aske his; though truth and falsehood bee
> Neare twins, yet truth a little elder is;
>
> (Ll. 71-73)

The attitude toward human authority in "Satyre III" also parallels the casuists' treatment of the relationship of the individual conscience to civil law. The satirist grants the legitimacy of some ecclesiastical authority by maintaining that true religion must be sought on earth in one of the visible churches. He satirizes indiscriminate rejection of all existing churches in the character of Phrygius, and in the character of Graccus dismisses with equal contempt the man who ignores completely the incompatibility of the claims of rival churches. The Christian must choose a church as the visible manifestation of Christian faith in the world, and the mutually exclusive positions of various existing churches force him logically to choose "but one" actual church.

By arguing that the one true Church is to be sought on earth and by endorsing human tradition as a guide to truth, the satirist acknowledges the moral force of some human authority, but his emphasis is on the inviolability of the individual conscience. The portrait of Graius who unthinkingly accepts the established Church is drawn with brilliant contempt:

> Graius stayes still at home here, and because
> Some Preachers, vile ambitious bauds, and lawes
> Still new like fashions, bid him thinke that shee
> Which dwels with us, is onely perfect, hee
> Imbraceth her, . . .

(Ll. 55-59)

The approach to individual moral responsibility is not quite that of the traditional satirist, however. The speaker exposes the sin and folly of naive acquiescence in governmental coercion of the conscience, and then, in casuistical fashion, stresses the theoretical basis for the limits of external authority. Although human rulers have legitimate authority, the individual conscience is the final judge. To transfer the responsibility of choice to civil or ecclesiastical authority is both morally and intellectually corrupt. No spiritual adviser will share responsibility on the Day of Judgment, he reminds his audience:

> Will it then boot thee
> To say a Philip, or a Gregory,
> A Harry, or a Martin taught thee this?

(Ll. 95-97)

To decide a moral problem on the basis of probabilism, which maintains that a man in doubt may act on the opinion of one qualified adviser, leads to logical chaos:

> Is not this excuse for mere contraries,
> Equally strong? cannot both sides say so?

(Ll. 98-99)

For a ruler to exceed his just authority is tyranny, and for a man to obey an unjust law against his conscience is idolatry.

> That thou may'st rightly 'obey power, her bounds know;
> Those past, her nature, and name's chang'd; to be
> Then humble to her is idolatrie.

(Ll. 100-102)

The conceit that ends the poem explains forcefully the theory of power behind the casuistical principle that to obey an unjust

165

human law instead of the law of God is to court damnation. Like the stream that becomes more tumultuous as it descends from its calm source to the sea, the exercise of power becomes less perfect as it descends from God, the source of all power. The man who obeys an unjust human law entrusts his soul to the "tyrannous rage" of human authority instead of to his conscience, the voice of God in him.

> So perish Soules, which more chuse mens unjust
> Power from God claym'd, then God himselfe to trust.
>   (Ll. 109-110)

In the third satire, then, Donne deals with a moral dilemma, as Perkins, Taylor, and other casuists do in their cases of conscience, by demonstrating the process by which it can be solved. He approaches the case of conscience without condoning moral or intellectual laxity and without indulging in excessively hair-splitting legalisms. He admits that the problem of choosing among existing churches is real and difficult but denies that its complexity absolves his questioner from the responsibility of choice. He treats the question of discovering the true Church as a particular man's personal problem of conscience while simultaneously showing it to be an instance of a universal moral question.

His tone is most personal at the beginning of the poem where he reacts emotionally and attacks personally the superficiality of his fictive audience. His primary intention, however, is not to denounce sin but to demonstrate the method by which the case of conscience can be resolved. First he clarifies the universal moral question involved and then narrows his focus to the specific instance of the problem in particular historical circumstances. He ridicules inadequate methods of dealing with the problem and vigorously recommends the process of rational inquiry. In the last third of the poem, he clarifies this process and recommends specific actions. He insists that while the ultimate mysteries of faith are not susceptible to rational analysis, the remoteness of truth in human experience necessitates tortuous intellectual exercise. He does not, like many casuists, suggest specific physical action; instead, he explains that thought and action are inseparable. He conceives of the conscience as rational activity based on knowledge and stresses the inviolability and ultimate responsibility of the individual conscience. The casuist-persona does not affirm personally the truth that he has found; rather he attempts to instill in another the necessary intellectual and moral courage to "stand inquiring right."

Looking at the third satire as a dramatization of a case of conscience explains features that have puzzled modern readers. In contrast to the personal quality of the sonnet on the Church, "Show me deare Christ, thy spouse, so bright and cleare," the third satire has seemed to some readers strangely unimpassioned. J. B. Leishman, for example, notes that in the satire, the "saving truth is, in a sense, factual rather than doctrinal, and to be attained, not in some beatific vision, but as the result of a long and laborious process. . . . by a careful comparison of rival arguments about matters of fact." [31] Understanding the poem's casuistical background makes clear that this approach to religious truth is not, as Leishman concludes, an instance of Donne's failure to portray a universal religious experience but an expression of the poet's sensitivity to the particular dramatic situation he creates. The speaker is not acting out his own spiritual struggle over religious commitment but advising another man. He sympathizes, mocks, and scolds, but primarily he explains calmly the rational process through which the problem can be solved.

Because he finds a satisfactory response to this particular case, the satirist's doubts about his vocation disappear from the poem after the first few lines. The problems of the distraction of the poet from his proper role of conferring with "God, and the Muses" and of the ineffectuality of poetry to reform men's actions do not come up. In this case, he does not try to protect another man from sin either by his physical presence or by communicating the repugnance that he feels. Instead, he asserts the individual's responsibility to choose and to act, and he provides a model of how to go about solving the problem, confident that right action presupposes clear thinking and that, in the midst of bewilderingly conflicting evidence, human reason can discover truth.

In satires two and three, the satirist speaks primarily as a guide to others and expresses his personal doubts indirectly. "Satyre IV" returns to the framework of "Satyre I," focusing directly on the satirist's case of conscience. The opening lines pose the question of whether his visit to the corrupt court is sinful, as Grierson suggests by noting their resemblance to the opening of Régnier's imitation of Horace's Ninth Satire:

[31] J. B. Leishman, *The Monarch of Wit* (London: Hutchinson & Co., 1962), p. 116.

Charles, des mes peches j'ay bien fait penitence;
Or, toy qui te cognois aux cas de conscience,
Juge si j'ay raison de penser estre absous.[32]

More precisely, the question is whether the particular circumstances of the satirist, his innocent motives and revulsion at the spectacle of vanity, free him from being implicated in the sinfulness of the court:

Well; I may now receive, and die; My sinne
Indeed is great, but I have beene in
A Purgatorie, such as fear'd hell is
A recreation to, 'and scant map of this.

(Ll. 1-4)

Although he confesses to the "sin of going" (l. 12), his self-accusation in the opening lines is not entirely serious. He so loathes court life that his sin is its own penance. Primarily, his emphases are on his innocent intentions and the disproportion between his sin and punishment.

My minde, neither with prides itch, nor yet hath been
Poyson'd with love to see, or to bee seene,
I had no suit there, nor new suite to shew,
Yet went to Court; But as Glaze which did goe
To'a Masse in jest, catch'd, was faine to disburse
The hundred markes, which is the Statutes curse,
Before he scapt, So'it pleas'd my destinie
(Guilty'of my sin of going,) to thinke me
As prone to'all ill, and of good as forget-
    full, as proud, as lustfull, and as much in debt,
As vaine, as witlesse, and as false as they
Which dwell at Court, for once going that way.

(Ll. 5-16)

When a foppish courtier with outlandish clothes and bizarre speech corners him, his first response is contemptuous amazement at a being so totally alien. He sees "A thing more strange, then on Niles slime, the Sunne / E'r bred" (ll. 18-19) and wonders "God! / How have I sinn'd, that thy wraths furious rod, / This fellow chuseth me?" (ll. 49-51).

32 Herbert J. C. Grierson, *The Poems of John Donne*, 2 vols. (London: Oxford University Press, 1912), II, 118.

Genuine anxiety, however, develops in the course of his sufferings. At first, he meets folly with irony. To the courtier's boast of linguistic skill, he responds:

'If you'had liv'd, Sir,
Time enough to have been Interpreter
To Babells bricklayers, sure the Tower had stood.'
(Ll. 63-65)

When the courtier, basking in closeness to the great, squeaks, " 'O Sir, / 'Tis sweet to talke of Kings,' " the satirist counters:

'At Westminster,'
Said I, 'The man that keepes the Abbey tombes,
And for his price doth with who ever comes,
Of all our Harries, and our Edwards talke,
From King to King and all their kin can walke:
Your eares shall heare nought, but Kings; your eyes meet
Kings only; The way to it, is Kingstreet.'
(Ll. 74-80)

But he soon finds that his irony falls on deaf ears and that in exercising his wit on so dull an object, he frustrates himself. As the bore's political gossip becomes increasingly malicious, the satirist's pride in witty rejoinders is replaced by a sense of helplessness: "I belch, spue, spit, / Looke pale, and sickly, like a Patient; Yet / He thrusts me more"; "I sigh, and sweat / . . . In vaine" (ll. 109-111, 116-117). The courtier, "like a priviledg'd spie" (l. 119), accuses the most powerful men in England of bribery, extortion, treason, and sodomy until the satirist feels himself being implicated:

I more amas'd then Circes prisoners, when
They felt themselves turne beasts, felt my selfe then
Becomming Traytor, and mee thought I saw
One of our Giant Statutes ope his jaw
To sucke me in. . . .
(Ll. 129-133)

He has discovered that he cannot remain a detached observer insulated from the evil of his society; corruption seems infectious:

for hearing him, I found
That as burnt venom'd Leachers doe grow sound

> By giving others their soares, I might growe
> Guilty, and he free. . . .

(Ll. 133-136)

Where he first protested innocence ("How have I sinn'd, that . . . / This fellow chuseth me?"), he now sees himself as part of sinful humanity: ". . . since I am in, / I must pay mine, and my forefathers sinne" (ll. 137-138). Where he first insisted on the courtier's strangeness, he now sees "All the court fill'd with more strange things then hee" (l. 152). Having recognized that innocence is not an invincible shield against evil, he loses confidence in being safe from "the vast reach of th'huge statute lawes" ("Satyre II", l. 112).[33] Boredom, contempt, and wit turn into fear and flight.

In the next section, he reflects on his experience at court. In the "wholesome solitarinesse" (l. 155) of home, fear gives way to pity at the wretchedness he has seen. Like Dante, he has a vision of hell populated with contemporary sinners. However powerful and menacing the courtiers seem, *sub specie aeternitatis* they are doomed. From this perspective, he realizes that since worldly power can threaten him physically but not corrupt him spiritually, his fear is cowardly: "Low feare / Becomes the guiltie, not th'accuser" (ll. 160-161). Thus, he reasons, in a society that uses language to cheat, lie, and betray, the satirist should not by withdrawing sacrifice the truth:

> Shall I, nones slave, of high borne, or rais'd men
> Feare frownes? And, my Mistresse Truth, betray thee
> To th'huffing braggart, puft Nobility?

(Ll. 162-164)

His doubts resolved, the satirist returns to court. Again, he has "no suit there, no new suite to shew" but, loyally serving his "Mistresse Truth," goes to report accurately how Englishmen behave at their sovereign's court. Because he no longer fears sin by contagion, he can treat standard satirical topics like women's cosmetics and bankrupt courtiers with amused detachment. He

[33] Howard Erskine-Hill has pointed out that throughout "Satyre IV" similes referring to prisoners, spies, and, most often, the persecution of outlawed religion imply that law is a threatening rather than protecting power. See "Satyre IV," in *John Donne: Essays in Celebration,* ed. A. J. Smith (London: Methuen and Co., 1972), pp. 273-307.

mocks the men and women engaged in the courtly rituals of seeing and being seen without trying to chastize them: "they each other plague" (l. 218). He emphasizes the self-punishing tawdriness of their obsession with surface and neglect of substance but does not forget the power wielded by small, vicious men. For example, Glorius, who affects a "rough carelessnesse" (l. 221) in dress, is an amusing contrast to Macrine's fastidiousness, but he is also a threatening figure: "he keepes all in awe; / Jeasts like a licenc'd foole, commands like law" (ll. 227-228). As he leaves court, the satirist passes the queen's guard:

> men big enough to throw
> Charing Crosse for a barre, men that doe know
> No token of worth, but 'Queenes man', and fine
> Living. . . .
>
> (Ll. 233-236)

In the presence of these imposing figures who represent to him the power and debased values of the courtly world, he feels his vulnerability as a critical intruder and shakes like "a spyed Spie" (l. 237).

The satirist has resolved the case of conscience posed first in "Satyre I." After having formulated in "Satyre III" man's duty to search for truth in spite of the deceptions and difficulties of the fallen world and his duty to follow his own conscience in spite of coercive human power, he concludes that, while "wholesome solitarinesse" is the poet's necessary and natural habitat, he must also fulfill his responsibility to tell the truth about the world he lives in. The satirist is no more convinced of the efficacy of poetry to effect reformation than he was at the end of "Satyre II," but he is confident that he can escape corruption and provide insight into reality:

> Preachers which are
> Seas of Wit and Arts, you can, then dare,
> Drowne the sinnes of this place, for, for mee
> Which am but a scarce brooke, it enough shall bee
> To wash the staines away; Though I yet
> With *Macchabees* modestie, the knowne merit
>   Of my worke lessen: yet some wise man shall,
>   I hope, esteeme my writs Canonicall.
>
> (Ll. 237-244)

Only preachers can change men's fallen wills, but perhaps the poet can help to supply their erected wits with a guide to truth, the text necessary for virtuous choice.

In the first four satires, Donne's poet-speaker struggles with the tension between his revulsion from the frivolity and corruption of society and his sense of responsibility to the world of men. He considers his doubts about his relation to society not as a *debat*, weighing the comparative advantages of the contemplative versus the active life, but as a case of conscience, a question of where his duty lies. He knows that involvement may be futile, corrupting, and dangerous, but he also knows that men must act in this imperfect world, that their salvation depends on acting in accordance with their consciences, and that conscience presupposes knowledge. His understanding of the corruption of the world, particularly the misuse of language and consequent obscuring of truth, convinces him of the need for a man of conscience who is also a poet. Although he has no assurance of success and no guarantee against spiritual and physical dangers, he is convinced that sin results from conscious choice, not physical contagion, and that ignorance and lack of moral awareness must be fought. Thus, in "Satyre V," he accepts the risks of involvement and assumes the responsibility of the satirist.

Since he has resolved his case of conscience, the last satire begins not with a question but with a firm announcement of purpose:

> Thou shalt not laugh in this leafe, Muse, nor they
> Whom any pitty warmes; He which did lay
> Rules to make Courtiers, (hee being understood
> May make good Courtiers, but who Courtiers good?)
> Frees from the sting of jests all who'in extreme
> Are wrech'd or wicked: of these two a theame
> Charity and liberty give me. What is hee
> Who Officers rage, and Suiters misery
> Can write, and jest?
>
> (Ll. 1-9)

He admits doubt about the possibility of effecting reformation but not about the moral nature of what he is doing. He identifies himself as a poet writing about extreme suffering and evil. Rapacious officers of the law and their wretched victims are his subject. Since their wickedness and misery are no laughing

matter, instead of witty caricatures or ironic dialogue, he proposes
a series of metaphors defining their relationship.

> Officers
> Are the vast ravishing seas; and Suiters,
> Springs; now full, now shallow, now drye; which, to
> That which drownes them, run: These selfe reasons do
> Prove the world a man, in which, officers
> Are the devouring stomacke, and Suiters
> Th'excrements, which they voyd.
>
> (Ll. 13-19)

Thus, the first section of "Satyre V" embodies the satirist's
resolution of the question of whether he ought to direct his
attention to worldly affairs and the related question of *how* he
should fulfill his responsibility to guide men to virtue. He has
discovered the futility of trying to make men good by dispensing
good advice. He has learned that ridicule may make men despise
folly and sin in others but not in themselves. Each man must
make his own decisions and will choose virtue only if he is able
to "stand inquiring right." The satirist's responsibility, then, is
to tell the truth, not just by persuading men to hate evil or by
identifying certain actions as evil, but by communicating a habit
of mind that enables men to discover truth in their particular
circumstances. His imagery expresses compassion for loss and
suffering and contempt for the evil and stupidity that cause them,
but its main force is to explain the mutually dependent relationship of exploiters and exploited.

> They [officers] are the mills which grinde you [suitors], yet you are
> The winde which drives them; and a wastfull warre
> Is fought against you, and you fight it; they
> Adulterate lawe, and you prepare their way
> Like wittals; th'issue your owne ruine is.
>
> (Ll. 23-27)

The suitors he addresses are both victims and perpetrators of
injustice.

The short, second section of the poem supplies a specific historical context for the poet's decision to participate actively in
his society. Donne translates commitment to making truth known
from an abstract, philosophical concept to specific action in a
particular time and place by referring directly to Elizabeth I—

"Greatest and fairest Empresse"—and to his own and Sir Thomas
Egerton's position in relation to the Queen:

> You Sir, whose righteousnes she loves, whom I
> By having leave to serve, an most richly
> For service paid. . . .
>
> (Ll. 28, 31-33) [34]

The satirist serves not only his "Mistresse Truth" but one of
Elizabeth's officers officially empowered to reform certain abuses
in the legal system. These references also provide the framework
for Donne's analysis of the relationship between individual conscience and legal authority. The Queen's unavoidable ignorance
of the abuses committed in her name shows that the government
hierarchy has an existence of its own beyond the control of any
single person, but the satirist's declaration that the righteous man
he serves is beginning "To know and weed out this enormous
sinne" (l. 34) asserts the significance of the individual conscience
and its efficacy in changing the system.

In the longest section of the poem, the satirist contributes to
this effort by making the "enormous sinne" known. He begins by
apostrophizing his society as an "Age of rusty iron" (l. 35) where
injustice sells higher than justice was sold in the mythological
Age of Iron. Then he analyzes this injustice in particular and
practical detail. Men seeking redress of grievances by appealing
to the judicial system are charged exorbitant fees and bribes, but
they still lose their cases. Where law is in a judge's word and
judges yield to political and financial influences, justice is lost.
Since the legal system is an integrated, hierarchical structure, the
actions of lower courts carry the force of the highest law in the
land and thus

> can throw
> Thee, if they sucke thee in, to misery,
> To fetters, halters. . . .
>
> (Ll. 46-48)

---

[34] Grierson identifies the historical context as Sir Thomas Egerton's attempt
to reform abuses in the administration of the Clerkship of the Star Chamber
(Grierson, *Poems of John Donne*, II, 126). Bald suggests that Egerton and
Donne were concerned also with abuses in the law courts, the Chancery, and
other government offices (Bald, *Donne: A Life*, pp. 100-101). What matters to
my argument, of course, is not the specific abuse being investigated but that
the poem evokes an actual situation.

Since the natural flow of power is downwards, taking one's case to a higher court is to go "Against the stream" (l. 50) and requires tremendous psychological effort and financial resources just when both have been exhausted by the corruption against which he is appealing.

Having described how the system works to the advantage of the wealthy—"only who have may'have more" (l. 56)—the satirist explains the moral significance of this perversion of the judicial system. "Judges are Gods," he reminds us, and human law is ordained by God to apply His will to particular situations:

> she is established
> Recorder to Destiny, on earth, and shee
> Speakes Fates words, and but tells us who must bee
> Rich, who poore, who in chaires, who in jayles.
> (Ll. 57, 70-73)

Men who steal in the name of the law are perverting the holy into the obscene.

> Shee [the law] is all faire, but yet hath foule long nailes,
> With which she scracheth Suiters; In bodies
> Of men, so'in law, nailes are th'extremities,
> So Officers stretch to more then Law can doe,
> As our nailes reach what no else part comes to.
> (Ll. 74-78)

After he has shrewdly explained the practical difficulties awaiting anyone appealing to the law and after he has indignantly denounced judges who take bribes, pursuivants who misrepresent evidence—all court officers who "stretch to more then Law can doe"—Donne's spokesman turns to the moral responsibility of suitors, the wretches who ruin themselves futilely seeking justice from human law. He charges them with ultimate responsibility for the corruption of the system that victimizes them. Avaricious men obsequiously pander to wealth and power. They use the courts dishonestly to acquire wealth and then are naively indignant when their greed and dishonesty recoil on their own heads: "Foole, twice, thrice, thou'hast bought wrong, 'and now hungerly/ Beg'st right" (ll. 81-82). The tone is harsh because even the most feckless of suitors is effectively perverting the law and spreading evil when he bribes officials and acquiesces in the corruption around him, but the anger is suffused with pity because the satirist realizes that not just bad poets and foolish courtiers but all sinners are deluded and are actively pursuing their own destruction:

> Thou'art the swimming dog whom shadows cosened,
> And div'st, neare drowning, for what vanished.
>
> (Ll. 90-91)

In "Satyre V," Donne examines the question of taking one's grievances to court, as does William Perkins in the case summarized in Chapter II, but Donne conducts his examination from a satirical, not a casuistical, perspective. While Perkins analyzes doubts rising from scriptural admonitions about the moral lawfulness of litigation and concludes with the assurance that going to court is morally innocent under certain conditions, Donne first estimates a plaintiff's chances of practical success and, through examining the difficulties of finding justice, concludes by accusing him of sin. In a sense, the satirist's function is the opposite of the casuist's. While the casuist attempts to resolve doubts and quiet troubled consciences, the satirist tries to overcome dangerous complacency by creating doubt. But, in spite of these differences in their immediate ends, their ultimate goals and their assumptions about human action are the same. Like a casuist, Donne's satirist tries to create in his readers a habit of mind at once intensely committed to virtuous action and intellectually disinterested. By providing a concrete model of rational analysis of the moral nature of human action, he tries to aid in the formation of men's consciences by overcoming their reluctance to think and their tendency to try to evade moral responsibility.

The distinctive quality of "Satyre V," its reflectiveness and absence of humor, has provoked a largely negative critical response,[35] perhaps partly because its echoes of the other satires have been seen as mere repetitions instead of as significant indications of the dramatic and thematic structures of the group of

---

[35] Sister Geraldine dismisses it as "shriller and less satisying than the other satires" ("Donne's *Notitia*," p. 31), and Milgate refers to it as "a series of spasmodic efforts" and as a "pathetic attempt" (*The Satires, Epigrams and Verse Letters*, p. xxiv). Shawcross has been the most perceptive about "Satyre V." Noting Donne's technique of communicating "an awareness crystalized in an image or allusion," he advises: "Those who find Satire 5 a failure (partially because of the lack of humor in it) would do well to recognize that the evil exposed is deeper, emboldened by the fabric of man's impoverished life and hopes of extrication through financial improvement" ("All Attest His Writs Canonical," p. 267).

satires, and partly because the unifying context of the speaker's case of conscience has been ignored. As satirist, Donne does not rest content with teaching virtue by presenting images of vice—even by presenting vice revealed in all its ugliness. Placing both institutional authority and individual conscience within the framework of divine law, he analyzes acutely the operation of the contemporary judicial system and the motives and consequences of individual action in those circumstances. His satire of official corruption and individual complicity depends on his fascination with the intricacies of the law and particular historical conditions as well as on his profound insight into the vagaries of the human mind. Out of these several kinds of knowledge he creates a horrified yet compassionate vision of greed and ignorance that is universal in scope.

Only "Satyre III" closely resembles the case of conscience structurally, but all of Donne's satires exhibit to a striking extent the casuist's double focus on self-examination and practical action. Even more significantly, the shifting tones and subjects of the satires and their unity as a group are intelligible only when we recognize that the speaker is working out his own case of conscience at the same time as he is exposing the evil around him. As a Christian poet, he must decide whether he ought to become involved in a shallow and sordid society. When he ponders whether to laugh or cry or rail at human folly, he is deciding not merely which tactic is most effective but which response is morally right. By showing the incipient recluse of "Satyre I" developing into the dedicated public servant of "Satyre V," Donne provides a model of a man discovering how to act according to his conscience in a perplexing situation.

The casuistical habit of mind informing the satires testifies not only to Donne's psychological insight and imaginative power but also to his independence and originality as moralist and churchman. During the 1590s, while he was writing the satires, troubled men took their cases of conscience to their pastors and preachers discussed casuistical problems in sermons, but Protestant casuistry was just beginning to appear in print. That Donne's poetic dramatization of casuistical material anticipates the attitudes and form of later English casuistry is further evidence for Helen Gardner's thesis that in his conversion to Anglicanism Donne did not merely prudentially capitulate to the *via media* but that he helped to create the English Protestant tradition. In the satires,

Donne insists on the supremacy of the individual mind operating morally among the unstable circumstances of the world and tries to clarify the process of resolving doubt as a way to truth, as Richard Baxter and Jeremy Taylor are to do later in works of casuistry. A. E. Malloch has observed that Donne's interest in casuistry shows "passionate concern for the reality and activity of the human self, and at the same time intellectual absorption in an external world of law." [36] This combination is also characteristic of the satires and of later prose cases of conscience.

THE *Songs and Sonnets* AND CASUISTRY

The casuistical habit of mind is not confined to Donne's satires. Less directly, it underlies much Renaissance poetry, as it does much political thought. Indeed, a summary of the salient characteristics of English casuistry has obvious similarities to most descriptions of metaphysical poetry. The casuists' yoking of individual conscience and particular circumstances with universal law and their emphasis at once on doubt and perplexity and on moral commitment, rational inquiry, and saving truth have clear affinities with the intensely personal and concrete yet intellectual poetry of Herbert as well as Donne. And the case of conscience, with its logical structure and plain statement complicated by subtle distinctions and explored ambiguities, suggests the form of many of their lyrics.

Arguing correctly that the casuistical habit of mind need not be limited to religious subject matter, Dwight Cathcart has investigated the broader implications of the casuistical tradition in Donne's *Songs and Sonnets,* showing how Donne's dual allegiance to the irreducible complexity of personal experience and to unified, harmonious truth from which moral certainty can be derived parallels the casuists' attempts to bridge the gap between the unique particularity of individual experience and universal moral law.[37] Cathcart demonstrates that much of the power of Donne's lyrics to disturb, excite, and delight comes from the speaker's assumption that truth is not self-evident and from his success in joining knowledge of universal law with knowledge of man's particular experience to discover truths about how to live that

[36] Malloch, "John Donne and the Casuists," p. 76.

[37] Dwight Cathcart, *Doubting Conscience: Donne and the Poetry of Moral Argument* (Ann Arbor: The University of Michigan Press, 1975).

violate or transcend merely conventional morality and unthinking common sense. Cathcart overstates the case, however, when he claims that the "speaker is a doubting conscience" and that the "structure of the argument and the assumptions about truth and law and the resolution of doubt are the same in the cases of conscience and in the speaker's words in the *Songs and Sonets.*" [38]

In "Womans Constancy," for example, Donne plays with sophistical arguments which plead that special circumstances create exceptions to moral law. When you break your promise and violate the law of fidelity, the speaker asks,

> Wilt thou then Antedate some new made vow?
>   Or say that now
> We are not just those persons, which we were?
> Or, that oathes made in reverentiall feare
> Of Love, and his wrath, any may forsweare?
> Or, as true deaths, true maryages untie,
> So lovers contracts, images of those,
> Binde but till sleep, deaths image, them unloose?
>   Or, your owne end to Justifie,
> For having purpos'd change, and falsehood; you
> Can have no way but falsehood to be true?
>
> (Ll. 3-13) [39]

But the poem does not exist for the sake of these parodies of casuistical reasoning; the parodies exist to dramatize the speaker's impudent cynicism. Characteristically Donne uses analysis and argument not to solve problems and to resolve doubt but to define and communicate emotion.[40]

[38] Cathcart, *Doubting Conscience*, pp. 141, 9, respectively.

[39] Quotations of the *Songs and Sonnets* are from Helen Gardner, ed., *John Donne: The Elegies and The Songs and Sonnets* (Oxford: Clarendon Press, 1965).

[40] Professor Cathcart's discovery of the casuistical paradigm in the lyrics often fails to convince me because his analysis of casuistry differs significantly from my own. While I see the casuists applying moral law to the perplexities of particular situations and creating a literary form that embodies the decision-making process, Cathcart sees them as engaged in making intelligible decisions already arrived at by a method that is essentially nonrational. Thus, his "the reasoned articulation of unreasonable truths" (p. 105) seems to me an apt description of many of Donne's love poems, but I do not recognize its applicability to English casuistry. Cathcart disagrees with me about the

"Loves Growth" is typical. The poem opens with the speaker raising moral doubts about his own actions ("I scarce beleeve my love to be so pure / As I had thought it was . . . Me thinkes I lyed all winter, when I swore, / My love was infinite," ll. 1-2, 5-6) and ends with a promise to act well in the future ("No winter shall abate the springs encrease," l. 28). But while the opening lines seem to denigrate the speaker, the completion of the first sentence reveals that the problem Donne raises is not really about the quality of his love but about how to describe it accurately. His winter protestations of infinite love are called in doubt by its springtime growth.

> I scarce beleeve my love to be so pure
>   As I had thought it was,
>   Because it doth endure
> Vicissitude, and season, as the grasse;
> Me thinkes I lyed all winter, when I swore,
> My love was infinite, if spring make'it more.
>   (Ll. 1-6)

The discrepancy between felt experience and verbal formulation creates doubt about the accuracy of traditional descriptions of love but not about the thing itself. While the casuist judges particular actions on the basis of general law, Donne judges general formulations against the authority of his own experience. The fact of his love's increase convinces him that Petrarchan attempts to limit love to an immutable, wholly spiritual union are misguided. Since the theory of love as pure essence has broken down, he poses an alternate theory.

> But if this medicine, love, which cures all sorrow
>   With more, not onely bee no quintessence,
>   But mixt of all stuffes, paining soule, or sense,
> And of the Sunne his working vigour borrow,
> Love's not so pure, and abstract, as they use
> To say, which have no Mistresse but their Muse,
> But as all else, being elemented too,
> Love sometimes would contemplate, sometimes do.
>   (Ll. 7-14)

---

relation of casuistry to the *Satyres*. "The satires are very little informed by this tradition; they thunder against wrong, but they do not argue about the nature of that wrong, and the speaker shows no doubt" (*Doubting Conscience*, p. 165).

Dissatisfied with his own description of love's mixed nature, in the second stanza, Donne qualifies his assertion that love, like everything else, is composed of various elements and thus capable of growth and action as well as of constancy and thought. The emotional experience he is trying to understand is not a matter of size or quantity but of perception.

> And yet not greater, but more eminent,
>> Love by the spring is growne;
>> As, in the firmament,
> Starres by the Sunne are not inlarg'd, but showne.
>> (Ll. 15-18)

But this image too is inadequate to capture the elusive sense that a love already strong and whole has grown, so he complements the idea of fuller manifestation with the idea of maturation.

> Gentle love deeds, as blossomes on a bough,
> From loves awaken'd root do bud out now.
>> (Ll. 19-20)

While the blossom image corrects the static implications of the star image, it misleadingly fragments love into a sequential progression in time. The series of images—grass, medicine, stars, blossoms—all illuminate partial truths about growing love, but they also distort the wholeness of experience. The last attempt to find a suitable analogy succeeds in unifying love's multiplicity because it focuses on love's cause and object—the beloved.

> If, as in water stir'd more circles bee
>> Produc'd by one, love such additions take,
>> Those like to many spheares, but one heaven make,
> For, they are all concentrique unto thee.
>> (Ll. 21-24)

Because he has succeeded in finding a way to talk about his love that combines its past, present, and future, its physicality and spirituality, its movement and growth as well as its permanence, Donne can bring love back to the mundane world with light-hearted assurance that it cannot be damaged by time or political jokes.

> And though each spring doe adde to love new heate,
> As princes doe in times of action get

New taxes, and remit them not in peace,
No winter shall abate the springs encrease.

(Ll. 25-28)

Like most of Donne's love lyrics, "Loves Growth" relates a particular human experience to general laws of behavior with the intellectual energy and subtlety characteristic of the best English casuistry. But Donne does not speak as a doubting conscience. He feels no doubt or confusion about whether to love, only about how to understand and describe his love. He argues not that his love's growth constitutes an exception to the law of love's immutability but that his experience reveals the true nature and operation of love. He analyzes his experience, pursuing the concept of growth through fine distinctions and intricate argument, not to resolve a moral dilemma but to compliment his beloved with the intensity and constancy of his love.[41]

As preacher, political controversialist, and poet, then, Donne exhibits the "moral diligence" recommended by casuists, assuming with Taylor that "he that searches, desires to find, and so far takes the right course." [42] In a broad sense, the casuistical habit of mind animates the intense self-exploration against a backdrop of the temporal and eternal conditions of men's lives in Donne's lyrics. But the lyrics are not casuistical in any precise, specific way; it is in the treatment of moral dilemmas in his verse satires that Donne is most significantly within the casuistical tradition. Indeed, the casuistical paradigm is more directly helpful in understanding Herbert's lyrics than Donne's. In the poetry of *The Temple*, Herbert devotes considerable attention to the moral theology that underlies casuistry as well as displaying a casuist's interest in particular, practical actions. Unlike the Donne of the lyrics, he uses the strategies of reasoned argument and self-analysis to resolve problems of moral doubt. Although Donne assumes a variety of roles in the *Songs and Sonnets,* neither a man struggling with moral doubt nor a casuist dispensing advice are among them. It is Herbert who undertakes the casuist's roles of comforter, guide, and healer and Herbert who resolves personal doubt in lyric poetry.

[41] Donald Guss makes this point in *John Donne, Petrarchist* (Detroit: Wayne State University Press, 1966), p. 167.
[42] Taylor, XI, 411.

Chapter V

CASUISTRY IN *THE TEMPLE*

After acknowledging an unfashionably high opinion of the scholastic philosophers, Richard Baxter qualifies his admiration:

> But how loath should I be to take such sauce for my food, and such recreations for my business! The jingling of too much and too false philosophy among them, often drowns the noise of Aaron's bells. I feel myself much better in Herbert's Temple.[1]

The great casuist's delight in *The Temple* testifies to an affinity of mind that would be evident even without George Herbert's specific endorsement of casuistry. Practical divinity is central to Herbert's description of the pastor and his duties in *A Priest to the Temple, or, the Country Parson:* "A Pastor is the Deputy of Christ for the reducing of Man to the Obedience of God." He has three basic duties:

> . . . the one, to infuse a competent knowledge of salvation in every one of his Flock; the other, to multiply, and build up this knowledge to a spirituall Temple; the third, to inflame this knowledge, to presse, and drive it to practice, turning it to reformation of life.[2]

Such a man probably would have found useful Baxter's *A Christian Directory*, designed to aid "the resolving of *practical Cases of Conscience*, and the reducing of Theoretical knowledge into *serious Christian Practice*, and promoting a *skilful facility* in the

---

[1] Richard Baxter, *The Practical Works of the Rev. Richard Baxter*, ed. William Orme, 23 vols. (London, 1830) XV, 16.

[2] F. E. Hutchinson, ed., *The Works of George Herbert* (Oxford: Clarendon Press, 1941), pp. 225, 255. All quotations of Herbert are from this edition and will be cited parenthetically in the text.

faithful exercise of universal obedience and Holiness of heart and life." [3]

Even more striking than Herbert's focus on the transformation of doctrine into virtuous living is his insistence on particularity. The country parson knows that "exactnesse lyes in particulars" (p. 275), and it comes as no surprise, as Arnold Stein observes, that he is a skillful casuist.[4] Herbert's praise of cases of conscience shows how closely he associates casuistry with precise observation and judgment of particular human actions:

> He greatly esteemes also of cases of conscience, wherein he is much versed. And indeed, herein is the greatest ability of a Parson to lead his people exactly in the wayes of Truth, so that they neither decline to the right hand, nor to the left. Neither let any think this a slight thing. For every one hath not digested, when it is a sin to take something for mony lent, or when not; when it is a fault to discover anothers fault, or when not; *when the affections of the soul in desiring and procuring increase of means, or honour, be a sin of covetousnes or ambition, and when not; when the appetites of the body in eating, drinking, sleep, and the pleasure that comes with sleep, be sins of gluttony, drunkenness, sloath, lust, and when not,* and so in many circumstances of actions. Now if a shepherd know not which grass will bane, or which not, how is he fit to be a shepherd? Wherefore the Parson hath throughly canvassed al the particulars of humane actions, at least all those which he observeth are most incident to his Parish.
>
> (P. 230)

Obviously Herbert agreed with William Perkins that *"Generall doctrine . . . is darke and obscure, and very hardly practised without the light of particular examples,"* and his list of cases of conscience suggests familiarity with Perkins's *The Whole Treatise of the Cases of Conscience,* which considers such questions as *"How farre a man may, with good conscience, proceede*

---

[3] Richard Baxter, *A Christian Directory: or a Summ of Practical Theology and Cases of Conscience* (London, 1673), sig. A2ᵛ. All quotations are from this edition and will be cited parenthetically in the text.

[4] Stein's brief but penetrating remarks linking Herbert's interest in cases of conscience with a general shift in the seventeenth century from speculative meditation to practical divinity and with the immediacy of experience in the lyrics of *The Temple* have been very valuable to me. Arnold Stein, *George Herbert's Lyrics* (Baltimore: The Johns Hopkins Press, 1968), pp. 23, 120.

in the desiring and seeking of Riches?" and *"How we may rightly use meates & drinkes . . . ?"* [5]

Herbert returns to these cases several times in *A Priest to the Temple.* Chapter 37, "Concerning detraction," explains the parson's resolution of the problem, "when it is a fault to discover anothers fault, or when not." Chapter 26 again stresses the difficulty of judging particular actions "because of the suddain passing from that which was just now lawfull, to that which is presently unlawfull, even in one continued action" (p. 264). The parson can lead his people through such perplexities because, having "exactly sifted the definitions of all vertues, and vices," he applies them to particular circumstances. In considering covetousness, for example, he lays the ground by defining the vice and explaining how it perverts divinely created order; then he illustrates this analysis with increasingly specific examples, concluding with the warning, "if a man hath wherewithall to buy a spade, and yet hee chuseth rather to use his neighbours, and wear out that, he is covetous." Although few people descend to such particularity, Herbert observes, it "yet ought to be done, since there is a Justice in the least things, and for the least there shall be a judgment" (pp. 264-265).

In poetry, Herbert's skill in observing "al the particulars of humane actions" in order to turn knowledge to the reformation of life is most obvious in "The Church-porch." Joseph Summers has noted that in the first section of *The Temple,* Herbert is a "subtle casuist, determining carefully the limits of rival moral claims," and Sheridan Blau has demonstrated in more detail that Herbert is undertaking just the kind of getting down to cases he advocates in *A Priest to the Temple.*[6] Stanzas 26 through 29, for example, try to define precisely the line between thrift and covetousness. Indeed, most of the particular actions evaluated have parallels in collections of cases of conscience. However, while Blau demonstrates that "The Church-porch" fulfills the casuistical purpose of giving moral advice through the casuistical

---

[5] William Perkins, *A Discourse of Conscience* and *The Whole Treatise of the Cases of Conscience,* in *The Workes of That Famous and Worthy Minister of Christ . . . Mr. William Perkins,* 3 vols. (London, 1612-1613). All references are to this edition and will be cited parenthetically in the text.

[6] Summers, *The Heirs of Donne and Jonson* (London: Chatto & Windus, 1970), p. 93; Blau, "The Poet as Casuist: Herbert's 'Church-Porch'," *Genre* 4 (1971): 142-152.

method of offering brief solutions to typical cases, his argument
that its structure and style can similarly be traced to the tradition
of casuistry is less convincing.[7] The concrete particularity and
calm, rational tone of "The Church-porch" ally it with casuistry
in the tradition of the plain style, but the succinctness and gnomic
point of Herbert's style probably owe more to the aphorism and
proverb than to the models of ingenious problem solving provided by casuistry.[8]

With their more intricate poetic logic, the poems of "The
Church," the long central section of *The Temple,* are less obviously but more deeply permeated with the casuistical habit of
mind. Throughout "The Church," Herbert draws on the moral
theology developed by such Protestant theologians as William
Perkins. In poems such as "Constancie" and "The Holdfast," he
presents fundamental casuistical principles about the relation
of divine law to human action in poetic forms that embody the
casuistical strategy of exemplary problem solving. Poems like
"The Windows" and "The Forerunners" not only exemplify
casuistical ideas and attitudes but employ casuistical methods to
present and resolve specific moral problems. Other poems, "Affliction (IV)" and "The Flower," for example, apply casuistical
methods to experiences of grief and doubt of salvation.

Although casuistry does not explain all of the complex and
varied forms of Herbert's creation, it provides a context that
reveals his characteristic concern with experiences of doubt and
his poetic strategies for achieving his equally characteristic tone
of calm assurance. Combining logical rigor with the concrete
particularity of individual experience, Herbert's lyrics embody
the careful, constant self-examination taught by the casuists. His

[7] Blau argues that the three-part structure suggested by Louis Martz—
individual conduct (stanzas 1-34), social behavior (stanzas 35-62), and religious
duties (stanzas 63-77)—significantly resembles William Perkins's divisions of
The Whole Treatise—Book I, man by himself, Book II, man in relation to
God, Book III, man in relation to other men. The similarity, however, is more
apparent than real. Although Perkins's Book II covers the topics of the last
third of "The Church-Porch" (tithing, behavior in church, the proper attitude
toward the preacher), his Book III includes the sorts of action Herbert surveys
in the rest of his poem. Book I considers questions about sin and salvation—
problems closer to Herbert's concerns in "The Church" than in "The Church-
porch." See Blau, "The Poet as Casuist," p. 144. See also Louis Martz, *The
Poetry of Meditation,* 2d ed. (New Haven: Yale University Press, 1962), p. 290.

[8] Margaret Bottrall suggests the influence of the proverb on "The Church-
porch" in *George Herbert* (London: John Murray, 1954), p. 59.

poems do not display the twentieth century's interest in the vagaries of the mind for their own sake, but, like the case of conscience, they move through problems, puzzles, and fine distinctions to conclusions that are models of spiritual peace.

PRACTICAL DIVINITY IN "THE CHURCH"

Most poems in "The Church" are less obviously and directly didactic than "The Church-porch." "Superliminare," the poem introducing "The Church," begins by suggesting a distinction between external, moral behavior and internal, mystical experience:

> Thou, whom the former precepts have
> Sprinkled and taught, how to behave
> Thy self in church; approach, and taste
> The churches mysticall repast.
>
> (Ll. 1-4)

A cursory reading of some of the most anthologized poems can even suggest explicit rejection of the casuist's emphasis on rational analysis and moral responsibility. In "Love (III)," for example, love triumphs over the guilt of the reluctant soul, whose self-judgment is apparently irrelevant to his participation in Love's banquet:

> let my shame
> Go where it doth deserve.
> And know you not, sayes Love, who bore the blame?
> My deare, then I will serve.
> You must sit down, sayes Love, and taste my meat:
> So I did sit and eat.
>
> (Ll. 13-18)

Similarly, divine power and love, not human reason, calm the wild rebellion of "The Collar."

But this is to oversimplify Herbert's stress on the emotional rather than the intellectual experience of devotion. He rejects the opposition of law and love, divine power and human responsibility. The speaker of "Love (III)" applies divine law to his own life, judges himself guilty and therefore not a "guest . . . worthy to be here" (l. 7). But Love's answer epitomizes the central paradox of Christian ethics: "Love said, You shall be he" (l. 8). The

187

speaker *will* be worthy, through God's grace, *because* he sees his guilt clearly. He can eat at the Lord's table because he wants only to serve. In "The Collar," only the disobedient man in his wildest rebellion contrasts joy and spontaneity with cold reason and narrow, restrictive law: "thy cold dispute/Of what is fit, and not" (ll. 20-21). The sense of loving and being loved at the end of the poem does not replace reason and obedience but reconciles the speaker to them.

Herbert makes no rigid distinction between spiritual and moral experience or between didactic and expressive poetry. While the structure of *The Temple* indicates a progression from the "precepts" of "The Church-porch" to the "mysticall repast" of "The Church" itself, the hierarchy implied is not the subordination of moral to arcane, mystical concerns. "The Dedication" to *The Temple* indicates an educative intention for the whole:

> *Turn their eyes hither, who shall make a gain:*
> *Theirs, who shall hurt themselves or me, refrain.*
>
> (Ll. 5-6)

Like most Renaissance poets, Herbert thinks of all poetry as didactic, and more than most, he attentively fits the lesson to the pupil. The audience presupposed for "The Church-porch" is the "sweet youth" (l. 1) who knows in a general way, as all people do, that good should be chosen and evil avoided, but who will learn most readily when the morally right can be presented as also the most prudent, when the good is also good taste. If the first stanza of "Superliminare" distinguishes learning "how to behave" from enjoying spiritual fulfillment, the second stanza complements this contrast with a subtler distinction:

> Avoid, Profanenesse; come not here:
> Nothing but holy, pure, and cleare,
> Or that which groneth to be so,
> May at his perill further go.
>
> (Ll. 5-8)

The fit audience stipulated for "The Church" is neither the worldling who needs to be persuaded that virtue pays nor the Christian who has mastered his obligations of obedience and is ready to go on to higher things. Rather, he is anyone who earnestly tries to do what is right in a sometimes bewildering world.

By pointing to the practical divinity that permeates *The Temple,* I am not trying to resurrect the image of a Herbert more notable for piety than poetry but rather to elucidate the poetry by describing the piety that is frequently its subject. Even for those who do not share his religious beliefs, the value of Herbert's poetry does not come solely from its formal elegance. The imaginative insights, discriminating intelligence, subtle craftsmanship, and superb control of tone and rhythm that we admire in Herbert are at least partially obscured unless we understand the terms in which he saw his art. Since Herbert's terms are Christian, we need to understand as precisely as possible the particular forms Christianity takes in his poems.

The same assumptions about the moral dimension of experience that underlie the practical advice of "The Church-porch" and prose casuistry inform "The Church." In "Christmas," Herbert presents allegorically the basic tenet that men are guided in all they do by God's will, revealed in His Word. Like Perkins, he places little trust in natural law. In "Nature," he confesses that, left to his own nature, he would be disobedient and self-destructive and prays to acquire "thy rev'rend Law and fear" (l. 14). In "Vanitie (I)," he refers to the "glorious law" God "Embosomes in us" (ll. 23-24), but his point is our perversity in ignoring it. And in spite of the centrality of the sacrament in the spiritual life pictured in "The Church," Herbert does not present the Church as an authoritative source of moral law. While the parallelism of Sanderson's "light innate, light inferred, and light acquired" suggests equivalence, for Herbert, as for Perkins and Ames, scripture is the single source of divine law. The clean, spare lines of "Discipline" describe Herbert's position:

> Not a word or look
> I affect to own,
>   But by book,
> And thy book alone.
>   (Ll. 9-12)

Nevertheless, he acknowledges that biblical interpretation and application to particular actions require all possible intelligence and learning. While "The H. Scriptures (I)" expresses awe in the Bible's rich applicability, "The H. Scriptures (II)" delights in the reader's complicated process of understanding. "Thy word is all, if we could spell," Herbert says in "The Flower" (l. 21), and draws on the multifaceted traditions of human learning to spell out God's presence everywhere.

"The Church" also endorses the efficacy of the conscience. Like William Ames, who defines conscience as "mans judgement of himselfe, according to the judgement of God of him," [9] Herbert says that, in spite of the ravages of "sin & passion," we can "prevent the last great day, / And judge our selves" ("Self-condemnation," ll. 19-20). In "The Storm," he describes the "strange force" of a "throbbing conscience" (ll. 9-10) to win forgiveness from a loving God. He shares too the casuists' emphasis on practical action. When he describes an ideally virtuous man, he presents this exemplary figure fulfilling his obligations to self, God, and others.

CONSTANCIE

Who is the honest man?
He that doth still and strongly good pursue,
To God, his neighbour, and himself most true:
Whom neither force nor fawning can
Unpinne, or wrench from giving all their due.
(Ll. 1-5)

He follows his own conscience regardless of the shifting winds of power and fashion:

Whose honestie is not
So loose or easie, that a ruffling winde
Can blow away, or glittering look it blinde:
Who rides his sure and even trot,
While the world now rides by, now lags behinde.
(Ll. 6-10)

He resolves his cases of conscience with calm, rational regard for duty and the demands of particular circumstances:

Who, when great trials come,
Nor seeks, nor shunnes them; but doth calmly stay,

[9] William Ames, *Conscience with the Power and Cases Thereof* (1639), Bk. I, p. 1.

Till he the thing and the example weigh:
    All being brought into a summe,
What place or person calls for, he doth pay.
(Ll. 11-15)

He is not a professional casuist skilled in untangling the snarls that sin ties in human lives, but he is thoughtful enough to be safe from fraud and self-deception and to exemplify his honesty in all the particular actions of his life:

        Whom none can work or wooe
    To use in any thing a trick or sleight;
    For above all things he abhorres deceit:
        His words and works and fashion too
    All of a piece, and all are cleare and straight.
(Ll. 16-20)

In "The Church," then, Herbert makes explicit the moral theology assumed in "The Church-porch": divine law, revealed in the Bible, defines human duty and demands total obedience. The mind is the join between God's law and human action, internalizing the law and applying it to specific situations. Still, while "The Church" and "The Church-porch" share this orthodox conception of moral law and action and a casuistical emphasis on intellectual effort and particular circumstances, they differ radically in form and substance. In *A Priest to the Temple,* Herbert's discussion of the relationship between the priest's private life and his teaching illuminates the relation of "The Church-porch" to "The Church." In the chapter called "The Parson's Library," instead of providing the expected list of recommended reading, Herbert argues that the parson's own life is his richest source of material. First he overcomes his own doubts and temptations; then he uses his experiences as models to help others. Particularly useful are those experiences of doubt or cases of conscience he has successfully resolved:

This Instruction and comfort the Parson getting for himself,
when he tels it to others, becomes a Sermon. The like he doth
in other Christian vertues, as of Faith, and Love, and the
Cases of Conscience belonging thereto.   (P. 279)

A similar relationship between private experience and instruc-

191

tion is implicit in *The Temple.* For the speaker, the struggles, doubts, and joys of "The Church" are preparation for the calm, self-assured public voice of "The Church-porch." This chronological progression is reversed for the reader. For him, "The Church-porch," with its clear, succinct, authoritative directives, is prologue to the more introspective, and frequently more difficult, lyrics of "The Church." The movement is not from moral to spiritual experience but from precepts or directions toward action to action itself—the mysterious particularity of actual experience. In the first section of *The Temple,* Herbert, in his role as pastor, tells others what they ought to do. In "The Church," he presents internal action in which the speaking voice is intimately involved in the moral dilemmas that it examines.

Even "Constancie," an idealized portrait of obedience, appears as part of the speaker's personal struggle when it is read in the context of "Frailtie," the preceding poem. In "Frailtie," the speaker fears his weakness. Withdrawn in meditation, he knows the ephemeral joys of the world for what they are:

> Lord, in my silence how do I despise
> What upon trust
> Is styled *honour, riches,* or *fair eyes;*
> But is *fair dust!*
> I surname them *guilded clay,*
> *Deare earth, fine grasse* or *hay;*
> In all, I think my foot doth ever tread
> Upon their head.
>
> (Ll. 1-8)

But he also knows his susceptibility when actually tempted:

> But when I view abroad both Regiments;
> The worlds, and thine:
> Thine clad with simplenesse, and sad events;
> The other fine,
> Full of glorie and gay weeds,
> Brave language, braver deeds:
> That which was dust before, doth quickly rise,
> And prick mine eyes.
>
> (Ll. 9-16)

The poem ends on a note of dread in spite of God's love and the speaker's good intentions:

> O brook not this, lest if what even now
> My foot did tread,
> Affront those joyes, wherewith thou didst endow
> And long since wed
> My poore soul, ev'n sick of love:
> It may a Babel prove
> Commodious to conquer heav'n and thee
> Planted in me.
>
> (Ll. 17-24)

Read after this confession of frailty, "Constancie" appears as an effort to solve a specific problem. Just as George Herbert, when assuming his duties as pastor of Bemerton, described "the Form and Character of a true Pastour" as "a Mark to aim at" (p. 224), so the speaker in "The Church," when suffering anxiety and self-doubt, constructs the character of "the honest man" as "the Mark-man, safe and sure." By posing the question, "Who is the honest man?" Herbert tries to show how ethical doctrine shapes a man's life. Translating abstract virtue into human form reveals that it is not an isolated quality or act but rather habitual action, a way of life. The question, "Who is the honest man?" implies the question, "How can I persevere in virtue?" [10] In this context, the details of the portrait emerge as conscious responses to particular difficulties.

When Herbert advises constancy in "The Church-porch," he extols it as sturdy integrity and self-reliance that protects one from self-destructive whims:

> When thou dost purpose ought within thy power,
> Be sure to doe it, though it be but small:
> Constancie knits the bones, and makes us stowre,
> When wanton pleasures becken us to thrall.
> Who breaks his own bond, forfeiteth himself:
> What nature made a ship, he makes a shelf.
>
> (Ll. 115-120)

In the poem "Constancie," the virtue is not a means of avoiding degradation and ruin but of constructively participating in the

---

[10] Cf. William Ames's questions under the heading "Constancy": *"Wherein doth perseverance, or constancy of vertue consist?"*; *"Which are the evills which are opposed to this Constancy?"*; *"How are men stirred up to constancy?"* Bk. III, pp. 73-74.

world. Aware that the test of virtue comes not when he contemplates the world "in my silence" but when he is "abroad," the speaker constructs a model of virtue surviving the temptations and duplicity of the world without self-protective withdrawal. In the stanzas already quoted, key words describing the honest man's life suggest active involvement: "pursue," "giving," "rides," "pay," "words and work and fashion." In the remaining stanzas, the emphasis on simultaneous independence and engagement is yet stronger:

> Who never melts or thaws
> At close tentations: when the day is done,
> His goodnesse sets not, but in dark can runne:
> The sunne to others writeth laws,
> And is their vertue; Vertue is his Sunne.
>
> Who, when he is to treat
> With sick folks, women, those whom passions sway,
> Allows for that, and keeps his constant way:
> Whom others faults do not defeat;
> But though men fail him, yet his part doth play.
>
> Whom nothing can procure,
> When the wide world runnes bias from his will,
> To writhe his limbes, and share, not mend the ill.
> This is the Mark-man, safe and sure,
> Who still is right, and prayes to be so still.
>
> (Ll. 21-35)

In "The Church-porch," inconstancy is self-destructive and perverse. In "The Church," Herbert's emphasis shifts from the common sense of perseverance to the considerable obstacles it must overcome: the "close tentations," the need to deal with "those whom passions sway," the times when "men fail him" and when "the wide world runnes bias from his will." In spite of pressures and temptations to compromise with the crooked world, the virtuous man plays his part honestly, a steady and unchanging "Mark-man" for others because he recognizes his weakness and the source of his strength.

I have discussed "Constancie" in some detail as a clear and relatively simple illustration of Herbert's practice in "The Church." Instead of presenting wisdom distilled from reflection and experience in lively, persuasive form as "The Church-porch" does, "The Church" presents a mind in the process of resolving the problematical. "Constancie" is no less didactic than "The Church-porch," but it teaches by exemplary problem solving rather than by direct prescription. The context of doubt and dread provided by "Frailtie," the stress on conditions making constancy difficult, and the deliberate choice of mundane involvement instead of detachment make us see the concept of constancy as a focal point of problems and questions rather than as a self-evident duty. Most poems in "The Church" are even more clearly the speaker's attempts, more or less successful, to work out personal problems. Instead of describing an ideal figure, Herbert more often creates a speaker essentially like the reader invited to enter "The Church"—someone struggling to be "holy, pure, and cleare" in a fallen world. These are the poems Herbert could describe as *"a picture of the many spiritual Conflicts that have past betwixt God and my Soul, before I could subject mine to the will of* Jesus my Master." He sent these poems to his friend Nicholas Ferrar with the proviso that they should be made public only if they could *"turn to the advantage of any dejected poor Soul."* [11] By presenting his own struggles as models for others, Herbert resembles casuists who teach the way to resolve moral doubts through model cases of conscience. His focus on problems and methods of resolving them makes the traditions of casuistry more pertinent to the poems of "The Church" than to the moral advice of "The Church-porch."

Not every poem in "The Church" portrays an overt spiritual conflict, but the process of resolving the problematical characterizes "The Church" as a whole. Sometimes, as in "The Collar," the problems are actual conflicts between self-will and God, but often they are subtle struggles within the self to understand and purify its relation to God. For this reason, although Herbert's portrayal of moral decision making is consistent throughout *The Temple,* his use of casuistical terms and categories in "The Church" is both more immediate and more oblique than his practice in "The Church-porch." Several poems explicitly examine such concepts as sin, virtue, law, and conscience, but instead of giving a straightforward exposition of moral theology, Herbert presents the process of analyzing the concepts in which man conceives of his moral life.

[11] Izaak Walton, "The Life of Mr. George Herbert," in *Lives,* The World's Classics (London: Oxford University Press, 1927), p. 314.

Often such concepts are the thematic center of a group of interrelated and complementary poems. "The Method" and "Divinitie," for example, put the case for practical divinity from opposite points of view. In "The Method," the speaker argues with painstaking logic the need for moral reflection and self-judgment: since the God of power and love could and would grant our prayers unless "there is some rub, some discontent," human dissatisfaction indicates human fault. Therefore, he advises examining the conscience in order to discover knowledge of past actions and of divine law:

> Go search this thing,
> Tumble thy breast, and turn thy book.
> If thou hadst lost a glove or ring,
>   Wouldst thou not look?
>   (Ll. 9-12)

Self-examination reveals previously overlooked sins of omission and commission—carelessness at prayers, things done in spite of doubt—and the speaker condemns the illogicality of expecting God to hear the prayer of a man who does not listen to Him or his own conscience. Inevitably, then, the proper response to unhappiness is moral analysis and repentance.

As though to qualify the laborious logicality of "The Method," the next poem, "Divinitie," mocks an overly intellectualized religion that attempts to "cut and carve" divinity with "the edge of wit" while "faith lies by" (ll. 7-8). Jeremy Taylor's advice that truth is easy but error intricate and hard and the taper of simplicity a better guide than the false fire of art might have been inspired by Herbert's ridicule of those who obscure the saving truth God has revealed clearly: [12]

> But all the doctrine, which he taught and gave,
>   Was cleare as heav'n, from whence it came.
> At least those beams of truth, which onely save,
>   Surpasse in brightnesse any flame.
>
> *Love God, and love your neighbour. Watch and pray.*
>   *Do as ye would be done unto.*
> O dark instructions; ev'n as dark as day!
>   Who can these Gordian knots undo?
>   (Ll. 13-20)

[12] The Taylor passage was previously quoted on p. 33.

"Obedience" and "Conscience" also take contrasting but complementary approaches to moral duty. "Obedience" uses legal language to express the thorough exactitude of the speaker's submission to God. The poem is the "speciall Deed" (l. 10) by which he conveys to God his heart and "all it hath" (l. 8). His model is Christ's sacrifice, a gift without hidden clauses or reservations:

> Besides, thy death and bloud
> Show'd a strange love to all our good:
> Thy sorrows were in earnest; no faint proffer,
> Or superficiall offer
> Of what we might not take, or be withstood.
> (Ll. 26-30)

In drawing up his deed of conveyance, he tries to cover every loophole, preventing defections and self-deceptions that might subsequently lead him to find exceptions to total submission. He even anticipates and rejects the pride implicit in his choice of metaphor:

> Wherefore I all forgo:
> To one word onely I say, No:
> Where in the Deed there was an intimation
> Of a gift or donation,
> Lord, let it now by way of purchase go.
> (Ll. 31-35)

Although he sees pleasure in the world as a temptation to be prevented, he concludes with hope of being effective in the world, leading others to God through his poem of self-scrutiny and renunciation:

> How happie were my part,
> If some kinde man would thrust his heart
> Into these lines; till in heav'ns Court of Rolls
> They were by winged souls
> Entred for both, farre above their desert!
> (Ll. 41-45)

In contrast, "Conscience" diagnoses the incessant fear of sin as itself a temptation, insidiously casting doubt on the worth of God's creation and His creature:

197

Peace pratler, do not lowre:
Not a fair look, but thou dost call it foul:
Not a sweet dish, but thou dost call it sowre:
Musick to thee doth howl.
By listning to thy chatting fears
I have both lost mine eyes and eares.

(Ll. 1-6)

The speaker can recover health, silencing the scrupulous conscience's nagging voice, not by careful, precise thought, but by participating in the sacrament:

And the receit shall be
My Saviours bloud: when ever at his board
I do but taste it, straight it cleanseth me,
And leaves thee not a word;

(Ll. 13-16)

The pleasures of the world and his human faculties are innocent, but he conquers neurotic doubt not through any overt deed or his own thoughts working in "harmonious peace" (l. 8), but through total and triumphant reliance on the mysteries of faith:

Yet if thou talkest still,
Besides my physick, know there's some for thee:
Some wood and nails to make a staffe or bill
For those that trouble me:
The bloudie crosse of my deare Lord
Is both my physick and my sword.[13]

(Ll. 19-24)

All of these poems are consistent doctrinally: each speaker accepts the duty to obey God while acknowledging that salvation is created by Christ's sacrifice, not earned by human merit. But Herbert presents lived experience, not doctrine, and the implications of Christ's death and the concept of moral obligation may be experienced in radically different ways. Herbert knew the

---

[13] Although Helen Vendler thinks the violent images of this last stanza weaken the poem, to a casuist, violence is an appropriate response to persistent scruples. Cf. Ames: "Many scruples when they cannot well be taken away by some *contrary reason*, ought to be laid downe as it were by *violence*, refusing to thinke or consider of them" (Bk. I, p. 20). See Helen Vendler, *The Poetry of George Herbert* (Cambridge, Mass.: Harvard University Press, 1975), pp. 236-238.

need for moral intelligence and self-knowledge and the dangers of rigid legalistic morality. He pictures conflicts between a paralyzing sense of sin and a liberating sense of love as well as between the tempting license of the world and the discipline of conscience. Within the body of "The Church," each poem completes and qualifies the partial truths of the others.

A problem that recurs frequently in Herbert's explorations of the ideas defining moral life is the inevitability of failure. The desire to obey God appears sometimes as agonizing guilt and sometimes as joyous love, but always Herbert recognizes that his obedience is imperfect. In "H. Baptisme (II)," his speaker prays to be completely malleable to God's will:

> O let me still
> Write thee great God, and me a childe:
> Let me be soft and supple to thy will,
> Small to my self, to others milde,
> Behither ill.

> (Ll. 6-10)

But significantly this nostalgic yearning for childlike innocence is followed by recognition of the inevitability of sin. After "H. Baptisme (II)" comes "Nature" ("Full of rebellion, I would die") and "Sinne (I)," a Shakespearean sonnet that for twelve lines catalogues all the warnings and enticements that guide people to virtue and in a final couplet acknowledges their ineffectuality against sin.

Herbert's emphasis on guilt, of course, is doctrinal as well as personal. According to Protestant theology, fallen humanity is sinful: people are saved by God's love, not their own righteousness. As Joseph Summers and others have shown, the contrast between condemnation under the law and freedom through Christ is a major theme in Herbert.[14] "Judgement," for example,

14 Joseph Summers, *George Herbert: His Religion and Art* (Cambridge, Mass.: Harvard University Press, 1968), pp. 57-64; William Halewood, *The Poetry of Grace: Reformation Themes and Structures in English Seventeenth-Century Poetry* (New Haven: Yale University Press, 1970), p. 95; Patrick Grant, *The Transformation of Sin: Studies in Donne, Herbert, Vaughan, and Traherne* (Montreal and London: McGill-Queen's University Press, 1974), pp. 123-125; Rosemond Tuve, *A Reading of George Herbert* (Chicago: University of Chicago Press, 1952), p. 123; Barbara Kiefer Lewalski, *Protestant Poetics and the Seventeenth-Century Religious Lyric* (Princeton: Princeton University Press, 1979), p. 286.

builds on the insufficiency of human merit. The first stanza imagines the dreadful time of reckoning:

> Almightie Judge, how shall poore wretches brook
>> Thy dreadfull look,
> Able a heart of iron to appall,
>> When thou shalt call
> For ev'ry mans peculiar book?
>> (Ll. 1-5)

The second stanza poses the possibility of perfect obedience with noncommittal irony:

> What others mean to do, I know not well:
>> Yet I heare tell,
> That some will turn thee to some leaves therein
>> So void of sinne,
> That they in merit shall excell.
>> (Ll. 6-10)

Herbert's speaker places his hope in Christ's atonement:

> But I resolve, when thou shalt call for mine,
>> That to decline,
> And thrust a Testament into thy hand:
>> Let that be scann'd.
> There thou shalt finde my faults are thine.
>> (Ll. 11-15)

The dread and irony of the first two stanzas are as necessary to Herbert's conception of judgment as the confidence of the last stanza. The speaker transcends fear and the folly of relying on human merit through his belief in justification by faith alone, but that doctrine does not make moral law irrelevant. As William Perkins explains, understanding the condemnation of the law is a step toward freedom from the law's curse:

> All justiciarie people, and persons that looke to bee saved and justified before God by the law, and the workes of the lawe, either in whole, or in part, are cast out of the church of God, and have no part in the kingdome of heaven. . . . We must learne to see, feele, acknowledge, and bewaile this bondage in ourselves. Deliverance belongs only to such captives, as know themselves to be captives . . . and labour

under this bondage. . . . To feele this bondage, is a step
out of it: and not to feele it, is to be plunged into it.

(II, 305-306)

Only through understanding his need for redemption through
Christ can the believer be regenerated in faith. Bondage to the
law under penalty of death then becomes voluntary service under-
taken out of love and gratitude.

The ethical implication of this conception of the human condition, stressed by the casuists and by Herbert, is not that man is
free to be a law to himself but that God's law becomes part of
the self. Indeed, "The Church" begins with a sequence of poems
establishing this relationship between God's law and human
action. "The Altar," the first poem after the introductory "Superliminare," introduces the idea of the internalization of the law
in the recurrent image of God forming the resistant human
heart:

> A Heart alone
> Is such a stone,
> As nothing but
> Thy pow'r doth cut.
> (Ll. 5-8)

In the second poem, "The Sacrifice," Christ describes the crucifixion, which contains "All that salvation" (l. 226) that men resist,
and the next three poems are human responses to the passion.
First, in "The Thanksgiving" the speaker tries to find an adequate
response in good works (giving alms, building a chapel, writing
poems) but recognizes the futility of merely human efforts. In
"The Reprisall," he admits "My sinnes deserve the condemnation" (l. 4) but finds consolation in the hope that he can share
in Christ's victory over sin:

> Yet by confession will I come
> Into thy conquest: though I can do nought
> Against thee, in thee I will overcome
> The man, who once against thee fought.
> (Ll. 13-16)

"The Agonie" develops the idea that only through imaginative
understanding of the passion can people understand the choices
open to them: sin and love.

201

The next four poems show that people can choose love only through the reforming of their hearts by God. "The Sinner" concludes with the image of God first carving His law in stone for Moses and then carving His image in the stony heart of man. "Good Friday," by transforming the image of carving into one of writing in blood, stresses the suffering and acknowledgment of guilt that this imprinting involves:

> Since bloud is fittest, Lord, to write
> Thy sorrows in, and bloudie fight;
> My heart hath store, write there, where in
> One box doth lie both ink and sinne:
>
>   (Ll. 21-24)

"Redemption" allegorizes the crucifixion as the granting of a new, more lenient contract to man. "Sepulchre" pulls together these ideas of sin, suffering, law, and love in a succinct statement of man's triumph over sin and death through internalization of God's will:

> And so of old the Law by heav'nly art
> Was writ in stone; so thou, which also art
> The letter of the word, find'st no fit heart
>   To hold thee.
> Yet do we still persist as we began,
> And so should perish, but that nothing can,
> Though it be cold, hard, foul, from loving man
>   Withhold thee.
>
>   (Ll. 17-24)

The ambiguity of the last three lines economically identifies the law with love and transforms sinful man, through internalization of the Word, into loving man. The partial stop at the end of line 22 ("but that nothing can,") causes us to read initially a reference to a primary law of nature: because none of God's creation can be utterly annihilated, sinful men will not destroy themselves completely but will suffer eternally. When the sentence continues, we have to revise our first reading: we should perish except that nothing, however sinful, can restrain an all-loving God from bestowing love on man. Simultaneously, "loving" functions as a participle as well as a gerund: nothing can keep

God away from a man who loves Him.[15] None of these meanings is rejected. The God of wrath is the God of love; man is sinful by nature, and he is also the son of God, loved and loving.

The first group of poems in "The Church" in which Herbert explores the internalization of divine law through Christ culminates in the Easter hymn, "I Got me flowers to straw thy way." Here the Christian fulfills his obligation to God in voluntary, self-fulfilling, and joyous song:

> I Got me flowers to straw thy way;
> I got me boughs off many a tree:
> But thou wast up by break of day,
> And brought'st thy sweets along with thee.
>
> (Ll. 19-22)

He praises divine, in contrast to human or physical, power, but man and God act together in the harmony of love. Indeed, this is the first poem in "The Church" that does not show human action as inadequate or perverse. Herbert's speaker does not presume to act without God's help but neither does he condemn his own actions as inevitably futile and sinful. Instead, he praises God, believing that he can rise with Christ to a life of value and justice:

> Rise heart; thy Lord is risen. Sing his praise
>   Without delayes,
> Who takes thee by the hand, that thou likewise
>   With him mayst rise:
> That, as his death calcined thee to dust,
> His life may make thee gold, and much more, just.
>
> (Ll. 1-6)

As Coburn Freer has noted, the poem insists on the difficulty of singing, but Herbert does not suggest that difficulty invalidates the enterprise.[16] Rather, the effort and tension of the singer's struggle (to find his part, to learn what key to play in) is the human analogue to the stretched sinews of the crucified Christ:

[15] Stanley Fish discusses the ambiguity of "loving" in *Self-Consuming Artifacts: The Experience of Seventeenth-Century Literature* (Berkeley and Los Angeles: University of California Press, 1972), pp. 172-173.

[16] Coburn Freer, *Music for a King: George Herbert's Style and the Metrical Psalms* (Baltimore: The Johns Hopkins Press, 1972), p. 138.

Awake, my lute, and struggle for thy part
　　　　　　With all thy art.
The crosse taught all wood to resound his name,
　　　　　　Who bore the same.
His stretched sinews taught all strings, what key
Is best to celebrate this most high day.
　　　　　　　　　　　　(Ll. 7-12)

While "Easter" relates to other poems where Herbert asserts that genuine feeling is more important than technical proficiency, Freer goes too far, I believe, when he says that the poem's "basic assertion" is that "the quality of a hymn is of less importance than its intent." [17] The speaker of "Easter" assumes that a pious intention cannot excuse a bad performance. He knows that men need divine mercy for all their imperfections, but he also urges using "all thy art" for major accomplishment. Man must struggle to create harmony out of the recalcitrant stuff of actuality. He can do nothing without God, but, in Herbert's figure, God is one of three: the heart and lute also have their parts to play.

Consort both heart and lute, and twist a song
　　　　　　Pleasant and long:
Or, since all musick is but three parts vied
　　　　　　And multiplied,
O let thy blessed Spirit bear a part,
And make up our defects with his sweet art.
　　　　　　　　　　　　(Ll. 13-18)

Herbert's combination of a high ethical standard with the doctrine of justification by faith alone often puzzles modern readers because of its contradictory emphases on strenuous moral effort and on the repudiation of human merit. Herbert resolves the paradox much as Perkins does. Perkins believed that it is "erroneous . . . that the promise of salvation depends upon the condition of our workes" (I, 545), but that man is not absolved of moral responsibility and is not merely the passive object of God's election:

I grant indeed, that to the promise [of salvation] there is annexed a condition of faith . . . and withall, repentance with the fruits thereof, are on our part required . . . as they

---

[17] Ibid., p. 138.

are necessary consequents of faith, and the signes and docu-
ments therof.   (I, 545)

Herbert is equally insistent that scripture promises salvation to
the children of God and that man is morally responsible for his
actions. In his poems, man's only hope is Christ, not his own
flawed actions, but man must cooperate with God. Stanley Fish's
influential reading of Herbert suffers by neglecting the reciprocal
basis of the man/God relationship worked out in the poems. His
analysis of "The Holdfast," for example, demonstrates beautifully
the rhetorical strategies by which Herbert's speaker learns and
teaches humility, but his conclusion that the lesson learned is
passivity and self-abnegation falsifies the peace and fulfillment
that the speaker achieves.[18]

As Fish shows, "The Holdfast" strips the speaker of his preten-
sions to self-sufficiency and ends with recognition of Christ's
power:

THE HOLDFAST

> I Threatned to observe the strict decree
>> Of my deare God with all my power & might.
>> But I was told by one, it could not be;
> Yet I might trust in God to be my light.
> Then will I trust, said I, in him alone.
>> Nay, ev'n to trust in him, was also his:
>> We must confesse that nothing is our own.
> Then I confesse that he my succour is:
> But to have nought is ours, not to confesse
>> That we have nought. I stood amaz'd at this,
>> Much troubled, till I heard a friend expresse,
> That all things were more ours by being his.
>> What Adam had, and forfeited for all,
>> Christ keepeth now, who cannot fail or fall.

Exploring the underlying question, "What can I do to be saved?"
the sonnet progresses by considering and rejecting answers that
allow man cause for self-satisfaction. The speaker is "Much
troubled" because discovering that God is the real source of his
every action destroys his sense of personal worth. But the poem

---

[18] Fish, *Self-Consuming Artifacts,* pp. 174-176.

does not culminate, as Fish suggests, in the speaker's humiliating realization that he can do nothing, that "the proper response to the dilemma . . . [is] not action, mental or physical, but humility and self-abnegation." [19] The speaker discovers his utter inability to do any good action in line nine. The sestet does not address his pride but rather his perplexity at being left with nothing to do. In the last three lines, the wisdom of "a friend" releases him from this bewildered passivity.

Perkins again provides a helpful gloss on Herbert's paradox: in one sense the Christian must give up all independence.

> He . . . must not thinke his owne thoughts, speake his owne words, nor doe his owne deeds; but he must think, speake, and doe that which Christ would have him.
>
> (III, 324)

But this subordination of self does not imply passivity:

> There is no vertue or gift of God in us, without our wils: and in every good act, Gods grace, & mans will, concurre: Gods grace, as the principall cause; mans will renewed, as the instrument of God. And therefore in all good things, industrie, and labour, and invocation on our parts is required.
>
> (I, 738)

Similarly, the speaker in "The Holdfast" learns that he cannot think his own thoughts; without God he cannot even understand his own unworthiness. But he is also disabused of the troubled sense of losing initiative and direction. After learning that all actions are ultimately God's, he also learns "That all things were more ours by being his" (1. 12). Since Adam lost for man the possibility of true action, Christ has redeemed and restored the ability to act significantly through Him. The speaker can and must do those actions he committed himself to in the first eight lines: obey God's law in a spirit of love, trust in God, confess his reliance on God. But he must do them, not with pride in his own merit, but with full awareness that Christ makes all possible.

---

[19] Ibid., p. 175. Sometimes Fish's formulations of the man/God relationship are closer to mine, suggesting self-fulfillment as well as humiliation. For example, on the conclusion of "The Crosse," he writes, "The words of Christ . . . are simultaneously and by right the words of those who accept Him as their Savior. . . . the figure before the cross *becomes* the figure on the cross and finds himself by totally losing himself" (p. 188).

He must let go of his pride but hold fast to his God, and, then because Christ cannot fail or fall, neither will he.

Herbert's understanding of human action is, then, essentially the same as the casuists'. The Christian dispensation binds man to a more, not less, perfect moral standard. God reveals His will and grants the grace that enables people to choose good; they either obey or rebel. This reciprocal relationship controls the fundamental unity and striking variety of "The Church." The poems all explore the intercourse of man and God, but this relationship includes all human life. Everything that happens, both afflictions and blessings, comes from God; everything people do, think, feel, and write expresses their response to Him.

CASES OF CONSCIENCE IN "THE CHURCH"

Reading "The Church" from the perspective of the casuistical tradition does not suggest radically new interpretations of the poems, but it does help to focus attention on the distinctive quality and strength of Herbert's religious lyrics. The poems are acts of obedience and love offered to God in humble gratitude; they are also, like William Perkins's casuistry, "paradigms of Christian response" offered as a means "of releeving and rectifying" the troubled consciences of his readers.[20] The poems I have been considering explore the personal implications of Christian doctrine in ways similar to contemporary Protestant casuistry. The moral theology they draw on is not exclusive to casuistry, but the yoking of knowledge of self with knowledge of God, the logically intricate structure, and the calm, rational tone of the case of conscience constitute a paradigm that informs these poems in which an individual consciousness struggles to understand its relationship with its Creator. Other poems in "The Church" show the influence of casuistry even more clearly by presenting and resolving practical moral problems. Herbert's speaker experiences doubts about what he ought to do as Christian, as preacher, and as poet. Sometimes he applies casuistical procedures clearly and directly; sometimes he radically trans-

[20] These phrases are applied to Perkins's casuistry by Ian Breward (see *The Works of William Perkins,* The Courtenay Library of Reformation Classics [Appleford, Eng.: The Sutton Courtenay Press, 1970], p. 66) and Thomas Pickering (see his dedication to Perkins's *The Whole Treatise of the Cases of Conscience*).

forms casuistical methods for resolving moral doubt. In all these poetic cases of conscience, intellectual activity is subordinate to faith and gratitude to a loving God, but it is the process of inquiry that enables the speaker to understand that relationship.

"To all Angels and Saints" is a relatively straightforward treatment of a casuistical problem, the lawfulness of invoking and praying to the saints. The poem begins by suggesting moral doubt about a particular course of action. The speaker does not direct prayers to the saints and is aware that his behavior may be interpreted as showing disrespect or even malice and envy for those God has glorified. He answers these anticipated objections by examining his conscience and testifying to the innocence of his motives:

> Not out of envie or maliciousnesse
> Do I forbear to crave your speciall aid:
>   I would addresse
> My vows to thee most gladly, Blessed Maid,
> And Mother of my God, in my distresse.
>   (Ll. 6-10)

He feels no resentment but rather a longing to find comfort in those closest to God; in particular, he would gladly seek the intercession of the Virgin:

> Thou art the holy mine, whence came the gold,
> The great restorative for all decay
>   In young and old;
> Thou art the cabinet where the jewell lay:
> Chiefly to thee would I my soul unfold:
>   (Ll. 11-15)

This self-analysis shows him that his love for the Virgin results from her relationship to Christ. She is the mine, the cabinet, deriving here value from the real jewel, her Son.

This perception leads, then, to his major argument: man must act in accordance with the revealed will of God.

> But now, alas, I dare not; for our King,
> Whom we do all joyntly adore and praise,
>   Bids no such thing:
> And where his pleasure no injunction layes,
> ('Tis your own case) ye never move a wing.
>   (Ll. 16-20)

Herbert again argues from Perkins's position:

> That which is done without good direction of Gods word,
> is a flat sinne . . . hence it appeares that all things devised
> by man for the worship of God, are flat sinnes; because
> conscience cannot say of them that they please God.   (I, 537)

This proposition not only clinches Herbert's defence but requires a new formulation of the problem. The question becomes not whether refraining from prayers is sinful but whether such praying is even lawful. That is, the first fifteen lines attack the minor premise of this implicit syllogism:

> Disrespect for holiness is sinful.
> Refusal to pray to the saints shows such disrespect.
> Refusal to pray to the saints is sinful.

In the second half of the poem, the evidence that God has not commanded such prayers reveals that the syllogism should be:

> All worship not commanded by God is sinful.
> Praying to the saints is not commanded by God.
> Praying to the saints is sinful.

As the speaker reasons himself into a clearer understanding of the moral issues involved, the action that initially appears as a duty neglected becomes a temptation resisted. The new moral perspective reveals misleading inaccuracies in the language he used to formulate the problem so that without relinquishing the traditional metaphors he is able to use them more precisely and to better purpose.

In the first half of the poem, the speaker demonstrates his veneration for all angels and saints by insisting on their freedom and power; in contrast to men, they are kings not subjected to God's wrath or the rigor of the law:

> OH glorious spirits, who after all your bands
> See the smooth face of God without a frown
>   Or strict commands;
> Where ev'ry one is king, and hath his crown,
> If not upon his head, yet in his hands:
>   (Ll. 1-5)

This contrast is still evident in the second half of the poem. Angels and saints are courted by men (l. 26), and men are controlled by their fear of God's law and wrath: "I dare not" (l. 16); "we dare not" (l. 24). But this contrast is relatively insignificant within the larger contrast between God and His creatures. The immediate case of conscience is resolved when the speaker realizes that his case is essentially that of the angels. Men and angels "all joyntly adore and praise." [21] All God's creatures are bound to serve Him according to His will: "('Tis your own case) ye never move a wing." Men may look toward heaven with envy or humble longing, but the condition aspired to is more immediate perception and implementation of God's will, not unlimited power or autonomy:

> All worship is prerogative, and a flower
> Of his rich crown, from whom lyes no appeal
> > At the last houre:
> Therefore we dare not from his garland steal,
> To make a posie for inferiour power.
>
> > > > (Ll. 21-25)

In heaven everyone is king and has his crown, but there, as here, all worship belongs to the King of kings. The poem concludes not with emphasis on the sin of those who disagree with this analysis of the question but with casuistical acknowledgement of differences and insistence on the certainty possible to the individual conscience:

> Although then others court you, if ye know
> What's done on earth, we shall not fare the worse,
> > Who do not so:
> Since we are ever ready to disburse,
> If any one our Masters hand can show.
>
> > > > (Ll. 26-30)

"To all Angels and Saints" is not among Herbert's most dramatic and moving poems, but its transformation of awe, apologetic self-doubt, and fear into serene confidence has a quiet power. Herbert did not learn from Protestant casuists the subtlety and tact with which he subordinates the crowned saints to "our King" and "his rich crown," but he probably did learn through the study and practice of casuistry to examine a particular con-

---

[21] See Rev. 22:8-9: "I fell down to worship before the feet of the angel which shewed me these things. Then saith he unto me, See thou do it not; for I am thy fellow servant."

troversial action so that doubt and fear yield to calm assurance. The central irony of the poem—that insistence on man's fearful subjection to God's strict commands produces the freedom of personal certainty—is implicit in the casuistical paradigm.

Like "To all Angels and Saints," "Lent" treats a question of religious observance, but it lacks the movement from doubt to certainty. Although the opening, "Welcome deare feast of Lent" (l. 1), suggests a lyric celebration, the poem immediately becomes a reasoned defense of the Lenten fast. The first two stanzas announce the speaker's position in the controversy and the principles on which such cases should be resolved. Scripture is the ultimate authority for religious duty, he argues, and the Church defines the form these duties take. When in doubt, men should assume a duty rather than evade it and should suspect themselves, rather than the Church, of causing scandal. The rest of the poem supports this basic argument by describing the physical and spiritual benefits of fasting and by answering objections. The last stanza warns against relying on penitential rituals for automatic spiritual improvement. The Lenten fast becomes a feast for the soul when one shares physical and spiritual nourishment in acts of Christian charity:

> Yet Lord instruct us to improve our fast
> By starving sinne and taking such repast
> As may our faults controll:
> That ev'ry man may revell at his doore,
> Not in his parlour; banquetting the poore,
> And among those his soul.
> (Ll. 43-48)

Structurally, then, "Lent," like "To all Angels and Saints," demonstrates the casuistical paradigm of analyzing a controversial action by clarifying the moral principles involved, anticipating objections, and providing specific directions to moral action. But it is a less successful poem because it does not make real the doubts it would overcome. The speaker anticipates and counters objections only in the vaguest terms:

> Neither ought other mens abuse of Lent
> Spoil the good use; lest by that argument
> We forfeit all our Creed.
> (Ll. 28-30)

211

He does not defend himself against imputed or potential moral dangers but simply diagnoses the moral failure of anyone who disagrees:

> who loves not thee,
>> He loves not Temperance, or Authoritie,
>>> But is composed of passion.
>>>> (Ll. 1-3)

Failing to establish actual doubt, "Lent" creates no tension or uncertainty to relax in the discovery of certainty, and the defence of Lent seems an exercise in conventional piety.

Herbert's most successful poetic cases of conscience are those in which his personal doubt seems strongest. For example, "The Windows," where Herbert grapples with doubts about his profession as preacher, opens with an anguished cry of doubt, at once universal and personal:

> Lord, how can man preach thy eternall word?
>> He is a brittle crazie glasse:
>>> (Ll. 1-2)

The remainder of the stanza is ambiguous, both answering and complicating the question of how man can presume to speak for God:

> Yet in thy temple thou dost him afford
>> This glorious and transcendent place,
>> To be a window, through thy grace.
>>> (Ll. 3-5)

In one sense, the fact that the preacher acts not through his own merit but through God's authority and grace counters the speaker's sense of unworthiness. It is irrelevant that man is weak and has no truth in him, "a brittle crazie glasse," for the preacher speaks God's word, not his own. By God's grace he is a transparent medium through which grace may pass. Yet, in another sense, because God has afforded preachers a "glorious and transcendent place" their responsibility increases.

The second stanza intensifies the dilemma by contrasting stained glass with ordinary glass, the priest who lives in imitation of Christ with the priest who merely speaks the word.

> But when thou dost anneal in glasse thy storie,
>> Making thy life to shine within

The holy Preachers; then the light and glorie
    More rev'rend grows, & more doth win:
    Which else shows watrish, bleak, & thin.
                    (Ll. 6-10)

Unworthiness does not excuse the preacher from the responsibility of his place; his place does not excuse his unworthiness. God's "light and glorie," passing through his deputies, may appear "watrish, bleak, & thin," or it may grow "More rev'rend," winning more souls to God. The opening line, we realize, is not merely a rhetorical query expressing man's unworthiness but really poses the question: *How* can man preach thy eternal word? The last stanza answers the question clearly and directly:

Doctrine and life, colours and light, in one
    When they combine and mingle, bring
A strong regard and aw: but speech alone
    Doth vanish like a flaring thing,
    And in the eare, not conscience ring.
                    (Ll. 11-15)

Only by fulfilling both roles—faithful teacher of doctrine and shining example of faith—can the preacher fulfill his purpose, preaching the eternal word so that it affects men's consciences.

As many readers have observed, Herbert links the priest and poet through their affinity in what Sidney calls the "wordish consideration." All men are obligated to praise God; poets and priests have special vocations to fulfill this duty, revealing truth and leading others to virtuous action through their words. In "The Church," Herbert shows poet and priest beset with similar doubts. Both are caught in a dilemma of duty and damnation, knowing their awesome responsibility and their inescapable unworthiness. Herbert's songs of praise are both the winged flight by which his soul rises to God and the flame of love returning to its source. This spiritual aesthetic, justifying and inspiring the efforts of the Christian poet, sharpens the perceptions and gives assurance to such poems as "Love (II)" or "The Quidditie," which assert with quiet confidence the superiority of the task of writing religious poetry as compared to other kinds of poetry and to other human activities. But the gifts of language carry responsibility, as Herbert explains in "Providence":

He that to praise and laud thee doth refrain,
Doth not refrain unto himself alone,

But robs a thousand who would praise thee fain,
And doth commit a world of sinne in one.

(Ll. 17-20)

Inspiration falters, and then the poet must face not only the frustrations of poetic failure but also guilt for failures of love and duty. In several poems ("The Temper [I]," "Employment [I]," "Dulnesse"), Herbert identifies inability to write with spiritual inadequacy, and in yet others he uses distortions in poetic order to embody spiritual disorder ("Deniall," "The Collar," "Grief").

Although he believes that failure to praise God is sinful in itself and a symptom of something wrong in his relationship with God, Herbert cannot enjoy verbal facility for long without self-doubt. In "The Thanksgiving," he finds the most satisfying response to Christ's love in his art:

My musick shall finde thee, and ev'ry string
    Shall have his attribute to sing;
That all together may accord in thee,
    And prove one God, one harmonie.
If thou shalt give me wit, it shall appeare,
    If thou hast giv'n it me, 'tis here.
Nay, I will read thy book, and never move
    Till I have found therein thy love,
Thy art of love, which I'le turn back on thee:
    O my deare Saviour, Victorie!

(Ll. 39-48)

But this exuberance is silenced abruptly:

Then for thy passion—I will do for that—
    Alas, my God, I know not what.

(Ll. 49-50)

In "Miserie," the song of praise is not merely negligible but presumptuous:

As dirtie hands foul all they touch,
    And those things most, which are most pure and fine:
So our clay hearts, ev'n when we crouch
    To sing thy praises, make them lesse divine.

(Ll. 37-40)

Thus Herbert questions the morality of writing poems more radically than Donne. While in the *Satyres* Donne fears the

214

preliminary involvement in the corrupt world necessary to the satiric poet, Herbert fears betrayals by language itself. *Whether* to write poems is a case of conscience for him; so too is *how* to write poems. In "Jordan (I)," he contrasts stylistic elaboration with straightforward statement of truth. Not merely denying that "all good structure [is] in a winding stair" (l. 3), he rejects poetic indirection and artifice as obscuring the truth and prefers to "plainly say, *My God, My King*" (l. 15). In "The Posie," although he makes no moral judgment on poetic artifice, he again dismisses it as irrelevant to his purpose:

> Invention rest,
> Comparisons go play, wit use thy will:
> *Lesse then the least*
> *Of all Gods mercies,* is my posie still.
> (Ll. 9-12)

"Brave language" is again a beguiling lower good in "Frailtie," but here, instead of confidently dismissing it, Herbert presents it as a temptation:

> But when I view abroad both Regiments;
> The worlds, and thine;
> Thine clad with simplenesse, and sad events;
> The other fine,
> Full of glorie and gay weeds,
> Brave language, braver deeds:
> That which was dust before, doth quickly rise,
> And prick mine eyes.
> (Ll. 9-16)

In "Jordan (II)," he confesses that he has been betrayed by his love of language. As Herbert the preacher fears the spiritual pride and futility of words that make a brilliant display but disappear "like a flaring thing" without affecting the conscience, so Herbert the poet condemns himself for obscuring "a plain intention" (l. 5) with the elaborate self-display of weaving himself into the sense "As flames do worke and winde, when they ascend" (l. 13).

In other poems, however, Herbert endorses using the "utmost art" ("Praise [II]," l. 9) to praise God. While he dismisses wit and invention in "The Posie," in "Love (II)," he prays that God will purify human love and "then shall our brain / All her invention on thine Altar lay" (ll. 6-7) and "all wits shall rise, / And praise him who did make and mend our eies" (ll. 13-14). In "Jordan (I)," the "winding stair" image of stylistic indirection and complexity is condemned, but in "Coloss. 3.3" oblique, indirect motion governs the poem's structure and represents man's spiritual life that "winds towards" (l. 6) God. Again in "The Starre," winding is the form that love and praise take.

This recurrent moral scrutiny of the poet's craft, extending from the very act of writing poems to the meaning and value of particular images, is a striking feature of "The Church." Perhaps it is possible to reconcile these apparently conflicting attitudes or to trace a developing poetic and so to summarize Herbert's basic or final position, but it is impossible to generalize accurately about his method of reaching it. He raises and resolves, or fails to resolve, his moral dilemma as a poet differently in each poem.

"An Offering," where Herbert's speaker is at once priest and poet, catechizer and maker of hymns, approaches moral questions in a manner very similar to that of the prose casuists. "An Offering" is a two-part poem. In the first part, the speaker raises and answers a series of doubts about the acceptability of human offerings to the divine; the second part is the hymn he offers. The first stanza, in dramatically compressed form, presents the assumptions about human worship that the poem builds on, and it poses the fundamental problem:

> Come, bring thy gift. If blessings were as slow
> As mens returns, what would become of fools?
> What hast thou there? a heart? but is it pure?
> Search well and see; for hearts have many holes.
> Yet one pure heart is nothing to bestow:
> In Christ two natures met to be thy cure.
>
> (Ll. 1-6)

What men can offer to God is not a gift but a "return," an inescapably small gesture in response to the bounty of His blessings. The only possible gift, whatever form it takes, is the heart's dedication to God. In rapid succession, Herbert's speaker accuses his audience of sloth in making its offering, of negligence in presenting damaged goods, and finally, of possessing nothing worth offering. Hurrying through charges of sluggishness and exhortations to zeal, the abrupt, impatient voice comes to a stop on the supremely perplexing problem—doubt of the worth of a merely human response to the Incarnation.

In stanza two, he presents two tentative solutions. First, he wistfully entertains the bizarre notion of a self-propagating heart. Next, he corrects himself, remembering that quality, not quantity, determines individual merit:

> O that within us hearts had propagation,
> Since many gifts do challenge many hearts!
> Yet one, if good, may title to a number;
> And single things grow fruitfull by deserts.
> In publick judgements one may be a nation,
> And fence a plague, while others sleep and slumber.
>
> (Ll. 7-12)

Stanza three combines the idea of number with the concept of purity set aside too quickly in the first stanza:

> But all I fear is lest thy heart displease,
> As neither good, nor one: so oft divisions
> Thy lusts have made, and not thy lusts alone;
> Thy passions also have their set partitions.
> These parcell out thy heart: recover these
> And thou mayst offer many gifts in one.
>
> (Ll. 13-18)

Through the first three stanzas, Herbert redefines his doubts without resolving them. First he fears the heart is unworthy because its single nature is inadequate in comparison with Christ's "two natures," human and divine. His answer to this problem, that "single things grow fruitfull by deserts," produces more doubt but also suggests a direction in which to look for a solution. In his last statement of the problem, the speaker fears that the heart is not single and fruitful but self-divided and self-destructive in its illusory and temporary pains and pleasures. Clearly, this disintegrating self cannot be "fruitfull by deserts," yet in the complexity of its nature, it can offer many gifts. The human heart is not merely a physical object, with or without holes, or merely a plant, capable of propagating and bearing fruit. Man can choose the objects of his desire and the direction of his change. The single human heart can decay or grow, love the world or God. By controlling and integrating his abilities to change and to love, man becomes capable of real giving. The last stanza explains how to realize this potential for love:

There is a balsome, or indeed a bloud,
Dropping from heav'n, which doth both cleanse and close
All sorts of wounds; of such strange force it is.
Seek out this All-heal, and seek no repose,
Untill thou finde and use it to thy good:
Then bring thy gift, and let thy hymne be this;

(Ll. 19-24)

All doubts and fears are resolved by the promise of regeneration through Christ's sacrifice. Realizing the mysterious complexity of the gift of life has led to understanding the even more wonderful mystery of the gift of grace, of "such strange force" that it cures all the various sorts of damage man can inflict on himself. By seeking and finding grace, man becomes able to give. His gift is the hymn that follows:

Since my sadnesse
Into gladnesse
Lord thou dost convert,
O accept
What thou hast kept,
As thy due desert.

Had I many,
Had I any,
(For this heart is none)
All were thine
And none of mine:
Surely thine alone.

Yet thy favour
May give savour
To this poore oblation;
And it raise
To be thy praise,
And be my salvation.

(Ll. 25-42)

While in part one, the speaker fears that man's indebtedness denies him the role of gift-giver, in the hymn, this indebtedness gives hope. Since he knows that Christ gave His blood to cure the human heart of "All sorts of wounds," he can now pray that God will accept as His what He has preserved—the converted human heart. Since everything, including his heart, belongs to God, the creator and redeemer, to count offerings is meaningless, and he no longer worries that a single heart is less than enough to give. His total dependence on God, even in the act of giving himself, is cause for both humility and hope. Through grace he can praise divine power and love and thus, in understanding his relationship to God, he can cooperate in God's plan for his salvation. The hymn, then, distills from the preceding stanzas man's essential relation to God. After struggling to the perception that, although the heart is neither good nor whole, Christ's blood cleanses and closes, Herbert's speaker ceases to worry about human dependence and unworthiness and rejoices without doubt or hesitation in God's power and love, man's humility and hope.

A radical shift in style reinforces this contrast in attitude. The first section is highly metaphorical; the language of the hymn is strikingly abstract and literal. Thus, "An Offering" implicitly comments on the problem of style. The metaphoric language of the first section is approximate and idiosyncratic, while the hymn speaks plainly without quaint words or curling metaphors. But the imagery of section one does not indicate proud self-deception, nor does the literal statement of section two suggest that appropriate offerings must be artless. In a sense, the hymn itself is a metaphor. The significant verbal form is the symbol for the human heart offered to God in love. The contrast is not between a false and a true style; rather it dramatizes distinguishable but complementary parts of a continuous performance—decision and action.

The first part is the process of discovery. Puzzling to understand man's value to God, Herbert's speaker uses images to express his misapprehensions, partial insights, and sudden perceptions about the human heart and its saviour. The concepts of human love as an object capable of having holes or dividing into discrete pieces and as an organism capable of propagating and bearing fruit express personal and partial truths. Weaving the self into the sense, these images show the self struggling to make sense out of the bewildering contradictions of its condition. The hymn is the statement of discovered truths. Avoiding metaphor or concrete imagery, it celebrates the reconciliation of conceptual paradoxes in harmonies of sound. Because the heart is nothing alone yet something of great value through Christ, the "sadnesse" of guilt becomes the "gladnesse" of hope. Where God is all, man can make no meaningful distinctions between "many" and "any," "thine" and "mine." Because man can give only what he receives and receive only by giving, his offering can have "savour" only through God's "favour," yet from his "oblation" may come "salvation."

In the first part of "An Offering," the problem-solving development, the resolution of doubt through reference to scripture,[22] and the concluding direction to specific action suggest the structural principles of the case of conscience. The speaker's moral awareness, his emphasis on self-examination, and his analytic approach to doubtful action reflect a casuistical habit of mind. The hymn itself is not casuistical in tone or structure, but, like the casuists' descriptions of individual action in particular circumstances, it serves as a model solution to the problems examined in the first part. As a model of right action, it is at once more personal and more universal than the preceding stanzas.

In the first four stanzas, as elsewhere in Herbert, the "you" addressed is both other people and the speaker himself.[23] While the analysis of the heart implies self-examination, or at least generalizations that include the speaker, the second person pronoun indicates an external audience. In either case, the voice is emotionally distanced from the wounds and impurities it diagnoses. Although the hymn is explicitly proposed as the proper course of action for another ("let thy hymne be this"), the self speaks directly to God, and the voice is personal and involved. This shift in pronoun reference emphasizes the movement from problem solving to action, from intellectual analysis to total assent. The impatience and detachment of part one reflect the tortuous examination and resolution of doubt that must precede

---

[22] The balsam dropping from heaven associates the balm of Gilead (Jer. 8:22) with manna (John 6:32-35), as Summers points out (*George Herbert*, p. 236, n. 38). Christ healing and cleansing through His blood are, of course, frequent New Testament images.

[23] Herbert explicitly dramatizes this ambiguity in "Miserie," where, after castigating the perversity of man for twelve stanzas, he concludes:

> But sinne hath fool'd him. Now he is
> A lump of flesh, without a foot or wing
> To raise him to a glimpse of blisse:
> A sick toss'd vessel, dashing on each thing;
>   Nay, his own shelf:
>   My God, I mean my self.
>   (Ll. 73-78)

virtuous action. The personal but nonindividualized voice of the hymn expresses the peace, personal wholeness, and universal truth men may achieve through their individual struggles. Both parts are necessary poetically as well as theologically. The irritability and detachment of the first part are unattractive in isolation. The collective "I" and bold paradoxes of the hymn would seem thin without the preparatory dissonances of the first four stanzas.[24] Together they constitute a model of doubt turning to hope, of decision and action.

"The Forerunners" also combines questions of morality and poetic style. While "An Offering" raises and resolves doubts about human action in general and indirectly comments on questions of style, "The Forerunners" explicitly discusses kinds of language as a moral problem. The speaker first reacts bitterly to death's harbingers—white hairs and the loss of poetic inspiration—until he realizes that even without verbal skill, he can still express his faith in God. Reassured by this permanence in the midst of mutability, he adopts an attitude of acquiescence, even nonchalant indifference, to the anticipated failure of his creative powers:

> The harbingers are come. See, see their mark;
> White is their colour, and behold my head.
> But must they have my brain? must they dispark
> Those sparkling notions, which therein were bred?
>   Must dulnesse turn me to a clod?
> Yet have they left me, *Thou art still my God.*
>
> Good men ye be, to leave me my best room,
> Ev'n all my heart, and what is lodged there:
> I passe not, I, what of the rest become,
> So *Thou art still my God,* be out of fear.

---

[24] Freer condemns the first part as "unpleasant and overbearing" and the hymn as "uncertain and repetitive" (*Music for a King*, p. 178). Vendler sees the possibility of self-criticism in the opening stanzas but complains of the detachment and irritability: "The self has so split off from itself that it no longer knows the part it is criticizing. The poem shows an ill-tempered Herbert" (*Poetry*, p. 185). Summers, rightly I think, emphasizes the complementariness of the two parts: "Throughout [the first] part of the poem the illusion of an individual 'voice' is preserved. . . . The hymn is by definition a collective expression of personal truth. The various metaphorical frames of reference of the opening speech would not be suitable for a 'true' expression of each individual" (*George Herbert* p. 168).

He will be pleased with that dittie;
And if I please him, I write fine and wittie.

                                                              (Ll. 1-12)

In these two stanzas, Herbert shows a religious poet facing a case of conscience, no less intense for concerning a choice of attitudes rather than of external action: How should one respond to the decay of mind and imagination? Is the Christian poet wrong to value his talent and grieve at its loss? To complain about or resent the loss of verbal facility seems to attribute an inordinately high value to merely human invention, but to relinquish creative power happily seems to denigrate life itself and to imply that all poetry is evidence of triviality and pride. The proper response is by no means obvious at this point. Although the speaker's self-correction, subordinating the inventions of his own wit to the simple, direct expression of the heart's truth, seems more pious, his first bitter response at turning "to a clod" seems natural and unavoidable. The heart's truth, *"Thou art still my God,"* is unquestionably most important, but it is not wholly satisfying. He needs to think through its relation to the rest of his experience. Loss of poetic inspiration forces him to face the emotional, moral, and philosophical implications of his theory of language, and in the next three stanzas he examines his assumptions from different angles that reveal further complications.

Saying good-bye to the arts of language evokes memories of earlier struggles to purify and discipline them in the service of God:

> Farewell sweet phrases, lovely metaphors.
> But will ye leave me thus? when ye before
> Of stews and brothels onely knew the doores,
> Then did I wash you with my tears, and more,
>   Brought you to Church well drest and clad:
> My God must have my best, ev'n all I had.

                                                              (Ll. 13-18)

Here the memory of past pain and joy undermines the speaker's theory of language, which assumed a dichotomy between the creative intelligence and verbal skill of the brain, on the one hand, and the faith and simple expression of the heart, on the other. Actual experience denies this rigid division. His heart lodges devotion to lovely language as well as to God. His mastery of language was not a superficial exercise of ingenuity but the product of his deepest suffering and love.

The next stanza predicts the future, again denying separation between "sparkling notions" and faith, between brain and heart:

> Lovely enchanting language, sugar-cane,
> Honey of roses, whither wilt thou flie?
> Hath some fond lover tic'd thee to thy bane?
> And wilt thou leave the Church, and love a stie?
> Fie, thou wilt soil thy broider'd coat,
> And hurt thy self, and him that sings the note.
> (Ll. 19-24)

The farewell to "sweet phrases, lovely metaphors" becomes a plea for them to stay. The poet describes the consequences of his personal loss in language both unashamedly personal and genuinely altruistic. He feels hurt and betrayed at being abandoned by the poetry he has served faithfully. And, no longer claiming indifference to "what of the rest become," he grieves for the English language itself and the poets enchanted by it. Without a dedicated and responsible poet re-creating it to God's glory, language is soon corrupted and corrupting to those who use it.

Since actual experience and his predictions based on it have refuted his original opposition between simple truth and beautiful language, Herbert next constructs a theory of language avowing the essential unity of beauty and truth:

> Let foolish lovers, if they will love dung,
> With canvas, not with arras, clothe their shame:
> Let follie speak in her own native tongue.
> True beautie dwells on high: ours is a flame
> But borrow'd thence to light us thither.
> Beautie and beauteous words should go together.
> (Ll. 25-30)

He evokes the world as he would have it, not without flaw, but morally, intellectually, and aesthetically coherent. This ideal, however, is not simply imaginative solace for an actuality where beautiful language does not always indicate spiritual beauty. It is a principle of action deriving from an accurate description of reality: "let" and "should" are moral imperatives. Because "True beautie dwells on high" and earthly beauty is "But borrow'd thence to light us thither," people *ought* to recognize and admit the baseness of their sin and folly and *ought* to use "beauteous words" to light their way to God. This moral theory of language justifies the poet's work. It also provides a way of understanding and accepting his present traumatic loss.

In the first movement of the poem, stanzas one and two, the speaker suffers age and loss. In this ruthlessly ephemeral world, he finds his only security in continuing faith in God, the unmoved mover, the still point of the turning world.[25] This attempt to find comfort in permanence, however, is futile, for absence of change or motion means confirmation of his deepest fears: silence and death.[26] Man is a pilgrim, not a permanent resident on earth, and beauty lights his way to his true home. Thus beauty of soul and beautiful words "go together," both in the sense that they are mutually suitable or harmonious and in the sense that both are by nature in the process of going, moving, becoming.[27] Poetry is a flame leading people back to the source of beauty, but it is not heaven itself. It is valuable as a means to an end. By articulating a theory that gives poetry its due and yet sees it as necessarily transitory, the speaker is able to accept the loss of inspiration as natural and inevitable:

> Yet if you go, I passe not; take your way:
> For, *Thou art still my God,* is all that ye
> Perhaps with more embellishment can say.
> Go birds of spring: let winter have his fee;
> > Let a bleak palenesse chalk the doore,
> So all within be livelier then before.

> > > (Ll. 31-36)

[25] A pun on "still," meaning "now as before" and "without movement," emphasizes this idea of permanence. Hutchinson notes that Psalms 31:14, the source for line 6, does not include "still" (*Works of George Herbert,* p. 539).

[26] As Psalm 31 continues, it expresses directly the association of evil, silence, and death that underlies the middle stanzas of "The Forerunners": "Let me not be ashamed, O lord; for I have called upon thee: let the wicked be ashamed, *and* let them be silent in the grave" (Ps. 31:17).

[27] Fish points out the pun on "go together" but understands the phrase to mean either " 'belong together' . . . or 'go *away* together' in the sense that they are to be let *go* of simultaneously" (*Self-Consuming Artifacts,* p. 221).

He returns to the acquiescence of stanza two, but the tone is different. The flippant bravado with which he assured himself that what was lost was not really worth having has disappeared. He does not hide his pain and regret at the extinguishing of the bright and beautiful flame borrowed from heaven, but neither does he feel that the loss dehumanizes him. Being alive means change. Aging leads to death, the final change that transforms becoming into being, and so the harbingers of death are the harbingers of eternal life. In the course of the poem, regret for genuine loss has generated increased spiritual insight and vitality.

"The Forerunners," then, does not resolve a traditional casuistical problem in a conventional manner. The question it poses is not what to do but how to respond to conditions one has no choice about. The reasoning is not overtly syllogistic, and, although biblical concepts and language permeate the poem, scripture is not cited as moral authority. The casuistical tradition is evident not in direct borrowing but in the basic conception of moral life as a process of solving problems in particular circumstances.

Herbert's readers have all been aware of his skill in depicting Christian misgivings and of the serenity with which his poems characteristically end. But they have not, I think, adequately studied how his exploration of complexity produces clear, unambiguous conclusions. Recent commentary on "The Forerunners" shows how Herbert creates the experience of doubt by reopening and complicating a problem apparently already solved, but it tends to look at the poem as an arrangement of contrasting but coexisting attitudes.[28] From the perspective of the casuistical tradition, however, "The Forerunners" shows a progressive development. Stanzas three through five modify the attitudes of the first two stanzas, preparing for the solution in the last stanza. By acknowledging the powerful beauty of language, its capacity for good and ill, as well as man's capacity to change and be changed by it, the speaker discovers the liberating perception of his essential self as traveling to true creative power rather than as statically

[28] Stanley Fish, for example, describes the poem as an inconclusive debate between competing values (ibid., p. 223), and Helen Vendler, although she makes clear that both love of language and its strict subordination to love of God are parts of Herbert's final position, argues that the poem does not resolve the alternative interpretations of loss (*Poetry*, p. 42).

awaiting the arrival of death. This enables him to accept the changing of spring to winter, youth to age, and life to death as natural processes on earth and to understand the end of productivity, the "bleak palenesse" of age, as the forerunner both of death and of his own movement toward "True beautie." "The Forerunners" thus is self-illustrating. It concludes that all other words are merely embellishments on the simple truth, *"Thou art still my God."* The lovely metaphors of the poetic form are peripheral to this central statement but are not therefore misleading or deceptive. They are the means of discovery, the flames lighting the way to understanding.

Herbert's renunciation of art is painful but sincere. In his poems, Herbert praises God, works out his relationship to God, and guides others in the ways of truth, but, like any responsible artist, he is aware that language is so tainted by our subconscious desires and fears, our pride and self-doubt, that it inevitably betrays us. Intensely sensitive to the enchantments of art, Herbert also knew its limits. A poem can create an experience that allows truth to emerge and can move us toward a fuller life, but it cannot encapsulate truth or become a substitute for life. Norman Rabkin's comment on Prospero's farewell to art is equally applicable to "The Forerunners": "We enjoy art as if it were life . . . ; yet after the spell has passed we remember that life is its subject and its goal." [29]

PROBLEMS OF SELF-KNOWLEDGE AND SALVATION

The influence of casuistry is most evident in poems where Herbert's speaker experiences bewilderment and doubt. In the poems I have discussed—those examining the personal implications of Christian doctrine and those confronting moral doubt— he struggles to reconcile apparent conflicts in his duties to God or to harmonize his personal actions and feelings with the principles of his religious belief: duty to obey God with knowledge of man's weakness and God's omnipotence in "The Holdfast," for example, or regret for waning poetic power with total and loving acceptance of God's will in "The Forerunners." Typically he resolves these dilemmas by reexamining and defining more precisely his own ideas and feelings.

[29] Norman Rabkin, *Shakespeare and the Common Understanding* (New York: The Free Press, 1967), p. 229.

The particular doubts he struggles with as Christian, priest, and poet are varying manifestations of the implicit problem of self-knowledge. In our time, the problem of self-definition is presented more often in psychological than in theological terms, but in the seventeenth century, understanding oneself meant understanding one's relationship with God as miserable sinner and as beloved child. It was primarily the casuist, or the parish priest acting as casuist, who performed the function of helping people to see themselves accurately and to accept what they saw. A sense of self free from flattering self-deception and from paralyzing guilt was no easier to achieve then than now. While the doctrine of justification by faith was the basis for joy, it also created intense fear. The obverse of faith in God's infinite power and love was the doctrine of the total depravity of mankind. The seventeenth-century Protestant's belief in the promise of eternal life freely given through grace was balanced by his sense of obligation and conviction of sin.[30] In spite of the promise of eternal life to all believers, agonies of guilt and spiritual desertion persisted. Assurance of salvation alternated with guilt and dread; despair was a constant temptation. Consequently, the need to relieve these anxieties was a primary emphasis of early Protestant casuistry.

A title such as *A Case of Conscience, the Greatest that ever was: how a man may know whether he be the child of God, or no* indicates Perkins's sensitivity to the problem.[31] The epigraph for *The Whole Treatise* shows the same concern: "*The Lord God hath given me a tongue of the learned, that I should knowe to minister a word in due time, to him that is wearie*" (Is. 50:4). Perkins explicates this text as giving scriptural authority for casuistry in the pastor's duty to comfort distressed consciences:

30 J.F.H. New, *Anglican and Puritan: The Basis of Their Opposition, 1558-1640* (Stanford, Calif.: Stanford University Press, 1964), p. 80.

31 Perkins's editors emphasize this point. Breward argues that Perkins's radical difference from traditional Roman Catholic casuistry grew from his "concern about pastoral problems raised by the doctrine and experience of justification. The fundamental question was whether a man was a child of God or not" (*Works of Perkins*, pp. 62-63). Merrill observes that "the most unique feature of Puritan casuistry [is] its preoccupation with the problem of assurance of election" and notes that "in all of Perkins's casuistry is the constant effort to relieve the pressure of conscience" (Thomas F. Merrill, ed., *William Perkins 1558-1602: English Puritanist* [Nieuwkoop: B. DeGraaf, 1966], pp. xiv-xv).

It was one speciall dutie of Christs propheticall office, to give comfort to the consciences of those that were distressed, as the Prophet here recordeth. Now as Christ had this power to execute and performe such a duty, so he hath committed the dispensation therof to the Ministers of the Gospell.

(II, sig. A)

This emphasis on comforting the troubled conscience is also present in Thomas Pickering's dedicatory letter, where he commends Perkins's treatise on the grounds that no doctrine is of "greater use and consequence" than that capable of "releeving and rectifying the Conscience," for "when once the Spirit is touched, and the heart . . . smitten with feare of the wrath of God for sinne; the griefe is so great, the burden so intollerable, that it will not by any outward meanes, be eased or asswaged." [32]

Perkins analyzes the cause and cure of a distressed conscience most directly in *The Whole Treatise,* where he asserts that all distress, whether grief or more extreme despair, is essentially a fear of condemnation and always results from temptation. The temptations causing fear and doubt of salvation are: God's wrath, outward affliction, one's own sins, blasphemies, and a corrupted imagination. William Ames's comparable list of "temptations . . . against FAITH" omits the last two and, to wrath, guilt, and affliction, adds the absence of "notable Fruits of . . . Faith" and the failure of faith to increase. Whatever the cause, the only remedy is God: "the *Applying of the promise* of life everlasting, in and by the blood of Christ." [33]

A similar concern to help "any dejected poor Soul" informs Herbert's "The Church." The spiritual conflicts he depicts often come not from reluctance to submit to God's will or from problems of behavior but from a sense of guilt and dread. Many of the best poems seek comfort for a distressed conscience by discovering causes and cures resembling closely those the casuists diagnose and prescribe. Herbert knew almost the full range of the casuists' catalogues of grief. He suffered afflictions from nature, when "Consuming agues dwell in ev'ry vein, / And tune my breath to grones," and afflictions from the wrath of God, "When he a torture hath design'd." He felt guilt and dread that his faith did not bear fruit: "My stock lies dead, and no increase /

[32] Perkins, II, Dedication to *The Whole Treatise.*
[33] Perkins, II, 22; Ames, Bk. II, pp. 16-18.

Doth my dull husbandrie improve"; that he sinfully misused God's blessings: "I have abus'd thy stock, destroy'd thy woods . . . my head did ake, / Till it found out how to consume thy goods"; that instead of growing in faith he belonged to a world of decay:

> I see the world grows old, when as the heat
> Of thy great love, once spread, as in an urn
> Doth closet up it self, and still retreat,
> Cold Sinne still forcing it, till it return,
>   And calling *Justice,* all things burn.[34]

Some poems, like "Grief" or "Sinnes round," express painful confusion without anticipating or even seeking comfort. More often, in "Grace," "Complaining," and "Longing," for example, spiritual agony leads to prayer for relief. When Herbert cures fear and doubt, the remedy is "the promise of life everlasting, in and by the blood of Christ": in "Justice (II)," where the speaker overcomes dread of judgment with confidence that "Gods promises have made thee mine" (l. 22); in "The Discharge," where he banishes anxiety over future grief with the thought, "My God hath promis'd; he is just" (l. 55); in "Church-lock and key," where crying sins are drowned out by Christ's blood pleading for fallen men; in "The Bag," where meditation on the crucifixion drives away despair.

Herbert's countering of grief and guilt with faith is, of course, standard Christian doctrine and proves nothing about his relation to casuistry. But he is strikingly casuistical in his presentation of grief as a case of conscience to be resolved, in his attentive consideration of the tortuous movement of the troubled mind, and in his demonstration of self-analysis as a means of recovery. While the casuists were unequivocal that "no physicke, no art or skill of man, can cure a wounded and distressed conscience, but only the blood of Christ" (Perkins, II, 22), they knew how difficult it could be for a troubled soul to apply the promise of redemption to his own case. They did not simply brush aside such spiritual anguish as a failure of faith. Thus Perkins advises:

He that is the comforter, must not be discouraged, though after long labour and paines-taking, there follow smal com-

[34] See "Affliction (I)," "Confession," "Grace," "Sighs and Grones," and "Decay."

fort and ease, to the party distressed. For . . . usually it is
long before comfort can bee received . . . because God hath
the greatest stroke in these distresses of mind, and brings
men through all the temptations, that hee hath appointed,
even to the last and upmost, before hee opens the heart to
receive comfort.   (II, 26)

Perkins's general advice for comforting a wounded conscience
is to delve into the fearful, despairing mind and to bring to
consciousness the causes of distress and the faith that can relieve
it. The procedure is, first, to disclose the cause of distress, next,
to bring about sorrow for sin and confession to God, and then to
offer comfort by recourse to the grace of God. The casuist thus
looks for relief within the conscience itself, the moral self-
awareness by which "a man knowes what he thinkes, what hee
willes and desires, [and] also in what manner he knoweth,
thinketh, or willeth, either good or evill" (II, 11). Discovering
the cause of grief may be difficult, since "sometime it is hid from
the party distressed," but it is crucial: "the very opening of the
cause is a great ease to the minde" (II, 22). The second step,
sorrow for sin, also necessitates rigorous self-examination, for the
sorrow must not be regret for worldly consequences or fear of
punishment but grief for "the very offence of God" (II, 23). The
grief for sin, moreover, must be for a particular sin, not a confused and general confession that one is "as other men are, a
sinner" (II, 23). The third step, offering comfort, is the most
difficult, for "the true children of God . . . have excellent measure of grace [but] when they are in distresse, feele litle or no
grace at all in themselves" (II, 24). The casuist can help them
discover seeds or beginnings of grace: "*A desire to repent, and
beleeve, in a touched heart and conscience, is faith and repentance
it selfe. . . .* If the partie be grieved for the hardnesse of his
heart . . . he hath undoubtedly received some portion of godly
sorrow" (II, 24). Thus, by searching himself, the sufferer can find
peace: "hee that can finde these beginnings, or any of them
truely in himselfe, hee may assure himselfe thereby, that he is the
childe of God" (II, 25).

Herbert analyzes doubt of salvation as a moral problem most
explicitly in "Assurance," where he identifies it, as Perkins does,
as a temptation to despair. The poem begins by denouncing a
"Spitefull bitter thought" (l. 1) as a dangerous temptation, which,

once accepted by the mind, would become "rank poyson" (l. 6). Only then does the speaker identify the thought as the fear that his hope in his union with God is illusory. Next he decries the diabolical purposes and consequences of such doubt and turns to "my Father" (l. 19) for "hope and comfort" (l. 21), explaining that, in spite of his personal unworthiness, assurance is possible because it rests on God, Who guides even man's part in the reciprocal relationship. Whereas "Assurance" demonstrates how faith withstands doubt, "The Method" proposes a solution for distress almost identical with Perkins's procedure of discovering cause, sorrow, and grace through self-examination. If you are unhappy, Herbert advises here, examine your conscience, confess distinct, particular sins, "and God will say, / *Glad heart rejoyce*" (ll. 31-32).

Although "Assurance" and "The Method" discuss grief in terms very close to those used by such casuists as Perkins and Ames, both poems explain rather than struggle with grief. In Herbert's best dejection poems, pain is not defeated so easily. In "Affliction (I)," resentment at suffering and disappointment builds to a threat of rebellion before recognition in the last couplet that the narrative of grievances has expressed not only a sense of betrayal by God but also a failure to love God. The "cold despairs, and gnawing pensivenesse" (l. 16) forestalled in "Assurance" are also intensely present in "Affliction (IV)." The speaker first thinks of himself as victim of divine malice (apparently hunted and abandoned by God simultaneously). But after the first stanza, he describes his affliction as self-torture: "My thoughts are all a case of knives, / Wounding my heart / With scatter'd smart" (ll. 7-9). Analyzing his internal chaos leads not to rebellion against God but to understanding that his fear and sense of isolation have incited rebellion within himself:

> All my attendants are at strife,
>   Quitting their place
>   Unto my face:
> Nothing performs the task of life:
>   The elements are let loose to fight,
>   And while I live, trie out their right.
>   (Ll. 13-18)

The rebellion metaphor expresses precisely the utter disorientation of physical and mental breakdown and, paradoxically, makes the experience comprehensible. Seeing himself as a rightful king threatened by rebellious attendants, the speaker can both confess his sinful destructiveness and assert his worth; while acknowledging the turmoil as his own, he can see it not simply as confusion ("scatter'd smart," "All . . . at strife," "elements . . . let loose") but as an isolatable, and hence opposable, plot against his life, a life that includes his essential identity and his God as well as his rebellious physical and mental powers:

> Oh help, my God! let not their plot
> Kill them and me,
> And also thee,
> Who art my life: dissolve the knot,
> As the sunne scatters by his light
> All the rebellions of the night.
> (Ll. 19-24)

By finding the potential for death and life within himself, he can share Richard II's vision of the "eye of heaven" by its very being revealing and frightening into submission all murders, treasons, and sins, without Richard's presumption or subsequent self-pity. Recognizing his dependence on God awakens faith in His power to disperse the rebellions of the night. Realizing then that God can re-create sinful man, he balances humility with self-respect and predicts a future where all the elements of his being perform their appropriate tasks, praising God and relieving his distress:

> Then shall those powers, which work for grief,
> Enter thy pay,
> And day by day
> Labour thy praise, and my relief;
> With care and courage building me,
> Till I reach heav'n, and much more, thee.
> (Ll. 25-30)

If these poems do not expressly depict complete spiritual recovery, they certainly anticipate those joys by discovering seeds of grace. But, while individual problems of doubt are resolved, they refuse to stay resolved. Just as Herbert's cases of conscience about the worth of his actions as priest and poet recur several times in "The Church," affliction poems appear repeatedly, frustrating critical attempts to discover a pattern of spiritual development in *The Temple*.[35] Guilt and fear do not cease abruptly once a Christian experiences certainty of God's love. Perkins, in fact, suggests that recurrent doubt distinguishes true assurance from presumption:

> Whereas presumption and the illusion of Satan use as well to tell a man that he is the childe of God, as the true testimonie of regenerate conscience: the way to put difference betweene them is this. . . . Presumption is peremptorie without doubting: whereas the testimonie of conscience is mingled with manifold doubtings . . . yea otherwhiles overcharged with them. (I, 548)

The temptation to doubt whether all is well "Betwixt my God and me" (l. 9) is not answered once and for all in the poem explicitly titled "Assurance" but takes various forms throughout "The Church," appearing as late as "A Parodie," which comes shortly before the concluding group of eschatological poems. Rather than trace a development from rebellion through resignation to acceptance, Herbert shows Christian life as a continuing effort to overcome self-doubt and doubt of God's love and to achieve peace in spite of affliction. It is not a linear progression of spiritual growth that unifies the work, but, as Earl Miner suggests, "the vicissitudes of the soul." [36]

---

[35] Individual poems exhibit varying degrees of spiritual awareness, and Herbert's statement, as reported by Walton, that his spiritual conflicts were resolved in submission to God supports Helen Vendler's argument for a biographical development in Herbert's responses to God (from self-abnegation, through emulation of Christ, to assimilation of Christ). See Vendler, *Poetry*, Chapter 8. However, if the arrangement of poems in both manuscripts and in the 1633 edition is Herbert's, he has taken care not to reflect that development in the structure of *The Temple*. Barbara Lewalski argues that the personal spiritual experience of Herbert's speaker epitomizes the Protestant-Pauline paradigm of salvation, but she also shows that this conventional pattern of spiritual life is not an orderly progression but an "essentially episodic sequence of trials, temptations, failures, successes, backslidings, until the end of life crowns all" (*Protestant Poetics*, p. 192; see also pp. 13-27, 286-287).

[36] *The Metaphysical Mode from Donne to Cowley* (Princeton: Princeton University Press, 1969), p. 237, n. 12. Although Miner traces the tradition of treating the soul's vicissitudes through commentary on Job, Psalms, and Canticles, he suggests the relevance of casuistry: "Herbert shows that he knew, both in himself and in others, what the seventeenth century called 'the case of conscience,' an inner turmoil and uncertainty" (p. 232).

233

Herbert celebrates times of joy when he escapes concern with self, but because joyous certainty alternates with grievous doubt, self-examination is a persistent mode of thought in the lyrics of "The Church." The poems do not apply mechanically the procedures recommended by casuists for discovering cause, sorrow, and grace, but many of the best transform doubt to hope through the casuists' introspective, problem-solving approach to grief. "The Crosse," for example, depicts a mind aware not only of what, but of how, it thinks, wills, and desires. The first five stanzas portray responses to incomprehensible experiences of frustration and disappointment. Initial reactions of anger and resentment at God's contradictions of His own will give way to self-pity and self-contempt at the contradictoriness of the speaker's own ambivalence and self-ignorance.[37] This self-recognition makes possible the final insight that resolves the problem and comforts the conscience:

> And yet since these thy contradictions
> Are properly a crosse felt by thy Sonne,
> With but foure words, my words, *Thy will be done.*
>
> (Ll. 34-36)

The interpretation of life's crossed purposes as "a crosse felt by thy Sonne" crystallizes in a single brilliant image the casuists' method of "applying the promise." The image of Christ on the cross symbolizes simultaneously the burden of sin, the remission of sin, the agonizing sense of being forsaken in suffering, and the grace present in the acceptance of God's will. Recognizing that he must bear his cross and that Christ bears it for him, the speaker obtains comfort by making Christ's words his own: "*Thy will be done.*"

Fluctuation between joy and grief defines the spiritual life portrayed in "The Church" and also constitutes one of Herbert's most characteristic spiritual dilemmas. Although casuists do not treat the question of how to live with the soul's vicissitudes as a case of conscience in itself (as distinct from particular manifestations of grief), in "The Flower" Herbert adapts the casuistical problem-solving, self-analytic approach to the fact of spiritual instability.

---

[37] See Fish, *Self-Consuming Artifacts,* pp. 184-186; Martz, *Poetry of Meditation,* pp. 134-135; and Vendler, *Poetry,* pp. 266-267, on this discovery of humility.

THE FLOWER

How fresh, O Lord, how sweet and clean
Are thy returns! ev'n as the flowers in spring;
    To which, besides their own demean,
The late-past frosts tributes of pleasure bring.
        Grief melts away
        Like snow in May,
As if there were no such cold thing.

    Who would have thought my shrivel'd heart
Could have recover'd greennesse? It was gone
    Quite under ground; as flowers depart
To see their mother-root, when they have blown;
        Where they together
        All the hard weather,
Dead to the world, keep house unknown.

    These are thy wonders, Lord of power,
Killing and quickning, bringing down to hell
    And up to heaven in an houre;
Making a chiming of a passing-bell.
        We say amisse,
        This or that is:
Thy word is all, if we could spell.

    O that I once past changing were,
Fast in thy Paradise, where no flower can wither!
    Many a spring I shoot up fair,
Offring at heav'n, growing and groning thither:
        Nor doth my flower
        Want a spring-showre,
My sinnes and I joining together.

    But while I grow in a straight line,
Still upwards bent, as if heav'n were mine own,
    Thy anger comes, and I decline:
What frost to that? what pole is not the zone,
        Where all things burn,
        When thou dost turn,
And the least frown of thine is shown?

    And now in age I bud again,
After so many deaths I live and write;

I once more smell the dew and rain,
And relish versing: O my onely light,
     It cannot be
     That I am he
On whom thy tempests fell all night.

These are thy wonders, Lord of love,
To make us see we are but flowers that glide:
     Which when we once can finde and prove,
Thou hast a garden for us, where to bide.
     Who would be more,
     Swelling through store,
Forfeit their Paradise by their pride.

Here the mind's capacity to reflect on its own processes both creates the moral problem and resolves it. "The Flower" begins with joy in spiritual renewal, but reflection on that experience shows how the overwhelming reality of the present distorts human understanding. In a time of joy, grief seems nonexistent, disappearing "As if there were no such cold thing" (l. 7). In a time of grief, joy is unimaginable: "Who would have thought my shrivel'd heart / Could have recover'd greennesse?" (ll. 8-9). Out of this multiple awareness of what seems and what is, of past and present emotional states, the third stanza concludes that the "Lord of power" (l. 15) controls the mutability of human life but that human knowledge is inadequate to an understanding of His mysterious ways. This sense of ignorance and helplessness at a time of growth and creativity is, as Herbert says in "The Crosse," "in the midst of delicates to need, / And ev'n in Paradise to be a weed" (ll. 29-30) and erupts in a wish to escape the confusing world of change.

The poet now reviews his spiritual life in a changed tone, emphasizing, as Helen Vendler says, the deadly repetitiveness of these fluctuations ("Many a spring I shoot up fair," l. 24).[38] His glad wonder at being surprised by joy and resurrected from a spiritual grave is transformed into fear. While grief seemed unreal in stanza one, in stanza five, the present tense ("Thy anger comes, and I decline," l. 31) makes it threateningly imminent, even momentarily present. But, while the cycle of growth and

[38] Vendler, *Poetry*, p. 51.

decline substantiates the desire to be "past changing" (l. 22), it also prepares for the resolution of the problem. This generalized account of the soul's vicissitudes interprets change morally. Periods of renewal include pain ("groning," l. 25) and sin (l. 28) as well as spiritual growth. Spiritual growth and rectitude, "I grow in a straight line" l. 29 (cf. "A Wreath": "life is straight, / Straight as a line, and ever tends to thee," ll. 5-6), imperceptibly become presumption: "Still upwards bent, as if heav'n were mine own" (l .30). Affliction comes as God's just anger, recalling the proud soul to the reality of its fallen condition and its dependence on God.

Moral analysis of God's killing and quickening brings the poet back to his present joy. Aware that in renewed self-confidence he risks forgetting his earthbound sinfulness and the source and goal of his vitality "as if heav'n were [his] own" (l. 30), he knows that God's anger will bring him back to earth. He has experienced grief before and will again, but for now he can savor human joys and the merciful blotting out of recent pain by present joy. Thus by joining a knowledge of past with a knowledge of present, of fact with emotion, of large pattern with immediate experience, of God's power to destroy with His power to create, he overcomes doubt and fear and defines moral action in a world of change. Fluctuations of fall and flight, of grief and joy, are not incomprehensible displays of God's power but wonders created by the God of love to make us see ourselves. Discovering that "we are but flowers that glide" (l. 44), that our human nature is to change, to grow, to learn, to die, and to live again, we enter the garden of peace.[39] Those who insist on inhuman perfection and security and refuse to understand that life includes birth and death, joy and pain, error and correction, forfeit this paradise within and the paradise beyond change.

Herbert's resolutions that direct to moral action in such poems as "The Crosse" and "The Flower" distinguish his poetry of spiritual conflict from Donne's. As Douglas Peterson has convincingly argued, in the *Holy Sonnets*, Donne addresses the

[39] "Glide" certainly means "fade away imperceptibly" as it is ordinarily glossed. It also has the more general meaning "move in a smooth manner," with connotations of the musical usage "blend one tone into the next" and refers to all the kinds of change in the poem. People are to accept and move smoothly and melodically through life's inescapable changes.

problem of how to achieve assurance, avoiding both despair and presumption.[40] Like Herbert, Donne approaches the dilemma through rigorous self-examination, relating the Christian commonplaces of grace and contrition to immediate personal experience. But, while both poets define universal truths in terms of the particular circumstances of individual experience and pursue spiritual simplicity through intellectual complexity, rejecting what is merely conventional in expression to eliminate what is spurious in feeling, their poems move in different directions. For example, Herbert's "The Crosse" and Donne's sonnet beginning "Batter my heart, three person'd God" both explore the ambivalence of fear and desire. Herbert resolves the tensions between sorrow and love in the paradox of the cross, finding evidence of grace in the recognition of guilt and intention to do God's will. Donne, in contrast, uses paradox not to resolve contradictions but to define the problem of simultaneously longing for and resisting grace, of loving and fearing God.[41] He uses meditative techniques to evoke the fear and love of true contrition, a necessary part of the redemptive process, but, for all the energy of self-analysis and intensity of feeling, his moral stance in the sonnets is passive. Reason misleads and will betrays; the helpless soul prays for grace. Herbert too has poems of unsatisfied longing, but in "The Crosse" and "The Flower," doubt yields to love, which directs future action—to endorsing the words *"Thy will be done"* and to seeing that "we are but flowers that glide" and so to avoiding forfeiting paradise through pride.

Herbert often resolves spiritual conflicts with insights recommended by casuists, and his religious lyrics approximate more closely than Donne's the casuistical paradigm of transforming confusion to clarity through understanding. Still, his poems are not rigidly or exclusively casuistical in subject or structure, and he never assumes the persona of the casuist as overtly as does Donne in *Biathanatos* or the *Satyres*. While the casuist typically

[40] *The English Lyric from Wyatt to Donne: A History of the Plain and Eloquent Styles* (Princeton: Princeton University Press, 1967), pp. 335-348.

[41] Dwight Cathcart argues that "the business of the poem is the reconciliation of that contradiction." Although I agree that in the rape metaphor Donne asks for "recognition . . . of the powers of both his reason and his physical nature," I believe that the metaphor expresses the violent tension between desire and fear, not the peace of reconciliation (Cathcart, *Doubting Conscience: Donne and the Poetry of Moral Argument* [Ann Arbor: The University of Michigan Press, 1975], pp. 161-162).

sees himself as a guide to the doubting conscience and a physician for the wounded conscience, Herbert, assuming that the best physician is the patient who has recovered, presents personal experience rather than helpful advice.

JOINING KNOWLEDGE WITH KNOWLEDGE: HERBERT'S CASUISTICAL STYLE

We have seen the casuistical tradition operating in a variety of ways in Herbert's poetry—in its concrete particularity and fine moral discriminations, in its balancing of individual moral responsibility with faith in divine omnipotence, in its emphasis on self-examination and on practical action, and in the problem-solving structure of many of the lyrics. Perhaps, however, Herbert's most significant debt to the casuistical habit of mind is the evolving poetic form that for one of his most attentive and perceptive readers is the distinctive quality of his poetry:

> Herbert "reinvents" the poem afresh as he goes along. He is constantly criticizing what he has already written, and he often finds the original conception inadequate, whether the original conception be the Church's, the Bible's, or his own.[42]

Herbert's self-correcting poems constantly redefine general truths in terms of growing understanding of his particular case, and his style, his original and personal choice and arrangement of words, is firmly related to the moral theology that applies general laws to specific circumstances and insists on the duty of constantly reexamining "our actions and state" because "a bare and naked *knowledge* is not sufficient for this act of Conscience, but things

[42] This formulation is Helen Vendler's (*Poetry*, p. 29), but Herbert's self-correcting form has been discussed in other terms by other critics. See, for example, Arnold Stein's analysis of Herbert's art of questioning (*Herbert's Lyrics*, pp. 182-201); Valerie Carnes's observation that "although a Herbert poem may refer to a completed act of perception, more often it re-enacts that act and thus is less a description of reality than a realization" ("The Unity of George Herbert's *The Temple:* A Reconsideration," *ELH* 35 [1968]: 524); and Stanley Fish's descriptions of Herbert's self-consuming poems in "Letting Go: the Dialectic of the Self in Herbert's Poetry," Chap. 3, in *Self-Consuming Artifacts*; in "Catechizing the Reader: Herbert's Socratean Rhetoric," in *The Rhetoric of Renaissance Poetry*, ed. Thomas O. Sloan and Raymond B. Waddington (Berkeley and Los Angeles: University of California Press, 1974); and in *The Living Temple: George Herbert and Catechizing* (Berkeley and Los Angeles: University of California Press, 1978).

must bee weighed over and over."[43] Herbert's poetic skill, then, is inseparable from his moral commitment. As L. C. Knights explains:

> The effort of craftsmanship involved was one with the moral effort to know himself, to bring his conflicts into the daylight and, so far as possible, to resolve them.[44]

This self-correcting poetic form is not confined to poems that resolve doubt and illuminate moral choice but also shapes such a poem as "Employment (II)" where cheerful self-congratulation for active virtue reveals its hollowness and dissolves in despair.

Perhaps the best demonstration of how Herbert's self-correcting poetry resembles and differs from prose casuistry is "The Elixir." This poem presents no spiritual conflict, but it immediately follows "A Parodie," where fear and grief appear for the last time in "The Church." In "A Parodie," the speaker is torn between faith and doubt. He states his dilemma as a paradox:

> Souls joy, when thou art gone,
>   And I alone,
>   Which cannot be,
> Because thou dost abide with me,
>   And I depend on thee;
>
>   (Ll. 1-5)

He believes that fearing "thou art not here" (l. 20) is sinful and false, but he cannot deny the experiential reality of feeling "That I may seek, but thou art lost" (l. 24). He can be rescued from this impasse only by God's grace:

> O what a deadly cold
>   Doth me infold!
>   I half beleeve,
> That Sinne says true: but while I grieve,
>   Thou com'st and dost relieve.
>
>   (Ll. 26-30)

If the dominant idea of "A Parodie" is man's helplessness without grace, the following poem, "The Elixir" explores how that grace operates in human experience by making possible a full human response to God's will. "The Elixir" is Herbert's

---

[43] Ames, Bk. I, p. 25.

[44] *Explorations* (New York: Chatto and Windus, 1946), p. 113.

version of the First Epistle of John, where the apostle teaches
that keeping God's commandments is a sign of faith and gives
assurance of salvation:

> And hereby we do know that we know him, if we keep his
> commandments. . . . whoso keepeth his word, in him verily
> is the love of God perfected. . . . And every man that hath
> this hope in him purifieth himself, even as he is pure. . . .
> And he that keepeth his commandments, dwelleth in him,
> and he in him. And hereby we know that he abideth in us,
> by the Spirit which he hath given us. . . . Herein is our
> love made perfect, that we may have boldness in the day of
> judgment: because as he is, so are we in this world. . . .
> These things have I written unto you that believe on the
> name of the Son of God; that ye may know that ye have
> eternal life.   (1 John 2:3,5; 3:3,24; 4:17; 5:13)

The First Epistle of John is William Perkins's favorite scriptural reference for treating the case of "how a man may know
whether he be the child of God, or no" and provides, according
to Perkins, *"full resolution to the conscience of man, touching
the certentie of his salvation"* (II, 19).[45] While Perkins's method
is to quote directly, to schematize his interpretation of the text
by dividing and subdividing the grounds and signs of assurance,
and to refute anticipated objections and misinterpretations,
Herbert characteristically takes the stance of learner rather than
teacher and, without alluding directly to the text, discovers
gradually a conception of human action analogous to Saint John's
version of perfect love manifested in obedience.

THE ELIXIR

Teach me, my God and King,
In all things thee to see,
And what I do in any thing,
To do it as for thee:

Not rudely, as a beast,
To runne into an action;

---

[45] In *A Discourse of Conscience* (I, 542), in *The Whole Treatise* (II, 19-20),
and throughout *The Greatest Case*, in which he recasts 1 John and Psalm 15
in dialogue form, Perkins draws heavily on 1 John to show that the conscience
may have certainty of salvation.

But still to make thee prepossest,
    And give it his perfection.

A man that looks on glasse,
    On it may stay his eye;
Or if he pleaseth, through it passe,
    And then the heav'n espie.

All may of thee partake;
    Nothing can be so mean,
Which with his tincture (for thy sake)
    Will not grow bright and clean.

A servant with this clause
    Makes drudgerie divine:
Who sweeps a room, as for thy laws,
    Makes that and th'action fine.

This is the famous stone
    That turneth all to gold:
For that which God doth touch and own
    Cannot for lesse be told.

Louis Martz traces "The Elixir" to the meditative traditions' "search for the presence of God in spiritual retirement." But because Herbert presents not spiritual detachment but acting "as for thy laws" (l. 19) as the elixir that transforms dross to gold, the casuists' study of lawful action brings us closer to the poem than instructions for meditation.[46] The speaker's prayer to learn how to act always in a spirit of loving service recognizes the need for conscious knowledge of God's will. Indeed, Herbert's revisions show him emphasizing intellectual effort.[47] In the early Williams manuscript, stanza two is absent and stanza one reads:

Lord teach mee to referr
All things I doe to thee
That I not onely may not erre
    But allso pleasing bee.

In the final version, Herbert has substituted "see," with connotations of knowledge and understanding, for "referr," with its

[46] Martz, *Poetry of Meditation,* p. 257.

[47] Hutchinson prints the variants in the Williams manuscript, apparently an early copy of Herbert's poems with corrections in the poet's hand (see *Works of George Herbert*).

suggestion of submission and obedience. He has dropped the qualitative distinction between avoiding sin and pleasing God and introduced a sequential distinction between perception (to see) and action (to do). The implication that such seeing and doing will not be easy or obvious is reinforced by the new second stanza with its contrast between acting "as a beast" (l. 5) and acting with intelligent forethought. Submitting one's will to God is not primarily a matter of resisting temptation but of giving human actions their perfection by perceiving God in them. Divine law is so internalized that "A servant with this clause" (l. 17) always acts "as for" God's laws.

Herbert's description of acting "for thy sake" (l. 15) conveys the casuistical idea of the conscience more accurately than the casuists themselves sometimes do. Although they define conscience as the internalization of God's will, their language often implies a separation not only of law from man but of man's moral awareness from his essential self. The common trial metaphor, in which the conscience is law, witness, and judge, may imply a self that acts and an external conscience that rewards or punishes. For example, Perkins's metaphor of the conscience as like "a Notarie, or a Register" that records all one's thoughts and deeds and "doth it continually" (I, 518) suggests a poem like Robert Herrick's "To his Conscience," where Herrick seems to be the "I," tempted to sin, and conscience appears as an external voice that prevents the temptation:

> Can I not sin, but thou wilt be
> My private *Protonotarie?*
> Can I not wooe thee to passe by
> A short and sweet iniquity?
>
> .   .   .   .
>
> It will not be: And, therefore, now,
> For times to come, I'le make this Vow,
> From aberrations to live free;
> So I'le not feare the Judge, or thee.[48]

Herbert, in "Conscience," distances himself from the voice of conscience only to satirize this legalistic idea of conscience as a joyless harping on the ubiquity of sin. In "The Elixir," man does not grudgingly accede to the promptings of conscience; he and his actions become God-like: "All may of thee partake" (l. 13).

[48] L. C. Martin, ed., *The Poetical Works of Robert Herrick* (Oxford: Clarendon Press, 1956), p. 357.

The sacramental and alchemical images of stanza four introduce the idea of a marvelous union of the material and the
spiritual in human life, implicitly correcting the wish to pass
beyond earth to heaven suggested by the sight images of stanza
three. Herbert's revisions also show him rejecting images of
progressive growth in time and developing images of transformation. The earlier version, originally called "Perfection," included
another stanza between stanzas three and four:

> He that does ought for thee,
> Marketh yᵗ deed for thine:
> And when the Divel shakes yᵉ tree,
> Thou saist, this fruit is mine.

The present stanza four used to read:

> All may of thee partake:
> Nothing can be so low,
> Which with his tincture (for thy sake)
> Will not to Heaven grow.

The tone of the last stanza was caution, not wonder:

> But these are high perfections:
> Happy are they that dare
> Lett in the Light to all their actions
> And show them as they are.

By changing the title from "Perfection" to "The Elixir"
Herbert has directed our attention to the means of perfecting
instead of to the result. By dropping the images of organic
growth and hierarchical ascent in the cancelled stanza and in
the "low / grow" rhyme and by substituting the "mean / clean"
rhyme and developing the alchemical image, Herbert brings the
search for perfection back to earth, locating it not in a condition
men may aspire to in a life beyond but in the purification and
transformation of thought and action on earth. The casuistical
principle that even the most trivial actions are morally significant,
far from implying dreary proscription, gives value to what people
do. The miraculous transformation results from mutual divine
and human love. God is the source of value: He teaches, touches,
and owns. People acting on their own are bestial or shallow, but
those acting "as for thy laws" may reach perfection.

The perfectionism of "The Elixir" exceeds the casuists' more cautious estimates of human achievement, and Herbert's success in creating a delicate balance of humility and assurance in talking about the reciprocal relationship of God and man surpasses their more modest achievements.[49] But here, as elsewhere in "The Church," the casuistical habit of mind shapes the poetry. As the speaker relates knowledge of Christian doctrine to knowledge of the particular turns of his own mind, he realizes that clarity of thought and purity of intention are realized in holiness of action. This gradual refining of thought and feeling, what Helen Vendler calls the "self-critical dialogue of the mind with itself" that underlies even those poems that do not overtly state a problem or dramatize a conflict, relates "The Church," more than "The Church-porch," with its aphoristic wisdom, to the casuistical practice of resolving problems in man's response to God's will.[50]

Studying the extensive revisions of "The Elixir" reveals that the subtle discriminations and self-corrections that define the formal development of the poems also characterize Herbert's personal way of dealing with the particular problems he confronted as a poet. This problem-solving habit of mind and the concentration on redefining general moral laws in terms of individual cases demonstrate an affinity between Herbert and the English casuists that goes beyond the moral theology they shared with most of their contemporaries. The conclusions that William Perkins's most recent editor has reached about the first English casuist apply aptly to Herbert as moralist in "The Church":

> Ethical imperatives were given their shape from men's relationship to God and one another, not by loyalty to abstract principles rationally arrived at. . . . Perkins presented an ethical system which reflected the great obligation imposed by God's gift of Christ, rather than fostering an interest in a host of minor pieties and duties which led to self-satisfaction rather than to humility and gratitude.[51]

Herbert rejoices in God's love but is never complacent or self-righteous. He experiences guilt but never acquiesces reluctantly

---

[49] J.F.H. New cites "The Elixir" as an illustration of the strain of perfectionism in Anglicanism in contrast to the characteristic Puritan emphasis on human depravity (*Anglican and Puritan,* pp. 83-84).

[50] Vendler, *Poetry,* p. 7.

[51] Breward, *Works of Perkins,* pp. 59, 63.

to particular prohibitions in fear of punishment. His characteristic tone includes humble gratitude to Him,

> Who of the Laws sowre juice sweet wine did make,
> Ev'n God himself being pressed for my sake.
>   ("The Bunch of Grapes," ll. 27-28)

and wonder that "All may of thee partake." The readers most capable of making "a gain" from reading Herbert's poems are not necessarily those who share his abstract beliefs but those who can imitate the models of self-discovery that Herbert provides, re-creating in the circumstances of their own lives moments of peace and wholeness out of the conflicts and confusions of living, as Herbert created comely forms and harmonies out of the conflicts between himself and his God.

Chapter VI

MILTON'S HERO OF
CONSCIENCE

The casuistical paradigm pervades almost everything that Milton wrote. This recent summary of Milton's ethical position accurately summarizes that of the Protestant casuists:

> His fundamental ethical conviction was that the good is discoverable by making a series of rational choices, issuing in actions which limit subsequent options but do not destroy the freedom to choose, upon which the ethical value of action must depend. The good is always contingent, always relative to circumstances, but the individual is free and always capable of renewing virtuous action. Virtue is not an abstract state of mind but an active state involving deeds answerable to insights.[1]

Believing, like Taylor, that "the act of choosing is the foundation of all morality,"[2] Milton addressed himself in poetry and prose to the problems perplexing men's consciences and applied the law of God to moral choices in particular circumstances. He championed the freedom and responsibility of the individual conscience, while presenting divine law as an exacting measure of human action. He consistently regarded human doubts and perplexities as problems to be solved through the exercise of right reason rather than as sins to be avoided. He resolved doubts not by rigid application of codified law but by diligent inquiry into how God's will could be realized in the changing circumstances of men's lives.

---

[1] Mary Ann Radzinowicz, *Toward "Samson Aganistes": The Growth of Milton's Mind* (Princeton: Princeton University Press, 1978), p. 186.

[2] Jeremy Taylor, *Ductor Dubitantium: or the Rule of Conscience*, in *The Whole Works of the Right Rev. Jeremy Taylor*, ed. Reginald Heber, 15 vols. (London, 1828), XIV, 348.

In 1654 when Milton looked back over his prose efforts in defense of human liberty, he listed them according to three areas of social life: religious, domestic, and civil:

> Reflecting, therefore, that there are in all three species of liberty, without which it is scarcely possible to pass any life with comfort, namely, ecclesiastical, domestic or private, and civil; that I had already written on the first species, and saw the magistrate diligently employed about the third, I undertook the domestic which was the one that remained.[3]

This scheme is similar to Perkins's classification of his cases of conscience concerning man "as he is a member of some societie, whether it bee the Familie, the Church, or the Commonwealth," [4] and to Baxter's organization of *A Christian Directory*, Books I and II treating private and family duties, Book III church duties, and Book IV duties to rulers and neighbors. Milton's formulation of these conventional groupings stresses liberty and the casuists' duty, but they all assume that obedience to God's law and liberty of conscience are complementary dimensions of moral choice.

Milton and the casuists share more than their attempt to discover how to fulfill God's will in problematic cases in these three areas. When Milton turned his attention to domestic liberty, he produced the divorce pamphlets, where, as Arthur Barker has pointed out, he treated the question of divorce as a case of conscience.[5] Invoking the casuistical principle "that every command giv'n with a reason, binds our obedience no otherwise then that reason holds" (C.E., III, 457), Milton argues that when incompatibility obstructs the purpose of marriage to provide men with the happiness of spiritual companionship, divorce becomes lawful. He answers doubts about the lawfulness of divorce raised by Christ's admonition to the Pharisees ("Whosoever shall put away his wife, except it be for fornication, and shall marry another, committeth adultery" [Matt. 19:9]) by warning against

[3] Frank Allen Patterson et al., 18 vols. *The Works of John Milton* (New York: Columbia University Press, 1931-1938), VIII, 131; hereafter cited parenthetically as C.E.

[4] William Perkins, *A Discourse of Conscience* and *The Whole Treatise of the Cases of Conscience*, in *The Workes of That Famous and Worthy Minister of Christ . . . Mr. William Perkins*, 3 vols. (London 1612-1613), II, 112. Quotations are from this edition and will be cited parenthetically in the text.

[5] Arthur Barker, *Milton and the Puritan Dilemma* (Toronto: University of Toronto Press, 1942), p. 69.

a literalist reading of scripture and insisting instead that Christ's words must be interpreted in the context of their particular circumstances as a reprimand to the Pharisees who divorced for trivial and temporary causes. The divine command that man shall "cleave to his wife, and they twain shall be one flesh" (Matt. 19:5) can apply only where circumstances permit the fulfillment of its intention to provide "a meet help against lonelines" (C.E., III, 386).

While Milton's conclusion is not the one reached by other casuists, he obviously conceives of the issue in casuistical terms. Similarly the ecclesiastical and political pamphlets try to resolve doubts and settle consciences by showing that such doubtful actions as defying bishops or executing a king do not in actual fact break divine law but fulfill its intention. The casuistical habit of mind is perhaps most striking in *Areopagitica*. Milton describes truth as absolute and immutable but often obscured and elusive in the changing circumstances of human history. In the perplexing world of mixed good and evil, truth assumes many shapes, and God's will can be discovered only through diligent inquiry. Doubt and confusion, though inevitable, can be resolved through the search for knowledge and the exercise of right reason. Each man's conscience must discern God's will and apply it to the particular practical problems he encounters. The man who, by relying on external authority, tries to avoid this responsibility to think is an object of ridicule and contempt, for

> A man may be a heretick in the truth; and if he beleeve things only because his Pastor sayes so, or the Assembly so determins, without knowing other reason, though his belief be true, yet the very truth he holds, becomes his heresie.
>
> (C.E., IV, 333)

And the man who tries to avoid applying the truth he perceives to practical problems possesses only

> a fugitive and cloister'd vertue, unexercis'd & unbreath'd, that never sallies out and sees her adversary, but slinks out of the race, where that immortall garland is to be run for, not without dust and heat.   (C.E., IV, 311)

The conception of conscience shared by Milton and the casuists leads to a defense of liberty, for, as Taylor puts it:

Difficulty makes virtue . . . and liberty is the hand and fingers of the soul by which she picks and chooses; and if she gathers flowers she makes herself a garland of immortality.[6]

Thus, the conceptual framework supporting Milton's argument for unlicensed printing in *Areopagitica* demonstrates how the complex of ideas germane to casuistry—the inviolability of individual conscience, the resolution of doubt through reason, the need for strenuous intellectual effort to apply divine law to actual circumstances—shapes Milton's thought and leads the Anglican bishop and the Puritan revolutionary to similar ethical perceptions. In tone and structure, however, *Areopagitica* is closer to the classical oration than to the case of conscience. While Milton's prose is primarily persuasive, the case of conscience is problem solving in form and intention. For example, in "The Case of the Engagement," Robert Sanderson presents the problem he attempts to solve as real and difficult. In his introductory remarks, he acknowledges that the point of inquiry is "great, both for difficulty and concernment." [7] He constantly reminds his reader of the possibility of doubt and disagreement. Throughout the case, his emphasis is as much on the method by which he disentangles the complexities of the problem as it is on his solution. In contrast, Milton presents his recommendations, whether for liberalized divorce laws, unlicensed printing, or educational reform, as positive suggestions for the improvement of society. He certainly acknowledges the complexity of the issues, the difficulty of reassembling the scattered bones of truth, and the practical difficulties that accompany the responsibility of freedom, but his emphasis is on the positive merits of his proposal. He anticipates objections to his argument, but he subordinates these and shows that they do not, in fact, offer a possible alternative. Thus, while Protestant casuistry illuminates the intellectual context of Milton's prose as it does most Renaissance political and didactic literature, Milton's pamphlets are not rightly cases of conscience.

MORAL CHOICE IN *Paradise Lost* AND *Paradise Regained*

The casuistical habit of mind also permeates Milton's poetry within the controlling forms of other genres. *Paradise Lost*

[6] Taylor, XIV, 282-283.

[7] William Jacobson, ed., *The Works of Robert Sanderson,* 6 vols. (Oxford: Oxford University Press, 1854), V, 20.

narrates the mythic core of man's relation to divine law—the disobedience that brings death and the obedience that actualizes grace in faith and action; moreover, it dramatizes the decision-making process in a series of exemplary and cautionary models. The councils in hell and in heaven define the extremes of moral choice, contrasting the fallen angels, who perversely and maliciously decide to destroy, with Christ, who freely chooses to create salvation through loving obedience. The simplicity and spontaneity of Christ's offer of service and sacrifice illuminate the deviousness of the perverted reasoning and manipulative rhetoric of the debate in hell, but the contrast does not suggest that choice is or should be easy or automatic. Milton has not recanted his conviction that "Where there is much desire to learn, there of necessity will be much arguing, much writing, many opinions" (C.E., IV, 341), but he also believes that reason is properly used in a specifically casuistical way, that is, to apply knowledge of the divine will to the particular actions of one's life. Thus, Milton mocks the devilish exercise of reason as an end in itself in his description of the fallen angels who:

> sat on a Hill retir'd,
> In thoughts more elevate, and reason'd high
> Of Providence, Foreknowledge, Will, and Fate,
> Fixt Fate, Free will, Foreknowledge absolute,
> And found no end, in wand'ring mazes lost.
>   (II, 557-561) [8]

In *Paradise Lost* reason is properly used not to speculate idly but to analyze experience. The consult in hell is evil not because Satan and his followers debate what they should do but because they debate without intending to obey God's law. Denying their own experience of bliss and pain and their intuitive knowledge of their own natures and their proper end, they pervert their reason. Transforming the major premise of the syllogism by which conscience relates law to action from "Good is to be done, evil eschewed" into "Evil is to be done, good eschewed," they consider how to act in the context of their particular circumstances. In this demonic parody of the casuistical process, the reasoning of Belial is as specious and futile as the passion of Moloch.

The perfection of Christ's dedication to fulfilling the divine

---

[8] Quotations from the poetry are from Merritt Y. Hughes, ed., *John Milton: Complete Poems and Major Prose* (New York: Odyssey Press, 1957).

intention in Book III prevents dramatizing the decision-making process, for, as Perkins explains, "the proper subjects of conscience are reasonable creatures, that is, men and Angels. . . . God the creator, who beeing righteousnes itselfe, needeth not conscience to order and governe his actions" (I, 517). Although angelic reason is intuitive rather than discursive, angels go through a reasoning process. Abdiel's debate with Satan in Book V, then, provides a more complete model of the operation of conscience. At this point before the fall, Satan has not yet decided to dedicate himself to evil, but his pride and envy have initiated the transformation. He falsifies the minor premises of the syllogism of conscience, misinterpreting the nature of the actions he considers, God's exaltation of Christ and his own rebellion. Abdiel corrects Satan, explaining that to honor God's "only Son" is just, a fulfillment of angelic glory, not servile degradation, and that to oppose God's Word is "perfidious fraud" (V, 880), not an assertion of reason and right. Abdiel scornfully exposes Satan's distorted judgment as an attempt to "give Law to God" (V, 822) and a falsification of his intuitive knowledge of the creative source of his being and of his direct experience of divine goodness and beneficence.

Abdiel also functions as a model of the right conscience in holding to the truth. While Satan's followers "all obey'd / The wonted signal, and superior voice / Of thir great Potentate" (V, 704-706), Abdiel acts according to his own judgment, disobeying his immediate superior in order to obey God. The rebellious angels demonstrate the danger of habitual, unreasoned submission to any of God's creatures; Abdiel shows the courage to think and act in spite of the scorn and anger of his leader and his peers. His "constant mind" rationally applies divine law to a particular case in opposition to those who "reason for thir Law refuse" (VI, 41), providing a paradigm of absolute obedience to divine law and of complete independence of conscience.

The reader of *Paradise Lost* reaches the crucial decisions of Book IX through these perspectives of demonic and angelic choice. Adam and Eve live innocently in Paradise under one command, a pledge of obedience, but the drama of decision making is essentially the same in heaven and hell, in Eden and in the fallen world. Adam and Eve, like the rest of God's rational creatures, know their purpose is:

> to observe
> Immutably his sovran will, the end
> Of what we are . . .
>
> (VII, 78-80)

They have knowledge and reason sufficient to discern good, and wills free to choose evil if passions sway their judgments. The prelapsarian universe does not present the fallen world's perplexing tangles of good and evil, but neither is Paradise static. Unprecedented situations occur in heaven and in Eden; in them especially obedience is tried.

Eve chooses and falls, deceived by the serpent, not because her feminine intellect was incapable of penetrating his fraud but because she willfully interrupts the analytic process of her conscience. William Ames explains:

> The *Will* can turn away the understanding from the *consideration* of any object. . . . By reason of this commanding power, the *Will* is the first cause of unadvisednesse, and blame-worthy error in the Understanding.[9]

So Eve voluntarily disregards what she knows about the offered fruit, refuses to examine her motives, ignores the circumstances of her life, the love and obedience she owes to her creator and husband. Unlike Abdiel, she chooses to believe Satan's lies. Adam, who disobeys God undeceived, sins against his conscience. Knowing that he should obey God and that to eat the forbidden fruit is to disobey, he eats. Preferring Eve to God, following her judgment, not his own, he imitates Satan instead of Abdiel. Adam's "if Death / Consort with thee, Death is to mee as Life" (IX, 953-954) is an unconscious parody of Satan's "Evil be thou my Good" (IV, 110).

Satan and Adam also suffer similarly the effects of an evil conscience: shame, sadness, horror, despair, and anguish of spirit (Ames, Bk. I, p. 33). Even Satan, dedicated to evil and self-delusion, cannot arrest the ravages of conscience. Indeed, according to the casuists, a desperate conscience is characteristic of the damned:

A *Desperate Conscience* is that which so *accuseth* and *con-*

---

[9] William Ames, *Conscience with the Power and Cases Thereof* (1639), Bk. I, pp. 23-24. Quotations are from this edition and will be cited parenthetically in the text.

demneth, that it taketh away not onely *quietnes* and *peace*, but *hope* also of any quietnesse, or remedy. . . . The *Despaire* of the damned, which utterly rooteth out all *hope of* remedy, is the *bottomlesse* pit of misery.

(Ames, Bk. I, p. 46)

Thus, as Milton's Satan pauses in his course to ruin mankind, his conscience reflects on his past actions, accuses and condemns him:

> horror and doubt distract
> His troubl'd thoughts, and from the bottom stir
> The Hell within him, for within him Hell
> He brings, and round about him, nor from Hell
> One step no more than from himself can fly
> By change of place: Now conscience wakes despair
> That slumber'd, wakes the bitter memory
> Of what he was, what is, and what must be
> Worse; of worse deeds worse sufferings must ensue.

(IV, 18-26)

Adam also reviews his past actions in the light of his knowledge of God's will and ends by condemning himself. Suffering confusion, guilt, terror, and despair, he exclaims:

> O Conscience, into what Abyss of fears
> And horrors hast thou driv'n me; out of which
> I find no way, from deep to deeper plung'd!

(X, 842-844)

The crucial difference, of course, is that while Satan's evil conscience leads to renunciation of hope, Adam's leads to contrition, the first step in the regenerative process. Again, the casuists offer a relevant commentary:

> When the accusation of the conscience is more forcible and violent, it is called a *wounded* or *troubled conscience:* which though of it selfe it be not good nor any grace of God; yet by the goodnesse of God it serveth often to be an occasion or preparation to grace. (Perkins, I, 550)

Shortly afterwards, then, when Eve suggests suicide, Adam "To better hopes his more attentive mind / Laboring had rais'd," and he is able to reject Eve's counsel of despair "That cuts us off from hope" and to seek a "safer resolution," contrition and confession (X, 1010-1096).

Through grace and repentance, Adam is prepared to receive from Michael the knowledge he needs to live in a fallen world. He learns that the Savior's obedience atones for his and all men's disobedience. In casuistical terms, "Conscience since the fall, or after sinne, is made good againe," not simply by repentance but "by the blood of Christ applyed through Faith" and "by the *witnesse* of the *Spirit,* whereby we are assured of the grace of God, not onely for the present, but also for the continuance of it, to the doing of every good worke" (Ames, Bk. I, pp. 37-38). Adam learns also that "a good Conscience is maintained by . . . exercise" (Ames, Bk. I, p. 38)—that he must express his faith in action. "Reason is also choice," Michael tells him, and the stories of Abel, Enoch, and Noah show him that choice is action.

Michael's account of history shows Adam the changing circumstances in which he and his descendants must choose and act in a world diminished by sin and death. The vision Adam receives is of a world where men know evil as well as good, where reason is impaired, where man is subjected to the tyranny of unreason within and to political tyranny without. The particular circumstances of man's trial of obedience change in the violent, confusing world Adam sees, but, while each historical phase requires difficult decisions, each affords examples of heroic virtue. Abel, Enoch, Noah, Abraham, and Moses are able to find favor with God without faith in redemption through Christ, for "the understanding must first of all conceive, or at the least have meanes of conceiving, before conscience can constraine; because it bindeth by vertue of knowne conclusions in the mind" (Perkins, I, 522). But complete peace of conscience can be achieved only through Christ's sacrifice. Thus Michael explains that the Law was given to Israel to discipline men to receive a "better Cov'nant," the Christian liberty that frees them from the bondage of the law. So Perkins explains that a conscience is good either by creation, as Adam's originally was, or by regeneration through faith in Christ and that the properties of the regenerate conscience are certainty of salvation and Christian liberty, which consists of "freedome from the justification of the morall law," "freedome from the rigour of the law," and freedom from "the bond of the ceremoniall law" (Perkins, I, 538).

While Adam lived in Paradise, a simple pledge was his only

law, angels were witnesses testifying to the nature of his actions, and God was his judge. After the fall, he is subjected to corrupt human authority, to the Mosaic law he cannot perform, to false witnesses and judges. Still, Michael shows him that man can regain a paradise within by relying on his own conscience, an internalized law, witness, and judge, which judges men in this life "as they shal be arraigned for their offences at the Tribunal seat of the everliving God in the day of judgement" (Perkins, I, 519). Adam learns, in terms accommodated to his understanding, the Father's plan for men:

> And I will place within them as a guide
> My Umpire *Conscience,* whom if they will hear,
> Light after light well us'd they shall attain,
> And to the end persisting, safe arrive.
>
> (III, 194-197)

Although idle speculation is more dangerous to the fallen Adam than when Raphael warned him to "be lowly wise" (VIII, 173), he urgently needs to know what concerns him and his being. Satan can create mazes of doubt and can make "intricate seem straight" (IX, 632), so that virtuous choice is frequently difficult, requiring moral discernment as well as good will. Thus Michael functions as the casuist, presenting in calm, unadorned language the knowledge essential to moral action, the nature of the law binding men in changing historical circumstances, and the nature of human action. Michael comforts Adam and creates in him a habit of mind able to deal with the problems he will face. He sends him from Eden with a peaceful conscience and with a specific direction to "add / Deeds to thy knowledge answerable" (XII, 581-582).

The casuistry of Milton's near contemporaries, then, provides us with a set of terms for talking about the central subject of Milton's major poems—moral choice. Looking at *Paradise Lost* in the context of casuistry focuses our attention on the rational and ethical emphases that Milton's epic shares with his prose. The inspired bard of *Paradise Lost,* like the theologian of *De Doctrina,* conceives of faith as knowledge and of worship as good works. He sees man's life as a trial of obedience in confusing circumstances and shows that the "rule of judgment will be the conscience of each individual, according to the measure of light which he has enjoyed" (C.E., XVI, 357). Through the dramatized cases of conscience and Michael's tutoring of Adam, *Paradise Lost* creates in the responsive reader understanding of the obligations of the Christian conscience and thus a habit of mind prepared to discriminate among the perplexities of his world, to follow his conscience as guide through the mazes of sin and error, and to act according to the dictates of his conscience, the God in him. *Paradise Lost* presents the archetype that all casuistry assumes:

> Every man is as Adam, his good conscience is his paradise; the forbidden fruit, is the strong desire of these earthly things; the serpent is the old enemie the divel: who if he may be suffered to intangle us with the love of the world, will straight way put us out of our paradise, and barre us from all good conscience. (Perkins, I, 553)

Yet to argue that Renaissance Protestant casuistry is relevant and helpful in our reading of *Paradise Lost* is not to deny radical differences in conception and mode. Where Milton's poetry is "simple, sensuous, and passionate," casuistical prose is discursively intricate, logical, and emotionally detached. Where Milton's subject is universal, an experience recurring constantly throughout history, casuistry is devoted to the uniqueness of each action in particular circumstances. Where Milton emphasizes eternal time transcending and giving significance to historical time, casuistry emphasizes the vagaries of human history as they manifest eternal values. When Adam and Eve leave Paradise at the close of the poem, they walk into the world that needs and produces casuists.

Paradise Regained and *Samson Agonistes* are set in this fallen world, a world of doubt. The moral choices in *Paradise Lost* are exemplary because, although psychologically complex, they are intellectually and morally simple. In the two later poems, issues are less clear, and the heroes face the question not of whether to obey God's will but of how to know His will for them in particular circumstances. From the cosmic setting of *Paradise Lost*, *Paradise Regained* moves to the world of human history foretold by Michael, a particular time and place where the paradise of a peaceful conscience can be reached only by discovering truth in the midst of deception and ambiguity and by acting according to God's will in situations where Satan's way may appear remarkably like God's. Christ supplies a pattern of a right conscience in a fallen world. It is part of God's eternal plan "To exercise him in the Wilderness" (*PR,* I, 156), just as it is part of His plan for man to exercise his conscience in each choice he makes. *Paradise Lost* shows Adam losing paradise by disobedience, sinning against his conscience; *Paradise Regained* shows Christ recovering paradise by "firm obedience fully tried" (*PR,* I, 4), following his conscience.

The action of Milton's brief epic develops through a series of spiritual and intellectual conflicts. Satan's weapons are fraud and guile, and Christ vanquishes him not by force but by wisdom. Satan proposes actions with some plausible appearance of virtue; Christ rejects the proposed actions in terms of their implicit intention and the circumstances of time, place, and person. He does not, for example, dismiss the transformation of stone into bread as evil in itself (he will perform similar miracles in the course of his ministry). But he understands that to do so at Satan's urging, in the wilderness to which the Spirit has led him to prepare for his life work, would involve distrust of God. When Satan urges precipitous action to establish his kingdom on earth, Christ refuses on the basis of the inappropriateness of the suggested means, time, and place:

> Means I must use thou say'st, prediction else
> Will unpredict and fail me of the Throne:
> My time I told thee (and that time for thee
> Were better farthest off) is not yet come;
> When that comes think not thou to find me slack
> On my part aught endeavoring, or to need
> Thy politic maxims, or that cumbersome
> Luggage of war there shown me, argument
> Of human weakness rather than of strength.
>
> (*PR,* III, 394-402)

His kingdom will be built in the mind of man, not in the world.

Confident of "knowing what I ought" (*PR,* IV, 288), Christ applies general ethical principles to the particular actions of his life with infallible acuity. He defeats Satan and erects Eden in the wilderness of sin by following his knowledge of God's will as his only guide. Through perfect faith and obedience, he achieves the paradise of the calm, peaceful conscience in a world of doubt. Joan Webber has demonstrated that in the world of *Paradise Regained,* good is not self-evident, doubt is universal experience, and Christ's "resistance to temptation is largely resistance to doubt." [10] As Christ enters the wilderness, he is not certain how to act; but he never doubts himself or God, nor does he hesitate in rejecting the actions Satan proposes. Through resisting Satan's temptations, he progresses from uncertainty to full understanding of his mission to teach God's will as the only truth and guide for men and "to dwell / In pious Hearts" (*PR*, I, 462-463), illuminating men's understanding and so defeating Satan. Christ solves the riddles of a fallen world; he considers with care how best to fulfill the Father's will in every act he does; and he thinks and acts with the perfect assurance of a good conscience. Thus, *Paradise Regained* dramatizes the condition that the casuists try to help create.

In *Samson Agonistes,* Milton dramatizes casuistical material itself, presenting mimetically the activities the casuists discuss discursively. In each scene, characters pass judgment on specific past actions and consider future ones. Many of the actions they discuss, such as marrying an unbeliever, sacrificing family obligations to the public good, rebelling against unjust political authority, and causing one's own death, are traditional cases of conscience. More significantly, the major episodes, which are often discussed as a series of temptations, are also steps in the process of learning to make moral decisions. In the first scene, Samson is bewildered and helpless; in his final speech, he is decisive and confident of the rightness of his actions; through the intervening dialogues, he discovers the casuistical principles and procedures that enable him to decide on a course of action with a right conscience. Thus, the casuistical tradition makes its most important contribution to Milton studies when brought to bear on Milton's tragedy.

SAMSON'S WOUNDED CONSCIENCE

Most critics agree that Milton's Samson begins in despair and ends as a hero of faith and that his movement from one state to the other provides the middle that Dr. Johnson was unable to discover in the dramatic action of *Samson Agonistes*. Despite this ground of agreement and the concentrated simplicity of the dramatic structure, the nature and significance of the process of regeneration cannot be defined easily. Martin Mueller describes

[10] Joan Webber, "The Son of God and Power of Life in Three Poems by Milton," *ELH* 37 (1970): 187.

the central action as "the change from reason to faith," yet he also points out that "Milton's drama is so intellectual that it often approaches the nature of a debate." [11] Samson's final act seems to be a heroic assertion of self, free from internal and external bondage; but from another perspective it is the expression of humility, the loss of self in obedience to God. The dramatic structure consists of Samson's spiritual growth—internal action rather than external events; but some Miltonists have argued persuasively that, in contrast with Christ in *Paradise Regained*, Samson's actions remain external and physical and ironically achieve dramatic force and moral significance through their very inadequacy.[12]

Scholarship has shown that Samson is a type of Christ, that is, an Old Testament figure whose experience adumbrates the pattern for salvation to be realized in Christ for all men; yet Milton's use of typology remains elusive.[13] Sherman Hawkins, for example, stressing the universality of Samson's tragedy, describes it as "a mimesis of the redemptive process . . . an action not of men but of man," and Albert Cirillo argues that the setting is not historical time and place but eternity: the particular "setting merely emphasizes the fact that the patterns of the Christian dispensation transcend the particular historical moments." [14] On the other hand, William Madsen warns that if "Samson is viewed

[11] Martin Mueller, *"Pathos* and *Katharsis* in *Samson Agonistes,"* in *Critical Essays on Milton from ELH* (Baltimore: Johns Hopkins Press, 1969), pp. 242-243. Reprinted from *ELH* 31 (1964): 156-174.

[12] William Madsen, *From Shadowy Types to Truth* (New Haven: Yale University Press, 1968), pp. 181-202, and Irene Samuel, *"Samson Agonistes* as Tragedy," in *Calm of Mind: Tercentenary Essays on "Paradise Regained" and "Samson Agonistes" in Honor of John S. Diekhoff,* ed. Joseph A. Wittreich, Jr. (Cleveland: Case Western Reserve Press, 1971), pp. 235-257.

[13] F. M. Krouse, *Milton's Samson and the Christian Tradition* (Princeton: Princeton University Press, 1949), surveys the Renaissance traditions that parallel Samson with Christ. The typological dimension is explored further with different approaches and emphases in Madsen's *From Shadowy Types to Truth* and in Arthur Barker, "Structural and Doctrinal Pattern in Milton's Later Poems," in *Essays in English Literature . . . Presented to A.S.P. Woodhouse,* ed. Millar MacLure and F. W. Watt (Toronto: University of Toronto Press, 1964), pp. 169-179. Mary Ann Radzinowicz argues persuasively that in *Samson Agonistes,* Milton's emphasis is less typological than exemplary (*Toward "Samson Agonistes,"* pp. 283-284).

[14] Hawkins, "Samson's Catharsis," in *Milton Studies* 2 (1970): 227; Cirillo, "Time, Light, and the Phoenix: The Design of *Samson Agonistes,"* in *Calm of Mind,* ed. Wittreich, pp. 209-210.

first of all as a concrete individual living in a concrete historical situation, then his significance for the Christian reader lies primarily in his inability to measure up to the heroic norm delineated in *Paradise Regained*." [15] To dismiss these conceptual tensions simply as conventional Christian paradoxes or differences in critical emphasis would be to ignore the distinctive texture of Milton's tragedy. Samson's career is not unique in its embodiment of the Christian paradox that man must lose his life in order to find it or in the tragic irony of wisdom through suffering and victory in defeat. But Milton's tragedy is distinctive in the interplay of reason and faith, the freedom of the individual conscience and the requirements of the law, internal and external action, and particular historical circumstances and immutable moral reality.

Like *Oedipus at Colonus*, *Samson Agonistes* presents a blind, despised hero who has violated divine law and who achieves glory in death; but, unlike Samson, Oedipus does not acknowledge personal guilt or present rational arguments justifying the lawfulness of his present actions as Samson does. Oedipus simply asserts his continued innocence and perseveres in his suffering humanity until the gods too acknowledge his glory. Samson is more like Job in his trial of faith, his effort to understand his suffering and to reconcile it with God's justice. But, while Job's crisis remains internal, Samson acknowledges divine justice very quickly; his torment is his inability to serve his God in action in a particular historical situation. Samson is like Christ in *Paradise Regained* in his consciousness of heroic vocation and his acquisition of self-knowledge through meditation and resistance to temptation; unlike Christ, however, Samson experiences agonizing doubt as he learns to choose. [16]

In *Samson Agonistes*, Milton shows us the fallen world where doubting men struggle among the bewilderingly deceptive forms taken by good and evil and where virtue is possible only when doubt is overcome. Samson is not primarily the hero who suffers or the hero who resists temptation but the hero who doubts and

---

[15] Madsen, *From Shadowy Types to Truth*, pp. 201-202.

[16] Joan Webber sees Christ's victory as that of "any man so in touch with himself that the world's distractions cannot betray him" (see "The Son of God and Power of Life," p. 194). I disagree only in emphasis. Christ is the only man so perfect in his faith and self-knowledge; Samson experiences the universal human problem of dealing with internal doubt.

by resolving doubt finally becomes free to act. Samson understands that his duty and his fulfillment is to act in accordance with the will of God; his problem, at once spiritual, moral, intellectual, and practical, is that his particular circumstances, "Eyeless in *Gaza* at the Mill with slaves," seem to make his duty impossible to perform. The central action of the tragedy is the process by which Samson decides what to do next, or, in the terminology of casuistry, the resolving of a doubtful conscience.

Milton's drama opens in the world the casuists describe, where men's consciences attempt to relate particular human actions to universal divine law in difficult situations that make men of goodwill disagree. In the first major movement, from Samson's opening soliloquy through his conversation with Manoa, all the characters are engaged in essentially the same activity, reflecting on the particular circumstances of Samson's plight in the light of their common assumption that man owes obedience to the will of God. The dramatis personae are joined by ties of family, friendship, country, and religion; and they share a common enemy and a common grief. Yet they interpret the same events differently and trade accusations of disobedience. In their responses to the immediate situation, they seem to share only their doubt, confusion, and perplexity.

Direction and pattern emerge, however, as they tell and retell their versions of Samson's marriages, his exploits as a champion of Israel, and his bondage. Milton is no Pirandello showing that each man is right if he thinks he is and that the more the past is explored the more pasts there are. Out of their disagreements about whether Samson should have married Dalila, about who bears the responsibility for Israel's continued servitude, and about the wisdom of Monoa's ransom attempt, the characters develop fuller understanding of the significance of what has happened and clearer conceptions of the moral nature of human actions to guide them in the future. No blinding flash of truth dispels their doubts and anxieties. Indeed, at the conclusion of the dialogue with Manoa, Samson reaches his lowest point of despair and the Chorus concludes that divine providence is unjust to the human eye. But we realize that these men are not statically defined by their weaknesses and that in spite of, or perhaps because of, their disagreements they have at least been able to learn important partial truths.

In his first soliloquy, Samson does not even understand that he

262

has a decision to make. He is bewildered about the nature of God's will, the basis of all human morality. Indeed, Samson exhibits the emotional and intellectual characteristics of what casuists call a troubled or wounded conscience. Although casuistry defines conscience as a function of reason, the practical intellect operating morally, its activities are not confined to the intellect. The conscience examines a particular action in the light of divine law and then draws a conclusion either to accuse and condemn or to excuse and absolve. The effects of these actions are seen in the affections. The absolving conscience produces boldness, confidence, joy, and peace; the condemning conscience causes shame, sadness, fear, and desperation, and is called a wounded or troubled conscience (Perkins, I, 536, 550). The medical analogy describes not only the defective nature of action, which deviates from divine law, but also the self-destructive psychological effects of a guilty conscience, which "will in a lingring manner wast the conscience, the soule, and the whole man" (Perkins, I, 553).

Samson is wounded in conscience as well as body. His anguish is bred in his own mind "From restless thoughts, that like a deadly swarm / Of Hornets" torment him with the contrast between "what once I was, and what am now" (ll. 19-20, 22). He tries to examine his actions in relation to God's will, but his festering conscience has wasted the whole man so that reason and faith have decayed and his thoughts are erratic and confused. He is perplexed about where truth is to be found and what guidelines for human behavior exist. His earlier understanding of God's will—his belief that he was chosen to be God's champion and to deliver Israel from Philistine oppression—has apparently proved false, and he is left in a universe without moral order. He does not complain, as Manoa and the Chorus later do, that God unjustly allows great men to suffer; but he is tempted to complain that God's will is inconsistent or unintelligible. Yet even as this abyss of moral chaos is glimpsed, the memory of his own action saves Samson. He quickly realizes that the apparent discrepancy between God's promise and his actual situation is more easily explained by his own failure:

> what if all foretold
> Had been fulfill'd but through mine own default,
> Whom have I to complain of but myself?
>
> (Ll. 44-46)

For all the angelic prophecies of his birth and his "order'd and prescrib'd" training as a Nazarite, he is not, he realizes, merely a passive receptacle of supernatural blessings. His relationship with God involves his own actions as well as God's. The divine prediction of his great exploits is conditional on his proving himself worthy of responsibility. Although he has failed, Samson's faith in divine prediction is reaffirmed.[17]

By reflecting on his past actions in his first soliloquy, Samson realizes the basic assumption of casuistry: he lives in a morally comprehensible universe. Divine law is intelligible and consistent, and human action can be judged on its basis. In spite of his reaffirmation of his belief in divine prediction, however, Samson still does not fully understand his sin. His next thought is to attribute his "own default" to inborn weakness, to impotence of mind. Half-aware that he is shifting the blame to his Creator, his thoughts recoil from the examination of the past and focus on the present. Samson suffers most from his sense of powerlessness. Blindness is the chief of his miseries because it renders him impotent:

> In power of others, never in my own;
> Scarce half I seem to live, dead more than half.
> O dark, dark, dark, amid the blaze of noon,
> Irrecoverably dark, total Eclipse
> Without all hope of day!
>
> (Ll. 78-82)

Ironically, his conviction of powerlessness in the past prevents his full repentance. He knows that he has sinned, broken the divine commandment of silence; but he has not admitted that his sin was voluntary, a free choice in the context of adequate knowledge. He is helplessly in darkness in the midst of blazing light because he is ignorant, even though God's will has been sufficiently revealed to him.[18] He feels "In power of others, never

---

[17] Similarly, in *The Christian Doctrine,* Milton argues that the divine decree of predestination is conditional upon the human response but that this condition does not "attribute mutability either to God or his decrees" (C.E., XIV, 107).

[18] Casuists differ in their descriptions of how men know God's will, but they agree that it is sufficiently revealed that men have the knowledge necessary to avoid sin. See Perkins, I, 519; Ames, Bk. III, p. 92. In *The Christian Doctrine,* Milton speaks of the conscience as the "judgment of the mind respecting its own actions, formed according to the light which we have received either from nature or from grace" (C.E., XVII, 41).

in my own," even though morally significant action, obedience to God's law, is always within his power. The pathos of Samson's suffering is intensified by his failure to recognize that while God is light and has given light to man, the light of divine truth in man is more easily extinguished than physical sight. Samson bewails the vulnerability of the eye: "why was the sight / To such a tender ball as th'eye confin'd? / So obvious and so easy to be quench't" (ll. 93-95), but William Perkins more aptly notes: "The good conscience is the most tender part of the soule; like to the apple of the eye; which being pierced by the least pin that may be, is not only blemished, but also looseth his sight" (I, 554).

The wounded conscience is not incurable however. When believers like Samson have evil consciences, "there is a principle of grace, by strength whereof they are *upholden,* they *wrastle* and *withstand,* and by little and little are *healed* of it" (Ames, Bk. I, p. 42). The progress of Samson's recovery is marked by the entrance of the Chorus. When they interrupt his distracted reflections, they recognize that he is suffering from a wounded conscience and assume the role and language of the casuist:

> Counsel or Consolation we may bring,
> Salve to thy Sores; apt words have power to swage
> The tumors of a troubl'd mind,
> And are as Balm to fester'd wounds.
>
> (Ll. 183-186)

Counsel and consolation are the traditional offices of the casuist, and his activities are frequently described as the "curing of a wounded conscience." [19] To the Chorus, Samson confesses that the pangs of conscience, not physical blindness, are his greatest torment:

> Yet that which was the worst now least afflicts me,
> Blindness, for had I sight, confus'd with shame,
> How could I once look up, or heave the head,
> Who like a foolish Pilot have shipwreck't
> My Vessel trusted to me from above,
> Gloriously rigg'd; . . .
>
> (Ll. 195-200)

[19] Titles such as the following are common: *The Wounded Conscience Cured, the Weak One strengthened and the doubting satisfied* (London, 1642); Thomas Fuller, *Cause and Cure of a Wounded Conscience* (1647). See also Perkins, II, 2, and Thomas Pickering's dedication to Perkins's *The Whole Treatise of the Cases of Conscience.*

The shipwreck metaphor is common in casuistry. Perkins analyzes the figure explicitly:

> Now we are all as passengers; the world is an huge sea, through which we must passe: our ship is the conscience of every man, I.Tim.1.19 and 3.12. the wares are our religion and salvation, and all other gifts of God. Therefore it stands us in hand to be alwaies at the helme, and to carrie our ship with as even a course as possibly we can, to the intended port of happines, which is the salvation of our soules.   (I, 554)

Samson's metaphor implies that he was gloriously endowed with gifts from God, but instead of using his talents well for their true purpose, he abandoned the helm, neglected his duty, and irresponsibly shipwrecked his conscience.

Although the foolish-pilot image implies a fuller acceptance of his moral responsibility than he has shown before, Samson still tries to avoid the full burden of his guilt by attributing his failure to lack of intelligence. The Chorus responds to his guilt and confusion like conventional casuists. William Perkins's directions for how to deal with a troubled conscience mention such tactics as mingling comfort with the "tartnesse of the law," reducing grief for sin in general to understanding and grief for a particular distinct offence, and reminding the sufferer of the universality of sin (II, 22-25, 42). Accordingly, the Chorus of Danites first offers friendship and sympathy and then warns Samson of the impiety of his complaints. They try to assuage the intensity of his self-recrimination by reminding him that he is not alone in his guilt. Then they probe into the particularities of his sin, questioning Samson's motives in marrying an unbeliever. As their probing leads Samson back to reconsider his actions, he explains his marriage choices and in the process proves a better casuist than the wholly conventional Chorus. While they think simply in terms of technical conformity with the letter of the law, Samson defends his decisions on the basis of the casuistical concept of the significance of the intention, the surrounding circumstances, and the probable consequences of an action.

Samson explains that he knew by "intimate impulse" from God that his first marriage with an unbeliever was lawful for him in order to fulfill his vocation to "begin *Israel's* Deliverance." His conclusion is consistent with casuistical principles and with Protestant cases of conscience. Most Protestant casuists do not absolutely condemn marriage to an unbeliever but resolve these cases on the basis of intention and circumstances, stressing the circumstances unfavorable to the ends of matrimony.[20] Samson has assumed the same latitude of choice in spite of the Mosaic proscription of marriage with an unbeliever. No casuists advocate the transgression of a divine law, but they recognize that, in the infinite variety of circumstances in actual human experience, laws cannot be applied mechanically. A guideline in resolving problems of doubt is the concept of equity:

> Legall Justice taken strictly, considereth the words just as they are written, but Equity considereth the End, scope and intent of the Law, and so hath more Law in it, then Legall Justice, when taken strictly. (Ames, Bk. V, p. 111)

The point, of course, is not that a firm sense of one's good intentions justifies an act that is evil in itself but that the honest intention to fulfill the intent or purpose of the law is the essence of lawful action. In Samson's case, the prohibition against mixed marriage is intended to preserve the true faith and prevent the dispersal of God's people. The circumstances of Samson's vocation, intention, and talents make it most probable that he will use the occasion to deliver Israel from oppression. Thus his decision that his unorthodox marriage does not transgress but rather fulfills divine law is reasonable.

Although Samson's decision can be justified in terms of Protestant casuistry and anticipates his later, crucial decision to contradict the restrictions of the law, he still does not fully understand the significance of his actions. He seems to believe that God dispensed with His Law in the case of his first marriage, and he seems to be unsure about whether or not he sinned in his second one. He fails to understand that God does not dispense with His immutable law and that every individual is responsible for judging how to fulfill that law.[21] He still cannot formulate clearly the principles that can help men make the moral decisions confronting them.

In spite of Samson's confusion, the Chorus who came to give

[20] See, for example, Sanderson's "The Case of Marrying with a Recusant," in *Works*, V, 75-80.

[21] Milton "was convinced that even the will of God himself could not make an unlawful act lawful or a lawful unlawful" (Arthur Barker, *Milton and the Puritan Dilemma*, p. 169).

counsel is now being instructed by him. Although he cannot correct their idea about special dispensation from divine law or their denunciation of reason, he does show them that divine justice is not contained by the narrow boundaries of "National obstriction," that morally right action involves more than conformity to the letter of the law, and that an attempt to reduce man's knowledge of God's will to a rigid code regardless of individual circumstances produces contradictions that mislead men into futile "wand'ring thought." Their suggestion that the source of his trouble was marrying an infidel has led him to see clearly that his sin was not his marriage, which he judged to be lawful, but giving up his "fort of silence," which he knew to be forbidden. He, not Dalila, was the prime cause of his fall. The woman who might have served to further Israel's liberty became the means of Samson's bondage through his own action. This distinction between the sin and the means of sin leads simultaneously to Samson's deepening sense of responsibility for his own sin and to his awareness of the limits of his responsibility. Having grasped the principle of individual responsibility in his own case, he can apply it in others. When the Chorus reproaches him for Israel's continued servitude, he can confidently defend his innocence. He provided the Israelites with the opportunity to struggle for liberty; the responsibility for choosing bondage is theirs.

Gradually, then, as he reflects on his own actions, Samson learns that the moral nature of human action depends on man's voluntary cooperation with God's will, not on external achievements. The increased clarity of his thought about divine law and human action makes possible the firmness of his response to Manoa in the next episode. In the early speeches, Samson had struggled to reconcile his faith in God with his bitterness that God's promise had proved false and with his feeling that somehow he had been tricked. In contrast to this confusion, he replies firmly to Manoa's questioning of divine justice, confessing fully and unequivocally his responsibility. The point, he knows, is that he broke the law of God, not that God is treating His hero inappropriately. Samson knew that to reveal the secret of his strength was to violate his vow to God; he knew through ample experience that Dalila was tempting him to that sin. The circumstances of his action, moreover, increase rather than extenuate his guilt because he betrayed his secret to a worshipper of Dagon.

Thus he was not tricked into violating a taboo; he sinned against his own conscience, his understanding of God's will. While he had acknowledged earlier that his fall from God's favor was his own fault, he had attributed that fault to innate weakness. Now in answering his father, he realizes that he had the necessary strength and knowledge for free choice. He voluntarily chose spiritual servitude and blindness, a torment far worse than the physical bondage imposed on him.

As Samson and Manoa turn from judging the past to considering what to do next, the concept of the weight of circumstances in moral choice assumes a new and horrible significance for Samson. Manoa warns that the Philistines will hold a feast honoring Dagon for Samson's defeat:

> So *Dagon* shall be magnified, and God,
> Besides whom is no God, compar'd with Idols,
> Disglorified, blasphem'd, and had in scorn
> By th'Idolatrous rout amidst thir wine;
> Which to have come to pass by means of thee,
> *Samson,* of all thy sufferings think the heaviest,
> Of all reproach the most with shame that ever
> Could have befall'n thee and thy Father's house.
> (Ll. 440-447)

Manoa is perhaps overly concerned with the outrage to personal pride and family honor, but he understands the moral responsibility to avoid being manipulated by Dagon's followers. Better than his father, Samson knows that the problem is not his loss of glory or God's, which does not depend on him; but Manoa's warning that the present situation perpetuates his guilt jolts Samson into new awareness of the consequences of his present position. He knows that he has already sinned by breaking divine law; now he realizes that he continues to sin by causing scandal, presenting a stumbling block to the faith of others. He confesses that he has

> brought scandal
> To *Israel,* diffidence of God, and doubt
> In feeble hearts, propense enough before
> To waver, or fall off and joyn with Idols:
> Which is my chief affliction, shame and sorrow.
> (Ll. 453-457)

Manoa's solution to the problem deals with his own responsibility, not Samson's. To him, the question is "But for thee what shall be done?" (l. 478). His proposal to ransom Samson and take him home ignores another important circumstance, Samson's vocation to work for Israel's deliverance. Manoa ignores his son's need to serve, but Samson understands that if he should retire to his father's house "a burdenous drone" he would be guilty of abandoning his calling altogether.

Samson's analysis of his present situation demonstrates the renewal of his understanding of divine justice and of his confidence in his own intellectual and moral faculties, but it also precipitates his most agonized sense of despair. He knows that God's word is truth and will prevail and that he has sufficient knowledge and understanding to distinguish good from evil, but he doubts his ability to act on his own judgment. He understands more fully than Manoa that through divine law he is obligated not simply to uphold a rigid national code of conduct but to respond creatively to his calling in God's service. He does not, however, see how any course of action open to him can avoid sin. He can find no way out of the dilemma of either causing scandal by serving the Philistines with his God-given talents or becoming a "burdenous drone." He cannot answer his question of how to act in his particular circumstances on his understanding of God's will:

> by which means,
> Now blind, disheart'n'd, sham'd, dishonour'd, quell'd,
> To what can I be useful, wherein serve
> My Nation, and the work from Heav'n impos'd.
>
> (Ll. 562-565)

Death is "the welcome end" because he no longer hopes to serve.

Manoa's argument that Samson should not seek his own punishment and destruction is sound casuistry, but he is addressing the wrong problem. It is not excessive and neurotic guilt over the past that drives Samson to despair. He is contrite for his sin and accepts his suffering, but he cannot achieve a peaceful conscience either as a captive among the Philistines or as a helpless parasite in his father's house. The consolation Manoa offers externalizes the problem:

> Believe not these suggestions which proceed
> From anguish of the mind and humors black,

That mingle with thy fancy. I however
Must not omit a Father's timely care
To prosecute the means of thy deliverance
By ransom or how else: meanwhile be calm,
And healing words from these thy friends admit.

(Ll. 599-605)

Rescue from physical bondage and the solace of friends cannot help, as Samson knows, because the disease is internal:

My griefs not only pain me
As a ling'ring disease,
But finding no redress, ferment and rage,
Nor less than wounds immedicable
Rankle, and fester, and gangrene,
To black mortification.
Thoughts my Tormentors arm'd with deadly stings
Mangle my apprehensive tenderest parts,
Exasperate, exulcerate, and raise
Dire inflammation which no cooling herb
Or med'cinal liquor can assuage.

(Ll. 617-627) [22]

When Samson can find no way to live virtuously, death must seem the only solution: "The close of all my miseries, and the balm" (l. 651).

In the first two episodes, then, men try to relate particular human situations to their conception of moral order. The contrasts among their judgments of what Samson has done and should do next suggest the problematic nature of moral choice, the intellectual difficulties of the decision-making process, and the possibility of solving moral dilemmas through reason. The varying judgments are dramatic models both of the human failure to judge wisely and of the adequacy of human reason for

[22] Samson's description echoes the comparison of the wounded conscience with physical disease that is pervasive in casuistry. Perkins, for example, describes a guilty conscience as "a worme that never dieth, but alwaies lies gnawing and grabbling, and pulling at the heart of man, Mark 9.44. and causeth more paine and anguish, then any disease in the world can doe" (I, 536). Milton uses this image in his Commonplace Book: "The cause of valour [is] a good conscience, for an evil conscience, as an English author noteth well, will otherwise knaw at the roots of valour like a worm and undermine all resolutions" (C.E., XVIII, 135).

the duty of applying divine law to particular situations. Those who offer Samson counsel and consolation lack the moral depth to provide guidance, but they provoke him to rethink his own judgments. Paradoxically, through dialogue with other men, Samson learns that finally each man is alone with his own conscience before God.

The tension between human achievement and human failure created by the dramatic action is reflected in the choric ode that follows the scene with Manoa. The Chorus reflects Samson's hopelessness and helplessness. "Many are the sayings of the wise," they begin, but they go on to lament the futility of human wisdom in the face of the uncontrollable calamities man is subject to. Men can bear their sufferings with patience only through "consolation from above"; and God's ways to man are, to limited human reason, unjust. The Danites' answer to the question "what is man" almost seems a deliberate inversion, a Puritan parody, of the ringing humanism of the ode in the *Antigone,* which Bernard Knox has called "A Hymn to Man." [23]

The Sophoclean ode begins with wonder at man the doer:

Many the marvelous things; but none that can be
   More of a marvel than man! This being that braves
With the south wind of winter the whitened streaks of the sea.
                         (Ll. 308-310) [24]

The Miltonic ode begins with wonder at what is done to man. Unlike other orders of created life, man is treated by God with bewildering inconsistency:

        God of our Fathers, what is man!
     That thou towards him with hand so various,
     Or might I say contrarious,
     Temper'st thy providence through his short course,
     Not evenly, as thou rul'st
     Th' Angelic orders and inferior creatures mute,
     Irrational and brute.

                         (Ll. 667-673)

The subject of Sophocles' ode is generic man. Each particular

[23] *Oedipus at Thebes: Sophocles' Tragic Hero and His Time* (New Haven: Yale University Press, 1957), pp. 107-108.

[24] All *Antigone* quotations are from *Three Theban Plays,* trans. Theodore Howard Banks (New York: Oxford University Press, 1956).

human skill demonstrates general human ability: "Wild creatures he catches," "the salt-sea brood he nets in his woven coils," "The tireless bull he has tamed," "He is master of all through his skills" (ll. 318-323). Milton's Chorus quickly excludes from their complaint "the common rout" of men and speaks of heroes who, with great "gifts and graces" have worked for God's glory and the "people's safety," yet still are subjected to divine displeasure (ll. 674-681). Sophocles' ode traces the "progress of man from primitive ignorance to civilized power. He conquers the elements . . . masters animate nature . . . communicates and combines with his fellows to found society; protects himself against the elements; begins to conquer disease—there seems to be no limit to his advance except his own death." [25] Milton's ode reverses the process, showing once-exalted heroes subject first to uncivilized brutality, then to corrupt human society, and finally to the unaided suffering of their own physical frailty:

> to the hostile sword
> Of Heathen and profane, thir carcases
> To dogs and fowls a prey, or else captiv'd:
> Or to th'unjust tribunals, under change of times,
> And condemnation of th'ingrateful multitude.
> If these they scape, perhaps in poverty
> With sickness and disease thou bow'st them down,
> Painful diseases and deform'd,
> In crude old age.
>
> (Ll. 692-700)

The chorus of Thebans concludes that the laws of the land are the mainstay of human dignity:

> When he holds the canons of justice high in his heart
>   And has sworn to the gods the laws of the land to defend,
> Proud stands his city.
>
> (Ll. 334-336)

In contrast, the Danites lament the injustice of the human condition:

> Just or unjust, alike seem miserable,
> For oft alike, both come to evil end.
>
> (Ll. 703-704)

---

[25] Knox, *Oedipus at Thebes*, p. 108.

Sophocles' chorus celebrates human talents and achievements, and Milton's laments the vulnerability and failure of even the greatest men. Ironically, however, the two odes function dramatically in ways almost opposite to what this analysis suggests. The chorus in *Antigone* turns immediately from their exalted praise of justice to condemn Antigone for having foolishly defied Creon's tyranny, and their praise of human mastery and control echoes ironically as Creon's efforts to enforce the law and impose rational control over his world degrade his subjects and reveal his lack of knowledge and control of even his own nature. The dramatic context affects the ode in *Samson* in a similarly ironic way. The ode stresses the limitations of human power, but in its immediate context, it sounds a strongly positive note:

> Behold him in this state calamitous, and turn
> His labors, for thou canst, to peaceful end.
>
> (Ll. 708-709)

However bitter their response to Samson's calamity, the Chorus assumes that his labors can have significant consequences. Their emphasis on God's mystery and power ultimately augments rather than degrades the significance and dignity of human actions. The Chorus reminds the reader of the crucial points of faith that Samson must discover before he can resolve his doubts: circumstances cannot obliterate the possibility of moral action, and God always can turn man's labors to His ends.

The principle that sinless action is always possible in any set of circumstances is a necessary complement and inevitable consequence of the concept of divine law and human moral responsibility that Samson has already been able to apply in judging his own actions. He has learned that divine law is just and that it is the moral basis of human action, that it is not a narrow proscription of human actions but the obligation of each man to respond to God's call with love and service in his own unique circumstances, and that men have adequate knowledge and reason to know good from evil and to choose through their free will. Taken together, these principles necessarily imply that "The precepts of God doe never so jarre of their own nature, that it is necessary to break one of them by sin" (Ames, Bk. III, p. 87). This conceptual relationship helps to account for the change in direction in the middle of *Samson Agonistes*. In the first half of the tragedy, Samson falls more and more deeply into despair. After the "God of our Fathers" ode Samson shows growing confidence in the possibility of virtuous, effective action and directs his attention to making decisions about what to do next. We can account for this positive change by understanding that the regenerative process Samson undergoes involves not simply humiliation of sinful pride but also the restoration of his human faculties. Once Samson's confidence in his own ability to choose virtue is restored and the question is reformulated as what to do next, it is inevitable that he will overcome his sense of powerlessness and hence his desire for death. He needs only to understand that circumstances cannot force him to sin. Dalila's arguments function as the catalyst revealing this corollary to responsibility.

SAMSON'S RECOVERY

In the dialogues with Manoa and the Chorus, Samson meets their judgments of past and future action with his own, but he does not explain fully the basis for his judgment or the inadequacy of theirs. He gropes for the correct formulation of the moral issues involved and through this process gains understanding. In subsequent scenes, he is able to apply these principles to particular cases; moral issues are defined more clearly, and each moral judgment is analyzed in precise detail in the second half of the tragedy.

During Dalila's visit, Samson betrays his anger, bitterness, fear, and fascination through the abuse and heavy-handed sarcasm he hurls at the woman he has loved and been betrayed by; but the dramatic force of the scene is created by his control of these powerful, destructive emotions. Most of the episode consists of close, logical analysis of complex moral questions. Unlike the Chorus and Manoa, Dalila formulates her judgments as cases of conscience. She explicitly relates particular doubtful actions in certain circumstances to moral law. She bases her argument on the assumption that moral law cannot be applied mechanically and that a human action can be judged only in the full light of its surrounding circumstances and the state of mind of the human agent. Although Dalila's casuistical practice is sophistical, her basic assumptions are sound, and so Samson does not ignore or dismiss her arguments; he carefully refutes her in her own terms. He meets her arguments directly, explaining exactly the flaw in her argument and the principle he is applying in each case.

275

Her first argument is that while her betrayal of Samson was wrong, the sinfulness of the action is mitigated by two circumstances, her female weakness and her love for Samson. Samson, who has painfully thought through the relation of circumstances to moral law in his own case, refutes her easily. Although circumstances alter the way man fulfills the law, they never release him from his duty to obey it. Weakness is the description of sin, not an excuse for it. Desire that attempts to possess and control the beloved against his will is lust, not love. Dalila then shifts her evasion of moral responsibility from the plea of private passion to civil and religious duty. She argues that she was caught in a conflict between love for her husband and duty to her country and religion. She resolved the dilemma on the principle "that to the public good / Private respects must yield." The case of conscience she poses was familiar to Milton's contemporaries. The axiom that "the public good is the supreme law" was frequently invoked in polemical literature and in cases of conscience.[26] Samson not only sneers at the feigned sincerity of her love and her religion but analyzes carefully the moral dilemma she posits and the ethical principle by which she resolves it:

> Being once a wife, for me thou wast to leave
> Parents and country; nor was I their subject,
> Nor under their protection but my own,
> Thou mine, not theirs: if aught against my life
> Thy country sought of thee, it sought unjustly,
> Against the law of nature, law of nations,
> No more thy country, but an impious crew
> Of men conspiring to uphold thir state
> By worse than hostile deeds, violating the ends
> For which our country is a name so dear;
> Not therefore to be obey'd.

(Ll. 885-895)

[26] The maxim *salus populi suprema lex* was invoked variously in Henry Parker, *Observations upon some of his Majesties Late Answers and Expresses* (1642); in Samuel Rutherford, *Lex, Rex* (1644); in John Goodwin, *Right and Might well met* (1648); in Milton, *The Tenure of Kings and Magistrates* (1649); and in Thomas Hobbes, *Leviathan* (1651). Robert Sanderson devotes two of his ten lectures on casuistry to explaining it. See *Several Cases of Conscience Discussed in Ten Lectures* (1660).

Samson's analysis of "the public good" is similar to Milton's own in the prose.[27] Since the state exists to uphold justice, an unjust law is a violation of the public good and of the ends for which the state exists. A human law or command that violates universal moral law is unjust and hence invalid. With her marriage, Dalila voluntarily assumed a primary allegiance to her husband, and betrayal of that bond is a violation of universal moral law. A political command to betray her husband is thus contrary to the public good, and the moral dilemma she poses is illusory.

After her sophistical judgments of past action are refuted logically, Dalila turns to the future. When she suggests that Samson can choose solace in domestic tranquillity with her instead of prison and hard labor, he realizes that in spite of the power of external circumstances to limit his physical freedom of movement, he still is able to reject her and to choose physical rather than spiritual bondage:

> This Gaol I count the house of Liberty
> To thine whose doors my feet shall never enter.
> (Ll. 949-950)

In rejecting her proposal, Samson extends the distinction between physical and spiritual bondage he made in talking with Manoa to the choices still available to him and sees scope for freedom in his present situation.

In responding to Dalila, Samson does not merely condemn his betrayer but applies to particular cases the moral principles that have emerged from analysis of his own actions. In doing so, he clarifies the role of circumstances in ethical judgments. The interrelations of domestic, political, and religious obligations raise complex moral questions, but these circumstances do not obliterate moral responsibility or free choice.

Samson's handling of Dalila's cases of conscience contrasts with the relative obtuseness of the Chorus as well as with his wife's deviousness. Appropriating the ship metaphor that Samson had used (ll. 198-200), the Chorus shows that they have grasped the point that Samson allowed himself to be guided by Dalila rather than his own conscience:

---

[27] On Milton and "the public good," see Barker, *Milton and the Puritan Dilemma,* pp. 109-110, 163-165, 281-282, 300-303.

What Pilot so expert but needs must wreck
Embark'd with such a Steers-mate at the Helm?
(Ll. 1044-1045)

But their hostility toward Dalila prevents their seeing Samson's sin and folly, and their moral insight is almost lost in their grumbling about the moral and intellectual inferiority of women. Whether or not Milton sympathized with their misogyny, it is noteworthy that, while the Chorus insists on female inferiority and male "despotic power," Samson does not speculate on women's incapacity for rational thought and moral choice. On the contrary, his denunciation of Dalila assumes that she is capable of and hence responsible for her moral choices.

Samson's interview with Dalila is the pivotal point in the drama. The dialogue in the remaining scenes continues the detailed analysis of doubtful moral problems. In discussing them, Samson shows no uncertainty about the reliability of his judgments and no longer looks for guidance from without. He continues to anticipate his death but never again refers to it in a tone of despair, for he does not doubt his freedom to choose to act in accordance with God's will. In the encounters with his avowed enemies, he shows increasing skill in devising means to control circumstances for his own ends instead of despairing that he is controlled by them.

Samson dismisses contemptuously Harapha's contention that blindness and imprisonment prevent him from fighting as the champion of his God and suggests simple expedients to make a duel possible. To Harapha's taunts that Samson's strength derives from black magic and that he has been deserted by his God, Samson confidently answers that his ability to act comes from the human strength of trust in "the living God . . . Whose ear is ever open." Harapha's next ploy, accusing Samson of murder, revolt, and robberty for his acts of hostility against the Philistines, involves Samson again in a case of conscience familiar to Milton's first readers. The moral obligations to a de facto government were, of course, not only debated hotly by committed royalists and revolutionaries but were pressing ethical questions for most citizens from the outbreak of hostilities in England until after the Restoration. Casuists were in agreement that the moral nature of certain actions is affected by their political context and that the preservation of society demands at least some degree of obedience to law even under the most tyrannical and unjust government. But there was no consensus, even among casuists with identical political and ecclesiastical allegiances, on how to resolve problems of when one is morally obligated to obey or to resist unlawful authority.

Samson approaches the problem by carefully detailing the particular circumstances of the case in question as well as the theoretical basis for his decision. His description of the wedding feast emphasizes his willingness to relate to Philistines on a personal basis without hostility:

> Among the Daughters of the *Philistines*
> I chose a Wife, which argu'd me no foe;
> And in your City held my Nuptial Feast.
> (Ll. 1192-1194)

By their treachery, the "ill-meaning Politician Lords" politicized the event and chose their roles as enemies of Israel. Samson responded appropriately; his revenge was not murder and robbery but war.

He next replies to Harapha's argument that the Philistines were rulers of Israel and Samson a rebel, treated as such by his compatriots. He divides the question into two parts. First:

> My Nation was subjected to your Lords.
> It was the force of Conquest; force with force
> Is well ejected when the Conquer'd can.
> (Ll. 1205-1207)

The argument that force does not constitute a lawful government is familiar. Second, Samson considers the standard argument that crime is distinguished from public service on the basis of the office of the agent (for example, a private citizen may not pass sentence on the life or property of another, but a duly constituted judge may).[28]

> But I a private person, whom my Country
> As a league-breaker gave up bound, presum'd
> Single Rebellion and did Hostile Acts.
> (Ll. 1208-1210)

[28] In *The Tenure of Kings and Magistrates,* Milton accepted this distinction: "To doe justice on a lawless King, is to a privat man unlawful, to an inferior Magistrate lawfull" (C.E., V, 58). Cf. Henry Parker, *Observations upon some of his Majesties Late Answers and Expresses* (1642).

Samson's answer to this charge may at first seem to accept the private person / public official distinction and to challenge merely the facts, but his argument is more subtle than this.

> I was no private but a person rais'd
> With strength sufficient and command from Heav'n
> To free my Country; if their servile minds
> Me their Deliverer sent would not receive,
> But to thir Masters gave me up for nought,
> Th'unworthier they; whence to this day they serve.
>
> (Ll. 1211-1216)

Instead of justifying his hostility to Philistine oppression on the basis of his official position as judge, he cites his conscience and implies that all Israelites should have followed his example.[29] Samson's answer to the question of the private citizen's obligation to an unlawful authority is radical. He recognizes no difference between ruler and subject morality and no moral obligation to obey unlawful authority. In circumstances of civil disorder, then, the individual owes obedience to no authority but divine law. Samson's gradual recognition of the traditional principles and practices of Protestant casuistry has led him to a revolutionary political position.

In his interview with the Philistine officer, Samson takes the final step in his assertion of the supremacy of the individual conscience and the harmony between thought and action. When the officer and the Chorus warn him against the risks of defying his conquerors, Samson explains his judgment more fully. To the officer's fatuous advice to "Regard thyself," Samson counters that

[29] Barbara Lewalski has shown that in the Protestant typology Milton draws on in *Samson Agonistes,* Samson and other Israelite judges are types of the Christian elect, both in their suffering in this life and their participation with Christ as judges of the world at the Apocalypse. Israelite judges and Christian magistrates are correlative types whose vocation to deliver God's people from oppression and to wreak vengeance on his enemies is fulfilled by the antitype, the Last Judgment. While seventeenth-century Puritans usually associated Samson as judge specifically with their own magistrates, the main force of the typological reverberations of the judge figure that Lewalski examines supports the emphasis on individual conscience instead of official position. In Milton's mature view, the Millennial Kingdom and the rule of Saints is achieved only at the end of time; until then the kingdom of the elect is internal and spiritual rather than outward and political. See Barbara Kiefer Lewalski, "*Samson Agonistes* and the 'Tragedy' of the Apocalypse," *PMLA* 85 (1970): 1050-1062.

his truest "self" is his conscience, making clear that he understands "conscience" to be at once his moral guide, the basis for
emotional health, and the intellectual ability to distinguish a
lawful command from an unlawful one.

> Myself? my conscience and internal peace.
> Can they think me so broken, so debas'd
> With corporal servitude, that my mind ever
> Will condescend to such absurd commands?
> (Ll. 1334-1337)

Samson's answer to the Chorus shows them and us that his decision is not based on mechanical obedience to the letter of the
law but on his understanding of the purpose or spirit of the law
and the inherent evil in the action it prohibits:

> Shall I abuse this Consecrated gift
> Of strength, again returning with my hair
> After my great transgression, so requite
> Favor renew'd, and add a greater sin
> By prostituting holy things to Idols;
> A *Nazarite* in place abominable
> Vaunting my strength in honor to thir *Dagon?*
> Besides, how vile, contemptible, ridiculous,
> What act more execrably unclean, profane?
> (Ll. 1354-1362)

The Chorus then raises objections to Samson's judgment, and
he answers them like a casuist resolving anticipated doubts in a
traditional case of conscience.[30] When they suggest that his willingness to serve the Philistines in some ways and not in others is
logically inconsistent, he explains the difference between compliance in indifferent things and actually participating in unjust
actions:

> *Chorus*   Yet with this strength thou serv'st the *Philistines,*
> Idolatrous, uncircumcis'd, unclean.
> *Samson*   Not in thir Idol-Worship, but by labor
> Honest and lawful to deserve my food
> Of those who have me in thir civil power.
> (Ll. 1363-1367)

---

[30] Compare Perkins's treatment of the case of conscience, *"Whether it be
lawfull for a man being urged, to go toe idol-service . . . so as he keepe his
heart to God?"* (II, 87). See also Ames, Bk. IV, pp. 7-8.

Next the Chorus suggests that outward compliance with evil is lawful if the heart is pure: "Where the heart joins not, outward acts defile not" (l. 1368). And Samson patiently explains that the relevant distinction is not between thought and deed but between a voluntary and an involuntary action:

> Where outward force constrains, the sentence holds;
> But who constrains me to the Temple of *Dagon*,
> Not dragging? the *Philistian* Lords command.
> Commands are no constraints. If I obey them,
> I do it freely; venturing to displease
> God for the fear of Man, and Man prefer,
> Set God behind: which in his jealousy
> Shall never, unrepented, find forgiveness.
> Yet that he may dispense with me or thee
> Present in Temples at Idolatrous Rites
> For some important cause, thou needst not doubt.
>
> (Ll. 1369-1379)

This speech succinctly reviews many of the basic principles that Samson's crisis of conscience has clarified for him: men are free to choose good or evil, and sin is always voluntary; no threat of force can justify the willing violation of divine law; the decision to obey an unlawful command against one's conscience is to obey man rather than God; repentance is possible since God is merciful, but circumstances cannot turn idolatry into virtue. At this point, Samson is finally able to articulate the principle inherent in the divine sanction of his marriage choice: obedience to divine law is totally obligatory, but the method of fulfilling the law may vary according to circumstances. Thus one might violate the letter of the law against attending idolatrous rites in order to obey its spirit that forbids "prostituting holy things to Idols."

Samson has been accused of logic chopping in this discussion,[31] but the fine distinctions he makes between lawful work and unlawful compliance and between commands and constraints are a necessary part of the casuistical process of applying divine law to particular circumstances without moral laxity or legal rigidity. It is the same process, of course, that today enables a conscientious objector to serve willingly as a doctor or a janitor while refusing to fight as a soldier under the same government.

[31] Mason Tung, "Samson *Impatiens*: A Reinterpretation of Milton's *Samson Agonistes*," *Texas Studies in Literature and Language* 9 (1968): 489.

Samson's next speech is the thematic core of the tragedy, giving form in action to the ideas of human responsibility and freedom that he has been struggling to grasp.

> I begin to feel
> Some rousing motions in me which dispose
> To something extraordinary my thoughts.
> I with this Messenger will go along,
> Nothing to do, be sure, that may dishonor
> Our Law, or stain my vow of *Nazarite*.
> If there be aught of presage in the mind,
> This day will be remarkable in my life
> By some great act, or of my days the last.
>
> (Ll. 1381-1389)

Claiming the freedom to ignore the Mosaic prohibition and at the same time insisting that he will not break the law, Samson is distinguishing between the letter and the spirit of the law. He is asserting the supremacy of his own conscience over Judaic as well as over civil law. Samson is subject only to divine law and the final authority on knowledge of God's will is his own conscience, his own reason operating morally. As Arthur Barker has said, Christian liberty is finally what *Samson Agonistes* is all about. Samson, rooted in his historical context, cannot possess Christian liberty; yet he serves as a model for the Christian liberty that Milton sought to define for his countrymen in his attempts to resolve contemporary cases of conscience.[32]

After the firmness with which he announced and defended his first decision to resist the Philistine command, Samson's change of mind comes with great dramatic force, but the reversal does not shock or bewilder us. Samson's "rousing motions" surprise us just as events in most tragedies strike us as both inevitable and startling. The way has been elaborately prepared, and

[32] Barker, "Structural and Doctrinal Pattern in Milton's Later Poems," pp. 169-179; Samuel S. Stollman, "Milton's Samson and the Jewish Tradition," *Milton Studies* 3 (1971): 185-200, corroborates Barker's thesis. Stollman's account of the abrogation of the Old Law and internalization of divine law is valuable but does not discuss the process by which Samson discovers his liberty. Lynn Veach Sadler suggests that the appropriate term is " 'prophetic liberty,' the Old Testament equivalent of 'Christian Liberty'." See "Typological Imagery in *Samson Agonistes*: Noon and the Dragon," *ELH* 37 (1970): 196.

Samson's sudden inspiration results from the careful analysis that precedes it. Through reinterpreting his past actions and considering future alternatives, Samson has achieved understanding of his responsibility to obey divine law and through this process of repentance and discovery has experienced the renovation of his natural powers of judgment. By recognizing his guilt before the law, he has learned to transcend the law.

The "rousing motions" Samson feels are, of course, the effect of grace, as indeed is the whole process of regeneration. In Samson's case, grace works through reason, as it usually does in Milton's view. Samson's sudden perception that he will be able to do something extraordinary does not miraculously translate him out of the human condition; on the contrary, it marks his full involvement in the experiential situation. Instead of trying to mitigate physical suffering and waiting for a miracle, Samson uses his human faculties to discover a solution to his dilemma in the mire of complexities of his actual situation. He has realized that by remaining a prisoner of the Philistines he would provide a stumbling block to the faith of the Hebrews and that by withdrawing to the care of Manoa he would reject the opportunity to respond to his calling by opposing the oppressors of Israel. He discovers an exit from the apparently impossible situation by deciding to appear at the festival of Dagon in order to defy the Philistines by some "great act." The way out that he discovers exacts a great price, but he acts with a clear conscience.

Changed circumstances necessitate new tactics. When Samson thought of himself as a national hero predestined to continuing success, a "petty God" invulnerable to his enemies and beyond the perplexities of ordinary mortals, he could fight his enemies simply and openly. Now, as a defeated champion in the power of his enemies, he can act virtuously only by dissembling. The lawfulness of deception was, of course, a recurrent problem for casuists. Their solutions varied from the concepts of equivocation and mental reservation associated with the Jesuits to Perkins's concept of the good deceit and Sanderson's position that only the literal truth is lawful, but they all tried to face the moral problem raised by the possibility of evil consequences resulting from the simple truth. The *locus classicus* for the innocent deception is the story of the Egyptian midwives' deception of the Pharoah to save the children of the Israelites (Exod. 1:19). In *The Christian*

Doctrine, Milton judges lying to the enemy in war as lawful.[33] Samson cannot explain, in the presence of the Philistine officer, how he resolved the case; but it is obvious that he pretends compliance and conceals his intention.[34]

> Masters' commands come with a power resistless
> To such as owe them absolute subjection;
> And for a life who will not change his purpose?
>
> (Ll. 1404-1406)

As Samson and any casuist know, subjection does not necessarily imply obedience.[35]

This episode epitomizes the complex relationships between absolute truth and the mutable ways of man in Samson's drama. By analyzing his own imperfect actions, Samson has gained new understanding of his relationship with God that supersedes all ties to family and nation. Paradoxically, this realization of absolute commitment to the unchanging law of God leads in turn to greater involvement in the actual human situation. In the first part of the scene, Samson demonstrates his obedience to the law and his courage to defy unlawful human authority; when the messenger returns, he transcends the dictates of the law and shows his cleverness in outwitting tyranny.

The Philistine officer contrasts vividly with Samson in both respects. He is at once detached from the complexities of human involvement and limited by the mutable human power structure. He is completely submissive to political authority, qualifying every thought with "our Lords thus bid me say" and "this will offend them highly." He is also totally naive, morally and politically, both in his underestimation of Samson and in his misunderstanding of freedom:

---

[33] Milton, C.E., XVII, 303. Cf. Ames, Bk. V, pp. 192, 269-277; Richard Baxter, *A Christian Directory: or a Summ of Practical Theology and Cases of Conscience* (London, 1673), Bk. I, pp. 421-430; Perkins, II, 116-117.

[34] See Paul R. Sellin, "Milton's Epithet *Agonistes,*" *SEL* 4 (1964): 137-162.

[35] For example, according to Ames: "For subjection in common, respects the authority, and power of the Superiour; but obedience respects the precept, or command which proceeds from the power. Hence . . . there may bee subjection, where there is not obedience, as in the humble denying of obedience, when that which is commanded by the Superiour, is manifestly unlawfull" (Bk. V, p. 155).

> By this compliance thou wilt win the Lords
> To favor, and perhaps to set thee free.
>
> > (Ll. 1411-1412)

The officer has won sympathy as a fundamentally decent man who reluctantly follows orders; but while Milton evokes pity for common human weakness, the banality of evil does not excuse it. The contrast between Samson, who will not "displease / God for the fear of Man" and exercises all his wit and courage to act effectively, and the officer, who obeys orders unquestioningly while expressing distaste for the cruelty involved, is not to Samson's discredit.

As he moves toward his death, Samson is isolated. He no longer looks for fame, comfort, or moral guidance from human relationships; but at no time is he more sensitive to the human situation. He carefully analyzes the motives behind the behavior of others and calculates shrewdly the consequences of his own actions.[36] He skillfully outmaneuvers his captors, ingeniously allowing them to deceive themselves while communicating to the Chorus the significance of his actions. Samson can never again be so naive and full of pride that he thinks he can be immune to the mischances of the human condition. He cannot control circumstances enough to predict completely the consequences of his own actions, or even to guarantee his own life. He is not able to create the world he wants, where the laws of nature are miraculously set aside and blind eyes see again and where sin is always punished and virtue rewarded. But he is able to predict with absolute certainty that he can act without sin:

> Happ'n what may, of me expect to hear
> Nothing dishonorable, impure, unworthy
> Our God, our Law, my Nation, or myself;
> The last of me or no I cannot warrant.
>
> > (Ll. 1423-1426)

Samson has learned that he does not have the power of a god but that he does have the human power that is freedom of conscience, a freedom that cannot be taken away from him.

The Chorus consistently regards Samson as an example whose fate somehow illuminates the human condition. They see in his

---

[36] Sellin demonstrates this point. See "Milton's Epithet *Agonistes*," pp. 153-154.

experience signs of divine power and glory as well as divine wrath, but they are limited throughout the tragedy by their conventional and legalistic view of man's moral obligations. Samson is therefore of greater service to them as an example of a man throwing off "mind-forg'd manacles" and making an independent decision in an unprecedented situation than he was as a military champion. His repeated insistence that he will obey the law and that unusual circumstances require extraordinary action has its effect. The Chorus is not equal to the freedom of acting to fulfill the spirit by transcending the letter of the law on the responsibility of their own consciences, but they can understand that Samson is. They know that Samson's suffering has been mental:

> This Idol's day hath been to thee no day of rest,
>> Laboring thy mind
> More than the working day thy hands.
>> (Ll. 1297-1299)

And they realize, even before the messenger enters, that Samson's struggle is of heroic proportions and that, whether God puts into his hands the power to defeat his enemies or whether he must suffer "all / That tyranny or fortune can inflict," Samson's victory will be won by his spiritual, not his physical strength—his "Heroic magnitude of mind" or the "patience" that is "more oft the exercise / Of Saints." After he has made his heroic decision, the Chorus's benediction acknowledges that Samson will now listen only to the voice of God and that conventional labels and codes of conduct will not serve to predict or describe how he will act:

> Go, and the Holy One
> Of *Israel* be thy guide
> To what may serve his glory best.
>> (Ll. 1427-1429)

Samson's carefully considered decision to appear before the Philistines is the last step in his regeneration. He has judged himself, repented, learned to understand the significance of his actions, and felt the renewal of God's favor. Deciding to act on the judgment of his conscience unsupported by an external authority completes the process. His courageous choice demonstrates his heroism. The external success or failure of his act is irrelevant to Samson's restoration, but his action assumes its full significance only in its effect on others. Milton brilliantly uses the convention of the messenger to give dramatic form to the meaning of Samson's history. Samson is unique in his talents, isolated from other men by his experience, enveloped in silence and mystery in his final relationship to his God; yet he serves as an example to other men, enlarging their understanding of the potentialities of their common human experience. The final scene gives dramatic form to these paradoxes of isolation / community and mystery / understanding.

Several critics have pointed out that the report of Samson's death is ironically preceded by the highest hopes of Manoa and the Chorus. As the roars of horror from the arena punctuate their predictions of Samson's release and regained eyesight, their optimism sounds facile and their ignorance pathetic. The dialogue between Manoa and the Chorus, however, does not show merely the limitations of the ordinary human perspective. If it is the world Samson transcends, it is also the world he loses and the world he serves. The focus is on human love and community. Manoa's hopes grow out of the intensity of his love for his son. He is eager to share his good news with his kinsmen, and they eagerly participate in his hope and joy. The sense of love and unity is interrupted by doubt and confusion, first about what has happened and then about its significance. After registering his first shock at the report of Samson's death, Manoa's immediate concern is to learn how he died, for the fact of death can be understood only in the context of its surrounding circumstances:

> Yet ere I give the reins to grief, say first,
> How died he? death to life is crown or shame.
>
> (Ll. 1578-1579)

Manoa is horrified at the answer that Samson died by his own hand; yet still he asks for particulars.

As we saw in the discussions of *Biathanatos* and *Julius Caesar*, Manoa's concern—whether suicide can be justified—is a classic question in casuistry, and Samson's case is frequently cited in the casuists' discussions.[37] Manoa and the Chorus wait silently through the messenger's long report to learn whether in Samson's particular case self-destruction was right or wrong. Until his account

[37] See Chapter IV, p. 143; also Ames, Bk. V, pp. 180-181 (mispaged 186-187); Perkins, II, 336. Cf. D. C. Allen, *The Harmonious Vision* (Baltimore: Johns Hopkins Press, 1954), pp. 83-84 and Krouse, *Milton's Samson*, pp. 74-75.

satisfies them that Samson's death was not shameful, there is no rejoicing at the destruction of their enemies. The messenger's methodical report of what he saw and heard makes clear that Samson did not act rashly in a furious moment of self-loathing but that he deliberately resolved upon his course of action and shrewdly misled his captors in order to carry out his decision:

> he his guide requested
> (For so from such as nearer stood we heard)
> As overtir'd to let him lean a while
> With both his arms on those two massy Pillars
> That to the arched roof gave main support.
> He unsuspicious led him; which when *Samson*
> Felt in his arms, with head a while inclin'd,
> And eyes fast fixt he stood, as one who pray'd,
> Or some great matter in his mind revolv'd.
> (Ll. 1630-1638)

The messenger also testifies that the Philistines were using the occasion of Samson's captivity to exalt the power of Dagon and that Samson's announced intention was not to kill himself but to prove that he had yet greater strength:

> At sight of him the people with a shout
> Rifted the Air clamoring thir god with praise,
> Who had made thir dreadful enemy thir thrall.
> (Ll. 1620-1622)

> At last with head erect thus cried aloud,
>   "Hitherto, Lords, what your commands impos'd
> I have perform'd, as reason was, obeying,
> Not without wonder or delight beheld.
> Now of my own accord such other trial
> I mean to show you of my strength, yet greater;
> As with amaze shall strike all who behold."
> (Ll. 1639-1645)

> *Samson* with these immixt, inevitably
> Pull'd down the same destruction on himself;
> (Ll. 1657-1658)

The Chorus rejoices that in Samson's case self-destruction was not a shameful flight from suffering but a glorious fulfillment of his vocation. They stress the innocence of Samson's intention:

289

        self-kill'd
Not willingly, but tangl'd in the fold
Of dire necessity, whose law in death conjoin'd
Thee with thy slaughter'd foes . . .

                    (Ll. 1664-1667)

And the Semichorus contrasts the blind, irrational frenzy of the
Philistine mob with Samson's conscious, independent virtue:

        But he though blind of sight,
        Despis'd and thought extinguish't quite,
        With inward eyes illuminated
        His fiery virtue rous'd
        From under ashes into sudden flame,
        And as an ev'ning Dragon came,
        Assailant on the perched roosts,
        And nests in order rang'd
        Of tame villatic Fowl.

                    (Ll. 1687-1695)

The much-debated gloss of "Dragon" as serpent in these lines
seems to me entirely appropriate as the Chorus realizes that, even
without the miraculous escape from the laws of nature that they
had hoped for, Samson has used his own wit to achieve victory
within the laws of "dire necessity." [38] The biblical admonition
to be as wise as serpents had naturally long been associated with
casuistry, since the case of conscience is essentially an attempt to
discover how to act innocently through the exercise of reason in
the labyrinthine confusions of a fallen world.[39] The progression

[38] Sellin discusses the appropriateness of the serpent image in relation to
Samson's feigning in "Milton's Epithet *Agonistes*," p. 159.

[39] See Jeremy Taylor, *Whole Works*, ed. Heber, VI, 95; George Starr, *Defoe
and Casuistry* (Princeton: Princeton University Press, 1971), p. 191; George L.
Mosse, *The Holy Pretence: A Study in Christianity and Reason of State from
William Perkins to John Winthrop* (Oxford: B. Blackwell, 1957), pp. 132-133.
Milton's "ev'ning Dragon" who is also eagle and phoenix is most reminiscent
of Donne's *Serpens exaltatus*:

So, if he who is *Serpens serpens humi*, the Serpent condemned to creep
upon the ground, doe transforme himselfe into a flying Serpent, and
attempt our noble faculties, there is *Serpens exaltatus*, a Serpent lifted
up in the wildernesse to recover all them that are stung, and feel that
they are stung with this Serpent, this flying Serpent, that is, these high
and continued sinnes. The creeping Serpent, the groveling Serpent, is
Craft; the exalted Serpent, the crucified Serpent, is Wisdome. All your

of images from serpent to eagle to phoenix crystalizes Samson's outwitting of his physically superior enemies, thus making his strength effective to achieve the immortality of glorious achievement. Like the self-begotten phoenix, Samson achieves immortality without external aid. He transcends the support and guidance of human political and religious authority and discovers within himself the wisdom and strength to overcome all obstacles to fulfilling his duty to obey God and serve his fellow men.

The last two speeches establish the final tone of concord and understanding within the human community. Manoa plans to gather "all my kindred, all my friends" for the burial rites and looks forward to Samson serving as a source of inspiration to posterity. More specifically, he sees that Samson has offered Israel the opportunity for freedom but that the Israelites, like Samson, can win freedom only through their own efforts. Samson fulfills the glorious prophecies of his birth not by winning battles and not by making their decisions for them or by teaching them what to do in particular situations. Rather, he serves as a model for others by his very uniqueness. What Samson does in his particular circumstances other men will be able to do in theirs, not by applying his decision to their lives, but by imitating the process by which he decided. When Samson "quit himself / Like *Samson*" (ll. 1709-1710), he showed that in spite of sin and weakness man can distinguish good from evil and judge himself without laxity and that in spite of the power of evil in the fallen world he can act vigorously and innocently. He can choose virtue in even the most limiting circumstances by transcending inapplicable codifications of right conduct and by following the dictates of his own conscience. Samson's life and death have not changed the basic conditions of life nor have they revealed new truths that answer any of the agonizing questions men perennially must ask. But through the experience of sharing vicariously Samson's doubts and the process of resolving them, his survivors also share the

---

worldly cares, all your crafty bargaines, . . . savour of the earth, and of the craft of that Serpent, that creeps upon the earth: But crucifie this craft of yours, bring all your worldly subtilty under the Crosse of Christ Jesus, . . . and then you have changed the Serpent, from the Serpent of perdition creeping upon the earth, to the Serpent of salvation exalted in the wildernesse.

John Donne, *Sermons,* ed. G. R. Potter and E. M. Simpson (Berkeley and Los Angeles: University of California Press, 1953-1962), X, 189-190.

peace, consolation, and calm of mind won by Samson's regenerated conscience.

The Casuistical Paradigm in *Samson Agonistes*

Reducing *Samson Agonistes* to a dramatized case of conscience would be as misleading as reducing it to a fictionalized life of Milton. Like the traditions of Renaissance poetics, classical drama, and biblical typology, Protestant casuistry is part of the intellectual context that helps to illuminate the distinctive qualities of Milton's tragedy and to resolve some of the critical problems it presents to modern readers. Casuistry provides the basic concepts with which Milton's contemporaries thought about moral decision making whatever their political and ecclesiastical allegiances. The parallels between case divinity and *Samson Agonistes* are striking and illuminating, perhaps most significantly so when they throw into clear relief Milton's distance from conventional positions.

In subject matter, structure, and language, Milton's tragedy strongly resembles the prose cases of conscience in which English clergymen analyzed the workings of the Christian conscience and created models of the decision-making process. Discussions of past and present moral judgments constitute the dramatic action. Since the characters' judgments are inseparable from their particular circumstances and since they differ significantly, the reader perceives the moral issues as complex problems requiring careful thought rather than as clear choices between good and evil. The conflicting judgments among modern critics about the lawfulness of such decisions as Samson's second marriage testify to Milton's success in communicating the casuistical habit of mind that sees such decisions both as morally significant, voluntary actions and as difficult problems eluding easy common sense or simple piety.

The obvious links with casuistry in such traditional cases of conscience as marriage with an infidel and suicide are less important than Samson's gradual enlightenment about how to resolve moral problems. The casuistical habit of mind, with its focus on the individuality of each case of conscience, can tend to fragment the narrative line, as George Starr has found in his study of the influence of casuistry on Defoe's novels.[40] Milton avoids this

[40] Starr, *Defoe and Casuistry*, p. ix.

problem because particular cases are subordinated to Samson's regeneration, the process of resolving doubts about his relationship with God, which William Perkins calls "the greatest [case of conscience] that ever was." [41]

Prompted by the judgments and proposals of the Chorus and Manoa, Samson reconsiders his past judgments and his present actions and learns the basic principles of applying universal divine law to particular human actions. This understanding leads to remorse and repentance, and it also equips Samson intellectually to contend with the arguments of his enemies. As Dalila, Harapha, and the officer attempt to exert authority and control over him, Samson discovers experientially the freedom of his own conscience and finally asserts it triumphantly in action.

This movement from doubt to resolution, from general to particular, from thought to action, from law as external code to law as internal self-judgment, roughly parallels the structure of traditional cases of conscience. *Samson Agonistes* begins by posing doubts and questions, presents general formulations of moral law relatively early, moves to moral judgments of specific types of human action, anticipates and answers objections to these judgments, and ends, not with an ethical precept, but with a model of a particular individual acting with a right conscience in a specific set of circumstances. The conclusion of *Samson Agonistes* does not recommend Samson's vengeance or Samson's way of death to others, but it does ask us to accept the ethical rightness of Samson's actions in his particular time and place.

Although the casuistical paradigm is evident in the subject matter and shape of *Samson Agonistes,* the eloquence and passion of Milton's poem contrast sharply with the plain style and calm voice of the casuist. Nevertheless, *Samson Agonistes* and prose casuistry are stylistically similar in one important respect: they draw on the store of traditional Christian images in strikingly similar ways. The images of darkness and light, bondage and freedom, disease and health permeate the casuists' discussions of how to transform doubt to certainty, to cure wounded con-

---

[41] Perkins, *A Case of Conscience, the greatest that ever was: how a man may know whether he be the child of God, or no,* in *Workes,* I. Thomas F. Merrill points out that the effort to combat despair is not confined to this work but permeates Perkins's casuistry and is the most distinctive feature of Puritan casuistry as a whole. Thomas F. Merrill, ed., *William Perkins 1558-1602: English Puritanist* (Nieuwkoop: B. DeGraaf, 1966), pp. xiv-xv.

sciences, and to make action possible in the confusions of the
fallen world. These images embody the unifying action of *Samson
Agonistes,* Samson's progress from error to truth, despair to faith,
and impotence to action.

In addition to the obvious and inevitable differences in scope
and form between the literary modes, the role played by reason
provides the most apparent contrast between *Samson Agonistes*
and prose cases of conscience. Traditionally, the movement from
general law to particular action proceeded by logical demonstration. In Milton's poetic drama, the transition is more complex,
since the resolution of particular cases of conscience combines
with the psychological recovery of the conscience, processes the
casuists treat separately. After all of Samson's vocal debates and
self-analysis, silence envelopes the crucial moments of his last
decisions. He enunciates the concept of freedom from the letter of
the law before he decides to accompany the officer, but the actual
process of applying the concept to his own situation defies analysis. The "rousing motions" signal his breakthrough, but the
respective roles of reason and divine grace remain mysterious.
The messenger's report of his final moment of decision is also
ambiguous:

> with head a while inclin'd,
> And eyes fast fixt he stood, as one who pray'd,
> Or some great matter in his mind revolv'd.
>
> (Ll. 1636-1638)

We need not conclude from these passages that Milton uncharac-
teristically abandoned an ethic of reason and will for a *deus ex
machina* of divine compulsion.[42] For Milton, reason and grace are
complementary. His view of the relation between divine grace
and human judgment and valor is essentially the same as Donne's:

> Consider we alwaies the grace of God, to be the Sun it selfe,
> but the nature of man, and his naturall faculties to be the
> Sphear, in which that Sun, that Grace moves.[43]

[42] Compare Radzinowicz, who argues that "Samson's 'rouzing motions,' is
not a seizing of power by an external, even if transcendental, force over a
dazzled mind, it is rather an inward prompting to a radical ecumenical
faith" (*Toward "Samson Agonistes,"* p. 349).

[43] *Sermons,* VII, 305. In *Biathanatos,* Donne is skeptical about reading into
the Samson story any "particular inspiration, or new commission" other than
"that resident and inherent grace of God, by which he excites us to works
of morall, or higher vertues" ([New York: The Facsimile Text Society, 1930],
p. 108). Cf. p. 201.

The whole process of regeneration that Samson experiences is possible only through God's grace, and the final inspired choices are logically compatible with the moral understanding that Samson has earned through hard thought.

Milton uses the traditional principles and approaches of casuistry to create a model of the troubled human conscience, which, through God's grace, overcomes doubt and judges particular actions calmly and confidently according to its understanding of God's will. Milton's dramatic form emphasizes Samson's intention and the circumstances surrounding his moral choices, and it celebrates the supremacy of his conscience over all human law and power. In this harmony of individual judgment and action, Samson illustrates the right conscience described by the Protestant casuists. But the casuistical paradigm is transformed by Milton's radical imagination while it informs his rendering of the Samson story.

The Protestant casuists insist that the individual conscience is supreme, but they also maintain that to defy lawful authority is sinful. They agree that the conscience is bound only by the word of God, that individual interpretations of God's word differ, and that failing to follow the dictates of one's conscience is sinful. Yet they also warn that one may err in interpreting God's word and sin by following an erroneous conscience. The conflicting claims of the individual conscience and the absolute truth created a dilemma they were unable to resolve.[44] As Arthur Barker has demonstrated, Milton's mature interpretation of Christian liberty "as depending solely on the inner light, and as releasing the believer from all outward rules whatsoever, human or divine, save for the Scriptures" together with his insistence that Scripture "can be interpreted only according to the divine illumination within the believer" allies Milton with the extreme leftwing of the Puritan group.[45] Milton's hero of conscience is more radical than any models offered by conventional casuists. Samson not only resists the unjust authority of his persecutors, he disregards all the authority and advice of his own people. He claims the freedom to interpret divine law itself solely on the basis of his own judgment. In this he is entirely consistent with casuistical

[44] H. R. McAdoo, *The Structure of Caroline Moral Theology* (London: Longmans, Green, and Co., 1949), pp. 85-87.

[45] Barker, *Milton and the Puritan Dilemma*, pp. 302, 225, respectively. See also Christopher Hill, *Milton and the English Revolution* (London: Faber and Faber, 1977), p. 105.

principles, but Milton has carried those principles to logical conclusions that the casuists tried to avoid.

In a sense, then, *Samson Agonistes* is a case of conscience that transcends the limitations of the form, reconciling the conflict between the theoretical individuality of each case and the casuist's formulation of general rules and models intended to guide many men. As Arnold Stein has shown, the opening lines introduce thematic materials and symbolically foreshadow the significant form of the whole, as well as initiating the literal action.[46]

> A little onward lend thy guiding hand
> To these dark steps, a little further on;
> For yonder bank hath choice of sun or shade.
>
> (Ll. 1-3)

In his doubt and confusion, Samson relies on others for moral and spiritual guidance while he, without realizing it, points the direction to a position where he can exercise choice. After learning to understand the relation between his actions and his God, he chooses deliberately and courageously, thus demonstrating to the Chorus that he has outgrown their counsel and consolation: "Go, and the holy One / Of *Israel* be thy guide." While Jeremy Taylor warned against placing too much reliance on spiritual advisers, he nevertheless concluded that "men will for ever need a living guide" (XI, 363). Samson learns that the living God who speaks within him is the one guide he must follow, even to his death. Samson's choice is not one we would expect to see recommended by a casuist. Although they acknowledge that the choice of virtue may necessitate sacrifice, they do not often advise men to become tragic heroes. Samson's experience does guide men to the dual perception of tragedy. It is horrible that man lives in a world where his understanding of God, his fellow man, and himself is difficult and incomplete, where freedom may be possible only through violence and destruction, where the innocent suffer with the guilty, and where following one's conscience may mean isolation and death. It is right that men can discover truth and choose good among the doubtful confusions of circumstances and conflicting authorities and that they can harmonize their actions with their judgments and so achieve the "calm of mind" of a peaceful conscience.

[46] Arnold Stein, *Heroic Knowledge* (Minneapolis: University of Minnesota Press, 1957), pp. 138-139.

Conclusion

The efforts by Renaissance casuists to chart the way to perfection in action in a far from perfect world are not entirely persuasive. The body of English casuistry includes cases of conscience like some of Thomas Barlow's where the intricacy of the casuistical method masks an underlying cynicism about the possibility of uncompromised virtuous action. Moreover, by trying to treat in detail spiritual, moral, psychological, and practical facets of the decision-making process and in doing so to demonstrate the universal and ideal through the actual and particular, even the best casuists sometimes attempted more than they could accomplish within the limits of literal exposition. Still, more recent attempts to balance traditional truths with the demands of new situations and to reconcile the rights of the individual with the prerogatives of the group have not been demonstrably more successful.

Instead of trying to resolve these tensions in universally applicable formulas, casuists tried to develop a method or approach to moral problems that would make them bearable. The casuists' goal was to transform doubt into the absolute assurance of the inviolate conscience, and, paradoxically, they tried to achieve this authoritative conviction without the support of any infallible authority, either of inward illumination or of external law. Casuistry is paradoxical too in presenting cases of conscience simultaneously as demonstrations of the principle that each human action is unique and as models of the decision-making process to be imitated by all men with similar cases of conscience. Casuists insisted that there are certain actions that are morally reprehensible—some things that we cannot do and live at peace with ourselves—and that circumstances alter cases so profoundly that no particular action can be judged apart from its context of human motives, surrounding circumstances, and probable consequences. While this approach does not lead them to explore motives and moral imperatives with a psychoanalyst's insight or to assess consequences with the thoroughness of utilitarian ethics, it frequently combines perceptive psychological and social analysis with traditional ethics, and it remains remarkably true to felt experience.

In this study, I have tried to show how the casuistical view of morality as problematic action to be analyzed in terms of divine law, particular circumstances, and individual conscience permeates the ethical and political thought of the time and also how this habit of mind informs major fictional works. Although the poems and plays I have discussed are not pure casuistry and must be read in relation to such literary types as verse satire, lyric, epic, and tragedy, the casuistical tradition provides a relevant commentary on their treatment of moral choice and illuminates their forms. Examining the consciences of Shakespeare's characters in the terms of casuistry helps us understand the distinctive qualities and crucial decisions of each as well as to see a consistent interpretation of moral choice that links these plays to contemporary intellectual currents without denying the terror of man's predicament. Reading Donne's satires in this context reveals a more comprehensive formal structure and a more subtle and perceptive moral vision than the conventions of verse satire prepare us for. Knowledge of the case of conscience helps us not only to understand how Herbert's lyrics resolve doubt and perplexity in clarity and certainty but also to avoid making a misleading separation between Herbert's Christian thought and his self-correcting poetic forms. Placing *Samson Agonistes* in this tradition corrects a current tendency to see Milton abandoning in despair the rational and ethical emphasis of his life's work for a transcendent mysticism. Familiarity with the tradition of English casuistry and with the cases of the 1640s and 1650s shows that *Samson* is not a departure from Milton's dominant attitudes and themes but rather his most daring experiment in creating symbolic myth out of the stuff of actual human situations.

Thus, the works by major poets most faithful to the center of casuistical thought and closest to the case of conscience in form are those which transform the tradition most radically. Indeed, studying their use of casuistical concepts and methods leads to the conclusion that the contradictions inherent in the formal case of conscience can best be resolved in fiction. The literal moralism of Herbert's "The Church-porch" is less successful in leading people "exactly in the wayes of Truth" than the more imaginative poems of "The Church." While the tension between individual conscience and universal law weakens in different ways both *Biathanatos* and *Pseudo-Martyr,* in the satires, Donne creates a model of the decision-making process that does justice to the integrity and complexity of the casuists' theoretical vision.

I have not offered the approach to poetry by way of case divinity as a radically new way of seeing Renaissance literature. The casuistical paradigm substantiates much that we have learned from traditional approaches through Christian humanism. It complements Mary Ann Radzinowicz's study of Samson's "achievement of integrity through progressive moral choices" and corroborates her conclusion that *Samson Agonistes* is the culmination of Milton's intellectual and political development.[1] The casuistical context supports, and I hope extends, Barbara Lewalski's demonstration that the most important influences on the great religious poetry of seventeenth-century England were not medieval, continental, and Roman Catholic, but contemporary, English, and Protestant.[2] It complements and sometimes qualifies such studies as Helen Vendler's and Stanley Fish's work on Herbert and Leslie Brisman's and Douglas Peterson's discussions of how, in Milton and Shakespeare respectively, the understanding of choice relates to the concept of time.[3]

Brisman, for example, shows that in Milton and his poetic heirs, conscious choice is an aesthetic as well as an ethical process reflected in imagery and syntax as well as in larger patterns of temptation and decision in poetic fable. He demonstrates convincingly that for Milton, choice involves renunciation, a turning "from the complexities of experience to the unity and direction of art." Brisman oversimplifies, however, when he contrasts Milton's reduction of "the multiplicity of possibilities to singleness of choice" with Shakespeare's "unnegating fullness."[4] Sensitivity to the casuistical paradigm in the poetry reveals that Milton's conception of moral decision making is more complex

---

[1] Mary Ann Radzinowicz, *Toward "Samson Agonistes": The Growth of Milton's Mind* (Princeton: Princeton University Press, 1978), p. 230.

[2] Barbara Kiefer Lewalski, *Protestant Poetics and the Seventeenth-Century Religious Lyric* (Princeton: Princeton University Press, 1979).

[3] Leslie Brisman, *Milton's Poetry of Choice and Its Romantic Heirs* (Ithaca: Cornell University Press, 1973), Douglas Peterson, *Time, Tide, and Tempest: A Study of Shakespeare's Romances* (San Marino, Calif.: The Huntington Library, 1973).

[4] Brisman, *Milton's Poetry of Choice,* pp. 14, 33.

than Brisman's either / or formulation allows. While Milton never underestimates the sacrifice demanded by choice in the limited fallen world, he does not present right choice as primarily a matter of selecting between alternatives. Each action must be analyzed thoroughly in the light of the conscience's knowledge of divine will, and virtuous action may require breaking through the either / or dilemma and formulating multiple alternatives in order to discover an action innocent in matter, intention, and circumstances. Perhaps, as Brisman argues, Eve is "unable to make the kind of renunciation needed in facing temptation" and thus may fall "from a desire for unlimited experience," [5] but Samson can be redeemed only by breaking through obvious limits. He triumphs by refusing both to serve Dagon and to live parasitically and by imaginatively creating fresh possibilities for action. Conversely, Shakespeare's broad, inclusive vision of human experience does not deny that in a world of ambiguities men must choose and that choice inevitably narrows possibilities. Like Samson, Hamlet must accept guilt for the evil he does, analyze the moral quality of every action he considers, and refuse both evil alternatives. He must discover a new possibility of action in harmony with divine will and die as a consequence of his choice. Macbeth suffers the still greater horror of forfeiting his ability to choose.

The casuistical vision may be comic or tragic, lyric or satiric, for the casuistical paradigm is not a comprehensive interpretation of human experience but a habit of mind, a way of approaching experience. Like any perspective, it distorts as well as reveals. The prominence that casuistry gives to duties and obligations, to firm resolution and practical action, may neglect the unresolvable ambivalences, the unarticulated and unformulated dimensions of our passional and contemplative lives. Yet, while love may not "know what conscience is," when we reflect that love expresses itself in caring attention and response, we realize that casuists, both theologians and poets, were aware that "conscience is born of love."

[5] Ibid., p. 15.

Index

Aldus, Paul J., 79n
Allen, D. C., 288n
Ames, William, xi, xiii, xvii, xviii, 7, 10n, 13, 33n, 35, 36n, 40n, 62, 189, 231, 288n; on cases of conscience, 32, 41; on casuistry, 5; on circumstances, 16; on conscience, 12, 13, 70, 78n, 79, 190, 239-240, 253-254, 255; on constancy, 193n; on doubt of salvation, 228; on equity, 25-26, 262; on forms of worship, 28; on ignorance, 18; on intention, 18; organization of *Conscience with the Power and Cases Thereof*, 37; on Perkins, 40; on precepts of God, 274; on scruples, 198n; on subjection, 285n; on will, 253
Andreasen, N.J.C., 150
Aristotle, 53
Ascham, Anthony, 46-47, 48, 49
Augustine, St., 17
Aylmer, G. E., 47n
Azor, Juan, 133, 142

Bacon, Francis, xi, 4-5, 10
Bagshawe, Christopher, 109
Bald, R. C., 145n, 174n
Banks, Theodore Howard, 272n
Barker, Arthur, 248, 260n, 267n, 277n, 283, 295
Barlow, Thomas, 17, 31, 33n, 37, 61, 62-63, 297
Batten, J. Minton, 58n
Battles, Ford Lewis, 23n
Baxter, Richard, xiii, xv, 7, 9n, 10n, 35, 36n, 62, 64, 178, 285n; on casuistry, 33-34, 38; on erroneous conscience, 65; on Herbert, 183; on hypocrites, 19; on God's law, 20; organization of *A Christian*

Directory, 37-38, 248; on scriptural law, 21-22; on unlawful commands, 24, 26
Bellette, A. F., 150
Birch, Thomas, 62n
Blau, Sheridan, D., xviii, 185-186
Bosher, Robert S., 44n, 45n
Bottrall, Margaret, 186n
Boyce, Benjamin, 57n
Boyle, Robert, 61n, 62n
Bradley, A. C., 114, 123-124n
Breward, Ian, xvii, 207n, 227n, 245n
Brisman, Leslie, 299-300
Brooke, Nicholas, 68n
Brooks, Cleanth, 107n
Brown, Thomas, xviii, 56
Bullough, Geoffrey, 135
Burrell Margaret, 111-112

Calderwood, James L., 67n
Calvin, John, 23n
Campbell, Lily B., xviii
Carbo, Ludovico, 133, 147
Carnes, Valerie, 239n
case divinity, *see* cases of conscience and casuistry
cases of conscience: Ames on, 32; attending *"idol-service,"* 281n; Baxter on, 38; *Biathanatos* as, 137-144; *A Case of Conscience, the Greatest that ever was*, 227, 241, 293; "The Case of the Engagement," 43-59, 250; "The Case of Marrying with a Recusant," 267n; "The Case of the Use of the Liturgy," 60; definition, 3, 13, 17, 41; Donne's lost book, 133; Esther's disobedience, 135-137; form, 38-43, 49-50, 52, 56, 59-66, 297-298; as genre, xiii-xiv; Herbert on, 184;

innocent deception, 124-125, 284-285; legal defense, 41-43;* organization of books of, 31, 36-38, 64; *Pseudo-Martyr* as, 145-149; readmission of Jews, 60-62; relation to other genres, 49, 56-57, 250; style, 39-40, 53-54; suicide, 142n, 288. *See also* casuistry and conscience.

casuistry: characteristics of, xii-xv, 35-36, 48-49, 60-66, 178, 297-298; circumstances in, 15-16, 23, 42, 84; conscience in, 10-13, 16-17, 19-20, 40-41, 79, 84-85, 98, 190, 227-228, 229-230; definition, xi, 3; development, xiv-xv, 4-9; Donne on, 133-135, 139-142, 146; doubt in, 13-15, 233; Herbert on, 3, 183-184; intention in, 18, 28, 84; knowledge in, 16-19, 94, 239-240; law in, 19-27; logic in, 40-41; metaphors in, 104n, 243, 266, 271n, 290, 293-294; popularity, 7-8, 9; Puritan and Anglican, 28-33; Roman Catholic, xiv, 4, 6, 8, 32, 35-36, 42-43, 139-142; scriptural authority in, 21-22, 29-30. *See also* cases of conscience and conscience.

Cathcart, Dwight, xviii, 178-179, 179-180n, 238n

The Changeling, 67

Charles I, 7, 8, 44, 47n

Charles II, 44, 53, 62

Charney, Maurice, 89n

A Christian Directory: or a Summ of Practical Theology and Cases of Conscience, xv, 7, 9n, 10n, 38, 183, 248. *See also* Baxter, Richard

Cirillo, Albert, 260

Codrington, Robert, 9n

Coffin, Charles, 137n

Coleridge, Samuel Taylor, 66, 106, 127

Colie, Rosalei, 111n, 129n, 138n, 143n

conscience: comforting or healing, 227-228, 229-230, 265-266; definition, 10-12, 79, 190; desperate, 69, 76-78, 129, 253-254; Donne on, 134, 148; doubting or doubtful, 12, 13, 52, 98, 101; erring, 12-13, 65, 94, 253; evil, 10, 67, 69-78, 96,

116-120, 127-129, 253; Milton on, 256, 264n; operation of, 16-17, 19-20, 40-41, 70, 84-85, 98, 239-240; right or good, 10, 12-13, 105, 252, 255, 257, 265; scrupulous, 12-13, 69, 198n; sinning against, 12, 67, 69, 89, 116, 253; wounded or troubled, 254, 263, 265-266, 271. *See also* cases of conscience, casuistry, *syneidesis,* and *synteresis.*

Conscience with the Power and Cases Thereof, 10n, 37. *See also* Ames, William

Cromwell, Oliver, 47, 60

Danson, Lawrence, 111, 112n, 121n

Dante Alighieri, 163, 170

De Conscientia, eius Jure et Casibus, 7. *See also* Ames, William, and *Conscience with the Power and Cases Thereof*

De Obligatione Conscientiae, 9n. *See also* Sanderson, Robert, and *Several Cases of Conscience Discussed in Ten Lectures*

DeQuincey, Thomas, 3-4, 106n

Digges, Sir Dudley, 8

A Discourse of Conscience, 7, 10n. *See also* Perkins, William

Donne, John, xi, xvi
    Biathanatos, xvi, xviii, 137-144, 146, 238, 288, 294n, 299
    on conscience, 133, 134, 148
    on doubt, 134
    Holy Sonnets, 237-238
    interest in casuistry, 133-135
    Pseudo-Martyr, xvi, 134, 144-149, 299
    on probabilism, 140, 147
    Satyres, xvi, 149-150, 177-178, 182, 214-215, 238, 298-299; "Satyre I," 150, 151-156, 157, 158, 160, 167, 171, 177; "Satyre II," 156-160, 161, 167, 170, 171; "Satyre III," 160-167, 171, 177; "Satyre IV," 167-172; "Satyre V," 172-177
    Sermons, 56, 134-137, 152n, 290-291n, 294
    Songs and Sonnets, 178-182;

Library of Congress Cataloging in Publication Data

Slights, Camille Wells.
    The casuistical tradition in Shakespeare, Donne,
Herbert, and Milton.

    1. English literature—Early modern, 1500-1700—His-
tory and criticism.   2. Casuistry—History.   3. Conscience in literature.   4. Ethics in literature.
5. Protestantism and literature. I. Title.
PR428.C28S57 1981   820'.9'384   80-8576
ISBN 0-691-06463-6